studysync®

Reading & Writing Companion

GRADE 11 UNITS 1–3

Breaking Away

The Highway

No Strangers Here

studysync

studysync.com

Send all inquiries to:
BookheadEd Learning, LLC
610 Daniel Young Drive
Sonoma, CA 95476

ISBN 978-1-94-973921-3
MHID 1-94-973921-X

3 4 5 6 7 8 9 10 LWI 25 24 23 22 21

C

Contents

Breaking Away

How does independence define
the American spirit?

The Highway

How do journeys influence perspective?

No Strangers Here

How does place shape the individual?

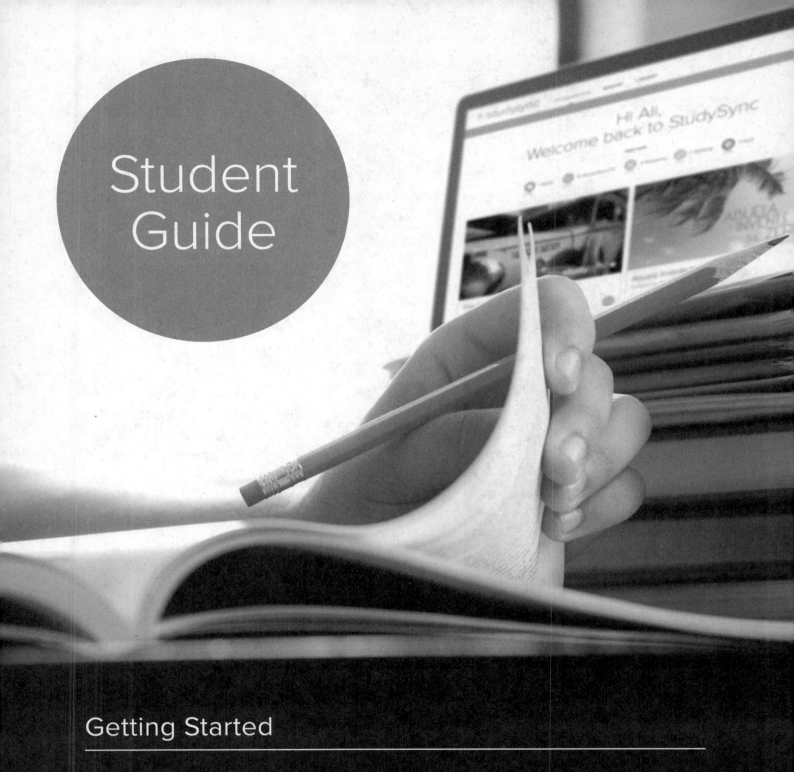

Student Guide

Getting Started

Welcome to the StudySync Reading & Writing Companion! In this book, you will find a collection of readings based on the theme of the unit you are studying. As you work through the readings, you will be asked to answer questions and perform a variety of tasks designed to help you closely analyze and understand each text selection. Read on for an explanation of each

Close Reading and Writing Routine

In each unit, you will read texts that share a common theme, despite their different genres, time periods, and authors. Each reading encourages a closer look through questions and a short writing assignment.

Introduction

① An Introduction to each text provides historical context for your reading as well as information about the author. You will also learn about the genre of the text and the year in which it was written.

Notes

② Many times, while working through the activities after each text, you will be asked to **annotate** or **make annotations** about what you are reading. This means that you should highlight or underline words in the text and use the "Notes" column to make comments or jot down any questions you have. You may also want to note any unfamiliar vocabulary words here.

You will also see sample student annotations to go along with the Skill lesson for that text.

Reading & Writing Companion

First Read

During your first reading of each selection, you should just try to get a general idea of the content and message of the reading. Don't worry if there are parts you don't understand or words that are unfamiliar to you. You'll have an opportunity later to dive deeper into the text.

Think Questions

These questions will ask you to start thinking critically about the text, asking specific questions about its purpose, and making connections to your prior knowledge and reading experiences. To answer these questions, you should go back to the text and draw upon specific evidence to support your responses. You will also begin to explore some of the more challenging vocabulary words in the selection.

Skills

Each Skill includes two parts: Checklist and Your Turn. In the Checklist, you will learn the process for analyzing the text. The model student annotations in the text provide examples of how you might make your own notes following the instructions in the Checklist. In the Your Turn, you will use those same instructions to practice the skill.

The Story of an Hour

First Read

Read "The Story of an Hour." After you read, complete the Think Questions below.

THINK QUESTIONS

1. At the beginning of paragraph 9, Mrs. Mallard senses "something coming to her." What is it? What physical effect does it have on her? Cite evidence from the text to support your response.

2. In paragraphs 5 through 9, how do the details about the natural setting outside of Mrs. Mallard's room relate to her emotional state? Point to specific evidence from the text to support your response.

3. At the end of the story, why do the doctors think that Mrs. Mallard died of "the joy that kills"? Do you think their diagnosis is accurate? Cite evidence from the text to support your answer.

4. Use context clues to determine the meaning of the word **elixir**. Then write your best definition of the word here, along with the clues that helped you find it.

5. Use context clues to determine the meaning of the word **absolutely** as it is used in "The Story of an Hour." Write your best definition of *absolutely* here. Then consult a print or online dictionary to confirm its meaning.

The Story of an Hour

Skill:
Story Elements

Use the Checklist to analyze Story Elements in "The Story of an Hour." Refer to the sample student annotations about Story Elements in the text.

CHECKLIST FOR STORY ELEMENTS

In order to identify the impact of the author's choices regarding how to develop and relate elements of a story or drama, note the following:

✓ where and when the story takes place, who the main characters are, and the main conflict, or problem, in the plot

✓ the order of the action

✓ how the characters are introduced and developed

✓ the impact that the author's choice of setting has on the characters and their attempt to solve the problem

✓ the point of view the author uses, and how this shapes what readers know about the characters in the story

To analyze the impact of the author's choices regarding how to develop and to relate elements of a story or drama, consider the following questions:

✓ How do the author's choices affect the story elements? The development of the plot?

✓ How does the setting influence the characters?

✓ Which elements of the setting impact the plot, and in particular the problem the characters face and must solve?

YOUR TURN

1. How does Mrs. Mallard's character develop over the course of the short story?

○ A. Mrs. Mallard begins to recognize that prayer is powerful and that she should begin to pray more so that she can live a long life.

○ B. Mrs. Mallard begins to recognize that she is now a free and independent women who has escaped a confined, unhappy life, and this brings her relief, hope, and excitement.

○ C. Mrs. Mallard begins to recognize that she is an independent women, and this scares her and makes her feel very sad and alone.

○ D. Mrs. Mallard transforms from feeling like an uninteresting, boring women to a goddess who will easily be able to find another husband.

2. How does Mrs. Mallard's character development over the course of the short story impact the story's outcome?

○ A. Mrs. Mallard's shift from feeling trapped to feeling free is snatched from her at the very end of the story, causing her death because her new found joy is taken from her.

○ B. Mrs. Mallard shifts from feeling trapped to feeling enraged when she finds out her husband is alive, and her anger causes her death.

○ C. Mrs. Mallard's shift from feeling trapped to feeling free is snatched from her at the very end of the story, and it causes her death because she is overjoyed that her husband is alive.

○ D. Mrs. Mallard shifts from feeling very sad about her husband's death to feeling comforted and relieved that he is alive.

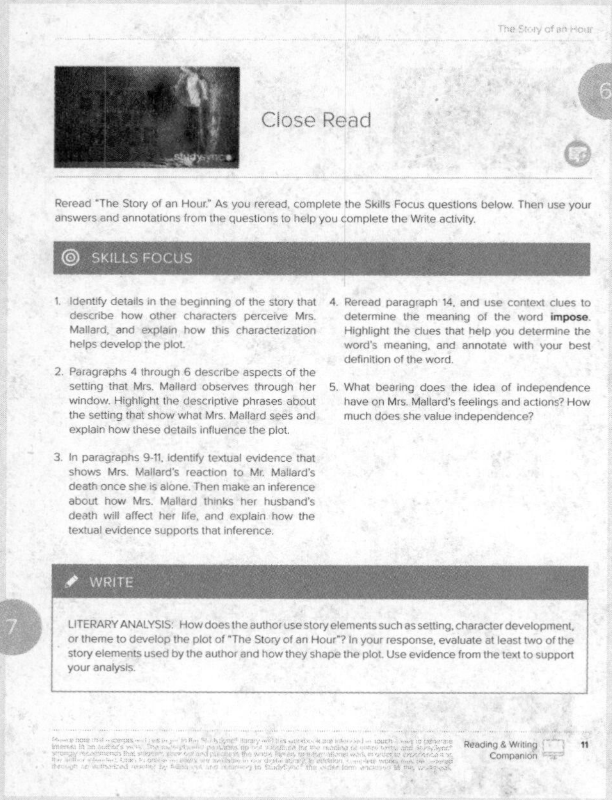
The Story of an Hour

Close Read

Reread "The Story of an Hour." As you reread, complete the Skills Focus questions below. Then use your answers and annotations from the questions to help you complete the Write activity.

SKILLS FOCUS

1. Identify details in the beginning of the story that describe how other characters perceive Mrs. Mallard, and explain how this characterization helps develop the plot.
2. Paragraphs 4 through 6 describe aspects of the setting that Mrs. Mallard observes through her window. Highlight the descriptive phrases about the setting that show what Mrs. Mallard sees and explain how these details influence the plot.
3. In paragraphs 9-11, identify textual evidence that shows Mrs. Mallard's reaction to Mr. Mallard's death once she is alone. Then make an inference about how Mrs. Mallard thinks her husband's death will affect her life, and explain how the textual evidence supports that inference.
4. Reread paragraph 14, and use context clues to determine the meaning of the word **impose**. Highlight the clues that help you determine the word's meaning, and annotate with your best definition of the word.
5. What bearing does the idea of independence have on Mrs. Mallard's feelings and actions? How much does she value independence?

WRITE

LITERARY ANALYSIS: How does the author use story elements such as setting, character development, or theme to develop the plot of "The Story of an Hour"? In your response, evaluate at least two of the story elements used by the author and how they shape the plot. Use evidence from the text to support your analysis.

Reading & Writing Companion 11

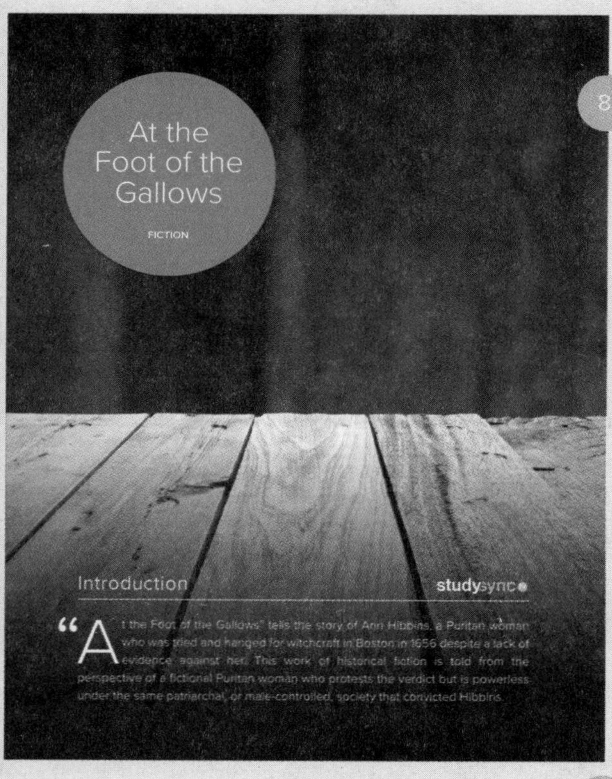
At the Foot of the Gallows

FICTION

Introduction

studysync

"At the Foot of the Gallows" tells the story of Ann Hibbins, a Puritan woman who was tried and hanged for witchcraft in Boston in 1656 despite a lack of evidence against her. This work of historical fiction is told from the perspective of a fictional Puritan woman who protests the verdict but is powerless under the same patriarchal, or male-controlled, society that convicted Hibbins.

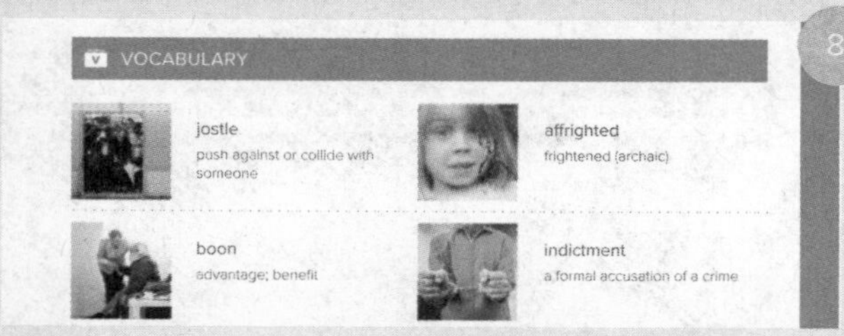
VOCABULARY

jostle
push against or collide with someone

affrighted
frightened (archaic)

boon
advantage; benefit

indictment
a formal accusation of a crime

6 Close Read & Skills Focus

After you have completed the First Read, you will be asked to go back and read the text more closely and critically. Before you begin your Close Read, you should read through the Skills Focus to get an idea of the concepts you will want to focus on during your second reading. You should work through the Skills Focus by making annotations, highlighting important concepts, and writing notes or questions in the "Notes" column. Depending on instructions from your teacher, you may need to respond online or use a separate piece of paper to start expanding on your thoughts and ideas.

7 Write

Your study of each selection will end with a writing assignment. For this assignment, you should use your notes, annotations, personal ideas, and answers to both the Think and Skills Focus questions. Be sure to read the prompt carefully and address each part of it in your writing.

8 English Language Learner

The English Language Learner texts focus on improving language proficiency. You will practice learning strategies and skills in individual and group activities to become better readers, writers, and speakers.

Extended Writing Project and Grammar

This is your opportunity to use genre characteristics and craft to compose meaningful, longer written works exploring the theme of each unit. You will draw information from your readings, research, and own life experiences to complete the assignment.

1 Writing Project

After you have read all of the unit text selections, you will move on to a writing project. Each project will guide you through the process of writing your essay. Student models will provide guidance and help you organize your thoughts. One unit ends with an **Extended Oral Project** which will give you an opportunity to develop your oral language and communication skills.

2 Writing Process Steps

There are four steps in the writing process: Plan, Draft, Revise, and Edit and Publish. During each step, you will form and shape your writing project, and each lesson's peer review will give you the chance to receive feedback from your peers and teacher.

3 Writing Skills

Each Skill lesson focuses on a specific strategy or technique that you will use during your writing project. Each lesson presents a process for applying the skill to your own work and gives you the opportunity to practice it to improve your writing.

1 Extended Writing Project and Grammar

EXTENDED WRITING PROJECT
NARRATIVE WRITING

2 Narrative Writing Process: Plan

PLAN | DRAFT | REVISE | EDIT AND PUBLISH

3 Skill: Organizing Narrative Writing

••• CHECKLIST FOR ORGANIZING NARRATIVE WRITING

As you consider how to organize your writing for your narrative, use the following questions as a guide:

- Who is the narrator, and who are the characters in the story?
- Where will the story take place?
- Have I created a problem that characters will have to face and resolve, while noting its significance to the characters?
- Have I created a smooth progression of experiences or plot events?

studysync®

UNIT 1

Breaking Away

How does independence define the American spirit?

Genre Focus: **FICTION**

Texts

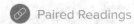 Paired Readings

Extended Writing Project and Grammar

English Language Learner Resources

Unit 1: Breaking Away
How does independence define the American spirit?

KATE CHOPIN

A popular short story writer, Kate Chopin (1850–1904) sparked controversy with the publication of her novel, *The Awakening,* in 1899. Though it was consistent with much of her previous work probing the inner lives of strong, independent female characters, the novel scandalized audiences with its frank depiction of female sexuality. Married at age twenty, Chopin moved from St. Louis, Missouri, to Louisiana, where most of her stories are set. She only began to write after being widowed at the age of thirty-one.

OLAUDAH EQUIANO

Olaudah Equiano's (c. 1745–1797) autobiography, *The Interesting Narrative of the Life of Olaudah Equiano, or Gustavus Vassa, the African* (1789) is one of the earliest books published by a black African writer. At a young age, Equiano was kidnapped from his home in what is now southern Nigeria and sold into slavery. He bought his own freedom in 1766 and settled in England, where he became an ardent abolitionist. His autobiography was a major contribution to the anti-slavery movement.

LOUISE ERDRICH

Born in Little Falls, Minnesota, Louise Erdrich (b. 1954) was raised in Wahpeton, North Dakota, by a German American father and a mother of Ojibwe descent. Both of Erdrich's parents taught at a Bureau of Indian Affairs boarding school, one of a number of schools established with the intent of assimilating Native American youth into Euro-American culture. In her poems, novels, and short stories, Erdrich explores both sides of her dual heritage.

NATHANIEL HAWTHORNE

Born in Salem, Massachusetts, Nathaniel Hawthorne (1804–1864) set most of his novels and short stories in colonial New England, as his ancestors had been some of its original founders. In his best-known work, *The Scarlet Letter* (1850), he scrutinizes the staunch moralism of the Puritan tradition he had inherited. Taking up the theme of guilt in the novel, Hawthorne probes his characters' psychology and the hypocrisy of dominant social values.

THOMAS JEFFERSON

The third president of the United States, Thomas Jefferson (1743–1826) also drafted the Declaration of Independence. This foundational document, ratified on July 4, 1776, established the thirteen American British colonies' independence from Great Britain. In writing the text, Jefferson drew on political philosopher John Locke's theory of "natural law," which suggested that human beings are "by nature free, equal and independent." Jefferson was a staunch advocate of individual freedom, which he considered to be a key tenet of the American Revolution.

JHUMPA LAHIRI

In many of her works, English-born American novelist and short story writer, Jhumpa Lahiri (b. 1967) examines themes related to identity and the East Indian immigrant experience. Both *Interpreter of Maladies* (1999), her debut short-story collection set between India and the United States, and *The Namesake* (2003), her novel about a Bengali family in New England, deal with the experience of being caught between these two distinct cultures.

HERMAN MELVILLE

Best known for his novel *Moby-Dick* (1851), Herman Melville (1819–1891) also wrote short stories and poems. "Bartleby the Scrivener: A Story of Wall Street" (1853), now considered to be one of the first great stories of corporate discontent, deploys an absurdist humor—notably, Bartleby's iconic refrain "I would prefer not to"—to reflect on modern American work culture. Melville died in relative obscurity, his work only beginning to receive critical acclaim in the 1920s.

PHILLIS WHEATLEY

Phillis Wheatley's (1753–1784) *Poems on Various Subjects, Religious and Moral* (1773) was the first volume of poetry by an African American published in modern times. Wheatley was forcibly brought to the United States from West Africa in 1761 and ended up in Boston, as an enslaved person in the home of the Wheatley family. Like much of her work, her best-known poem, "On Being Brought from Africa to America," uses biblical symbolism to comment on slavery. Wheatley may have written as many as 145 poems, most of which are now lost.

ANNE BRADSTREET

Anne Bradstreet (c. 1612–1672) immigrated to America from England at the age of eighteen with her husband and parents to join the Puritans at the Massachusetts Bay Colony. They were met with distressing conditions such as sickness and food scarcity when they arrived, but settled there regardless. Bradstreet returned to the theme of women in Puritan society throughout her many volumes of poetry. She became the first published American poet when her brother-in-law had some of her poems published in England in 1650 without her knowledge.

DEKANAWIDAH

Dekanawidah, known as the Great Peacemaker, united five Iroquois nations torn apart by fighting in present-day New York to form the Iroquois Confederacy, now considered to be one of the world's oldest participatory democracies. Dekanawidah's name, meaning "Two River Currents Flowing Together," symbolizes the peacemaking legacy for which he is remembered. Along with his spokesman Hiawatha, he formulated the Great Law of Peace, the oral constitution of the Iroquois Confederacy originally written on wampum belts before being translated into English, which ultimately inspired the framers of the U.S. Constitution.

JUPITER HAMMON

The first African American poet published in the United States, Jupiter Hammon (1711–c. 1806) was a devout Christian born into slavery in New York. His second poem, a direct address to Phillis Wheatley, expressed the controversial opinion that it was through the mercy of the Lord that she had left "the heathen shore" and entreated her to better herself in the eyes of God. Hammon was never emancipated, though he supported the abolitionist movement.

The Story of an Hour

FICTION

Kate Chopin

1894

Introduction

American author Kate Chopin (1850–1904) wrote feminist literature before the term even existed. Her writing is famous for depicting strong, independent women, liberated to a degree that made many in her time uncomfortable. Considered today to be a widely influential work of proto-feminist literature, "The Story of an Hour"—first published in *Vogue* magazine in 1894—is a quintessential Chopin narrative. In this brief, powerful tale, a wife learns that her husband has died suddenly. But her reaction after digesting the news might not be what you'd expect.

"Free! Body and soul free!"

1   Knowing that Mrs. Mallard was afflicted with a heart trouble, great care was taken to break to her as gently as possible the news of her husband's death.

2   It was her sister Josephine who told her, in broken sentences; veiled hints that revealed in half concealing. Her husband's friend Richards was there, too, near her. It was he who had been in the newspaper office when intelligence of the railroad disaster was received, with Brently Mallard's name leading the list of "killed." He had only taken the time to assure himself of its truth by a second telegram, and had hastened to **forestall** any less careful, less tender friend in bearing the sad message.

Kate Chopin

3   She did not hear the story as many women have heard the same, with a paralyzed inability to accept its significance. She wept at once, with sudden, wild abandonment, in her sister's arms. When the storm of grief had spent itself she went away to her room alone. She would have no one follow her.

4   There stood, facing the open window, a comfortable, roomy armchair. Into this she sank, pressed down by a physical exhaustion that haunted her body and seemed to reach into her soul.

5   She could see in the open square before her house the tops of trees that were all aquiver with the new spring life. The delicious breath of rain was in the air. In the street below a peddler was crying his wares. The notes of a distant song which some one was singing reached her faintly, and countless sparrows were twittering in the eaves.

6   There were patches of blue sky showing here and there through the clouds that had met and piled one above the other in the west facing her window.

 NOTES

Skill:
Story Elements

Words such as "comfortable," "roomy," and "delicious breath" describe the setting in a positive way. This seems to contrast with the terrible news Mrs. Mallard has received and how she must be feeling.

Reading & Writing
Companion   1

NOTES

Skill:
Textual Evidence

The labor Mrs. Mallard put into her marriage shows on her face, which is lined but strong. She is tired from enduring a lack of freedom. The phrase "But now" signals a transition in her state of mind.

Skill:
Text-Dependent Responses

Mrs. Mallard has contradictory feelings in response to her husband's death. She both grieves for him and celebrates her freedom. She imagines that she will cry at his funeral. However, she does not focus on her loss. She sees her independence beyond it.

7   She sat with her head thrown back upon the cushion of the chair, quite motionless, except when a sob came up into her throat and shook her, as a child who has cried itself to sleep continues to sob in its dreams.

8   She was young, with a fair, calm face, whose lines bespoke repression and even a certain strength. But now there was a dull stare in her eyes, whose gaze was fixed away off yonder on one of those patches of blue sky. It was not a glance of reflection, but rather indicated a suspension of intelligent thought.

9   There was something coming to her and she was waiting for it, fearfully. What was it? She did not know; it was too subtle and elusive to name. But she felt it, creeping out of the sky, reaching toward her through the sounds, the scents, the color that filled the air.

10 Now her bosom rose and fell **tumultuously**. She was beginning to recognize this thing that was approaching to possess her, and she was striving to beat it back with her will—as powerless as her two white slender hands would have been.

11 When she abandoned herself a little whispered word escaped her slightly parted lips. She said it over and over under the breath: "free, free, free!" The vacant stare and the look of terror that had followed it went from her eyes. They stayed keen and bright. Her pulses beat fast, and the coursing blood warmed and relaxed every inch of her body.

12 She did not stop to ask if it were or were not a monstrous joy that held her. A clear and exalted perception enabled her to dismiss the suggestion as trivial.

13 She knew that she would weep again when she saw the kind, tender hands folded in death; the face that had never looked save with love upon her, fixed and gray and dead. But she saw beyond that bitter moment a long procession of years to come that would belong to her **absolutely**. And she opened and spread her arms out to them in welcome.

14 There would be no one to live for during those coming years; she would live for herself. There would be no powerful will bending hers in that blind persistence with which men and women believe they have a right to impose a private will upon a fellow-creature. A kind intention or a cruel intention made the act seem no less a crime as she looked upon it in that brief moment of illumination.

15 And yet she had loved him—sometimes. Often she had not. What did it matter! What could love, the unsolved mystery, count for in the face of this possession of self-assertion which she suddenly recognized as the strongest impulse of her being!

NOTES

16   "Free! Body and soul free!" she kept whispering.

17   Josephine was kneeling before the closed door with her lips to the keyhole, imploring for admission. "Louise, open the door! I beg; open the door—you will make yourself ill. What are you doing, Louise? For heaven's sake open the door."

18   "Go away. I am not making myself ill." No; she was drinking in a very **elixir** of life through that open window.

19   Her fancy[1] was running riot along those days ahead of her. Spring days, and summer days, and all sorts of days that would be her own. She breathed a quick prayer that life might be long. It was only yesterday she had thought with a shudder that life might be long.

20   She arose at length and opened the door to her sister's **importunities**. There was a feverish triumph in her eyes, and she carried herself unwittingly like a goddess of Victory. She clasped her sister's waist, and together they descended the stairs. Richards stood waiting for them at the bottom.

21   Some one was opening the front door with a latchkey. It was Brently Mallard who entered, a little travel-stained, composedly carrying his grip-sack and umbrella. He had been far from the scene of the accident, and did not even know there had been one. He stood amazed at Josephine's piercing cry; at Richards' quick motion to screen him from the view of his wife.

22   But Richards was too late.

23   When the doctors came they said she had died of heart disease—of the joy that kills.

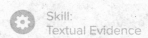

Skill:
Textual Evidence

Louise Mallard locks herself in her room because she is distraught by her husband's death. When she exits her room, the words "triumph" and "Victory" show that she feels like she endured a battle and that she won the fight.

---

1. **fancy** a particular liking, interest or desire one has

Skill:
Text-Dependent Responses

Use the Checklist to analyze Text-Dependent Responses in "The Story of an Hour." Refer to the sample student annotations about Text-Dependent Responses in the text.

••• CHECKLIST FOR TEXT-DEPENDENT RESPONSES

In order to identify strong and thorough textual evidence that supports an analysis, note the following:

✓ strong and thorough details from the text that help to make a strong inference or draw a conclusion. Inferences are sound and logical assumptions about information in a text that is not explicitly stated by the author. To practice, you should:

- read closely and critically and consider why an author provides or excludes particular details and information

- apply your own knowledge and experiences, along with textual evidence to help you figure out what the author does not state directly

- cite several pieces of textual evidence that offer strong and thorough support for your analysis

- note where textual evidence is lacking, leaving certain matters uncertain

✓ strong and thorough details that you can use to support your ideas and opinions about a text

✓ explicit evidence of a character's feelings or motivations, or the reasons behind an historical event in a nonfiction text

- explicit evidence is stated directly in the text and must be cited accurately to support a text-dependent response or analysis

To cite strong and thorough textual evidence to support an analysis, including determining where the text leaves matters uncertain, consider the following questions:

✓ What strong and thorough textual evidence can I use to support an analysis of the text?

✓ Where does the text leave matters uncertain? How will that impact my analysis?

✓ If I infer things in the text that the author does not state directly, what evidence can I use to support my analysis?

Skill:
Text-Dependent Responses

Reread paragraphs 9–14 from "The Story of an Hour." Then, using the Checklist on the previous page, answer the multiple-choice questions below.

 YOUR TURN

1. In paragraph 9, it is revealed that "There was something coming to her and she was waiting for it, fearfully." Which commentary best responds to this textual evidence?

   ○ A. This textual evidence shows that Mrs. Mallard has heart problems and is worried about having a heart attack.

   ◉ B. This textual evidence shows that Mrs. Mallard is worried that a bird might enter her room through the window.

   ○ C. This textual evidence shows that Mrs. Mallard is afraid there will be another train accident.

   ○ D. This textual evidence shows that Mrs. Mallard's feeling is far from her usual experiences.

2. Which quotation best supports the reader's response that claims Mrs. Mallard dies from disappointment when she discovers her husband is still living?

   ○ A. "She knew that she would weep again when she saw the kind, tender hands folded in death."

   ○ B. "There was something coming to her and she was waiting for it, fearfully."

   ○ C. "There would be no one to live for during those coming years; she would live for herself."

   ◉ D. "The vacant stare and the look of terror that had followed it went from her eyes."

Please note that excerpts and passages in the StudySync® library and this workbook are intended as touchstones to generate interest in an author's work. The excerpts and passages do not substitute for the reading of entire texts, and StudySync® strongly recommends that students seek out and purchase the whole literary or informational work in order to experience it as the author intended. Links to online resellers are available in our digital library. In addition, complete works may be ordered through an authorized reseller by filling out and returning to StudySync® the order form enclosed in this workbook.

Reading & Writing Companion

5

First Read

Read "The Story of an Hour." After you read, complete the Think Questions below.

☁ THINK QUESTIONS

1. At the beginning of paragraph 9, Mrs. Mallard senses "something coming to her." What is it? What physical effect does it have on her? Cite evidence from the text to support your response.

2. In paragraphs 5 through 9, how do the details about the natural setting outside of Mrs. Mallard's room relate to her emotional state? Point to specific evidence from the text to support your response.

3. At the end of the story, why do the doctors think that Mrs. Mallard died of "the joy that kills"? Do you think their diagnosis is accurate? Cite evidence from the text to support your answer.

4. Use context clues to determine the meaning of the word **elixir**. Then write your best definition of the word here, along with the clues that helped you find it.

5. Use context clues to determine the meaning of the word **absolutely** as it is used in "The Story of an Hour." Write your best definition of *absolutely* here. Then consult a print or online dictionary to confirm its meaning.

Skill:
Textual Evidence

Use the Checklist to analyze Textual Evidence in "The Story of an Hour." Refer to the sample student annotations about Textual Evidence in the text.

••• CHECKLIST FOR TEXTUAL EVIDENCE

In order to support an analysis by citing evidence that is explicitly stated in the text, do the following:

- ✓ read the text closely and critically

- ✓ identify what the text says explicitly

- ✓ find the most relevant textual evidence that supports your analysis

- ✓ cite the specific words, phrases, sentences, or paragraphs from the text that support your analysis

- ✓ determine where evidence in the text still leaves certain matters uncertain or unresolved

In order to interpret implicit meanings in a text by making inferences, do the following:

- ✓ combine information directly stated in the text with your own knowledge, and observations

- ✓ cite the specific evidence from the text that led to and support this inference

In order to cite textual evidence to support an analysis of what the text says explicitly as well as inferences drawn from the text, consider the following questions:

- ✓ Have I read the text closely and critically?

- ✓ What inferences am I making about the text?

- ✓ What textual evidence am I using to support these inferences?

- ✓ Am I quoting the evidence from the text correctly?

- ✓ Does my textual evidence logically relate to my analysis or the inference I am making?

- ✓ Does evidence in the text still leave certain matters unanswered or unresolved? In what ways?

Skill:
Textual Evidence

Reread paragraphs 3–7 from "The Story of an Hour." Then, using the Checklist on the previous page, answer the multiple-choice questions below.

🔁 YOUR TURN

1. According to the text, Mrs. Mallard's initial response to her husband's death is different from that of other women because—

   ● A. she weeps immediately.
   ○ B. she wants to grieve alone.
   ○ C. she sobs like a child.
   ○ D. she would rather be outside.

2. In paragraph 5, which pair of words best supports the claim that the scene outside the window is a symbol of renewal?

   ○ A. distant, faintly
   ○ B. twittering, crying
   ○ C. tops, aquiver
   ● D. open, life

Reading & Writing Companion

Skill:
Story Elements

Use the Checklist to analyze Story Elements in "The Story of an Hour." Refer to the sample student annotations about Story Elements in the text.

••• CHECKLIST FOR STORY ELEMENTS

In order to identify the impact of the author's choices regarding how to develop and relate elements of a story or drama, note the following:

✓ where and when the story takes place, who the main characters are, and the main conflict, or problem, in the plot

✓ the order of the action

✓ how the characters are introduced and developed

✓ the impact that the author's choice of setting has on the characters and their attempt to solve the problem

✓ the point of view the author uses, and how this shapes what readers know about the characters in the story

To analyze the impact of the author's choices regarding how to develop and to relate elements of a story or drama, consider the following questions:

✓ How do the author's choices affect the story elements? The development of the plot?

✓ How does the setting influence the characters?

✓ Which elements of the setting impact the plot, and in particular the problem the characters face and must solve?

✓ Are there any flashbacks or other story elements that have an effect on the development of events in the plot? How does the author's choice of utilizing a flashback affect this development?

✓ How does the author introduce and develop characters in the story? Why do you think the author made these choices?

Skill:
Story Elements

Reread paragraphs 17–22 from "The Story of an Hour." Then, using the Checklist on the previous page, answer the multiple-choice questions below.

🔁 YOUR TURN

1. How does Mrs. Mallard's character develop over the course of the short story?

   ○ A. Mrs. Mallard begins to recognize that prayer is powerful and that she should begin to pray more so that she can live a long life.

   ◉ B. Mrs. Mallard begins to recognize that she is now a free and independent women who has escaped a confined, unhappy life, and this brings her relief, hope, and excitement.

   ○ C. Mrs. Mallard begins to recognize that she is an independent women, and this scares her and makes her feel very sad and alone.

   ○ D. Mrs. Mallard transforms from feeling like an uninteresting, boring women to a goddess who will easily be able to find another husband.

2. How does Mrs. Mallard's character development over the course of the short story impact the story's outcome?

   ◉ A. Mrs. Mallard's shift from feeling trapped to feeling free is snatched from her at the very end of the story, causing her death because her new found joy is taken from her.

   ○ B. Mrs. Mallard shifts from feeling trapped to feeling enraged when she finds out her husband is alive, and her anger causes her death.

   ○ C. Mrs. Mallard's shift from feeling trapped to feeling free is snatched from her at the very end of the story, and it causes her death because she is overjoyed that her husband is alive.

   ○ D. Mrs. Mallard shifts from feeling very sad about her husband's death to feeling comforted and relieved that he is alive.

Close Read

Reread "The Story of an Hour." As you reread, complete the Skills Focus questions below. Then use your answers and annotations from the questions to help you complete the Write activity.

◎ SKILLS FOCUS

1. Identify details in the beginning of the story that describe how other characters perceive Mrs. Mallard, and explain how this characterization helps develop the plot.

2. Paragraphs 4 through 6 describe aspects of the setting that Mrs. Mallard observes through her window. Highlight the descriptive phrases about the setting that show what Mrs. Mallard sees and explain how these details influence the plot.

3. In paragraphs 9-11, identify textual evidence that shows Mrs. Mallard's reaction to Mr. Mallard's death once she is alone. Then make an inference about how Mrs. Mallard thinks her husband's death will affect her life, and explain how the textual evidence supports that inference.

4. Reread paragraph 14, and use context clues to determine the meaning of the word **impose**. Highlight the clues that help you determine the word's meaning, and annotate with your best definition of the word.

5. What bearing does the idea of independence have on Mrs. Mallard's feelings and actions? How much does she value independence?

✎ WRITE

LITERARY ANALYSIS: How does the author use story elements such as setting, character development, or theme to develop the plot of "The Story of an Hour"? In your response, evaluate at least two of the story elements used by the author and how they shape the plot. Use evidence from the text to support your analysis.

Please note that excerpts and passages in the StudySync® library and this workbook are intended as touchstones to generate interest in an author's work. The excerpts and passages do not substitute for the reading of entire texts, and StudySync® strongly recommends that students seek out and purchase the whole literary or informational work in order to experience it as the author intended. Links to online resellers are available in our digital library. In addition, complete works may be ordered through an authorized reseller by filling out and returning to StudySync® the order form enclosed in this workbook.

Reading & Writing Companion   11

Introduction

This informational text offers background about the history and culture that defined early American literature, including written and oral pieces from indigenous, European, and African voices. Readers will explore early, groundbreaking literature about self-government and consider the progressive ideals of the time, which influenced its most memorable works. What great texts, for example, inspired America's foundational documents? Amidst the different religious and philosophical movements of their respective times, works like the Constitution of the Iroquois Nations and the Declaration of Independence set the framework for a new democracy.

"...new, never-before-seen ideas emerge from the interactions of diverse cultures."

1   American culture is characterized by its blend of features from other cultures. Barbecue, for example, is based upon a native Caribbean cooking technique, uses European ingredients, and was popularized and spread by African Americans. Jazz and blues make use of European-inspired harmonies and African-inspired rhythms. In many aspects of American life, you can find influences from the cultures of Native Americans, European colonists, and Africans. Even the earliest examples of American literature show how new, never-before-seen ideas emerge from the interactions of diverse cultures.

The First Peoples

2   Between about 40,000 and 10,000 BCE, small bands of people crossed a land bridge between Asia and North America—where the Bering Strait exists today—and began to settle in North America. Over time, the population grew and spread to form hundreds of diverse indigenous cultures in North and South America. For thousands of years, the cultures of indigenous peoples of North America flourished. Some societies developed writing systems, especially those in modern-day Mexico and Central America, but the majority of Native American peoples maintained a rich oral literature tradition to preserve their beliefs and histories. The Constitution of the Iroquois Nations, which contained some of the original ideas about **self-government** and later influenced the creation of the founding documents of the United States of America, was passed down for hundreds of years through Native American oral traditions.

Painting by Henry Bruckner (ca. 1855) depicting the marriage of British colonist John Rolfe to Pocahontas, the daughter of Chief Powhatan of the Algonquian tribe, in 1614

NOTES

Colonization

3   The existence of North and South America was largely unknown to Europeans until the voyages of Christopher Columbus in the late fifteenth century brought widespread attention to the region. In the ensuing rush to gain economic and territorial power, Spain, England, and other countries began to establish **colonies** in what Amerigo Vespucci called *Mundus Novus*, or the New World. Initial accounts from early colonists told stories of a land rich in resources and opportunity, compelling people from all over Europe to cross the Atlantic to seek a new life in North America.

4   When the early settlers arrived, they began interacting with the indigenous peoples who had long inhabited the land. The desire of European settlers to claim physical territory and establish colonial culture often resulted in widespread violence against Native Americans. This oppression of others was also spurred by a desire for economic gain. For example, as early as 1501, the Spanish started kidnapping and enslaving Africans, forcibly bringing them from their native continent to the Americas as as part of a widespread slave trade that was both extremely profitable and inhumane.

5   What resulted was a society of people from wide-ranging backgrounds, comprised of the oppressed and the oppressors, all speaking a multitude of languages including Spanish, English, German, Portuguese, Dutch, French, a variety of African languages, and, of course, indigenous languages. The tumultuous, and at times violent, interaction of these diverse cultures in North America during the early colonial period contributed to the formation of a unique and fraught American cultural identity.

6   Eventually, as England colonized the entire eastern seaboard north of Florida, English became the most common language and literature in the colonies. Much of the literature the colonists read and drew from in their own writings originated in Britain. England had a well-established literary tradition at the time—Shakespeare had died only four years before the Pilgrims landed at Plymouth in 1620. By contrast, because North American settlers were occupied with establishing the colonies and had little time to devote to the creation of original works of fiction, the majority of early colonial literature was utilitarian—observations of North American geography, biographies, and treatises. There was also a significant body of religious literature because many of the English colonists were Puritans who had come to North America seeking religious freedom. **Puritanism** was a religious movement of Reformed Protestants who felt that the Church of England, which had split from the Roman Catholic Church in 1534, was still too similar to Catholicism and needed further reform. While colonial literature was still heavily influenced by the English, the Puritans' efforts to differentiate themselves from English religious culture had a strong influence on new ideas that had begun to percolate in the colonial imagination.

7   In the eighteenth century, two important movements had a defining influence on colonial culture: the **Enlightenment** and **the Great Awakening**. The Enlightenment was a philosophical movement that promoted the use of reason in all areas of intellectual life. Enlightenment ideas swept through the entire Western world and had revolutionary effects on both sides of the Atlantic. European Enlightenment philosophers, including John Locke and Thomas Hobbes, introduced a political philosophy concerned with equality and the natural rights of man, which provided a foundation for the creation of modern democracies. In North America, Benjamin Franklin, Thomas Paine, and Thomas Jefferson incorporated Enlightenment ideas into their rhetoric, urging the Thirteen British Colonies to break their ties to England and eventually leading to the **Revolutionary War** and the Declaration of Independence.

8   What's more, in the 1730s and 1740s, a growing religious movement, known as the Great Awakening, began to gain popularity in the colonies. Reform Protestants, like George Whitefield and Jonathan Edwards, preached to large groups about a more personal approach to faith and successfully converted large numbers of people from a variety of religious, social, and racial backgrounds. Both the Enlightenment and the Great Awakening helped to shape a distinctively American sense of identity, encouraging people to find their own way rather than subject themselves to the power of traditional governments and religious institutions. In the process of intellectual exploration and debate, the colonists ultimately formulated dramatic new ideas about reason, religion, and independence that led to the founding of the United States of America and changed the world.

9   **Major Concepts**

- **The Sacred Earth and the Power of Storytelling** — The oral literature of Native American peoples reflected the deep connection to the earth that was at the heart of their belief system. Some stories had practical functions such as helping to keep track of seasons, animal migrations, harvest times, and other periodic phenomena, but other narratives had a more spiritual purpose. Creation myths described how the earth began and origin myths explained how things like the moon or mountains were made. Many stories emphasized the sacred harmony, or interdependence, between humans and the natural world.

- **Life in the New World** — Many of the inhabitants of North America during the colonial period were struggling to adapt to unfamiliar circumstances. Native Americans saw the land they had inhabited for thousands of years overrun by newcomers; they saw their populations being decimated by European diseases and colonization, which culminated in violent battles over territory. Early European settlers sought to establish themselves and tame what they viewed as a wild and alien environment, documenting

NOTES

their efforts in diaries, letters, and books. Enslaved Africans passed on oral and written accounts of their daily struggle to survive the violence and degradation imposed on them by colonial masters.

- **The Road to Independence** — In order to fund the Seven Years' War with France, Great Britain imposed high taxes on the colonists. They also sent soldiers to the colonies to enforce regulations and maintain control of the territory. Without representation in the British Parliament—England's legislative body—colonists had no power to voice their opposition to the taxes and policies imposed on them. The colonists shared the view of Enlightenment philosophers who believed that a government's authority was dependent upon the consent of the governed. Literature of the late colonial period dealt with these conflicts as well as ideas of justice, independence, and how to create a better society.

John Trumbull's 1818 painting depicting the presentation of the Declaration of Independence to Congress in 1776

Style and Form

Native American Literature

10

- Native American oral literature incorporated pattern, repetition, and structural formulas as mnemonic devices, or memory aids. How these elements were used in a given story influenced the story's style and form.

- Native American oral literature was comprised of many genres, including creation and origin myths, prayers, songs, folktales, and narratives of heroism and transformation. Native American oral literature was performed, not read. Thus, the translation of indigenous stories into written English sometimes caused certain aspects of the stories to be lost or recorded in a different form than how they were originally performed.

Puritans

11

- William Bradford was a Puritan who served as governor of the Plymouth colony for over thirty years. His *Of Plymouth Plantation* provides insight into colonial life. He defined Puritan style as a "plain style, with singular regard unto the simple truth in all things."

- This plain, simple, truthful style was employed first by the Puritans but became a hallmark of early American literature. For instance, Jonathan Edwards and George Whitfield used it in their sermons.

12 **Significance of Rhetoric and Rhetorical Devices**

- Rhetoric is the art of speaking and writing persuasively. Classical rhetoric uses three types of appeals: *logos*, an appeal to logic; *pathos*, an emotional appeal to the audience; and *ethos*, an appeal based the author's expertise. Revolutionaries like Thomas Paine and Thomas Jefferson expertly adopted these rhetorical methods in their speeches and writings, most famously in Paine's *Common Sense* and in the Declaration of Independence, which was drafted by Jefferson.

- Authors use rhetorical devices like similes, metaphors, and irony, among a long list of other things, to convince their audiences in more subtle ways. Thomas Jefferson was a learned student of literature and philosophy and had a keen sense of how to use these devices. In the Declaration of Independence, he employed a straightforward style but used rhetorical devices such as alliteration, allusion, euphony, and repetition to drive home his points. The rhetoric used during the late colonial period was instrumental in fostering the revolutionary spirit that defined the times and formed the basis of the arguments that led to the founding of the United States of America.

Phillis Wheatley

13 **Biblical Symbolism, Neoclassical Couplets, and Iambic Pentameter**

- Early American poets, such as the enslaved poet, Phillis Wheatley, sometimes took inspiration from English writers such as Alexander Pope. Neoclassical poetry, like Pope's, often used the heroic couplet. Couplets are two successive lines in which the last words rhyme. Heroic couplets are couplets written in iambic pentameter, a poetic meter with five "beats," or stressed syllables.

- Biblical symbolism also appears in poems written in the period. For example, in Wheatley's "On Being Brought from Africa to America,"she compares Africans to the biblical figure Cain, to whom God showed mercy.

14 Early American literature was influenced by a variety of cultures and traditions, but it also incorporated new ideas and interpreted them in a uniquely American way. People from diverse backgrounds built a new culture that was based on a foundation of Old World literary custom and invigorated by the exploration and adoption of new ideas. Combining ideas to create something new continues to fuel America's gift for innovation. Where else in modern-day America can you recognize the concepts and ideas that defined early American literature? How do diverse opinions about the guiding principles of early American culture—reason, religious freedom, and independence—continue to shape America today?

Literary Focus

Read "Literary Focus: Early America." After you read, complete the Think Questions below.

THINK QUESTIONS

1. Explain how rhetoric can be used to convince an audience. Provide examples of early American literature in which the authors utilize rhetoric. Be sure to cite evidence directly from the text.

2. What are some of the cultural differences among the various groups that inhabited the early American colonies, and how are these differences reflected in their literature? Explain, citing evidence from the text to support your response.

3. What effect did religion have on different works of early American literature? Cite evidence from the text to support your explanations.

4. Use context clues to determine the meaning of the word **colonies**. Write your best definition here, along with the words and phrases that were most helpful in determining the word's meaning. Then, check a dictionary to confirm your understanding.

5. The word **puritanism** likely stems from the Latin *puritas*, meaning "purity." With this information in mind along with context from the text, write your best definition of the word *puritanism* as it used in this text. Cite any words or phrases that were particularly helpful in coming to your conclusion.

On Being Brought from Africa to America

POETRY
Phillis Wheatley
1773

Introduction

Seized from her home in West Africa by slave traders when she was no more seven years of age, Phillis Wheatley (ca. 1753–1784) nevertheless learned to read and write in a hostile, unfamiliar land. Named for the ship (Phyllis) that brought her to America in chains, she would become the first African American writer to have a book of poetry published. Due to prejudices at the time, Wheatley's authorship of her poems was quickly contested. Seventeen Boston men (including John Hancock) signed a preface to Wheatley's volume, verifying her authorship. Wheatley's poems are stylistically complex and sophisticated, with themes focusing on faith, perseverance, and morality. This poem, "On Being Brought from Africa to America," is an autobiographical reflection of Wheatley's journey to America.

"Some view our sable race with scornful eye . . ."

NOTES

1 'Twas mercy brought me from my *Pagan* land,
2 Taught my **benighted** soul to understand
3 That there's a God, that there's a *Saviour* too:
4 Once I redemption neither sought nor knew.
5 Some view our **sable** race with **scornful** eye,
6 "Their colour is a **diabolic** die."
7 Remember, *Christians*, *Negros*[1], black as *Cain*[2],
8 May be refin'd, and join th' angelic train.

Phillis Wheatley

✏ WRITE

PERSONAL RESPONSE: Consider the emotions and events described in the poem. In your opinion, what would be an appropriate alternate title to convey the speaker's perspective and experiences? Why? Use evidence from the text to support your response.

---

1. **Negros** common terminology at the time for peoples of African descent
2. **Cain** In the book of Genesis, Cain, the son of Adam, kills his brother, Abel.

An Address to Miss Phillis Wheatley

POEM
Jupiter Hammon
1778

Introduction

Jupiter Hammon (1711–ca. 1806) was America's first published black poet. His first poem appeared in a broadside in 1761; his second, featured here, was not published until 17 years later. Hammon was born into slavery; although supportive of the abolitionist movement, he was never himself emancipated. A devout Christian, he encouraged enslaved people to look to heaven for salvation from the evils of slavery on Earth. "An Address to Miss Phillis Wheatley" was a direct entreaty to America's first published black female poet, herself an emancipated Christian. In the poem, Hammon encourages Wheatley to improve as a Christian and become more devout. In the original publication, each stanza was accompanied by a corresponding Bible verse.

"Dear Phillis, seek for heaven's joys, Where we do hope to meet."

I

1   O come you pious youth! adore
2   The wisdom of thy God,
3   In bringing thee from distant shore,
4   To learn His holy word.

II

5   Thou mightst been left behind
6   Amidst a dark abode;
7   God's tender mercy still combin'd
8   Thou hast the holy word.

III

9   Fair wisdom's ways are paths of peace,
10   And they that walk therein,
11   Shall reap the joys that never **cease**
12   And Christ shall be their king.

IV

13   God's tender mercy brought thee here;
14   Tost o'er the raging main;[1]
15   In Christian faith thou hast a share,
16   Worth all the gold of Spain.

V

17   While thousands tossed by the sea,
18   And others settled down,
19   God's tender mercy set thee free,
20   From dangers that come down.

VI

21   That thou a pattern still might be,
22   To youth of Boston town,
23   The blessed Jesus set thee free,
24   From every sinful wound.

---

1. **main** (archaic) the ocean

Copyright © BookheadEd Learning, LLC

VII

25 The blessed Jesus, who came down,
26 Unvail'd his sacred face,
27 To cleanse the soul of every wound,
28 And give repenting grace.

VIII

29 That we poor sinners may obtain
30 The pardon of our sin;
31 Dear blessed Jesus now constrain
32 And bring us flocking in.

IX

33 Come you, Phillis, now aspire,
34 And seek the living God,
35 So step by step thou mayst go higher,
36 Till perfect in the word.

X

37 While thousands mov'd to distant shore,
38 And others left behind,
39 The blessed Jesus still adore,
40 Implant this in thy mind.

XI

41 Thou hast left the **heathen** shore;
42 Thro' mercy of the Lord,
43 Among the heathen live no more,
44 Come magnify thy God.

XII

45 I pray the living God may be,
46 The shepherd of thy soul;
47 His tender mercies still are free,
48 His mysteries to unfold.

XIII

49 Thou, Phillis, when thou hunger hast,
50 Or pantest for thy God;
51 Jesus Christ is thy **relief**,
52 Thou hast the holy word.

XIV

53 The bounteous mercies of the Lord
54 Are hid beyond the sky,

55 And holy souls that love His word,
56 Shall taste them when they die.

XV
57 These bounteous mercies are from God,
58 The merits of His Son;
59 The humble soul that loves his word,
60 He chooses for His own.

XVI
61 Come, dear Phillis, be advis'd
62 To drink Samaria's flood,[2]
63 There's nothing that shall **suffice**
64 But Christ's redeeming blood.

XVII
65 While thousands muse with earthly toys;
66 And range about the street;
67 Dear Phillis, seek for heaven's joys,
68 Where we do hope to meet.

XVIII
69 When God shall send his summons down
70 And number saints together
71 Blest angels chant (Triumphant sound)
72 Come live with me forever.

XIX
73 The humble soul shall fly to God,
74 And leave the things of time.
75 Stand forth as 'twere at the first word,
76 To taste things more divine.

XX
77 Behold! the soul shall waft away,
78 Whene'er we come to die,
79 And leave its cottage made of clay,
80 In twinkling of an eye.

XXI
81 Now glory be to the Most High,
82 United praises given
83 By all on earth, **incessantly**,
84 And all the hosts of heav'n.

---

2. **Samaria's flood** In Biblical times, Samaria was the capital of the northern kingdom of Israel.

First Read

Read "An Address to Miss Phillis Wheatley." After you read, complete the Think Questions below.

THINK QUESTIONS

1. Who are the "pious youth[s]" the poet addresses in stanza 1? Cite evidence from the text to support your answer.

2. When does the poem first mention Phillis Wheatley (outside of the title)? Why do you think her name appears where it does, relative to the beginning of the poem? Cite evidence from the text to support your answer.

3. What is the poet's prevailing attitude toward Phillis Wheatley? Is this attitude straightforward, or conflicted? Cite evidence from the text to support your answer.

4. Read the following dictionary entry:

   relief
   re•lief /rɪˈliːf/

   noun

   1. financial assistance to a state, organization, or individual
   2. release from anxiety, pain, or stress
   3. a person replacing another on duty
   4. the state of being accentuated by a backdrop

   Which definition most closely matches the meaning of **relief** as it is used in the text? Write the correct definition of *relief* here, and explain how you figured out its meaning.

5. Use context clues to determine the meaning of **suffice** as it is used in the text. Write your definition here, and describe which clues helped you arrive at it.

Skill:
Compare and Contrast

Use the Checklist to analyze Compare and Contrast in "An Address to Miss Phillis Wheatley" and "On Being Brought from Africa to America."

••• CHECKLIST FOR COMPARE AND CONTRAST

In order to determine how to compare and contrast texts from the same period, and how these texts treat similar themes or topics, use the following steps:

✓ first, identify two or more foundational works of American literature written during the eighteenth-, nineteenth- or early-twentieth-century

✓ next, identify the topic and theme in each work, and any central or recurring topics that each author presents

✓ after, explain how each text reflects and represents the time period in which it was written, including its historical events, customs, beliefs, or social norms

✓ finally, explain the similarities or differences between each of the texts written during the same time period including how they address related themes and topics

To demonstrate knowledge of and compare and contrast eighteenth-, nineteenth- and early-twentieth-century foundational works of American literature, consider the following questions:

✓ Are the texts from the same time period in American literature?

✓ In what ways does each text reflect and represent the time period in which it was written?

✓ How does each work treat themes or topics representative of the time period in which it was written?

✓ How is the treatment of the themes or topics in these literary works similar and different?

Please note that excerpts and passages in the StudySync® library and this workbook are intended as touchstones to generate interest in an author's work. The excerpts and passages do not substitute for the reading of entire texts, and StudySync® strongly recommends that students seek out and purchase the whole literary or informational work in order to experience it as the author intended. Links to online resellers are available in our digital library. In addition, complete works may be ordered through an authorized reseller by filling out and returning to StudySync® the order form enclosed in this workbook.

Reading & Writing
Companion

27

Skill:
Compare and Contrast

Reread stanzas 14 through 17 of "An Address to Miss Phillis Wheatley" and the entirety of "On Being Brought from Africa to America." Then, using the Checklist on the previous page, answer the multiple-choice questions below.

↻ YOUR TURN

1. How does each poet describe his or her experiences with religion in different ways?

   ○ A. Wheatley says that religion turned her away from a "pagan" life whereas Hammon says it made him feel discriminated against.

   ○ B. Wheatley uses religion as a metaphor for her experience, whereas Hammon uses scripture to give his argument credibility.

   ○ C. Wheatley views religion as offering personal enlightenment, whereas Hammon uses his beliefs to offer advice to others.

   ○ D. Wheatley uses less religious imagery in her poem than Hammon does.

2. Since the two poems are autobiographical, which inference about each poet's experience is best supported by comparing and contrasting the language in the text?

   ○ A. Both poets seem thankful for their religious experiences in America.

   ○ B. Both poets show ambivalence about their experiences with conversion.

   ○ C. Both poets experienced uncertainty about their Christian faith.

   ○ D. Both poets use rhyme as a humorous technique in their poems.

Close Read

Reread "An Address to Miss Phillis Wheatley" and "On Being Brought from Africa to America." As you reread, complete the Skills Focus questions below. Then use your answers and annotations from questions to help you complete the Write activity.

◎ SKILLS FOCUS

1. Identify Hammon's commands in the first three stanzas. What is he advising his reader to do? Cite evidence to support your answer.

2. How does Hammon's repetitious discussions of God, Jesus, and Christ differ from Wheatley's language?

3. In her poem "On Being Brought from Africa to America," Wheatley states, "'Twas mercy brought me from my *Pagan* land / Taught my benighted soul to understand." Explain whether Hammon and Wheatley have similar perspectives. Find evidence from Hammon's poem to support your answer.

4. How do Hammon and Wheatley's relationship with religion support or challenge the concept of independence? Cite evidence from the poems to support your answer.

✏ WRITE

COMPARE AND CONTRAST: Citing clear, supporting evidence from both texts, compare and contrast the overall attitude toward religion in each poem. In which ways do the authors agree about religion, and in which ways do they disagree? Then, tell how both poems represent early American literature.

Life After High School

ARGUMENTATIVE TEXT
Point/Counterpoint
2018

Introduction

Are you thinking of moving away from home after graduating from high school? In the two argumentative essays presented here, each writer makes a case for what's best. One discusses the positive opportunities of moving away from home, whereas the other explores why staying near home might be more beneficial in the long run. Both writers present strong arguments and support their claims with evidence. Which of the arguments do you find more convincing?

"In a new place, young adults can meet people they never would have met online."

Life After High School: Is it better to move far away or stay close to home?

Point: It is better to move far away from home after high school.

1   For a recent high school graduate, now is the best time to move far away from home because moving to a new place offers more independence, new experiences, and increased awareness about the world.

Gain Independence

2   According to Eurobarometer and the 2005 Current Population Survey, almost 12% of people in the United States move each year. This percentage puts Americans only slightly behind the most frequent movers in the world, the Finnish and the Danish. Considering that the United States was founded by people moving from England to escape the restraints of their old lives and begin anew, moving seems to be an important part of our national character.

3   One of the main reasons to move far away from home after high school is to gain more independence. At home, young adults have to follow their parents' or guardians' rules. Even if these young adults move but stay close to home, they may find themselves encountering similar rules and hearing unwanted advice from family and old friends. In another place, whether at a college or at a new job in a new city, young adults will be able to make their own rules and form their own habits.

4   Some people argue that moving far away will make it harder for young adults to get help if they need it. It's true that parents cannot easily rush to aid their children if they live hundreds of miles apart, but depending on the situation, this may actually be a benefit. For example, if young adults have always had meals prepared by a parent or guardian, then living far away means that they must learn to provide meals for themselves that suit their individual tastes and budgets. Besides, parents or guardians will not always be available to help, even if young adults live close by, so it is important for young adults to learn how to pay bills, communicate with others, and solve problems on their own.

Expand Understanding

Skill:
Media

This summary of statistical evidence supports the claim that moving increases one's awareness of the world. The chart provides the specific data points in a clear visual format, which serves to reinforce the author's statement.

5   Another reason to move away is to have new experiences. Many students spend the majority of their childhood and adolescence in one place; they may have even spent their entire lives in the same house or apartment and learned alongside students a lot like themselves from elementary school through high school. Yet, most respondents to a 2015 Allstate/Atlantic Media Heartland Monitor Poll indicated that they would value living in an area where there are people from many different ethnic and racial backgrounds.

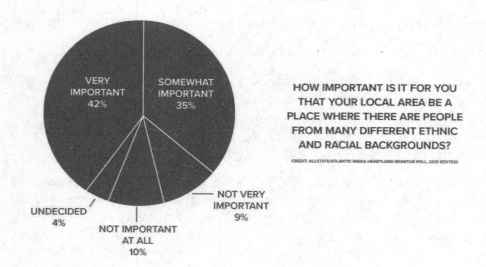

VERY IMPORTANT 42%

SOMEWHAT IMPORTANT 35%

UNDECIDED 4%

NOT IMPORTANT AT ALL 10%

NOT VERY IMPORTANT 9%

HOW IMPORTANT IS IT FOR YOU THAT YOUR LOCAL AREA BE A PLACE WHERE THERE ARE PEOPLE FROM MANY DIFFERENT ETHNIC AND RACIAL BACKGROUNDS?

CREDIT: ALLSTATE/ATLANTIC MEDIA HEARTLAND MONITOR POLL, 2015 (EDITED)

6   Once students move away from home, they will have the opportunity to meet new people. A college campus has people from all around the country and even from other countries; likewise, living in a new city allows young adults to explore new places, such as museums, restaurants, and venues for entertainment. As part of their military experience, some young adults may travel to distant bases or move to other parts of the country.

7   Moving to a new place also increases a person's awareness about the world. According to the Pew Research Center, 53% of people around the world and 60% of people in advanced world economies use social media as of 2017. Those numbers suggest that we already have increased connection to the world from our computers or smartphones. While it is possible to make new friends from around the world via social media, those numbers also show that 47% of people worldwide are not posting pictures, watching videos, and chatting on the Internet. In a new place, young adults can meet people they never would have met online. By taking a chance and exploring, young people may discover a whole new world; they may walk into a new favorite restaurant and meet fascinating people who help them see an entirely different way of experiencing the world.

Seize the Moment

8   Although it may seem scary at first, moving far away may be one of the most **beneficial** things young adults can do for themselves. Many young adults have not settled down with a partner, had children, or purchased property yet, which means that young adulthood is the perfect time to seize the moment and try living in an exciting, new place. Maybe the new place will become their new home—a place to settle down and raise their own family— or maybe the place will give them **unique** insight about the world that they can take back to their hometowns and share with others.

9   **Takeaways:**

- Moving far away is a great way to gain and **assert** independence.
- Moving far away will expand young adults' understanding of the world.
- Moving right after high school allows young adults to take advantage of the freedom of youth.

10   Being on their own, meeting new people, and learning new things are valuable experiences for young adults. After living in a new place, young adults will discover that the rewards of moving far away from home far outweigh any reason to stay behind.

"Still, nothing can replace time spent together in person . . ."

NOTES

Counterpoint: It is better to stay close to home after high school.

11 The struggle to leave childhood behind is difficult enough without having to acclimate to a new environment and create a new support system, so new high school graduates should stay close to home as they transition into their new roles as adults.

Stay Nearby, Save Money

12 In "Out of High School, Into Real Life," *New York Times* reporter Jack Healy reveals that 30% of the graduating class of 2017 did not plan to go directly to college. For many, this decision was based on the following criteria:

- Finances: some did not have enough money to pay for higher education, and others wanted to help support their parents or other family members.

- Employment: some young adults already have jobs before graduating, which allows them to contribute to their household's income.

13 Additionally, moving far away, whether it is to attend college or to pursue job opportunities in another city, involves moving expenses. Shipping furniture and electronics can be prohibitively expensive, so young adults will likely

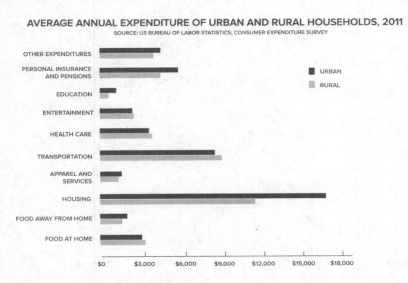

AVERAGE ANNUAL EXPENDITURE OF URBAN AND RURAL HOUSEHOLDS, 2011
SOURCE: US BUREAU OF LABOR STATISTICS, CONSUMER EXPENDITURE SURVEY

OTHER EXPENDITURES
PERSONAL INSURANCE AND PENSIONS
EDUCATION
ENTERTAINMENT
HEALTH CARE
TRANSPORTATION
APPAREL AND SERVICES
HOUSING
FOOD AWAY FROM HOME
FOOD AT HOME

■ URBAN
■ RURAL

$0 $3,000 $6,000 $9,000 $12,000 $15,000 $18,000

Copyright © BookheadEd Learning, LLC

need to purchase such essentials once they've arrived at their new homes. Some say that living in a new city is exciting, and while it's true that urban environments often afford young people new opportunities, a new graduate has to consider whether or not a new lifestyle is worth the cost. The cost of living for **fundamental** requirements, such as food, clothing, and housing, can be more expensive in an urban environment.

14   By staying close to home, students can contribute to their families as well as save money for their future plans instead of spending money on traveling or moving.

Use an Existing Network

15   Some people move to be closer to friends or distant relatives, but for most, moving away means starting over and losing networking connections. According to Healy's article, one graduating senior mentioned that he already works for a car detailing business and that his plan is to take advantage of the connections he already has in his hometown in order to start a career. He is already working to build a life for himself, so leaving to search for a new opportunity in a new place does not appeal to him.

16   Although not all families have the same business ventures, young adults can still benefit from family and friend connections. Young adults can ask people they know if someone is hiring or request advice when approaching local businesses for opportunities. Young adults may also have connections from their own experiences. Being a trusted member of the community could lead to other opportunities if people see and appreciate the young adult's work. These kinds of connections must start from scratch when young adults move somewhere new, unless they have pre-existing connections before moving.

Maintain Relationships with Family and Friends

17   Some may claim that living in a digital world means we don't need to live physically near friends and family in order to stay connected to them. Social media and technological advancements like Skype and FaceTime do make it easier to spend virtual time with faraway loved ones. Still, nothing can replace time spent together in person; seeing a person's face on a screen does not fulfill the same emotional needs as a hug or sharing an experience together. For some, it is more important to strengthen bonds with parents, siblings, grandparents, aunts, uncles, and cousins than it is to meet new people. This familial closeness can take the form of staying in the same area or living in multigenerational households, which as of 2016 make up 20% of all U.S. households according to the Pew Research Center.

18   Aside from being close and easily accessible, family and trusted friends can offer valuable moral support that can help ease young adults' transition from

Skill:
Media

The statistics shown in the bar graph counterpoint the claim that moving away is better. The presentation is clear and the source is reliable, but some figures do not directly support the claim, and "rural" may not correspond with "close to home." The media are not convincing.

NOTES

high school to the adult world. Everyone needs help sometimes, and knowing that a loved one is around to help at any time offers valuable peace of mind. A parent or guardian might be able to help with repairs around a nearby apartment or could offer roadside help with a flat tire, while trusted friends may be able to help you make important life decisions that a new acquaintance would not care to understand.

19 Looking at recent data regarding movement of different generations supports the assertion that it is better to stay close to home after high school. For the past three generations of Americans, fewer and fewer young adults are moving. For all of the reasons provided above, young adults are abandoning a transient lifestyle for the stability of home.

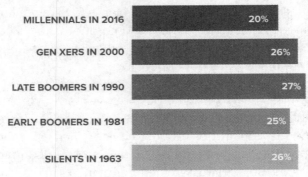

MILLENNIALS ARE LESS LIKELY TO MOVE THAN PRIOR GENERATIONS
% OF 25- TO 35-YEAR-OLDS WHO MOVED IN THE PREVIOUS YEAR

MILLENNIALS IN 2016	20%
GEN XERS IN 2000	26%
LATE BOOMERS IN 1990	27%
EARLY BOOMERS IN 1981	25%
SILENTS IN 1963	26%

"MILLENNIALS ARE LESS LIKELY TO MOVE THAN PRIOR GENERATIONS OF YOUNG ADULTS." PEW RESEARCH CENTER, WASHINGTON, D.C. FEBRUARY 10, 2017. <HTTP://WWW.PEWRESEARCH.ORG/FACT-TANK/2017/02/13/AMERI-CANS-ARE-MOVING-AT-HISTORICALLY-LOW-RATES-IN-PART-BECAUSE-MILLENNIALS-ARE-STAYING-PUT/FT_17-02-07_MILLENNIAL-MOBILITY_1/>

20 While the transition to full independence may be slower, staying close to home ultimately offers more benefits than drawbacks. Young adults can save money or contribute to their family's income, **maintain** lifelong networking connections, and strengthen the relationships with the people who mean the most to them. Travel can happen at any time, but the benefits of staying close to home are irreplaceable.

First Read

Read "Life After High School." After you read, complete the Think Questions below.

☁ THINK QUESTIONS

1. What are the benefits of moving away from home after high school? Cite at least three examples from the "Point" essay to support your answer.

2. What are some of the benefits of staying near home after high school? Cite at least three examples from the "Counterpoint" essay to support your answer.

3. Why might staying at home be an appealing choice for students who pursue higher education? Cite specific evidence from the appropriate essay to support your answer.

4. Keeping in mind that the Latin word *unus* means "one," determine the meaning of the word **unique** as it is used in paragraph 8 of the "Point" essay. Write your definition of *unique* here, and explain which context clues helped you figure it out.

5. Use context clues to determine the meaning of **assert** as it is used in paragraph 9 of the "Point" essay. Write your definition of *assert*, and explain which context clues helped you figure it out.

Please note that excerpts and passages in the StudySync® library and this workbook are intended as touchstones to generate interest in an author's work. The excerpts and passages do not substitute for the reading of entire texts, and StudySync® strongly recommends that students seek out and purchase the whole literary or informational work in order to experience it as the author intended. Links to online resellers are available in our digital library. In addition, complete works may be ordered through an authorized reseller by filling out and returning to StudySync® the order form enclosed in this workbook.

Reading & Writing Companion   37

Skill: Media

Use the Checklist to analyze Media in "Life After High School." Refer to the sample student annotations about Media in the text.

••• CHECKLIST FOR MEDIA

In order to determine how to integrate and/or evaluate multiple sources of information presented in different media or formats, note the following:

- ✓ whether multiple media are incorporated as support in a single document or are stand-alone versions or sources of the same information

- ✓ the key elements in each source of information

- ✓ the various elements of a particular medium and how the parts are put together

- ✓ how each medium or format presents information, e.g., visually and/or quantitatively

- ✓ what information is included or excluded in each media presentation

- ✓ the substantial differences in types of media presentation, e.g., tables, bar charts, infographics with newscast, documentary, made-for-TV docudrama

- ✓ the audience and the author's purpose of each media presentation

- ✓ the reliability and credibility of each presentation

To integrate and/or evaluate multiple sources of information presented in different media or formats as well as in words in order to address a question or solve a problem, consider the following questions:

- ✓ How is each media presentation reliable or credible?

- ✓ How can you use each media presentation?

- ✓ How can you integrate multiple sources of information presented in different media or formats to address a question, solve a problem, or support an argument?

Skill:
Media

Reread paragraph 19 from the "Counterpoint" essay and the text accompanying the chart comparing millennials' and prior generations' likelihood of moving. Then, using the Checklist on the previous page, answer the multiple-choice questions below.

⟳ YOUR TURN

1. The author's purpose for including millennials' comparative migration statistics is most likely to—

   ○ A. refute the "Point" author's claim that all generations prefer urban living.

   ○ B. contrast moving costs between urban and rural households.

   ○ C. prove that older generations prefer urban living.

   ○ D. show the relevance of the argument to the author's contemporaries.

2. What is the author's purpose in choosing these media as support?

   ○ A. The presentation is clear and provides detailed data on generational migration habits.

   ○ B. The data are supportive, clearly presented, and come from a reliable source.

   ○ C. The media provide statistical causes of the millennial choice to stay near home.

   ○ D. The author did not realize that the chart applies only to groups older than the audience.

Close Read

Reread "Life After High School." As you reread, complete the Skills Focus questions below. Then use your answers and annotations from the questions to help you complete the Write activity.

◎ SKILLS FOCUS

1. Both authors mention social media as a factor that contributes to decisions young people make about moving. Cite an example of this, and explain whether social media is a reason young adults should move or should not move.

2. Identify an example of visual or quantitative information that one of the authors uses to help the reader better understand an argument. Explain how this media element supports the author's claim.

3. What role do financial considerations play in the decision to stay close to home or to move away after high school? Support your response with evidence from the text.

4. Which of the two authors more effectively uses quantitative media to support an argument? Support your answer with evidence from the text.

5. Explain how moving can be related to the the American desire for independence. Cite textual evidence to support your response.

✏ WRITE

ARGUMENTATIVE: Each author chooses to address either the pros or cons of the decision to settle somewhere new or to stay close to home after high school. How does each author use both textual and graphic information to support his or her argument? Based on the information provided in each text, which argument do you find more convincing and why? Support your answer with both textual and graphic evidence.

Constitution of the Iroquois Nations

INFORMATIONAL TEXT
Dekanawidah (Oral Tradition)
Circa 1150

Introduction

Most information about Dekanawidah, co-founder of the Iroquois Confederacy, is lost to time. In Iroquois tradition, his name, meaning "two rivers flowing together," is used only under special circumstances. According to tradition, when the Iroquois tribes in present-day New York were torn apart by fighting, Dekanawidah stepped in to instill peace and unite the Iroquois nations. The oral constitution that followed represented an alliance among five tribes: the Seneca, Cayuga, Oneida, Onondaga, and Mohawk. A sixth tribe—the Tuscarora—later joined the union. Most historians believe that the democratic ideals of the Iroquois Constitution inspired the Constitution of the United States.

"I am Dekanawidah and with the Five Nations' Confederate Lords I plant the Tree of Great Peace."

The Great Binding Law, Gayanashagowa

1 **1.** I am Dekanawidah and with the Five Nations' Confederate Lords I plant the Tree of Great Peace. I plant it in your territory, Adodarhoh, and the Onondaga Nation, in the territory of you who are Firekeepers.

2 I name the tree the Tree of the Great Long Leaves. Under the shade of this Tree of the Great Peace we spread the soft white

Photo of a modern reproduction of an Iroquoian Longhouse

feathery down of the globe thistle as seats for you, Adodarhoh, and your cousin Lords.

3 We place you upon those seats, spread soft with the feathery down of the globe thistle, there beneath the shade of the spreading branches of the Tree of Peace. There shall you sit and watch the Council Fire of the Confederacy of the Five Nations, and all the affairs of the Five Nations shall be transacted at this place before you, Adodarhoh, and your cousin Lords, by the Confederate Lords of the Five Nations.

4 **2.** Roots have spread out from the Tree of the Great Peace, one to the north, one to the east, one to the south and one to the west. The name of these roots is The Great White Roots and their nature is Peace and Strength.

5 If any man or any nation outside the Five Nations shall obey the laws of the Great Peace and make known their **disposition** to the Lords of the Confederacy, they may trace the Roots to the Tree and if their minds are clean and they are obedient and promise to obey the wishes of the Confederate Council, they shall be welcomed to take shelter beneath the Tree of the Long Leaves. We place at the top of the Tree of the Long Leaves an Eagle who is able to see afar. If he sees in the distance any evil approaching or any danger threatening he will at once warn the people of the Confederacy.

. . .

6 **10.** In all cases the procedure must be as follows: when the Mohawk and Seneca Lords have **unanimously** agreed upon a question, they shall report their decision to the Cayuga and Oneida Lords who shall deliberate upon the question and report a unanimous decision to the Mohawk Lords. The Mohawk Lords will then report the standing of the case to the Firekeepers, who shall **render** a decision as they see fit in case of a disagreement by the two bodies, or confirm the decisions of the two bodies if they are identical. The Fire Keepers shall then report their decision to the Mohawk Lords who shall announce it to the open council.

7 **11.** If through any misunderstanding or obstinacy on the part of the Fire Keepers, they render a decision at variance with that of the Two Sides, the Two Sides shall reconsider the matter and if their decisions are jointly the same as before they shall report to the Fire Keepers who are then compelled to confirm their joint decision.

. . .

Rights, Duties and Qualifications of Lords

. . .

8 **19.** If at any time it shall be manifest that a Confederate Lord has not in mind the welfare of the people or disobeys the rules of this Great Law, the men or women of the Confederacy, or both jointly, shall come to the Council and **upbraid** the erring Lord through his War Chief. If the complaint of the people through the War Chief is not heeded the first time it shall be uttered again and then if no attention is given a third complaint and warning shall be given. If the Lord is contumacious the matter shall go to the council of War Chiefs. The War Chiefs shall then divest the erring Lord of his title by order of the women in whom the titleship is vested. When the Lord is deposed the women shall notify the Confederate Lords through their War Chief, and the Confederate Lords shall sanction the act. The women will then select another of their sons as a candidate and the Lords shall elect him. Then shall the chosen one be installed by the Installation Ceremony.

9 When a Lord is to be deposed, his War Chief shall address him as follows:

10 "So you, _____, disregard and set at naught the warnings of your women relatives. So you fling the warnings over your shoulder to cast them behind you.

11 "Behold the brightness of the Sun and in the brightness of the Sun's light I depose you of your title and remove the sacred emblem of your Lordship title. I remove from your brow the deer's antlers, which was the emblem of your position and token of your nobility. I now depose you and return the antlers to the women whose heritage they are."

. . .

NOTES

12   **25.** If a Lord of the Confederacy should seek to establish any authority independent of the jurisdiction of the Confederacy of the Great Peace, which is the Five Nations, he shall be warned three times in open council, first by the women relatives, second by the men relatives and finally by the Lords of the Confederacy of the Nation to which he belongs. If the offending Lord is still obdurate he shall be dismissed by the War Chief of his nation for refusing to conform to the laws of the Great Peace. His nation shall then install the candidate nominated by the female name holders of his family.

13   **26.** It shall be the duty of all of the Five Nations Confederate Lords, from time to time as occasion demands, to act as mentors and spiritual guides of their people and remind them of their Creator's will and words. They shall say:

14   "Hearken, that peace may continue unto future days! "Always listen to the words of the Great Creator, for he has spoken. "United people, let not evil find lodging in your minds. "For the Great Creator has spoken and the cause of Peace shall not become old. "The cause of peace shall not die if you remember the Great Creator." Every Confederate Lord shall speak words such as these to promote peace.

15   **27.** All Lords of the Five Nations Confederacy must be honest in all things. They must not idle or gossip, but be men possessing those honorable qualities that make true royaneh. It shall be a serious wrong for anyone to lead a Lord into trivial affairs, for the people must ever hold their Lords high in estimation out of respect to their honorable positions.

. . .

Names, Duties and Rights of War Chiefs

. . .

16   **37.** There shall be one War Chief for each Nation and their duties shall be to carry messages for their Lords and to take up the arms of war in case of emergency. They shall not participate in the proceedings of the Confederate Council but shall watch its progress and in case of an erroneous action by a Lord they shall receive the complaints of the people and **convey** the warnings of the women to him. The people who wish to convey messages to the Lords in the Confederate Council shall do so through the War Chief of their Nation. It shall ever be his duty to lay the cases, questions and propositions of the people before the Confederate Council.

. . .

Official Symbolism

...

17 **57.** Five arrows shall be bound together very strong and each arrow shall represent one nation. As the five arrows are strongly bound this shall symbolize the complete union of the nations. Thus are the Five Nations united completely and enfolded together, united into one head, one body and one mind. Therefore they shall labor, legislate and council together for the interest of future generations. The Lords of the Confederacy shall eat together from one bowl the feast of cooked beaver's tail. While they are eating they are to use no sharp utensils for if they should they might accidentally cut one another and bloodshed would follow. All measures must be taken to prevent the spilling of blood in any way.

...

Religious Ceremonies Protected

18 **99.** The rites and festivals of each nation shall remain undisturbed and shall continue as before because they were given by the people of old times as useful and necessary for the good of men.

...

✏ WRITE

PERSONAL RESPONSE: Most historians believe the Constitution of the Iroquois Nations inspired the framers of the U.S. Constitution. Whether you are inspired by these same ideals, or by ideals of your own, write a personal response on what you think the laws, ethics, and aspirations of an individual or nation should be. Use evidence from the text and your own experiences to support your response.

Declaration of Independence

ARGUMENTATIVE TEXT
Thomas Jefferson
1776

Introduction

On June 11, 1776, the delegates of the Second Continental Congress appointed a committee to draft a statement declaring independence from Britain. The committee included Benjamin Franklin, John Adams, and Thomas Jefferson, who was tasked with putting the committee's ideas to paper, inspired by the English political philosopher John Locke, whose theory of "natural law" states that human beings are "by nature free, equal and independent." Although the Declaration of Independence did not guarantee equality for *all* people, it was a significant first step toward establishing America's democracy.

"We hold these truths to be self-evident, that all men are created equal . . ."

1   In Congress, July 4, 1776

2   The unanimous Declaration of the thirteen united States of America[1]

3   When in the Course of human events, it becomes necessary for one people to **dissolve** the political bands which have connected them with another, and to assume, among the Powers of the earth, the separate and equal station to which the Laws of Nature and of Nature's God entitle them, a decent respect to the opinions of mankind requires that they should declare the causes which impel them to the separation.

The Declaration of Independence, 1776

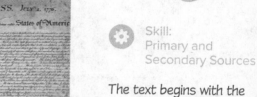

Skill:
Primary and Secondary Sources

The text begins with the date of writing, showing that this is a primary source because it indicates a time period. The text also says it is a declaration, or first hand account, which makes me think it is a primary source.

4   We hold these truths to be self-evident, that all men are created equal, that they are endowed by their Creator with certain unalienable Rights, that among these are Life, Liberty, and the pursuit of Happiness.—That to secure these rights, Governments are instituted among Men, deriving their just powers from the consent of the governed,—That whenever any Form of Government becomes destructive of these ends, it is the Right of the People to alter or to abolish it, and to institute new Government, laying its foundation on such principles and organizing its powers in such form, as to them shall seem most likely to effect their Safety and Happiness. Prudence, indeed, will dictate that Governments long established should not be changed for light and transient causes; and accordingly all experience hath shown, that mankind are more disposed to suffer, while evils are sufferable, than to right themselves by abolishing the forms to which they are accustomed. But when a long train of abuses and usurpations, pursuing invariably the same Object evinces a design to reduce them under absolute Despotism, it is their right, it is their duty, to throw off such Government, and to provide new Guards for their future security.—Such has been the patient sufferance of these Colonies;

Skill:
Author's Purpose and Point of View

Jefferson uses specific phrases to indicate that he believes that the king has treated the colonies poorly. Based on this treatment, I can infer that Jefferson is critical of the king's behavior.

---

1. **thirteen united States of America** the original thirteen British colonies on the east coast of America

Please note that excerpts and passages in the StudySync® library and this workbook are intended as touchstones to generate interest in an author's work. The excerpts and passages do not substitute for the reading of entire texts, and StudySync® strongly recommends that students seek out and purchase the whole literary or informational work in order to experience it as the author intended. Links to online resellers are available in our digital library. In addition, complete works may be ordered through an authorized reseller by filling out and returning to StudySync® the order form enclosed in this workbook.

Copyright © BookheadEd Learning, LLC

Skill:
Rhetoric

Jefferson repeats "he has" to show a pattern of offenses committed by King George III. Jefferson uses the rhetorical device of repetition to emphasize the number of ways that the colonies have been mistreated.

and such is now the necessity which constrains them to alter their former Systems of Government. The history of the present King of Great Britain[2] is a history of repeated injuries and usurpations, all having in direct object the establishment of an absolute Tyranny over these States. To prove this, let Facts be submitted to a candid world.

5   He has refused his Assent to Laws, the most wholesome and necessary for the public good.

6   He has forbidden his Governors to pass Laws of immediate and pressing importance, unless suspended in their operation till his Assent should be obtained; and when so suspended, he has utterly neglected to attend to them.

7   He has refused to pass other Laws for the accommodation of large districts of people, unless those people would relinquish the right of Representation in the Legislature, a right inestimable to them and formidable to tyrants only.

8   He has called together legislative bodies at places unusual, uncomfortable, and distant from the depository of their Public Records, for the sole purpose of fatiguing them into compliance with his measures.

9   He has dissolved Representative Houses[3] repeatedly, for opposing with manly firmness his invasions on the rights of the people.

10 He has refused for a long time, after such dissolutions, to cause others to be elected; whereby the Legislative Powers, incapable of Annihilation, have returned to the People at large for their exercise; the State remaining in the mean time exposed to all the dangers of invasion from without, and convulsions within.

11 He has endeavoured to prevent the population of these States; for that purpose obstructing the Laws of Naturalization of Foreigners; refusing to pass others to encourage their migration hither, and raising the conditions of new Appropriations of Lands.

12 He has obstructed the Administration of Justice, by refusing his Assent to Laws for establishing Judiciary Powers.

13 He has made judges dependent on his Will alone, for the tenure of their offices, and the amount and payment of their salaries.

---

2. **the King of Great Britain** King George III, whose exceptionally long reign over Britain and Ireland was marked by military conflict
3. **Representative Houses** organizations designed to give American colonists a voice in the British government

NOTES

14   He has erected a multitude of New Offices, and sent hither swarms of Officers to harass our People, and eat out their substance.

15   He has kept among us, in times of peace, Standing Armies without the Consent of our legislatures.

16   He has affected to render the Military independent of and superior to the Civil Power.

17   He has combined with others to subject us to a **jurisdiction** foreign to our constitution, and unacknowledged by our laws; giving his Assent to their Acts of pretended legislation:

18   For quartering large bodies of armed troops among us:

19   For protecting them, by a mock Trial, from Punishment for any Murders which they should commit on the Inhabitants of these States:

20   For cutting off our Trade with all parts of the world:

21   For imposing taxes on us without our Consent:

22   For depriving us, in many cases, of the benefits of Trial by Jury:

23   For transporting us beyond Seas to be tried for pretended offences:

24   For abolishing the free System of English Laws in a neighbouring Province, establishing therein an Arbitrary government, and enlarging its Boundaries so as to render it at once an example and fit instrument for introducing the same absolute rule into these Colonies:

25   For taking away our Charters, abolishing our most valuable Laws, and altering fundamentally the Forms of our Governments:

26   For suspending our own Legislatures and declaring themselves invested with Power to legislate for us in all cases whatsoever.

27   He has abdicated Government here, by declaring us out of his Protection and waging War against us.

28   He has plundered our seas, ravaged our Coasts, burnt our towns, and destroyed the lives of our people.

29   He is at this time transporting large armies of foreign mercenaries to complete the works of death, desolation and tyranny, already begun with circumstances of Cruelty & perfidy scarcely paralleled in the most barbarous ages, and totally unworthy of the Head of a civilized nation.

Copyright © BookheadEd Learning, LLC

30 He has constrained our fellow Citizens taken Captive on the high Seas to bear Arms against their Country, to become the executioners of their friends and Brethren, or to fall themselves by their Hands.

31 He has excited domestic insurrections amongst us, and has endeavoured to bring on the inhabitants of our frontiers, the merciless Indian Savages, whose known rule of warfare is an undistinguished destruction of all ages, sexes and conditions.

32 In every stage of these Oppressions We have Petitioned for Redress in the most humble terms: Our repeated Petitions have been answered only by repeated injury. A Prince, whose character is thus marked by every act which may define a Tyrant, is unfit to be the ruler of a free People.

33 Nor have We been wanting in attention to our British brethren. We have warned them from time to time of attempts by their legislature to extend an unwarrantable jurisdiction over us. We have reminded them of the circumstances of our emigration and settlement here. We have appealed to their native justice and **magnanimity,** and we have conjured them by the ties of our common kindred to disavow these usurpations, which would inevitably interrupt our connections and correspondence. They too have been deaf to the voice of justice and of **consanguinity**. We must, therefore, acquiesce in the necessity, which denounces our Separation, and hold them, as we hold the rest of mankind, Enemies in War, in Peace Friends.

34 We, therefore, the Representatives of the United States of America, in General Congress, Assembled, appealing to the Supreme Judge of the world for the **rectitude** of our intentions, do, in the Name, and by the Authority of the good People of these Colonies, solemnly publish and declare, That these United Colonies are, and of Right ought to be Free and Independent States; that they are Absolved from all Allegiance to the British Crown, and that all political connection between them and the State of Great Britain, is and ought to be totally dissolved; and that as Free and Independent States, they have full Power to levy War, conclude Peace, contract Alliances, establish Commerce, and to do all other Acts and Things which Independent States may of right do. And for the support of this Declaration, with a firm reliance on the Protection of Divine Providence, we mutually pledge to each other our Lives, our Fortunes and our sacred Honor.

First Read

Read the Declaration of Independence. After you read, complete the Think Questions below.

☁ THINK QUESTIONS

1. According to paragraph 3, what is the purpose of the Declaration of Independence beyond simply claiming freedom from British rule? Identify the phrase that states this purpose most clearly and relate it to the rest of the document.

2. In paragraph 4, what does Jefferson say about the treatment of the colonists under the king of Great Britain? According to Jefferson, what justifies a revolt against the existing government? Use evidence from the text to support your response.

3. Where in the document does Jefferson officially declare independence, and how does he define independence for the colonies? Use evidence from the text to support your response.

4. The Latin prefix *con-* means "with." The Latin root *sanguis* means "blood." Using this information and your knowledge of word patterns and relationships, write your best definition of the word **consanguinity** here.

5. The Latin root *rect* means "right" or "straight." With this information in mind and using context clues from the text, write your best definition of the word **rectitude** here. Then verify your meaning using a print or digital dictionary.

Skill:
Author's Purpose and
Point of View

Use the Checklist to analyze Author's Purpose and Point of View in the Declaration of Independence. Refer to the sample student annotations about Author's Purpose and Point of View in the text.

••• CHECKLIST LIST FOR AUTHOR'S PURPOSE AND POINT OF VIEW

In order to identify author's purpose and point of view, note the following:

- ✓ whether the writer is attempting to establish trust by citing his or her experience or education

- ✓ whether the evidence the author provides is convincing and whether the argument or position is logical

- ✓ what words and phrases the author uses to appeal to the emotions

- ✓ the author's use of rhetoric, or the art of speaking and writing persuasively, such as the use of repetition to drive home a point as well as allusion and alliteration

- ✓ the author's use of rhetoric to contribute to the power, persuasiveness, or beauty of the text

To determine the author's purpose and point of view, consider the following questions:

- ✓ How does the author try to convince me that he or she has something valid and important for me to read?

- ✓ What words or phrases express emotion or invite an emotional response? How or why are they effective or ineffective?

- ✓ What words and phrases contribute to the power, persuasiveness, or beauty of the text? Is the author's use of rhetoric successful? Why or why not?

AUTHOR'S PURPOSE AND
AUTHOR'S POINT OF VIEW

sync•skills

Skill:
Author's Purpose and
Point of View

Reread paragraphs 27–31 from the Declaration of Independence. Then, using the Checklist on the previous page, answer the multiple-choice questions below.

↻ YOUR TURN

1. What is Jefferson's purpose for listing all of the colonists' grievances against the king?

   ○ A. to show the audience that he keeps very meticulous records of events
   ○ B. to introduce his argument for independence
   ○ C. to share a personal experience in support of the argument for independence
   ○ D. to persuade the audience that they have just cause for choosing independence

2. Words such as "plundered," "ravaged," and "destroyed" support the idea that Jefferson's attitude towards the king is—

   ○ A. understanding.
   ○ B. hostile.
   ○ C. frustrated.
   ○ D. critical.

Skill:
Rhetoric

Use the Checklist to analyze Rhetoric in the Declaration of Independence. Refer to the sample student annotations about Rhetoric in the text.

In order to identify an author's point of view or purpose in a text and to analyze the rhetoric of the text, note the following:

✓ the purpose of the text

✓ details and statements that identify the author's point of view or purpose

✓ when the author uses rhetoric to advance his or her point of view or purpose. Rhetoric is the way by which writers phrase, or construct, what they want to say. Writers use many different kinds of rhetorical devices, and the style they employ can contribute to the power, persuasiveness, or beauty of the text. Look for:

- an author's use of sensory language

- words that appeal to the senses, which can create a vivid picture in the minds of readers and listeners, and persuade them to accept a specific point of view

- a specific style, such as the use of assonance or the repetition of certain words, which can be used to create catchphrases, phrases that can be widely or repeatedly used and that can be easily remembered

✓ when the author's use of rhetoric is particularly effective

To determine an author's point of view or purpose in a text in which the rhetoric is particularly effective, consider the following questions:

✓ Which rhetorical devices can you identify in the text?

✓ How does this writer or speaker use rhetorical devices to persuade an audience?

✓ Do the rhetorical devices work to make the argument or position sound? Why or why not?

✓ How does the use of rhetorical devices affect the way the text is read and understood?

✓ In what ways are the rhetorical devices particularly effective?

Skill:
Rhetoric

Reread paragraph 33 from the Declaration of Independence. Then, using the Checklist on the previous page, answer the multiple-choice questions below.

♻ YOUR TURN

1. The repetition of the phrase "We have" at the beginning of many sentences serves to—

   ○ A. provide a rhetorical shift for Jefferson to change topics.
   ○ B. appeal to readers' emotions about seeking independence.
   ○ C. emphasize the actions the colonists took to communicate and reason with the British.
   ○ D. offer an antithesis to the rest of Jefferson's argument about Britain's leadership.

2. The logical presentation of facts in this paragraph leads Jefferson to conclude that—

   ○ A. going to war is always the best way to solve problems.
   ○ B. there is hope for reconciliation with British leadership.
   ○ C. the British will be shocked by the complaints outlined in the Declaration.
   ○ D. the cause of independence is more important than past relationships.

Skill:
Primary and Secondary Sources

Use the Checklist to analyze Primary and Secondary Sources in the Declaration of Independence. Refer to the sample student annotations about Primary and Secondary Sources in the text.

••• CHECKLIST FOR PRIMARY AND SECONDARY SOURCES

In order to differentiate between primary and secondary sources, do the following:

- ✓ examine the source, noting the title, author, and date of publication
- ✓ identify the genre of the source
  - • Primary sources include letters, diaries, journals, speeches, eyewitness interviews, oral histories, memoirs, and autobiographies.
  - • Secondary sources include encyclopedia articles, newspaper and magazine articles, biographies, documentary films, history books, and textbooks.

If the source meets one or more of the following criteria, it is considered a primary source:

- ✓ original, first-hand account of an event or time period
- ✓ writing that takes place during the event or time period

If the source meets one or more of the following criteria, it is considered a secondary source:

- ✓ a book or an article that analyzes and interprets primary sources
- ✓ a second-hand account of a historical event
- ✓ a book or an article that interprets or analyzes creative work

To analyze seventeenth-, eighteenth-, and nineteenth-century foundational U.S. documents of historical and literary significance, consider the following questions:

- ✓ How is the source reliable and credible?
- ✓ What is the purpose of this source?
- ✓ What historical themes, such as patriotism or heroism, are brought out in the source?
- ✓ How does the author use anecdotes, interviews, allusions, or other rhetorical features?
- ✓ What gives this source literary or historical significance?

Skill:
Primary and Secondary Sources

Reread paragraph 34 from the Declaration of Independence. Then, using the Checklist on the previous page, answer the multiple-choice questions below.

⟳ YOUR TURN

1. This question has two parts. First, answer Part A. Then, answer Part B.

   Part A: What Early American values are emphasized in the closing of this document?

   ○ A. isolation and exclusion

   ○ B. participation in government and civic affairs

   ○ C. peace and prosperity

   ○ D. freedom and independence

   Part B: Which line from the passage best supports your answer in Part A?

   ○ A. "appealing to the Supreme Judge of the world for the rectitude of our intentions"

   ○ B. "That these United Colonies are, and of Right ought to be Free and Independent States"

   ○ C. "all political connection between them and the State of Great Britain, is and ought to be totally dissolved"

   ○ D. "with a firm reliance on the Protection of Divine Providence, we mutually pledge to each other our Lives, our Fortunes and our sacred Honor"

2. What gives this text historical significance?

   ○ A. It illustrates the government structures in place at the time of its writing.

   ○ B. It marks the transition from colonies to independent states, and the founding of our nation.

   ○ C. It is an important reminder of Great Britain's treatment of the colonies.

   ○ D. It is an example of how to make a strong argument.

Close Read

Reread the Declaration of Independence. As you reread, complete the Skills Focus questions below. Then use your answers and annotations from the questions to help you complete the Write activity.

◎ SKILLS FOCUS

1. What is Thomas Jefferson's point of view regarding the relationship between the colonies and the king? Identify evidence that demonstrates his attitude.

2. Identify Jefferson's call to action as he addresses his audience in the final paragraphs of this text. What is his purpose as a writer?

3. The repetition of a word or phrase is a kind of rhetorical device. Identify an example of the repetition of a word or phrase in the text, and analyze its effectiveness in persuading readers to support the claim.

4. How does this document highlight important American values? Identify examples throughout the text.

5. The ways in which Britain controlled the colonies influenced the laws and system of government that the founding fathers put into place. Find examples of specific grievances against the king that Jefferson cites, and explain how our constitution prevents such abuses.

✏ WRITE

COMPARE AND CONTRAST: "The Constitution of the Iroquois Nations" and the Declaration of Independence use rhetoric to reveal the author's purpose and point of view. Write a response in which you compare and contrast each text's purpose and the rhetoric used to support it. Then evaluate which rhetorical devices in each text are the most effective by using textual evidence and original commentary to support your response.

The Interesting Narrative of the Life of Olaudah Equiano, or Gustavus Vassa, the African

INFORMATIONAL TEXT
Olaudah Equiano
1789

Introduction

The achievements of Olaudah Equiano (ca. 1745–1797) continue to be studied and explored to this day. When he was eleven, he was kidnapped by slave traders in Africa and forced onto a ship to the Caribbean. Later in life, Equiano secured his freedom and settled in England, where he became an ardent abolitionist, fighting for the freedom of enslaved people. His autobiography accounts the inhumanity of the Middle Passage, and in part serves as a call to action: "I supplicate your Majesty's compassion for millions . . . who groan under the lash of tyranny in the West Indies." In this excerpt, Equiano describes the grueling conditions aboard

"Must every tender feeling be likewise sacrificed to your avarice?"

1   The first object which saluted my eyes when I arrived on the coast was the sea, and a slave ship, which was then riding at anchor, and waiting for its cargo. These filled me with astonishment, which was soon converted into terror when I was carried on board. I was immediately handled and tossed up to see if I were sound by some of the crew; and I was now persuaded that I had gotten into a world of bad spirits, and that they were going to kill me.

2   Their complexions too differing so much from ours, their long hair, and the language they spoke, (which was very different from any I had ever heard) united to confirm me in this belief. Indeed such were the horrors of my views and fears at the moment, that, if ten thousand worlds had been my own, I would have freely parted with them all to have exchanged my condition with that of the meanest slave in my own country. When I looked round the ship too and saw a large furnace of copper boiling, and a multitude of black people of every description chained together, every one of their countenances expressing dejection and sorrow, I no longer doubted of my fate; and, quite overpowered with horror and anguish, I fell motionless on the deck and fainted.

3   When I recovered a little I found some black people about me, who I believed were some of those who brought me on board, and had been receiving their pay; they talked to me in order to cheer me, but all in vain. I asked them if we were not to be eaten by those white men with horrible looks, red faces, and loose hair. They told me I was not; and one of the crew brought me a small portion of spirituous liquor in a wine glass; but, being afraid of him, I would not take it out of his hand. One of the blacks therefore took it from him and gave it to me, and I took a little down my palate, which, instead of reviving me, as they thought it would, threw me into the greatest **consternation** at the strange feeling it produced, having never tasted any such liquor before. Soon after this the blacks who brought me on board went off, and left me abandoned to despair.

4   I now saw myself deprived of all chance of returning to my native country, or even the least glimpse of hope of gaining the shore, which I now considered as friendly; and I even wished for my former slavery in preference to my present situation, which was filled with horrors of every kind, still heightened by my ignorance of what I was to undergo. I was not long suffered to indulge my grief;

I was soon put down under the decks, and there I received such a salutation in my nostrils as I had never experienced in my life: so that, with the **loathsomeness** of the stench, and crying together, I became so sick and low that I was not able to eat, nor had I the least desire to taste any thing. I now wished for the last friend, death, to relieve me; but soon, to my grief, two of the white men offered me eatables; and, on my refusing to eat, one of them held me fast by the hands, and laid me across I think the windlass, and tied my feet, while the other flogged me severely. I had never experienced any thing of this kind before; and although, not being used to the water, I naturally feared that element the first time I saw it, yet nevertheless, could I have got over the nettings, I would have jumped over the side, but I could not; and, besides, the crew used to watch us very closely who were not chained down to the decks, lest we should leap into the water: and I have seen some of these poor African prisoners most severely cut for attempting to do so, and hourly whipped for not eating. This indeed was often the case with myself. In a little time after, amongst the poor chained men, I found some of my own nation, which in a small degree gave ease to my mind. I inquired of these what was to be done with us; they gave me to understand we were to be carried to these white people's country to work for them. I then was a little revived, and thought, if it were no worse than working, my situation was not so desperate: but still I feared I should be put to death, the white people looked and acted, as I thought, in so savage a manner; for I had never seen among any people such instances of brutal cruelty; and this not only shewn towards us blacks, but also to some of the whites themselves. One white man in particular I saw, when we were permitted to be on deck, flogged so unmercifully with a large rope near the foremast, that he died in consequence of it; and they tossed him over the side as they would have done a brute. This made me fear these people the more; and I expected nothing less than to be treated in the same manner. I could not help expressing my fears and **apprehensions** to some of my countrymen: I asked them if these people had no country, but lived in this hollow place (the ship): they told me they did not, but came from a distant one. 'Then,' said I, 'how comes it in all our country we never heard of them?' They told me because they lived so very far off. I then asked where were their women? had they any like themselves? I was told they had: 'and why,' said I, 'do we not see them?' they answered, because they were left behind. I asked how the vessel could go? they told me they could not tell; but that there were cloths put upon the masts by the help of the ropes I saw, and then the vessel went on; and the white men had some spell or magic they put in the water when they liked in order to stop the vessel. I was exceedingly amazed at this account, and really thought they were spirits. I therefore wished much to be from amongst them, for I expected they would sacrifice me: but my wishes were vain; for we were so quartered that it was impossible for any of us to make our escape.

5   While we stayed on the coast I was mostly on deck; and one day, to my great astonishment, I saw one of these vessels coming in with the sails up. As soon as the whites saw it, they gave a great shout, at which we were amazed; and the

more so as the vessel appeared larger by approaching nearer. At last she came to an anchor in my sight, and when the anchor was let go I and my countrymen who saw it were lost in astonishment to observe the vessel stop; and were not convinced it was done by magic. Soon after this the other ship got her boats out, and they came on board of us, and the people of both ships seemed very glad to see each other. Several of the strangers also shook hands with us black people, and made motions with their hands, signifying I suppose we were to go to their country; but we did not understand them.

6   At last, when the ship we were in had got in all her cargo, they made ready with many fearful noises, and we were all put under deck, so that we could not see how they managed the vessel. But this disappointment was the least of my sorrow. The stench of the hold while we were on the coast was so intolerably loathsome, that it was dangerous to remain there for any time, and some of us had been permitted to stay on the deck for the fresh air; but now that the whole ship's cargo were confined together, it became absolutely pestilential. The closeness of the place, and the heat of the climate, added to the number in the ship, which was so crowded that each had scarcely room to turn himself, almost suffocated us. This produced copious perspirations, so that the air soon became unfit for respiration, from a variety of loathsome smells, and brought on a sickness among the slaves, of which many died, thus falling victims to the improvident **avarice**, as I may call it, of their purchasers. This wretched situation was again aggravated by the galling of the chains, now become insupportable; and the filth of the necessary tubs, into which the children often fell, and were almost suffocated. The shrieks of the women, and the groans of the dying, rendered the whole a scene of horror almost inconceivable. Happily perhaps for myself I was soon reduced so low here that it was thought necessary to keep me almost always on deck; and from my extreme youth I was not put in fetters. In this situation I expected every hour to share the fate of my companions, some of whom were almost daily brought upon deck at the point of death, which I began to hope would soon put an end to my miseries. Often did I think many of the inhabitants of the deep much more happy than myself. I envied them the freedom they enjoyed, and as often wished I could change my condition for theirs. Every circumstance I met with served only to render my state more painful, and heighten my apprehensions, and my opinion of the cruelty of the whites.

7   One day they had taken a number of fishes; and when they had killed and satisfied themselves with as many as they thought fit, to our astonishment who were on the deck, rather than give any of them to us to eat as we expected, they tossed the remaining fish into the sea again, although we begged and prayed for some as well as we could, but in vain; and some of my countrymen, being pressed by hunger, took an opportunity, when they thought no one saw them, of trying to get a little privately; but they were discovered, and the attempt procured them some very severe floggings. One day, when we had a smooth sea and moderate wind, two of my wearied

countrymen who were chained together (I was near them at the time), preferring death to such a life of misery, somehow made through the nettings and jumped into the sea: immediately another quite dejected fellow, who, on account of his illness, was suffered to be out of irons, also followed their example; and I believe many more would very soon have done the same if they had not been prevented by the ship's crew, who were instantly alarmed. Those of us that were the most active were in a moment put down under the deck, and there was such a noise and confusion amongst the people of the ship as I never heard before, to stop her, and get the boat out to go after the slaves. However two of the wretches were drowned, but they got the other, and afterwards flogged him unmercifully for thus attempting to prefer death to slavery. In this manner we continued to undergo more hardships than I can now relate, hardships which are inseparable from this accursed trade. Many a time we were near suffocation from the want of fresh air, which we were often without for whole days together. This, and the stench of the necessary tubs, carried off many.

8   During our passage I first saw flying fishes, which surprised me very much: they used frequently to fly across the ship, and many of them fell on the deck. I also now first saw the use of the quadrant; I had often with astonishment seen the mariners make observations with it, and I could not think what it meant. They at last took notice of my surprise; and one of them, willing to increase it, as well as to gratify my curiosity, made me one day look through it. The clouds appeared to me to be land, which disappeared as they passed along. This heightened my wonder; and I was now more persuaded than ever that I was in another world, and that every thing about me was magic. At last we came in sight of the island of Barbadoes, at which the whites on board gave a great shout, and made many signs of joy to us. We did not know what to think of this; but as the vessel drew nearer we plainly saw the harbour, and other ships of different kinds and sizes; and we soon anchored amongst them off Bridge Town. Many merchants and planters now came on board, though it was in the evening. They put us in separate parcels, and examined us attentively. They also made us jump, and pointed to the land, signifying we were to go there. We thought by this we should be eaten by these ugly men, as they appeared to us; and, when soon after we were all put down under the deck again, there was much dread and trembling among us, and nothing but bitter cries to be heard all the night from these apprehensions, insomuch that at last the white people got some old slaves from the land to pacify us. They told us we were not to be eaten, but to work, and were soon to go on land, where we should see many of our country people. This report eased us much; and sure enough, soon after we were landed, there came to us Africans of all languages.

9   We were conducted immediately to the merchant's yard, where we were all pent up together like so many sheep in a fold, without regard to sex or age. As every object was new to me every thing I saw filled me with surprise. What struck me first was that the houses were built with stories, and in every other

Please note that excerpts and passages in the StudySync® library and this workbook are intended as touchstones to generate interest in an author's work. The excerpts and passages do not substitute for the reading of entire texts, and StudySync® strongly recommends that students seek out and purchase the whole literary or informational work in order to experience it as the author intended. Links to online resellers are available in our digital library. In addition, complete works may be ordered through an authorized reseller by filling out and returning to StudySync® the order form enclosed in this workbook.

Reading & Writing Companion   63

respect different from those in Africa: but I was still more astonished on seeing people on horseback. I did not know what this could mean; and indeed I thought these people were full of nothing but magical arts. While I was in this astonishment one of my fellow prisoners spoke to a countryman of his about the horses, who said they were the same kind they had in their country. I understood them, though they were from a distant part of Africa, and I thought it odd I had not seen any horses there; but afterwards, when I came to converse with different Africans, I found they had many horses amongst them, and much larger than those I then saw.

10   We were not many days in the merchant's custody before we were sold after their usual manner, which is this:—On a signal given, (as the beat of a drum) the buyers rush at once into the yard where the slaves are confined, and make choice of that parcel they like best. The noise and clamour with which this is attended, and the eagerness visible in the countenances of the buyers, serve not a little to increase the apprehensions of the terrified Africans, who may well be supposed to consider them as the ministers of that destruction to which they think themselves devoted. In this manner, without scruple, are relations and friends separated, most of them never to see each other again. I remember in the vessel in which I was brought over, in the men's apartment, there were several brothers, who, in the sale, were sold in different lots; and it was very moving on this occasion to see and hear their cries at parting. O, ye nominal Christians! might not an African ask you, learned you this from your God, who says unto you, Do unto all men as you would men should do unto you? Is it not enough that we are torn from our country and friends to toil for your luxury and lust of gain? Must every tender feeling be likewise sacrificed to your avarice? Are the dearest friends and relations, now rendered more dear by their separation from their kindred, still to be parted from each other, and thus prevented from cheering the gloom of slavery with the small comfort of being together and mingling their sufferings and sorrows? Why are parents to lose their children, brothers their sisters, or husbands their wives? Surely this is a new refinement in cruelty, which, while it has no advantage to **atone** for it, thus aggravates distress, and adds fresh horrors even to the wretchedness of slavery.

✏ WRITE

DISCUSSION: *The Interesting Narrative of the Life of Olaudah Equiano, or Gustavus Vassa, the African* is both a description of the horrors of The Middle Passage and a passionate argument against slavery. What kind of rhetorical devices and appeals does Equiano use at the end of the last paragraph? How do the descriptions throughout the excerpt lend power to Equiano's ultimate argument that the cruel and inhumane separation of families "adds fresh horrors even to the wretchedness of slavery"? Be sure to support your response with evidence from the text.

Verses upon the Burning of Our House

POETRY
Anne Bradstreet
1666

Introduction

Anne Bradstreet (1612–1672) was born in England, but emigrated to America at age 18 to join the Puritans at the Massachusetts Bay Colony. Her "Verses upon the Burning of Our House" describes a real-life event: in 1666, her family's home actually did burn down, destroying most of their earthly possessions. Her faith in God, however, impelled her to see this great loss as part of a larger purpose. Bradstreet wrote volumes of poetry during her life, much of it reflecting her views on the roles of women in Puritan society. She was the first female poet to be published on both sides of the Atlantic, though her writing was not without controversy—especially among those who believed that writing was not an

And piteous shrieks of dreadful voice.
That fearful sound of "Fire" and "Fire,"

NOTES

1 In silent night when rest I took,
2 For sorrow near I did not look,
3 I wakened was with thundering noise
4 And piteous shrieks of dreadful voice.
5 That fearful sound of "Fire" and "Fire,"
6 Let no man know, is my desire.
7 I, starting up, the light did spy,
8 And to my God my heart did cry
9 To strengthen me in my distress,
10 And not to leave me succorless.
11 Then coming out, behold a space
12 The flame **consume** my dwelling place.
13 And when I could no longer look,
14 I blest His name that gave and took,
15 That laid my goods now in the dust;
16 Yea, so it was, and so 'twas just.
17 It was His own; it was not mine.
18 Far be it that I should repine.
19 He might of all justly bereft,
20 But yet **sufficient** for us left.
21 When by the ruins oft I passed
22 My sorrowing eyes aside did cast
23 And here and there the places spy
24 Where oft I sat and long did lie.
25 Here stood that trunk, and there that chest;
26 There lay that store I counted best,
27 My pleasant things in ashes lie,
28 And them behold no more shall I.
29 Under thy roof no guest shall sit,
30 Nor at thy table eat a bit;
31 No pleasant tale shall e'er be told,
32 Nor things recounted done of old;
33 No candle e'er shall shine in thee,
34 Nor bridegroom's voice e'er heard shall be.

Image of Anne Bradstreet or Puritan woman

NOTES

35 In silence ever shall thou lie.
36 **Adieu**, Adieu, all's vanity.
37 Then straight I 'gin my heart to **chide**:
38 And did thy wealth on earth abide?
39 Didst fix thy hope on mould'ring dust?
40 The arm of flesh didst make thy trust?
41 Raise up thy thoughts above the sky
42 That dunghill mists away may fly.
43 Thou hast a house on high erect;
44 Framed by that mighty Architect,
45 With glory richly furnishéd
46 Stands permanent though this be fled.
47 It's purchased, and paid for, too,
48 By him who hath enough to do-
49 A price so vast as is unknown,
50 Yet, by His gift, is made thine own.
51 There's wealth enough; I need no more.
52 Farewell, my **pelf**; farewell, my store;
53 The world no longer let me love.
54 My hope and treasure lie above.

✏ WRITE

NARRATIVE: "Verses upon the Burning of Our House" describes the speaker's resilience after losing her home. Write a narrative about a character who also demonstrates resilience during a time of trial, or write a personal narrative describing a similar experience from your own life in order to create a deeper connection to the themes of the text.

Please note that excerpts and passages in the StudySync® library and this workbook are intended as touchstones to generate interest in an author's work. The excerpts and passages do not substitute for the reading of entire texts, and StudySync® strongly recommends that students seek out and purchase the whole literary or informational work in order to experience it as the author intended. Links to online resellers are available in our digital library. In addition, complete works may be ordered through an authorized reseller by filling out and returning to StudySync® the order form enclosed in this workbook.

Reading & Writing
Companion

67

The Scarlet Letter

FICTION
Nathaniel Hawthorne
1850

Introduction

*T*he Scarlet Letter is a classic novel by Nathaniel Hawthorne (1804–1864), a towering figure in 19th-century American literature whose dark, allegorical fiction broods on America's deeply Puritanical origins. The protagonist of *The Scarlet Letter* is Hester Prynne, a young mother of a newborn baby living in the Puritan settlement of Boston in 17th-century New England. Branded as an adulteress and sentenced to wear a scarlet 'A' as her badge of shame, Hester must endure the judgment of the strict, mean-spirited townspeople. In this excerpt, after defiantly refusing to disclose the identity of the baby's father, Hester is led to the town square for public shaming.

"in fine red cloth, surrounded with an elaborate embroidery . . . , appeared the letter A."

from Chapter II. THE MARKET-PLACE

1   The grass-plot before the jail, in Prison Lane, on a certain summer morning, not less than two centuries ago, was occupied by a pretty large number of the inhabitants of Boston, all with their eyes intently fastened on the iron-clamped oaken door. Amongst any other population, or at a later period in the history of New England, the grim rigidity that petrified the bearded physiognomies of these good people would have augured some awful business in hand. It could have betokened nothing short of the anticipated execution of some noted culprit, on whom the sentence of a legal tribunal had but confirmed the verdict of public sentiment. But, in that early severity of the Puritan[1] character, an inference of this kind could not so indubitably be drawn. It might be that a

The Scarlet Letter by Hugues Merle, 1861

sluggish bond-servant, or an undutiful child, whom his parents had given over to the civil authority, was to be corrected at the whipping-post. It might be that an Antinomian, a Quaker, or other heterodox religionist, was to be scourged out of the town, or an idle or vagrant Indian, whom the white man's firewater had made riotous about the streets, was to be driven with stripes into the shadow of the forest. It might be, too, that a witch, like old Mistress Hibbins, the bitter-tempered widow of the magistrate, was to die upon the gallows. In either case, there was very much the same solemnity of demeanour on the part of the spectators, as befitted a people among whom religion and law were almost identical, and in whose character both were so thoroughly interfused, that the mildest and severest acts of public **discipline** were alike made venerable and awful. . .

2   "Goodwives," said a hard-featured dame of fifty, "I'll tell ye a piece of my mind. It would be greatly for the public behoof if we women, being of mature age

---

1. **Puritan** a Protestant religious group in New England marked by their rigid moral code

and church-members in good repute, should have the handling of such malefactresses as this Hester Prynne. What think ye, gossips? If the hussy stood up for judgment before us five, that are now here in a knot together, would she come off with such a sentence as the worshipful **magistrates** have awarded? Marry, I trow not."

3   "People say," said another, "that the Reverend Master Dimmesdale, her godly pastor, takes it very grievously to heart that such a scandal should have come upon his congregation."

4   "The magistrates are God-fearing gentlemen, but merciful overmuch—that is a truth," added a third autumnal matron. "At the very least, they should have put the brand of a hot iron on Hester Prynne's forehead. Madame Hester would have winced at that, I warrant me. But she—the naughty baggage—little will she care what they put upon the bodice of her gown! Why, look you, she may cover it with a brooch, or such like heathenish adornment, and so walk the streets as brave as ever!"

5   "Ah, but," interposed, more softly, a young wife, holding a child by the hand, "let her cover the mark as she will, the pang of it will be always in her heart."

6   "What do we talk of marks and brands, whether on the bodice of her gown or the flesh of her forehead?" cried another female, the ugliest as well as the most pitiless of these self-constituted judges. "This woman has brought shame upon us all, and ought to die; is there not law for it? Truly there is, both in the Scripture and the statute-book. Then let the magistrates, who have made it of no effect, thank themselves if their own wives and daughters go astray."

7   "Mercy on us, goodwife!" exclaimed a man in the crowd, "is there no virtue in woman, save what springs from a wholesome fear of the gallows? That is the hardest word yet! Hush now, gossips; for the lock is turning in the prison-door, and here comes Mistress Prynne herself."

8   The door of the jail being flung open from within there appeared, in the first place, like a black shadow emerging into sunshine, the grim and gristly presence of the town-beadle, with a sword by his side, and his staff of office in his hand. This personage prefigured and represented in his aspect the whole **dismal** severity of the Puritanic code of law, which it was his business to administer in its final and closest application to the offender. Stretching forth the official staff in his left hand, he laid his right upon the shoulder of a young woman, whom he thus drew forward, until, on the threshold of the prison-door, she repelled him, by an action marked with natural dignity and force of character, and stepped into the open air as if by her own free will. She bore in her arms a child, a baby of some three months old, who winked and turned aside its little face from the too **vivid** light of day; because its

existence, heretofore, had brought it acquaintance only with the grey twilight of a dungeon, or other darksome apartment of the prison.

9   When the young woman—the mother of this child—stood fully revealed before the crowd, it seemed to be her first impulse to clasp the infant closely to her bosom; not so much by an impulse of motherly affection, as that she might thereby conceal a certain token, which was wrought or fastened into her dress. In a moment, however, wisely judging that one token of her shame would but poorly serve to hide another, she took the baby on her arm, and with a burning blush, and yet a haughty smile, and a glance that would not be abashed, looked around at her townspeople and neighbours. On the breast of her gown, in fine red cloth, surrounded with an **elaborate** embroidery and fantastic flourishes of gold thread, appeared the letter A. It was so artistically done, and with so much fertility and gorgeous luxuriance of fancy, that it had all the effect of a last and fitting decoration to the apparel which she wore, and which was of a splendour in accordance with the taste of the age, but greatly beyond what was allowed by the sumptuary regulations of the colony.

✏ WRITE

LITERARY ANALYSIS: *The Scarlet Letter* depicts life in a society where Puritan values are the norm. What details about the historical and social setting of this society contribute to the plot and how people in the crowd perceive Hester? Use evidence from the text to support your response.

Please note that excerpts and passages in the StudySync® library and this workbook are intended as touchstones to generate interest in an author's work. The excerpts and passages do not substitute for the reading of entire texts, and StudySync® strongly recommends that students seek out and purchase the whole literary or informational work in order to experience it as the author intended. Links to online resellers are available in our digital library. In addition, complete works may be ordered through an authorized reseller by filling out and returning to StudySync® the order form enclosed in this workbook.

Reading & Writing Companion   71

Indian Boarding School: The Runaways

POETRY
Louise Erdrich
1984

Introduction

Born in North Dakota of German and Chippewa descent, Louise Erdrich (b. 1954) emerged as one of the leading figures in what is today known as the second wave of the Native American Renaissance. Her writing across genres highlights the complex and beautiful history of Native Americans and their perspectives in American life past and present. In this poem, Erdrich depicts Native American students in post-Civil-War America, many of whom who were forced to attend boarding schools established by Christian missionaries who sought to assimilate Native Americans into Euro-American culture.

"Home's the place we head for in our sleep."

NOTES

1 Home's the place we head for in our sleep.
2 Boxcars[1] stumbling north in dreams
3 don't wait for us. We catch them on the run.
4 The rails, old **lacerations** that we love,
5 shoot parallel across the face and break
6 just under Turtle Mountains[2]. Riding scars
7 you can't get lost. Home is the place they cross.

8 The lame guard strikes a match and makes the dark
9 less **tolerant**. We watch through cracks in boards
10 as the land starts rolling, rolling till it hurts
11 to be here, cold in **regulation** clothes.
12 We know the sheriff's waiting at midrun
13 to take us back. His car is dumb and warm.
14 The highway doesn't rock, it only hums
15 like a wing of long insults. The worn-down welts
16 of **ancient** punishments lead back and forth.

17 All runaways wear dresses, long green ones,
18 the color you would think shame was. We scrub
19 the sidewalks down because it's shameful work.
20 Our brushes cut the stone in watered arcs
21 and in the soak **frail** outlines shiver clear
22 a moment, things us kids pressed on the dark
23 face before it hardened, pale, remembering
24 delicate old injuries, the spines of names and leaves.

"Indian Boarding School: The Runaways" from ORIGINAL FIRE: SELECTED AND NEW POEMS by LOUISE ERDRICH. Copyright © 2003 by Louise Erdrich. Reprinted by permission of HarperCollins Publishers.

---

1. **boxcars** the freight cars on a train, usually with sliding doors and a roof
2. **Turtle Mountains** a mountainous area that continues from the northern border of North Dakota into Manitoba, Canada

Please note that excerpts and passages in the StudySync® library and this workbook are intended as touchstones to generate interest in an author's work. The excerpts and passages do not substitute for the reading of entire texts, and StudySync® strongly recommends that students seek out and purchase the whole literary or informational work in order to experience it as the author intended. Links to online resellers are available in our digital library. In addition, complete works may be ordered through an authorized reseller by filling out and returning to StudySync® the order form enclosed in this workbook.

Reading & Writing Companion

73

WRITE

NARRATIVE: This poem expresses the significance that home and setting have for one's sense of self. Write a narrative about a place, real or imagined, that has been integral to your identity.

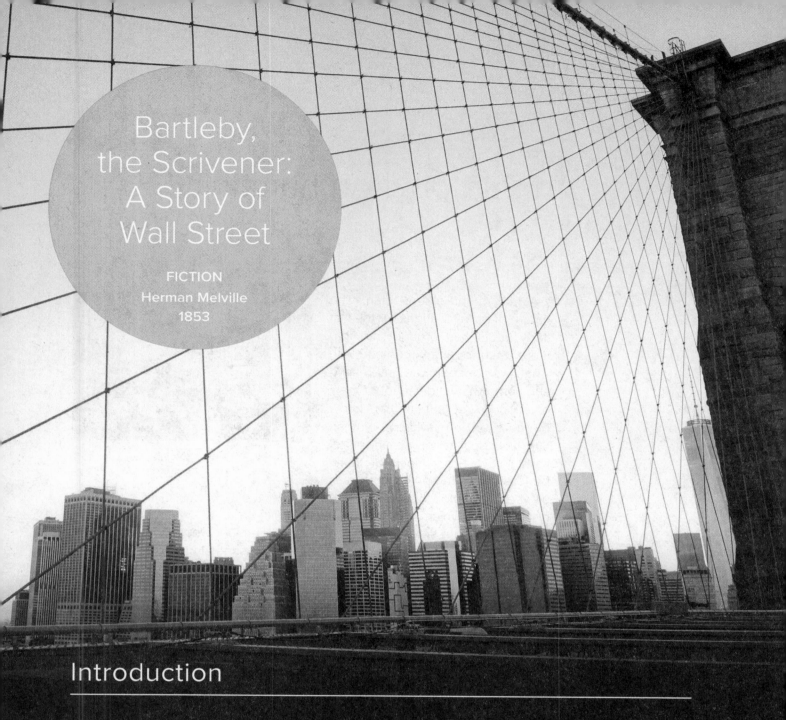

Bartleby, the Scrivener: A Story of Wall Street

FICTION
Herman Melville
1853

Introduction

Herman Melville (1819–1891) is best remembered for writing *Moby-Dick*, one of the great American novels, though he also wrote other novels and dozens of short stories and poems. In "Bartleby, the Scrivener: A Story of Wall-Street," our narrator is an aging lawyer who hires a talented copyist named Bartleby to work in his office as a legal clerk. Although Bartleby's hard work initially impresses his new employer, his unusual behavior soon extends beyond the limits of what the narrator can tolerate. Melville's story about depression and isolation in American work culture endures as a classic piece of short fiction. Though Melville's work was largely ignored during his lifetime, the centennial of his birth in 1919 revived critical interest.

"Ah Bartleby! Ah humanity!"

1   I AM A rather elderly man. The nature of my avocations for the last thirty years has brought me into more than ordinary contact with what would seem an interesting and somewhat singular set of men, of whom as yet nothing that I know of has ever been written:—I mean the law-copyists or scriveners.[1] I have known very many of them, professionally and privately, and if I pleased, could relate divers histories, at which good-natured

Engraving of a scene outside the New York Stock Exchange at the corner of Wall Street and Broad Street in downtown Manhattan, New York, New York, 1860s (Photo by FPG/ Getty Images)

gentlemen might smile, and sentimental souls might weep. But I waive the biographies of all other scriveners for a few passages in the life of Bartleby, who was a scrivener of the strangest I ever saw or heard of. While of other law-copyists I might write the complete life, of Bartleby nothing of that sort can be done. I believe that no materials exist for a full and satisfactory biography of this man. It is an irreparable loss to literature. Bartleby was one of those beings of whom nothing is ascertainable, except from the original sources, and in his case those are very small. What my own astonished eyes saw of Bartleby, *that* is all I know of him, except, indeed, one vague report which will appear in the sequel.

2   Ere introducing the scrivener, as he first appeared to me, it is fit I make some mention of myself, my *employees*, my business, my chambers, and general surroundings; because some such description is indispensable to an adequate understanding of the chief character about to be presented.

3   Imprimis:[2] I am a man who, from his youth upwards, has been filled with a profound conviction that the easiest way of life is the best. Hence, though I belong to a profession proverbially energetic and nervous, even to turbulence,

---

1. **law-copyists or scriveners** employees in a law office whose primary job was document production and reproduction
2. **Imprimis** an adverb used to introduce a list of things to think about

at times, yet nothing of that sort have I ever suffered to invade my peace. I am one of those unambitious lawyers who never addresses a jury, or in any way draws down public applause; but in the cool tranquillity of a snug retreat, do a snug business among rich men's bonds and mortgages and title-deeds. All who know me, consider me an eminently *safe* man. The late John Jacob Astor,[3] a personage little given to poetic enthusiasm, had no hesitation in pronouncing my first grand point to be prudence; my next, method. I do not speak it in vanity, but simply record the fact, that I was not unemployed in my profession by the late John Jacob Astor; a name which, I admit, I love to repeat, for it hath a rounded and orbicular sound to it, and rings like unto bullion. I will freely add, that I was not insensible to the late John Jacob Astor's good opinion.

4   Some time prior to the period at which this little history begins, my avocations had been largely increased. The good old office, now extinct in the State of New York, of a Master in Chancery, had been conferred upon me. It was not a very arduous office, but very pleasantly remunerative. I seldom lose my temper; much more seldom indulge in dangerous indignation at wrongs and outrages; but I must be permitted to be rash here and declare, that I consider the sudden and violent abrogation of the office of Master in Chancery, by the new Constitution, as a—premature act; inasmuch as I had counted upon a life-lease of the profits, whereas I only received those of a few short years. But this is by the way.

5   My chambers were up stairs at No.—Wall-street. At one end they looked upon the white wall of the interior of a spacious sky-light shaft, penetrating the building from top to bottom. This view might have been considered rather tame than otherwise, deficient in what landscape painters call "life." But if so, the view from the other end of my chambers offered, at least, a contrast, if nothing more. In that direction my windows commanded an unobstructed view of a lofty brick wall, black by age and everlasting shade; which wall required no spy-glass to bring out its lurking beauties, but for the benefit of all near-sighted spectators, was pushed up to within ten feet of my window panes. Owing to the great height of the surrounding buildings, and my chambers being on the second floor, the interval between this wall and mine not a little resembled a huge square cistern.

6   At the period just preceding the advent of Bartleby, I had two persons as copyists in my employment, and a promising lad as an office-boy. First, Turkey; second, Nippers; third, Ginger Nut. These may seem names, the like of which are not usually found in the Directory. In truth they were nicknames, mutually conferred upon each other by my three clerks, and were deemed expressive of their respective persons or characters. Turkey was a short, pursy Englishman of about my own age, that is, somewhere not far from sixty. In the morning,

3. **John Jacob Astor** a prominent American businessman

Skill:
Point of View

The narrator compares Turkey's face to a brightly burning Christmas fire and the daily route of the sun. He's using exaggeration to make fun of Turkey's anger as just habit and doesn't take it seriously. This is an example of satire.

one might say, his face was of a fine florid hue, but after twelve o'clock, meridian—his dinner hour—it blazed like a grate full of Christmas coals; and continued blazing—but, as it were, with a gradual wane—till 6 o'clock, P.M. or thereabouts, after which I saw no more of the proprietor of the face, which gaining its meridian with the sun, seemed to set with it, to rise, culminate, and decline the following day, with the like regularity and undiminished glory. There are many singular coincidences I have known in the course of my life, not the least among which was the fact, that exactly when Turkey displayed his fullest beams from his red and radiant countenance, just then, too, at that critical moment, began the daily period when I considered his business capacities as seriously disturbed for the remainder of the twenty-four hours. Not that he was absolutely idle, or averse to business then; far from it. The difficulty was, he was apt to be altogether too energetic. There was a strange, inflamed, flurried, flighty recklessness of activity about him. He would be incautious in dipping his pen into his inkstand. All his blots upon my documents, were dropped there after twelve o'clock, meridian. Indeed, not only would he be reckless and sadly given to making blots in the afternoon, but some days he went further, and was rather noisy. At such times, too, his face flamed with augmented blazonry, as if cannel coal had been heaped on anthracite. He made an unpleasant racket with his chair; spilled his sand-box; in mending his pens, impatiently split them all to pieces, and threw them on the floor in a sudden passion; stood up and leaned over his table, boxing his papers about in a most indecorous manner, very sad to behold in an elderly man like him. Nevertheless, as he was in many ways a most valuable person to me, and all the time before twelve o'clock, meridian, was the quickest, steadiest creature too, accomplishing a great deal of work in a style not easy to be matched—for these reasons, I was willing to overlook his eccentricities, though indeed, occasionally, I remonstrated with him. I did this very gently, however, because, though the civilest, nay, the blandest and most reverential of men in the morning, yet in the afternoon he was disposed, upon provocation, to be slightly rash with his tongue, in fact, insolent. Now, valuing his morning services as I did, and resolved not to lose them; yet, at the same time made uncomfortable by his inflamed ways after twelve o'clock; and being a man of peace, unwilling by my admonitions to call forth unseemly retorts from him; I took upon me, one Saturday noon (he was always worse on Saturdays), to hint to him, very kindly, that perhaps now that he was growing old, it might be well to **abridge** his labors; in short, he need not come to my chambers after twelve o'clock, but, dinner over, had best go home to his lodgings and rest himself till teatime. But no; he insisted upon his afternoon devotions. His countenance became intolerably fervid, as he oratorically assured me— gesticulating with a long ruler at the other end of the room—that if his services in the morning were useful, how indispensable, then, in the afternoon?

7   "With submission, sir," said Turkey on this occasion, "I consider myself your right-hand man. In the morning I but marshal and deploy my columns; but in

the afternoon I put myself at their head, and gallantly charge the foe, thus!"—and he made a violent thrust with the ruler.

8   "But the blots, Turkey," intimated I.

9   "True,—but, with submission, sir, behold these hairs! I am getting old. Surely, sir, a blot or two of a warm afternoon is not to be severely urged against gray hairs. Old age—even if it blot the page—is honorable. With submission, sir, we *both* are getting old."

10   This appeal to my fellow-feeling was hardly to be resisted. At all events, I saw that go he would not. So I made up my mind to let him stay, resolving, nevertheless, to see to it, that during the afternoon he had to do with my less important papers.

11   Nippers, the second on my list, was a whiskered, sallow, and, upon the whole, rather piratical-looking young man of about five and twenty. I always deemed him the victim of two evil powers—ambition and indigestion. The ambition was evinced by a certain impatience of the duties of a mere copyist, an unwarrantable usurpation of strictly professional affairs, such as the original drawing up of legal documents. The indigestion seemed betokened in an occasional nervous testiness and grinning irritability, causing the teeth to audibly grind together over mistakes committed in copying; unnecessary maledictions, hissed, rather than spoken, in the heat of business; and especially by a continual discontent with the height of the table where he worked. Though of a very ingenious mechanical turn, Nippers could never get this table to suit him. He put chips under it, blocks of various sorts, bits of pasteboard, and at last went so far as to attempt an exquisite adjustment by final pieces of folded blotting paper. But no invention would answer. If, for the sake of easing his back, he brought the table lid at a sharp angle well up towards his chin, and wrote there like a man using the steep roof of a Dutch house for his desk:—then he declared that it stopped the circulation in his arms. If now he lowered the table to his waistbands, and stooped over it in writing, then there was a sore aching in his back. In short, the truth of the matter was, Nippers knew not what he wanted. Or, if he wanted any thing, it was to be rid of a scrivener's table altogether. Among the manifestations of his diseased ambition was a fondness he had for receiving visits from certain ambiguous-looking fellows in seedy coats, whom he called his clients. Indeed I was aware that not only was he, at times, considerable of a ward-politician, but he occasionally did a little business at the Justices' courts, and was not unknown on the steps of the Tombs. I have good reason to believe, however, that one individual who called upon him at my chambers, and who, with a grand air, he insisted was his client, was no other than a dun, and the alleged title-deed, a bill. But with all his failings, and the annoyances he caused me, Nippers, like his compatriot Turkey, was a very useful man to me; wrote a neat, swift hand; and, when he chose, was not deficient in a gentlemanly sort

NOTES

of deportment. Added to this, he always dressed in a gentlemanly sort of way; and so, incidentally, reflected credit upon my chambers. Whereas with respect to Turkey, I had much ado to keep him from being a reproach to me. His clothes were apt to look oily and smell of eating-houses. He wore his pantaloons very loose and baggy in summer. His coats were execrable; his hat not to be handled. But while the hat was a thing of indifference to me, inasmuch as his natural civility and deference, as a dependent Englishman, always led him to doff it the moment he entered the room, yet his coat was another matter. Concerning his coats, I reasoned with him; but with no effect. The truth was, I suppose, that a man of so small an income, could not afford to sport such a lustrous face and a lustrous coat at one and the same time. As Nippers once observed, Turkey's money went chiefly for red ink. One winter day I presented Turkey with a highly-respectable looking coat of my own, a padded gray coat, of a most comfortable warmth, and which buttoned straight up from the knee to the neck. I thought Turkey would appreciate the favor, and abate his rashness and obstreperousness of afternoons. But no. I verily believe that buttoning himself up in so downy and blanket-like a coat had a pernicious effect upon him; upon the same principle that too much oats are bad for horses. In fact, precisely as a rash, restive horse is said to feel his oats, so Turkey felt his coat. It made him insolent. He was a man whom prosperity harmed.

12 Though concerning the self-indulgent habits of Turkey I had my own private surmises, yet touching Nippers I was well persuaded that whatever might by his faults in other respects, he was, at least, a temperate young man. But indeed, nature herself seemed to have been his vintner, and at his birth charged him so thoroughly with an irritable, brandy-like disposition, that all subsequent potations were needless. When I consider how, amid the stillness of my chambers, Nippers would sometimes impatiently rise from his seat, and stooping over his table, spread his arms wide apart, seize the whole desk, and move it, and jerk it, with a grim, grinding motion on the floor, as if the table were a perverse voluntary agent, intent on thwarting and vexing him; I plainly perceive that for Nippers, brandy and water were altogether superfluous.

13 It was fortunate for me that, owing to its peculiar cause—indigestion— the irritability and consequent nervousness of Nippers, were mainly observable in the morning, while in the afternoon he was comparatively mild. So that Turkey's paroxysms only coming on about twelve o'clock, I never had to do with their eccentricities at one time. Their fits relieved each other like guards. When Nippers' was on, Turkey's was off; and *vice versa*. This was a good natural arrangement under the circumstances.

14 Ginger Nut, the third on my list, was a lad some twelve years old. His father was a carman, ambitious of seeing his son on the bench instead of a cart, before he died. So he sent him to my office as student at law, errand boy, and cleaner and sweeper, at the rate of one dollar a week. He had a little desk to

Copyright © BookheadEd Learning, LLC

himself, but he did not use it much. Upon inspection, the drawer exhibited a great array of the shells of various sorts of nuts. Indeed, to this quick-witted youth the whole noble science of the law was contained in a nut-shell. Not the least among the employments of Ginger Nut, as well as one which he discharged with the most **alacrity**, was his duty as cake and apple purveyor for Turkey and Nippers. Copying law papers being proverbially dry, husky sort of business, my two scriveners were fain to moisten their mouths very often with Spitzenbergs to be had at the numerous stalls nigh the Custom House and Post Office. Also, they sent Ginger Nut very frequently for that peculiar cake—small, flat, round, and very spicy—after which he had been named by them. Of a cold morning when business was but dull, Turkey would gobble up scores of these cakes, as if they were mere wafers—indeed they sell them at the rate of six or eight for a penny—the scrape of his pen blending with the crunching of the crisp particles in his mouth. Of all the fiery afternoon blunders and flurried rashnesses of Turkey, was his once moistening a ginger-cake between his lips, and clapping it on to a mortgage for a seal. I came within an ace of dismissing him then. But he mollified me by making an oriental bow, and saying—"With submission, sir, it was generous of me to find you in stationery on my own account."

15   Now my original business—that of a conveyancer and title hunter, and drawer-up of recondite documents of all sorts—was considerably increased by receiving the master's office. There was now great work for scriveners. Not only must I push the clerks already with me, but I must have additional help. In answer to my advertisement, a motionless young man one morning, stood upon my office threshold, the door being open, for it was summer. I can see that figure now—pallidly neat, pitiably respectable, incurably forlorn! It was Bartleby.

16   After a few words touching his qualifications, I engaged him, glad to have among my corps of copyists a man of so singularly sedate an aspect, which I thought might operate beneficially upon the flighty temper of Turkey, and the fiery one of Nippers.

17   I should have stated before that ground glass folding-doors divided my premises into two parts, one of which was occupied by my scriveners, the other by myself. According to my humor I threw open these doors, or closed them. I resolved to assign Bartleby a corner by the folding-doors, but on my side of them, so as to have this quiet man within easy call, in case any trifling thing was to be done. I placed his desk close up to a small side-window in that part of the room, a window which originally had afforded a lateral view of certain grimy back-yards and bricks, but which, owing to subsequent erections, commanded at present no view at all, though it gave some light. Within three feet of the panes was a wall, and the light came down from far above, between two lofty buildings, as from a very small opening in a dome. Still further to a satisfactory arrangement, I procured a high green folding

Skill:
Theme

The narrator meets a pale "forlorn" young applicant who just stands "motionless" at the office door. This description reminds me of loneliness and isolation and makes me wonder if one of the themes may relate to loneliness.

NOTES

Skill:
Figurative
Language

This passage uses hyperboles to emphasize Bartleby's work habits. The hyperbole seems to suggest that the narrator finds Bartleby's behavior strange and off putting.

screen, which might entirely isolate Bartleby from my sight, though not remove him from my voice. And thus, in a manner, privacy and society were conjoined.

18   At first Bartleby did an extraordinary quantity of writing. As if long famishing for something to copy, he seemed to gorge himself on my documents. There was no pause for digestion. He ran a day and night line, copying by sun-light and by candle-light. I should have been quite delighted with his application, had he been cheerfully industrious. But he wrote on silently, palely, mechanically.

19   It is, of course, an indispensable part of a scrivener's business to verify the accuracy of his copy, word by word. Where there are two or more scriveners in an office, they assist each other in this examination, one reading from the copy, the other holding the original. It is a very dull, wearisome, and **lethargic** affair. I can readily imagine that to some sanguine temperaments it would be altogether intolerable. For example, I cannot credit that the mettlesome poet Byron would have contentedly sat down with Bartleby to examine a law document of, say five hundred pages, closely written in a crimpy hand.

20   Now and then, in the haste of business, it had been my habit to assist in comparing some brief document myself, calling Turkey or Nippers for this purpose. One object I had in placing Bartleby so handy to me behind the screen, was to avail myself of his services on such trivial occasions. It was on the third day, I think, of his being with me, and before any necessity had arisen for having his own writing examined, that, being much hurried to complete a small affair I had in hand, I abruptly called to Bartleby. In my haste and natural expectancy of instant compliance, I sat with my head bent over the original on my desk, and my right hand sideways, and somewhat nervously extended with the copy, so that immediately upon emerging from his retreat, Bartleby might snatch it and proceed to business without the least delay.

Skill:
Figurative
Language

The narrator describing Bartleby as having a "mild, firm voice" is paradoxical. These two adjectives seem to contradict each other emphasizing the idea that Bartleby is very peculiar.

21   In this very attitude did I sit when I called to him, rapidly stating what it was I wanted him to do—namely, to examine a small paper with me. Imagine my surprise, nay, my consternation, when without moving from his privacy, Bartleby in a singularly mild, firm voice, replied, "I would prefer not to."

22   I sat awhile in perfect silence, rallying my stunned faculties. Immediately it occurred to me that my ears had deceived me, or Bartleby had entirely misunderstood my meaning. I repeated my request in the clearest tone I could assume. But in quite as clear a one came the previous reply, "I would prefer not to."

23   "Prefer not to," echoed I, rising in high excitement, and crossing the room with a stride. "What do you mean? Are you moon-struck? I want you to help me compare this sheet here—take it," and I thrust it towards him.

NOTES

24   "I would prefer not to," said he.

25   I looked at him steadfastly. His face was leanly composed; his gray eye dimly calm. Not a wrinkle of agitation rippled him. Had there been the least uneasiness, anger, impatience or impertinence in his manner; in other words, had there been any thing ordinarily human about him, doubtless I should have violently dismissed him from the premises. But as it was, I should have as soon thought of turning my pale plaster-of-paris bust of Cicero out of doors. I stood gazing at him awhile, as he went on with his own writing, and then reseated myself at my desk. This is very strange, thought I. What had one best do? But my business hurried me. I concluded to forget the matter for the present, reserving it for my future leisure. So calling Nippers from the other room, the paper was speedily examined.

26   A few days after this, Bartleby concluded four lengthy documents, being quadruplicates of a week's testimony taken before me in my High Court of Chancery. It became necessary to examine them. It was an important suit, and great accuracy was imperative. Having all things arranged I called Turkey, Nippers and Ginger Nut from the next room, meaning to place the four copies in the hands of my four clerks, while I should read from the original. Accordingly Turkey, Nippers and Ginger Nut had taken their seats in a row, each with his document in hand, when I called to Bartleby to join this interesting group.

27   "Bartleby! quick, I am waiting."

28   I heard a slow scrape of his chair legs on the uncarpeted floor, and soon he appeared standing at the entrance of his hermitage.

29   "What is wanted?" said he mildly.

30   "The copies, the copies," said I hurriedly. "We are going to examine them. There"—and I held towards him the fourth quadruplicate.

31   "I would prefer not to," he said, and gently disappeared behind the screen.

32   For a few moments I was turned into a pillar of salt,[4] standing at the head of my seated column of clerks. Recovering myself, I advanced towards the screen, and demanded the reason for such extraordinary conduct.

33   "*Why* do you refuse?"

34   "I would prefer not to."

35   With any other man I should have flown outright into a dreadful passion, scorned all further words, and thrust him ignominiously from my presence. But there was something about Bartleby that not only strangely disarmed me,

 Skill:
Theme

Bartleby's repetition of the phrase "I would prefer not to" makes me think. It brings out the idea of passive resistance—refusing to conform to social norms. Is passive resistance another theme?

4. **pillar of salt** In the Bible, Lot's wife was turned into a pillar of salt when she disobeyed God's command not to look back at the destruction of Sodom and Gomorrah.

but in a wonderful manner touched and disconcerted me. I began to reason with him.

36 "These are your own copies we are about to examine. It is labor saving to you, because one examination will answer for your four papers. It is common usage. Every copyist is bound to help examine his copy. Is it not so? Will you not speak? Answer!"

37 "I prefer not to," he replied in a flute-like tone. It seemed to me that while I had been addressing him, he carefully revolved every statement that I made; fully comprehended the meaning; could not gainsay the irresistible conclusions; but, at the same time, some paramount consideration prevailed with him to reply as he did.

38 "You are decided, then, not to comply with my request—a request made according to common usage and common sense?"

39 He briefly gave me to understand that on that point my judgment was sound. Yes: his decision was irreversible.

40 It is not seldom the case that when a man is browbeaten in some unprecedented and violently unreasonable way, he begins to stagger in his own plainest faith. He begins, as it were, vaguely to surmise that, wonderful as it may be, all the justice and all the reason is on the other side. Accordingly, if any disinterested persons are present, he turns to them for some reinforcement for his own faltering mind.

41 "Turkey," said I, "what do you think of this? Am I not right?"

42 "With submission, sir," said Turkey, with his blandest tone, "I think that you are."

43 "Nippers," said I, "what do *you* think of it?"

44 "I think I should kick him out of the office."

45 (The reader of nice perceptions will here perceive that, it being morning, Turkey's answer is couched in polite and tranquil terms, but Nippers replies in ill-tempered ones. Or, to repeat a previous sentence, Nippers' ugly mood was on duty and Turkey's off.)

46 "Ginger Nut," said I, willing to enlist the smallest suffrage in my behalf, "what do *you* think of it?"

47 "I think, sir, he's a little *luny*," replied Ginger Nut with a grin.

48 "You hear what they say," said I, turning towards the screen, "come forth and do your duty."

NOTES

49   But he vouchsafed no reply. I pondered a moment in sore perplexity. But once more business hurried me. I determined again to postpone the consideration of this dilemma to my future leisure. With a little trouble we made out to examine the papers without Bartleby, though at every page or two, Turkey deferentially dropped his opinion that this proceeding was quite out of the common; while Nippers, twitching in his chair with a dyspeptic nervousness, ground out between his set teeth occasional hissing maledictions against the stubborn oaf behind the screen. And for his (Nippers') part, this was the first and the last time he would do another man's business without pay.

50   Meanwhile Bartleby sat in his hermitage, oblivious to every thing but his own peculiar business there.

51   Some days passed, the scrivener being employed upon another lengthy work. His late remarkable conduct led me to regard his ways narrowly. I observed that he never went to dinner; indeed that he never went any where. As yet I had never of my personal knowledge known him to be outside of my office. He was a perpetual sentry in the corner. At about eleven o'clock though, in the morning, I noticed that Ginger Nut would advance toward the opening in Bartleby's screen, as if silently beckoned thither by a gesture invisible to me where I sat. The boy would then leave the office jingling a few pence, and reappear with a handful of ginger-nuts which he delivered in the hermitage, receiving two of the cakes for his trouble.

52   He lives, then, on ginger-nuts, thought I; never eats a dinner, properly speaking; he must be a vegetarian then; but no; he never eats even vegetables, he eats nothing but ginger-nuts. My mind then ran on in reveries concerning the probable effects upon the human constitution of living entirely on ginger-nuts. Ginger-nuts are so called because they contain ginger as one of their peculiar constituents, and the final flavoring one. Now what was ginger? A hot, spicy thing. Was Bartleby hot and spicy? Not at all. Ginger, then, had no effect upon Bartleby. Probably he preferred it should have none.

53   Nothing so aggravates an earnest person as a passive resistance. If the individual so resisted be of a not inhumane temper, and the resisting one perfectly harmless in his passivity; then, in the better moods of the former, he will endeavor charitably to construe to his imagination what proves impossible to be solved by his judgment. Even so, for the most part, I regarded Bartleby and his ways. Poor fellow! Thought I, he means no mischief; it is plain he intends no insolence; his aspect sufficiently evinces that his eccentricities are involuntary. He is useful to me. I can get along with him. If I turn him away, the chances are he will fall in with some less indulgent employer, and then he will be rudely treated, and perhaps driven forth miserably to starve. Yes. Here I can cheaply purchase a delicious self-approval. To befriend Bartleby; to humor him in his strange willfulness, will cost me little or nothing, while I lay

up in my soul what will eventually prove a sweet morsel for my conscience. But this mood was not invariable with me. The passiveness of Bartleby sometimes irritated me. I felt strangely goaded on to encounter him in new opposition, to elicit some angry spark from him answerable to my own. But indeed I might as well have essayed to strike fire with my knuckles against a bit of Windsor soap. But one afternoon the evil impulse in me mastered me, and the following little scene ensued:

54 "Bartleby," said I, "when those papers are all copied, I will compare them with you."

55 "I would prefer not to."

56 "How? Surely you do not mean to persist in that mulish vagary?"

57 No answer.

58 I threw open the folding-doors near by, and turning upon Turkey and Nippers, exclaimed in an excited manner—

59 "He says, a second time, he won't examine his papers. What do you think of it, Turkey?"

60 It was afternoon, be it remembered. Turkey sat glowing like a brass boiler, his bald head steaming, his hands reeling among his blotted papers.

61 "Think of it?" roared Turkey; "I think I'll just step behind his screen, and black his eyes for him!"

62 So saying, Turkey rose to his feet and threw his arms into a pugilistic position. He was hurrying away to make good his promise, when I detained him, alarmed at the effect of incautiously rousing Turkey's combativeness after dinner.

63 "Sit down, Turkey," said I, "and hear what Nippers has to say. What do you think of it, Nippers? Would I not be justified in immediately dismissing Bartleby?"

64 "Excuse me, that is for you to decide, sir. I think his conduct quite unusual, and indeed unjust, as regards Turkey and myself. But it may only be a passing whim."

65 "Ah," exclaimed I, "you have strangely changed your mind then—you speak very gently of him now."

66 "All beer," cried Turkey; "gentleness is effects of beer—Nippers and I dined together to-day. You see how gentle I am, sir. Shall I go and black his eyes?"

67 "You refer to Bartleby, I suppose. No, not to-day, Turkey," I replied; "pray, put up your fists."

Copyright © BookheadEd Learning, LLC

NOTES

68   I closed the doors, and again advanced towards Bartleby. I felt additional incentives tempting me to my fate. I burned to be rebelled against again. I remembered that Bartleby never left the office.

69   "Bartleby," said I, "Ginger Nut is away; just step round to the Post Office, won't you? (it was but a three-minute walk,) and see if there is any thing for me."

70   "I would prefer not to."

71   "You *will* not?"

72   "I *prefer* not."

73   I staggered to my desk, and sat there in a deep study. My blind inveteracy returned. Was there any other thing in which I could procure myself to be ignominiously repulsed by this lean, penniless wight?—my hired clerk? What added thing is there, perfectly reasonable, that he will be sure to refuse to do?

74   "Bartleby!"

75   No answer.

76   "Bartleby," in a louder tone.

77   No answer.

78   "Bartleby," I roared.

79   Like a very ghost, agreeably to the laws of magical invocation, at the third summons, he appeared at the entrance of his hermitage.

80   "Go to the next room, and tell Nippers to come to me."

81   "I prefer not to," he respectfully and slowly said, and mildly disappeared.

82   "Very good, Bartleby," said I, in a quiet sort of serenely severe self-possessed tone, intimating the unalterable purpose of some terrible retribution very close at hand. At the moment I half intended something of the kind. But upon the whole, as it was drawing towards my dinner-hour, I thought it best to put on my hat and walk home for the day, suffering much from perplexity and distress of mind.

83   Shall I acknowledge it? The conclusion of this whole business was, that it soon became a fixed fact of my chambers, that a pale young scrivener, by the name of Bartleby, had a desk there; that he copied for me at the usual rate of four cents a folio (one hundred words); but he was permanently exempt from examining the work done by him, that duty being transferred to Turkey and Nippers, one of compliment doubtless to their superior acuteness; moreover, said Bartleby was never on any account to be dispatched on the most trivial

errand of any sort; and that even if entreated to take upon him such a matter, it was generally understood that he would prefer not to—in other words, that he would refuse point-blank.

84 As days passed on, I became considerably reconciled to Bartleby. His steadiness, his freedom from all dissipation, his incessant industry (except when he chose to throw himself into a standing revery behind his screen), his great stillness, his unalterableness of demeanor under all circumstances, made him a valuable acquisition. One prime thing was this,—*he was always there*;—first in the morning, continually through the day, and the last at night. I had a singular confidence in his honesty. I felt my most precious papers perfectly safe in his hands. Sometimes to be sure I could not, for the very soul of me, avoid falling into sudden spasmodic passions with him. For it was exceeding difficult to bear in mind all the time those strange peculiarities, privileges, and unheard of exemptions, forming the tacit stipulations on Bartleby's part under which he remained in my office. Now and then, in the eagerness of dispatching pressing business, I would inadvertently summon Bartleby, in a short, rapid tone, to put his finger, say, on the incipient tie of a bit of red tape with which I was about compressing some papers. Of course, from behind the screen the usual answer, "I prefer not to," was sure to come; and then, how could a human creature with the common infirmities of our nature, refrain from bitterly exclaiming upon such perverseness—such unreasonableness. However, every added repulse of this sort which I received only tended to lessen the probability of my repeating the inadvertence.

85 Here it must be said, that according to the custom of most legal gentlemen occupying chambers in densely-populated law buildings, there were several keys to my door. One was kept by a woman residing in the attic, which person weekly scrubbed and daily swept and dusted my apartments. Another was kept by Turkey for convenience sake. The third I sometimes carried in my own pocket. The fourth I knew not who had.

86 Now, one Sunday morning I happened to go to Trinity Church, to hear a celebrated preacher, and finding myself rather early on the ground, I thought I would walk around to my chambers for a while. Luckily I had my key with me; but upon applying it to the lock, I found it resisted by something inserted from the inside. Quite surprised, I called out; when to my consternation a key was turned from within; and thrusting his lean visage at me, and holding the door ajar, the apparition of Bartleby appeared, in his shirt sleeves, and otherwise in a strangely tattered dishabille, saying quietly that he was sorry, but he was deeply engaged just then, and—preferred not admitting me at present. In a brief word or two, he moreover added, that perhaps I had better walk round the block two or three times, and by that time he would probably have concluded his affairs.

87   Now, the utterly **unsurmised** appearance of Bartleby, tenanting my law-chambers of a Sunday morning, with his cadaverously gentlemanly *nonchalance*, yet withal firm and self-possessed, had such a strange effect upon me, that incontinently I slunk away from my own door, and did as desired. But not without sundry twinges of impotent rebellion against the mild effrontery of this unaccountable scrivener. Indeed, it was his wonderful mildness chiefly, which not only disarmed me, but unmanned me, as it were. For I consider that one, for the time, is a sort of unmanned when he tranquilly permits his hired clerk to dictate to him, and order him away from his own premises. Furthermore, I was full of uneasiness as to what Bartleby could possibly be doing in my office in his shirt sleeves, and in an otherwise dismantled condition of a Sunday morning. Was any thing amiss going on? Nay, that was out of the question. It was not to be thought of for a moment that Bartleby was an immoral person. But what could he be doing there?—copying? Nay again, whatever might be his eccentricities, Bartleby was an eminently decorous person. He would be the last man to sit down to his desk in any state approaching to nudity. Besides, it was Sunday; and there was something about Bartleby that forbade the supposition that he would by any secular occupation violate the proprieties of the day.

88   Nevertheless, my mind was not pacified; and full of a restless curiosity, at last I returned to the door. Without hindrance I inserted my key, opened it, and entered. Bartleby was not to be seen. I looked round anxiously, peeped behind his screen; but it was very plain that he was gone. Upon more closely examining the place, I surmised that for an indefinite period Bartleby must have ate, dressed, and slept in my office, and that too without plate, mirror, or bed. The cushioned seat of a rickety old sofa in one corner bore the faint impress of a lean, reclining form. Rolled away under his desk, I found a blanket; under the empty grate, a blacking box and brush; on a chair, a tin basin, with soap and a ragged towel; in a newspaper a few crumbs of ginger-nuts and a morsel of cheese. Yes, thought I, it is evident enough that Bartleby has been making his home here, keeping bachelor's hall all by himself. Immediately then the thought came sweeping across me, What miserable friendlessness and loneliness are here revealed! His poverty is great; but his solitude, how horrible! Think of it. Of a Sunday, Wall-street is deserted as Petra; and every night of every day it is an emptiness. This building too, which of week-days hums with industry and life, at nightfall echoes with sheer vacancy, and all through Sunday is forlorn. And here Bartleby makes his home; sole spectator of a solitude which he has seen all populous—a sort of innocent and transformed Marius[5] brooding among the ruins of Carthage!

89   For the first time in my life a feeling of overpowering stinging melancholy seized me. Before, I had never experienced aught but a not-unpleasing

---

5. **Marius** Gaius Marius, a Roman general and statesman, who was exiled to the destroyed city of Carthage

sadness. The bond of a common humanity now drew me irresistibly to gloom. A fraternal melancholy! For both I and Bartleby were sons of Adam. I remembered the bright silks and sparkling faces I had seen that day, in gala trim, swan-like sailing down the Mississippi of Broadway; and I contrasted them with the pallid copyist, and thought to myself, Ah, happiness courts the light, so we deem the world is gay; but misery hides aloof, so we deem that misery there is none. These sad fancyings—chimeras, doubtless, of a sick and silly brain—led on to other and more special thoughts, concerning the eccentricities of Bartleby. Presentiments of strange discoveries hovered round me. The scrivener's pale form appeared to me laid out, among uncaring strangers, in its shivering winding sheet.

90 Suddenly I was attracted by Bartleby's closed desk, the key in open sight left in the lock.

91 I mean no mischief, seek the gratification of no heartless curiosity, thought I; besides, the desk is mine, and its contents too, so I will make bold to look within. Every thing was methodically arranged, the papers smoothly placed. The pigeon holes were deep, and removing the files of documents, I groped into their recesses. Presently I felt something there, and dragged it out. It was an old bandanna handkerchief, heavy and knotted. I opened it, and saw it was a savings' bank.

92 I now recalled all the quiet mysteries which I had noted in the man. I remembered that he never spoke but to answer; that though at intervals he had considerable time to himself, yet I had never seen him reading—no, not even a newspaper; that for long periods he would stand looking out, at his pale window behind the screen, upon the dead brick wall; I was quite sure he never visited any refectory or eating house; while his pale face clearly indicated that he never drank beer like Turkey, or tea and coffee even, like other men; that he never went any where in particular that I could learn; never went out for a walk, unless indeed that was the case at present; that he had declined telling who he was, or whence he came, or whether he had any relatives in the world; that though so thin and pale, he never complained of ill health. And more than all, I remembered a certain unconscious air of pallid—how shall I call it?—of pallid haughtiness, say, or rather an austere reserve about him, which had positively awed me into my tame compliance with his eccentricities, when I had feared to ask him to do the slightest incidental thing for me, even though I might know, from his long-continued motionlessness, that behind his screen he must be standing in one of those dead-wall reveries of his.

93 Revolving all these things, and coupling them with the recently discovered fact that he made my office his constant abiding place and home, and not forgetful of his morbid moodiness; revolving all these things, a prudential feeling began to steal over me. My first emotions had been those of pure

melancholy and sincerest pity; but just in proportion as the forlornness of Bartleby grew and grew to my imagination, did that same melancholy merge into fear, that pity into repulsion. So true it is, and so terrible too, that up to a certain point the thought or sight of misery enlists our best affections; but, in certain special cases, beyond that point it does not. They err who would assert that invariably this is owing to the inherent selfishness of the human heart. It rather proceeds from a certain hopelessness of remedying excessive and organic ill. To a sensitive being, pity is not seldom pain. And when at last it is perceived that such pity cannot lead to effectual succor, common sense bids the soul rid of it. What I saw that morning persuaded me that the scrivener was the victim of innate and incurable disorder. I might give alms to his body; but his body did not pain him; it was his soul that suffered, and his soul I could not reach.

94   I did not accomplish the purpose of going to Trinity Church that morning. Somehow, the things I had seen disqualified me for the time from church-going. I walked homeward, thinking what I would do with Bartleby. Finally, I resolved upon this;—I would put certain calm questions to him the next morning, touching his history, etc., and if he declined to answer them openly and unreservedly (and I supposed he would prefer not), then to give him a twenty-dollar bill over and above whatever I might owe him, and tell him his services were no longer required; but that if in any other way I could assist him, I would be happy to do so, especially if he desired to return to his native place, wherever that might be, I would willingly help to defray the expenses. Moreover, if, after reaching home, he found himself at any time in want of aid, a letter from him would be sure of a reply.

95   The next morning came.

96   "Bartleby," said I, gently calling to him behind his screen.

97   No reply.

98   "Bartleby," said I, in a still gentler tone, "come here; I am not going to ask you to do any thing you would prefer not to do—I simply wish to speak to you."

99   Upon this he noiselessly slid into view.

100   "Will you tell me, Bartleby, where you were born?"

101   "I would prefer not to."

102   "Will you tell me *any thing* about yourself?"

103   "I would prefer not to."

104   "But what reasonable objection can you have to speak to me? I feel friendly towards you."

Please note that excerpts and passages in the StudySync® library and this workbook are intended as touchstones to generate interest in an author's work. The excerpts and passages do not substitute for the reading of entire texts, and StudySync® strongly recommends that students seek out and purchase the whole literary or informational work in order to experience it as the author intended. Links to online resellers are available in our digital library. In addition, complete works may be ordered through an authorized reseller by filling out and returning to StudySync® the order form enclosed in this workbook.

Reading & Writing Companion   91

105   He did not look at me while I spoke, but kept his glance fixed upon my bust of Cicero, which as I then sat, was directly behind me, some six inches above my head.

106   "What is your answer, Bartleby?" said I, after waiting a considerable time for a reply, during which his countenance remained immovable, only there was the faintest conceivable tremor of the white attenuated mouth.

107   "At present I prefer to give no answer," he said, and retired into his hermitage.

108   It was rather weak in me I confess, but his manner on this occasion nettled me. Not only did there seem to lurk in it a certain calm disdain, but his perverseness seemed ungrateful, considering the undeniable good usage and indulgence he had received from me.

109   Again I sat ruminating what I should do. Mortified as I was at his behavior, and resolved as I had been to dismiss him when I entered my offices, nevertheless I strangely felt something superstitious knocking at my heart, and forbidding me to carry out my purpose, and denouncing me for a villain if I dared to breathe one bitter word against this forlornest of mankind. At last, familiarly drawing my chair behind his screen, I sat down and said: "Bartleby, never mind then about revealing your history; but let me entreat you, as a friend, to comply as far as may be with the usages of this office. Say now you will help to examine papers to-morrow or next day: in short, say now that in a day or two you will begin to be a little reasonable:—say so, Bartleby."

110   "At present I would prefer not to be a little reasonable," was his mildly cadaverous reply. Just then the folding-doors opened, and Nippers approached. He seemed suffering from an unusually bad night's rest, induced by severer indigestion than common. He overheard those final words of Bartleby.

111   "*Prefer not*, eh?" gritted Nippers—"I'd *prefer* him, if I were you, sir," addressing me—"I'd *prefer* him; I'd give him preferences, the stubborn mule! What is it, sir, pray, that he *prefers* not to do now?"

112   Bartleby moved not a limb.

113   "Mr. Nippers," said I, "I'd prefer that you would withdraw for the present."

114   Somehow, of late I had got into the way of involuntarily using this word "prefer" upon all sorts of not exactly suitable occasions. And I trembled to think that my contact with the scrivener had already and seriously affected me in a mental way. And what further and deeper aberration might it not yet produce? This apprehension had not been without efficacy in determining me to summary means.

115 As Nippers, looking very sour and sulky, was departing, Turkey blandly and deferentially approached.

116 "With submission, sir," said he, "yesterday I was thinking about Bartleby here, and I think that if he would but prefer to take a quart of good ale every day, it would do much towards mending him, and enabling him to assist in examining his papers."

117 "So you have got the word too," said I, slightly excited.

118 "With submission, what word, sir," asked Turkey, respectfully crowding himself into the contracted space behind the screen, and by so doing, making me jostle the scrivener. "What word, sir?"

119 "I would prefer to be left alone here," said Bartleby, as if offended at being mobbed in his privacy.

120 "*That's* the word, Turkey," said I—"*that's* it." "Oh, *prefer*? oh yes—queer word. I never use it myself. But, sir, as I was saying, if he would but prefer—"

121 "Turkey," interrupted I, "you will please withdraw."

122 "Oh certainly, sir, if you prefer that I should."

123 As he opened the folding-door to retire, Nippers at his desk caught a glimpse of me, and asked whether I would prefer to have a certain paper copied on blue paper or white. He did not in the least roguishly accent the word prefer. It was plain that it involuntarily rolled from his tongue. I thought to myself, surely I must get rid of a demented man, who already has in some degree turned the tongues, if not the heads of myself and clerks. But I thought it **prudent** not to break the dismission at once.

124 The next day I noticed that Bartleby did nothing but stand at his window in his dead-wall revery. Upon asking him why he did not write, he said that he had decided upon doing no more writing.

125 "Why, how now? what next?" exclaimed I, "do no more writing?"

126 "No more."

127 "And what is the reason?"

128 "Do you not see the reason for yourself?" he indifferently replied.

129 I looked steadfastly at him, and perceived that his eyes looked dull and glazed. Instantly it occurred to me, that his unexampled diligence in copying by his dim window for the first few weeks of his stay with me might have temporarily impaired his vision.

NOTES

130   I was touched. I said something in condolence with him. I hinted that of course he did wisely in abstaining from writing for a while; and urged him to embrace that opportunity of taking wholesome exercise in the open air. This, however, he did not do. A few days after this, my other clerks being absent, and being in a great hurry to dispatch certain letters by the mail, I thought that, having nothing else earthly to do, Bartleby would surely be less inflexible than usual, and carry these letters to the post-office. But he blankly declined. So, much to my inconvenience, I went myself.

131   Still added days went by. Whether Bartleby's eyes improved or not, I could not say. To all appearance, I thought they did. But when I asked him if they did, he vouchsafed no answer. At all events, he would do no copying. At last, in reply to my urgings, he informed me that he had permanently given up copying.

132   "What!" exclaimed I; "suppose your eyes should get entirely well—better than ever before—would you not copy then?"

133   "I have given up copying," he answered, and slid aside.

134   He remained as ever, a fixture in my chamber. Nay—if that were possible—he became still more of a fixture than before. What was to be done? He would do nothing in the office: why should he stay there? In plain fact, he had now become a millstone to me, not only useless as a necklace, but afflictive to bear. Yet I was sorry for him. I speak less than truth when I say that, on his own account, he occasioned me uneasiness. If he would but have named a single relative or friend, I would instantly have written, and urged their taking the poor fellow away to some convenient retreat. But he seemed alone, absolutely alone in the universe. A bit of wreck in the mid-Atlantic. At length, necessities connected with my business tyrannized over all other considerations. Decently as I could, I told Bartleby that in six days' time he must unconditionally leave the office. I warned him to take measures, in the interval, for procuring some other abode. I offered to assist him in this endeavor, if he himself would but take the first step towards a removal. "And when you finally quit me, Bartleby," added I, "I shall see that you go not away entirely unprovided. Six days from this hour, remember."

135   At the expiration of that period, I peeped behind the screen, and lo! Bartleby was there.

136   I buttoned up my coat, balanced myself; advanced slowly towards him, touched his shoulder, and said, "The time has come; you must quit this place; I am sorry for you; here is money; but you must go."

137   "I would prefer not," he replied, with his back still towards me.

138   "You *must*."

NOTES

139   He remained silent.

140   Now I had an unbounded confidence in this man's common honesty. He had frequently restored to me sixpences and shillings carelessly dropped upon the floor, for I am apt to be very reckless in such shirt-button affairs. The proceeding then which followed will not be deemed extraordinary.

141   "Bartleby," said I, "I owe you twelve dollars on account; here are thirty-two; the odd twenty are yours.—Will you take it?" and I handed the bills towards him.

142   But he made no motion.

143   "I will leave them here then," putting them under a weight on the table. Then taking my hat and cane and going to the door I tranquilly turned and added— "After you have removed your things from these offices, Bartleby, you will of course lock the door—since every one is now gone for the day but you—and if you please, slip your key underneath the mat, so that I may have it in the morning. I shall not see you again; so good-bye to you. If hereafter in your new place of abode I can be of any service to you, do not fail to advise me by letter. Good-bye, Bartleby, and fare you well."

144   But he answered not a word; like the last column of some ruined temple, he remained standing mute and solitary in the middle of the otherwise deserted room.

145   As I walked home in a pensive mood, my vanity got the better of my pity. I could not but highly plume myself on my masterly management in getting rid of Bartleby. Masterly I call it, and such it must appear to any dispassionate thinker. The beauty of my procedure seemed to consist in its perfect quietness. There was no vulgar bullying, no bravado of any sort, no choleric hectoring, and striding to and fro across the apartment, jerking out vehement commands for Bartleby to bundle himself off with his beggarly traps. Nothing of the kind. Without loudly bidding Bartleby depart—as an inferior genius might have done—I *assumed* the ground that depart he must; and upon that assumption built all I had to say. The more I thought over my procedure, the more I was charmed with it. Nevertheless, next morning, upon awakening, I had my doubts,—I had somehow slept off the fumes of vanity. One of the coolest and wisest hours a man has, is just after he awakes in the morning. My procedure seemed as sagacious as ever—but only in theory. How it would prove in practice—there was the rub. It was truly a beautiful thought to have assumed Bartleby's departure; but, after all, that assumption was simply my own, and none of Bartleby's. The great point was, not whether I had assumed that he would quit me, but whether he would prefer so to do. He was more a man of preferences than assumptions.

146   After breakfast, I walked down town, arguing the probabilities *pro* and *con*. One moment I thought it would prove a miserable failure, and Bartleby would

NOTES

be found all alive at my office as usual; the next moment it seemed certain that I should see his chair empty. And so I kept veering about. At the corner of Broadway and Canal-street, I saw quite an excited group of people standing in earnest conversation.

147 "I'll take odds he doesn't," said a voice as I passed.

148 "Doesn't go?—done!" said I, "put up your money."

149 I was instinctively putting my hand in my pocket to produce my own, when I remembered that this was an election day. The words I had overheard bore no reference to Bartleby, but to the success or non-success of some candidate for the mayoralty. In my intent frame of mind, I had, as it were, imagined that all Broadway shared in my excitement, and were debating the same question with me. I passed on, very thankful that the uproar of the street screened my momentary absent-mindedness.

150 As I had intended, I was earlier than usual at my office door. I stood listening for a moment. All was still. He must be gone. I tried the knob. The door was locked. Yes, my procedure had worked to a charm; he indeed must be vanished. Yet a certain melancholy mixed with this: I was almost sorry for my brilliant success. I was fumbling under the door mat for the key, which Bartleby was to have left there for me, when accidentally my knee knocked against a panel, producing a summoning sound, and in response a voice came to me from within—"Not yet; I am occupied."

151 It was Bartleby.

152 I was thunderstruck. For an instant I stood like the man who, pipe in mouth, was killed one cloudless afternoon long ago in Virginia, by a summer lightning; at his own warm open window he was killed, and remained leaning out there upon the dreamy afternoon, till some one touched him, when he fell.

153 "Not gone!" I murmured at last. But again obeying that wondrous ascendancy which the inscrutable scrivener had over me, and from which ascendancy, for all my chafing, I could not completely escape, I slowly went down stairs and out into the street, and while walking round the block, considered what I should next do in this unheard-of perplexity. Turn the man out by an actual thrusting I could not; to drive him away by calling him hard names would not do; calling in the police was an unpleasant idea; and yet, permit him to enjoy his cadaverous triumph over me,—this too I could not think of. What was to be done? Or, if nothing could be done, was there any thing further that I could *assume* in the matter? Yes, as before I had prospectively assumed that Bartleby would depart, so now I might retrospectively assume that departed he was. In the legitimate carrying out of this assumption, I might enter my office in a great hurry, and pretending not to see Bartleby at all, walk straight against him as if he were air. Such a proceeding would in a singular degree

have the appearance of a home-thrust. It was hardly possible that Bartleby could withstand such an application of the doctrine of assumptions. But upon second thoughts the success of the plan seemed rather dubious. I resolved to argue the matter over with him again.

154   "Bartleby," said I, entering the office, with a quietly severe expression, "I am seriously displeased. I am pained, Bartleby. I had thought better of you. I had imagined you of such a gentlemanly organization, that in any delicate dilemma a slight hint would have suffice—in short, an assumption. But it appears I am deceived. Why," I added, unaffectedly starting, "you have not even touched that money yet," pointing to it, just where I had left it the evening previous.

155   He answered nothing.

156   "Will you, or will you not, quit me?" I now demanded in a sudden passion, advancing close to him.

157   "I would prefer *not* to quit you," he replied, gently emphasizing the *not*.

158   "What earthly right have you to stay here? Do you pay any rent? Do you pay my taxes? Or is this property yours?"

159   He answered nothing.

160   "Are you ready to go on and write now? Are your eyes recovered? Could you copy a small paper for me this morning? or help examine a few lines? or step round to the post-office? In a word, will you do any thing at all, to give a coloring to your refusal to depart the premises?"

161   He silently retired into his hermitage.

162   I was now in such a state of nervous resentment that I thought it but prudent to check myself at present from further demonstrations. Bartleby and I were alone. I remembered the tragedy of the unfortunate Adams and the still more unfortunate Colt in the solitary office of the latter; and how poor Colt, being dreadfully incensed by Adams, and imprudently permitting himself to get wildly excited, was at unawares hurried into his fatal act—an act which certainly no man could possibly deplore more than the actor himself. Often it had occurred to me in my ponderings upon the subject, that had that altercation taken place in the public street, or at a private residence, it would not have terminated as it did. It was the circumstance of being alone in a solitary office, up stairs, of a building entirely unhallowed by humanizing domestic associations—an uncarpeted office, doubtless, of a dusty, haggard sort of appearance;—this it must have been, which greatly helped to enhance the irritable desperation of the hapless Colt.

163   But when this old Adam of resentment rose in me and tempted me concerning Bartleby, I grappled him and threw him. How? Why, simply by recalling the

divine injunction: "A new commandment give I unto you, that ye love one another." Yes, this it was that saved me. Aside from higher considerations, charity often operates as a vastly wise and prudent principle—a great safeguard to its possessor. Men have committed murder for jealousy's sake, and anger's sake, and hatred's sake, and selfishness' sake, and spiritual pride's sake; but no man that ever I heard of, ever committed a diabolical murder for sweet charity's sake. Mere self-interest, then, if no better motive can be enlisted, should, especially with high-tempered men, prompt all beings to charity and philanthropy. At any rate, upon the occasion in question, I strove to drown my exasperated feelings towards the scrivener by benevolently construing his conduct. Poor fellow, poor fellow! thought I, he don't mean any thing; and besides, he has seen hard times, and ought to be indulged.

164   I endeavored also immediately to occupy myself, and at the same time to comfort my despondency. I tried to fancy that in the course of the morning, at such time as might prove agreeable to him. Bartleby, of his own free accord, would emerge from his hermitage, and take up some decided line of march in the direction of the door. But no. Half-past twelve o'clock came; Turkey began to glow in the face, overturn his inkstand, and become generally obstreperous; Nippers abated down into quietude and courtesy; Ginger Nut munched his noon apple; and Bartleby remained standing at his window in one of his profoundest dead-wall reveries. Will it be credited? Ought I to acknowledge it? That afternoon I left the office without saying one further word to him.

165   Some days now passed, during which, at leisure intervals I looked a little into "Edwards on the Will," and "Priestley on Necessity." Under the circumstances, those books induced a salutary feeling. Gradually I slid into the persuasion that these troubles of mine touching the scrivener, had been all predestinated from eternity, and Bartleby was billeted upon me for some mysterious purpose of an all-wise Providence, which it was not for a mere mortal like me to fathom. Yes, Bartleby, stay there behind your screen, thought I; I shall persecute you no more; you are harmless and noiseless as any of these old chairs; in short, I never feel so private as when I know you are here. At last I see it, I feel it; I penetrate to the predestinated purpose of my life. I am content. Others may have loftier parts to enact; but my mission in this world, Bartleby, is to furnish you with office-room for such period as you may see fit to remain.

166   I believe that this wise and blessed frame of mind would have continued with me, had it not been for the unsolicited and uncharitable remarks obtruded upon me by my professional friends who visited the rooms. But thus it often is, that the constant friction of illiberal minds wears out at last the best resolves of the more generous. Though to be sure, when I reflected upon it, it was not strange that people entering my office should be struck by the peculiar aspect of the unaccountable Bartleby, and so be tempted to throw out some

sinister observations concerning him. Sometimes an attorney having business with me, and calling at my office and finding no one but the scrivener there, would undertake to obtain some sort of precise information from him touching my whereabouts; but without heeding his idle talk, Bartleby would remain standing immovable in the middle of the room. So after contemplating him in that position for a time, the attorney would depart, no wiser than he came.

167 Also, when a Reference was going on, and the room full of lawyers and witnesses and business was driving fast; some deeply occupied legal gentleman present, seeing Bartleby wholly unemployed, would request him to run round to his (the legal gentleman's) office and fetch some papers for him. Thereupon, Bartleby would tranquilly decline, and yet remain idle as before. Then the lawyer would give a great stare, and turn to me. And what could I say? At last I was made aware that all through the circle of my professional acquaintance, a whisper of wonder was running round, having reference to the strange creature I kept at my office. This worried me very much. And as the idea came upon me of his possibly turning out a long-lived man, and keep occupying my chambers, and denying my authority; and perplexing my visitors; and scandalizing my professional reputation; and casting a general gloom over the premises; keeping soul and body together to the last upon his savings (for doubtless he spent but half a dime a day), and in the end perhaps outlive me, and claim possession of my office by right of his perpetual occupancy: as all these dark anticipations crowded upon me more and more, and my friends continually intruded their relentless remarks upon the apparition in my room; a great change was wrought in me. I resolved to gather all my faculties together, and for ever rid me of this intolerable incubus.

168 Ere revolving any complicated project, however, adapted to this end, I first simply suggested to Bartleby the propriety of his permanent departure. In a calm and serious tone, I commended the idea to his careful and mature consideration. But having taken three days to meditate upon it, he apprised me that his original determination remained the same in short, that he still preferred to abide with me.

169 What shall I do? I now said to myself, buttoning up my coat to the last button. What shall I do? what ought I to do? what does conscience say I *should* do with this man, or rather ghost. Rid myself of him, I must; go, he shall. But how? You will not thrust him, the poor, pale, passive mortal,— you will not thrust such a helpless creature out of your door? You will not dishonor yourself by such cruelty? No, I will not, I cannot do that. Rather would I let him live and die here, and then mason up his remains in the wall. What then will you do? For all your coaxing, he will not budge. Bribes he leaves under your own paperweight on your table; in short, it is quite plain that he prefers to cling to you.

170   Then something severe, something unusual must be done. What! Surely you will not have him collared by a constable, and commit his innocent pallor to the common jail? And upon what ground could you procure such a thing to be done?—a vagrant, is he? What! He a vagrant, a wanderer, who refuses to budge? It is because he will *not* be a vagrant, then, that you seek to count him *as* a vagrant. That is too absurd. No visible means of support: there I have him. Wrong again: for indubitably he *does* support himself, and that is the only unanswerable proof that any man can show of his possessing the means so to do. No more then. Since he will not quit me, I must quit him. I will change my offices; I will move elsewhere; and give him fair notice, that if I find him on my new premises I will then proceed against him as a common trespasser.

171   Acting accordingly, next day I thus addressed him: "I find these chambers too far from the City Hall; the air is unwholesome. In a word, I propose to remove my offices next week, and shall no longer require your services. I tell you this now, in order that you may seek another place." He made no reply, and nothing more was said.

172   On the appointed day I engaged carts and men, proceeded to my chambers, and having but little furniture, every thing was removed in a few hours. Throughout, the scrivener remained standing behind the screen, which I directed to be removed the last thing. It was withdrawn; and being folded up like a huge folio, left him the motionless occupant of a naked room. I stood in the entry watching him a moment, while something from within me upbraided me.

173   I re-entered, with my hand in my pocket—and—and my heart in my mouth.

174   "Good-bye, Bartleby; I am going—good-bye, and God some way bless you; and take that," slipping something in his hand. But it dropped upon the floor, and then,—strange to say—I tore myself from him whom I had so longed to be rid of.

175   Established in my new quarters, for a day or two I kept the door locked, and started at every footfall in the passages. When I returned to my rooms after any little absence, I would pause at the threshold for an instant, and attentively listen, ere applying my key. But these fears were needless. Bartleby never came nigh me.

176   I thought all was going well, when a perturbed looking stranger visited me, inquiring whether I was the person who had recently occupied rooms at No.—Wall-street.

177   Full of forebodings, I replied that I was.

178   "Then sir," said the stranger, who proved a lawyer, "you are responsible for the man you left there. He refuses to do any copying; he refuses to do any thing; he says he prefers not to; and he refuses to quit the premises."

179   "I am very sorry, sir," said I, with assumed tranquillity, but an inward tremor, "but, really, the man you allude to is nothing to me—he is no relation or apprentice of mine, that you should hold me responsible for him."

180   "In mercy's name, who is he?"

181   "I certainly cannot inform you. I know nothing about him. Formerly I employed him as a copyist; but he has done nothing for me now for some time past."

182   "I shall settle him then,—good morning, sir."

183   Several days passed, and I heard nothing more; and though I often felt a charitable prompting to call at the place and see poor Bartleby, yet a certain squeamishness of I know not what withheld me.

184   All is over with him, by this time, thought I at last, when through another week no further intelligence reached me. But coming to my room the day after, I found several persons waiting at my door in a high state of nervous excitement.

185   "That's the man—here he comes," cried the foremost one, whom I recognized as the lawyer who had previously called upon me alone.

186   "You must take him away, sir, at once," cried a portly person among them, advancing upon me, and whom I knew to be the landlord of No.— Wall-street. "These gentlemen, my tenants, cannot stand it any longer; Mr. B—" pointing to the lawyer, "has turned him out of his room, and he now persists in haunting the building generally, sitting upon the banisters of the stairs by day, and sleeping in the entry by night. Every body is concerned; clients are leaving the offices; some fears are entertained of a mob; something you must do, and that without delay."

187   Aghast at this torrent, I fell back before it, and would fain have locked myself in my new quarters. In vain I persisted that Bartleby was nothing to me—no more than to any one else. In vain:—I was the last person known to have any thing to do with him, and they held me to the terrible account. Fearful then of being exposed in the papers (as one person present obscurely threatened) I considered the matter, and at length said, that if the lawyer would give me a confidential interview with the scrivener, in his (the lawyer's) own room, I would that afternoon strive my best to rid them of the nuisance they complained of.

188   Going up stairs to my old haunt, there was Bartleby silently sitting upon the banister at the landing.

189   "What are you doing here, Bartleby?" said I.

190   "Sitting upon the banister," he mildly replied.

191   I motioned him into the lawyer's room, who then left us.

192   "Bartleby," said I, "are you aware that you are the cause of great tribulation to me, by persisting in occupying the entry after being dismissed from the office?"

193   No answer.

194   "Now one of two things must take place. Either you must do something, or something must be done to you. Now what sort of business would you like to engage in? Would you like to re-engage in copying for some one?"

195   "No; I would prefer not to make any change."

196   "Would you like a clerkship in a dry-goods store?"

197   "There is too much confinement about that. No, I would not like a clerkship; but I am not particular."

198   "Too much confinement," I cried, "why you keep yourself confined all the time!"

199   "I would prefer not to take a clerkship," he rejoined, as if to settle that little item at once.

200   "How would a bar-tender's business suit you? There is no trying of the eyesight in that."

201   "I would not like it at all; though, as I said before, I am not particular."

202   His unwonted wordiness inspirited me. I returned to the charge.

203   "Well then, would you like to travel through the country collecting bills for the merchants? That would improve your health."

204   "No, I would prefer to be doing something else."

205   "How then would going as a companion to Europe, to entertain some young gentleman with your conversation,—how would that suit you?"

206   "Not at all. It does not strike me that there is any thing definite about that. I like to be stationary. But I am not particular."

207   "Stationary you shall be then," I cried, now losing all patience, and for the first time in all my exasperating connection with him fairly flying into a passion. "If you do not go away from these premises before night, I shall feel bound— indeed I *am* bound—to—to—to quit the premises myself!" I rather absurdly concluded, knowing not with what possible threat to try to frighten his immobility into compliance. Despairing of all further efforts, I was precipitately leaving him, when a final thought occurred to me—one which had not been wholly unindulged before.

208 "Bartleby," said I, in the kindest tone I could assume under such exciting circumstances, "will you go home with me now—not to my office, but my dwelling—and remain there till we can conclude upon some convenient arrangement for you at our leisure? Come, let us start now, right away."

209 "No: at present I would prefer not to make any change at all."

210 I answered nothing; but effectually dodging every one by the suddenness and rapidity of my flight, rushed from the building, ran up Wall-street towards Broadway, and jumping into the first omnibus was soon removed from pursuit. As soon as tranquillity returned I distinctly perceived that I had now done all that I possibly could, both in respect to the demands of the landlord and his tenants, and with regard to my own desire and sense of duty, to benefit Bartleby, and shield him from rude persecution. I now strove to be entirely care-free and quiescent; and my conscience justified me in the attempt; though indeed it was not so successful as I could have wished. So fearful was I of being again hunted out by the incensed landlord and his exasperated tenants, that, surrendering my business to Nippers, for a few days I drove about the upper part of the town and through the suburbs, in my rockaway; crossed over to Jersey City and Hoboken, and paid fugitive visits to Manhattanville and Astoria. In fact I almost lived in my rockaway for the time.

211 When again I entered my office, lo, a note from the landlord lay upon the desk. I opened it with trembling hands. It informed me that the writer had sent to the police, and had Bartleby removed to the Tombs as a vagrant. Moreover, since I knew more about him than any one else, he wished me to appear at that place, and make a suitable statement of the facts. These tidings had a conflicting effect upon me. At first I was indignant; but at last almost approved. The landlord's energetic, summary disposition had led him to adopt a procedure which I do not think I would have decided upon myself; and yet as a last resort, under such peculiar circumstances, it seemed the only plan.

212 As I afterwards learned, the poor scrivener, when told that he must be conducted to the Tombs, offered not the slightest obstacle, but in his pale unmoving way, silently acquiesced.

213 Some of the compassionate and curious bystanders joined the party; and headed by one of the constables arm in arm with Bartleby, the silent procession filed its way through all the noise, and heat, and joy of the roaring thoroughfares at noon.

214 The same day I received the note I went to the Tombs, or to speak more properly, the Halls of Justice. Seeking the right officer, I stated the purpose of my call, and was informed that the individual I described was indeed within. I then assured the functionary that Bartleby was a perfectly honest man, and greatly to be compassionated, however unaccountably eccentric. I narrated all I knew, and closed by suggesting the idea of letting him remain in as

Please note that excerpts and passages in the StudySync® library and this workbook are intended as touchstones to generate interest in an author's work. The excerpts and passages do not substitute for the reading of entire texts, and StudySync® strongly recommends that students seek out and purchase the whole literary or informational work in order to experience it as the author intended. Links to online resellers are available in our digital library. In addition, complete works may be ordered through an authorized reseller by filling out and returning to StudySync® the order form enclosed in this workbook.

Reading & Writing Companion

103

indulgent confinement as possible till something less harsh might be done—though indeed I hardly knew what. At all events, if nothing else could be decided upon, the alms-house must receive him. I then begged to have an interview.

215 Being under no disgraceful charge, and quite serene and harmless in all his ways, they had permitted him freely to wander about the prison, and especially in the inclosed grass-platted yard thereof. And so I found him there, standing all alone in the quietest of the yards, his face towards a high wall, while all around, from the narrow slits of the jail windows, I thought I saw peering out upon him the eyes of murderers and thieves.

216 "Bartleby!"

217 "I know you," he said, without looking round,—"and I want nothing to say to you."

218 "It was not I that brought you here, Bartleby," said I, keenly pained at his implied suspicion. "And to you, this should not be so vile a place. Nothing reproachful attaches to you by being here. And see, it is not so sad a place as one might think. Look, there is the sky, and here is the grass."

219 "I know where I am," he replied, but would say nothing more, and so I left him.

220 As I entered the corridor again, a broad meat-like man, in an apron, accosted me, and jerking his thumb over his shoulder said—"Is that your friend?"

221 "Yes."

222 "Does he want to starve? If he does, let him live on the prison fare, that's all."

223 "Who are you?" asked I, not knowing what to make of such an unofficially speaking person in such a place.

224 "I am the grub-man. Such gentlemen as have friends here, hire me to provide them with something good to eat."

225 "Is this so?" said I, turning to the turnkey.

226 He said it was.

227 "Well then," said I, slipping some silver into the grub-man's hands (for so they called him). "I want you to give particular attention to my friend there; let him have the best dinner you can get. And you must be as polite to him as possible."

228 "Introduce me, will you?" said the grub-man, looking at me with an expression which seem to say he was all impatience for an opportunity to give a specimen of his breeding.

229 Thinking it would prove of benefit to the scrivener, I acquiesced; and asking the grub-man his name, went up with him to Bartleby.

230 "Bartleby, this is Mr. Cutlets; you will find him very useful to you."

231 "Your servant, sir, your servant," said the grub-man, making a low salutation behind his apron. "Hope you find it pleasant here, sir;—spacious grounds—cool apartments, sir—hope you'll stay with us some time—try to make it agreeable. May Mrs. Cutlets and I have the pleasure of your company to dinner, sir, in Mrs. Cutlets' private room?"

232 "I prefer not to dine to-day," said Bartleby, turning away. "It would disagree with me; I am unused to dinners." So saying he slowly moved to the other side of the enclosure, and took up a position fronting the dead-wall.

233 "How's this?" said the grub-man, addressing me with a stare of astonishment. "He's odd, ain't he?"

234 "I think he is a little deranged," said I, sadly.

235 "Deranged? deranged is it? Well now, upon my word, I thought that friend of yourn was a gentleman forger; they are always pale and genteel-like, them forgers. I can't pity 'em—can't help it, sir. Did you know Monroe Edwards?" he added touchingly, and paused. Then, laying his hand pityingly on my shoulder, sighed, "He died of consumption at Sing-Sing. So you weren't acquainted with Monroe?"

236 "No, I was never socially acquainted with any forgers. But I cannot stop longer. Look to my friend yonder. You will not lose by it. I will see you again."

237 Some few days after this, I again obtained admission to the Tombs, and went through the corridors in quest of Bartleby; but without finding him.

238 "I saw him coming from his cell not long ago," said a turnkey, "may be he's gone to loiter in the yards."

239 So I went in that direction. "Are you looking for the silent man?" said another turnkey passing me. "Yonder he lies—sleeping in the yard there. 'Tis not twenty minutes since I saw him lie down."

240 The yard was entirely quiet. It was not accessible to the common prisoners. The surrounding walls, of amazing thickness, kept off all sounds behind them. The Egyptian character of the masonry weighed upon me with its gloom. But a soft imprisoned turf grew under foot. The heart of the eternal pyramids, it seemed, wherein, by some strange magic, through the clefts, grass-seed, dropped by birds, had sprung.

NOTES

241 Strangely huddled at the base of the wall, his knees drawn up, and lying on his side, his head touching the cold stones, I saw the wasted Bartleby. But nothing stirred. I paused; then went close up to him; stooped over, and saw that his dim eyes were open; otherwise he seemed profoundly sleeping. Something prompted me to touch him. I felt his hand, when a tingling shiver ran up my arm and down my spine to my feet.

242 The round face of the grub-man peered upon me now. "His dinner is ready. Won't he dine to-day, either? Or does he live without dining?"

243 "Lives without dining," said I, and closed his eyes.

244 "Eh!—He's asleep, ain't he?"

245 "With kings and counselors," murmured I.

. . .

246 There would seem little need for proceeding further in this history. Imagination will readily supply the meager recital of poor Bartleby's interment. But ere parting with the reader, let me say, that if this little narrative has sufficiently interested him, to awaken curiosity as to who Bartleby was, and what manner of life he led prior to the present narrator's making his acquaintance, I can only reply, that in such curiosity I fully share, but am wholly unable to gratify it. Yet here I hardly know whether I should divulge one little item of rumor, which came to my ear a few months after the scrivener's decease. Upon what basis it rested, I could never ascertain; and hence, how true it is I cannot now tell. But inasmuch as this vague report has not been without certain strange suggestive interest to me, however sad, it may prove the same with some others; and so I will briefly mention it. The report was this: that Bartleby had been a subordinate clerk in the Dead Letter Office at Washington, from which he had been suddenly removed by a change in the administration. When I think over this rumor, I cannot adequately express the emotions which seize me. Dead letters! does it not sound like dead men? Conceive a man by nature and misfortune prone to a pallid hopelessness, can any business seem more fitted to heighten it than that of continually handling these dead letters, and assorting them for the flames? For by the cart-load they are annually burned. Sometimes from out the folded paper the pale clerk takes a ring:—the finger it was meant for, perhaps, moulders in the grave; a bank-note sent in swiftest charity:—he whom it would relieve, nor eats nor hungers any more; pardon for those who died despairing; hope for those who died unhoping; good tidings for those who died stifled by unrelieved calamities. On errands of life, these letters speed to death.

247 Ah Bartleby! Ah humanity!

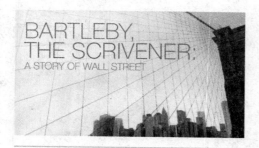

BARTLEBY,
THE SCRIVENER:
A STORY OF WALL STREET

First Read

Read "Bartleby, the Scrivener: A Story of Wall Street." After you read, complete the Think Questions below.

 THINK QUESTIONS

1. How does the narrator meet Bartleby? Cite specific evidence from the text to support your answer.

2. How does Turkey respond to Bartleby's refusal to have his work examined by the other scriveners? Cite evidence from the text in support of your answer.

3. What is one idea of Bartleby that the narrator has to rid himself of after the scrivener refuses to leave? Use evidence from the text to support your answer.

4. Use context clues to determine the meaning of the word **alacrity** as it is used in the text. Write your definition of *alacrity* here, and explain which clues helped you figure it out.

5. Keeping in mind that the Latin word *prūdēns* means "wise," determine the meaning of the word **prudent** as it is used in the text. Write your definition of *prudent* here, and explain how you figured it out.

Skill:
Theme

Use the Checklist to analyze Theme in "Bartleby, the Scrivener: A Story of Wall Street." Refer to the sample student annotations about Theme in the text.

••• CHECKLIST FOR THEME

In order to identify two or more themes of a text, note the following:

✓ the subject and how it relates to the themes in the text

✓ if one or more themes are stated directly in the text

✓ details in the text that help to reveal each theme:

- the title and chapter headings

- details about the setting

- the narrator's or speaker's tone

- characters' thoughts, actions, and dialogue

- the central conflict, climax, and resolution of the conflict

- shifts in characters, setting, or plot events

✓ when the themes interact with each other

To determine two or more themes of a text and analyze their development over the course of the text, including how they interact and build on one another to produce a complex account, consider the following questions:

✓ What are the themes in the text? When do they emerge?

✓ How does each theme develop over the course of the text?

✓ How do the themes interact and build on one another?

Skill:
Theme

Reread paragraphs 95–108 from "Bartleby, the Scrivener: A Story of Wall Street." Then, using the Checklist on the previous page, answer the multiple-choice questions below.

⟳ YOUR TURN

1. How does the dialogue between the narrator and Bartleby further develop the theme related to loneliness and isolation?

- ○ A. It shows that Bartleby's growing friendship with the narrator proves that even lonely people can make friends if they want to.
- ○ B. It reveals that the narrator accepts Bartleby's dangerous behavior, which may help Bartleby overcome his isolation.
- ○ C. It describes Bartleby as a person who thinks more of himself than others and how this attitude causes his relationships to fail.
- ○ D. It indicates Bartleby's entrenchment in his isolation and how his pride and refusal to talk only further separate him from people.

2. What impact does Bartleby's nonconformity to social norms have on the narrator's view of him?

- ○ A. He believes Bartleby's poor eyesight is responsible and offers to help him with medical expenses.
- ○ B. He is persuaded that Bartleby is violent and calls the police to take him to the Tombs.
- ○ C. He thinks Bartleby is ungrateful for his help, which increases the barrier between them.
- ○ D. He begins to see Bartleby as a free spirit and wishes to spend more time with him.

Please note that excerpts and passages in the StudySync® library and this workbook are intended as touchstones to generate interest in an author's work. The excerpts and passages do not substitute for the reading of entire texts, and StudySync® strongly recommends that students seek out and purchase the whole literary or informational work in order to experience it as the author intended. Links to online resellers are available in our digital library. In addition, complete works may be ordered through an authorized reseller by filling out and returning to StudySync® the order form enclosed in this workbook.

Reading & Writing Companion   109

Skill:
Point of View

Use the Checklist to analyze Point of View in "Bartleby, the Scrivener: A Story of Wall Street." Refer to the sample student annotations about Point of View in the text.

••• CHECKLIST FOR POINT OF VIEW

In order to determine a narrator's point of view through what is directly stated is different from what is really meant, note the following:

✓ literary techniques intended to provide humor or criticism. Examples include:

- sarcasm or the use of language that says one thing, but means the opposite

- irony or a contrast between what one expects to happen and what happens

- understatement or an instance where a character deliberately makes a situation seem less important or serious than it is

- satire or the use of humor, irony, exaggeration, or ridicule to expose and criticize people's foolishness or vices

✓ possible critiques an author might be making about contemporary society

✓ an unreliable narrator or character whose point of view cannot be trusted

To analyze a case in which grasping a point of view requires distinguishing what is directly stated in a text from what is really meant, consider the following questions:

✓ How do the cultural lens and experiences of the narrator or speaker shape his or her point of view? How do they shape what they say and how they say it?

✓ Is the narrator or speaker reliable? Why?

✓ How does a character's or narrator's point of view contribute to a non-literal understanding of the text?

✓ How does the use of sarcasm, understatement, or satire add meaning to the story?

Skill:
Point of View

Reread paragraphs 12 and 13 from "Bartleby, the Scrivener: A Story of Wall Street." Then, using the Checklist on the previous page, answer the multiple-choice questions below.

♻ YOUR TURN

1. This question has two parts. First, answer Part A. Then, answer Part B.

   Part A: What is the main aspect of office culture being satirized in this excerpt?

   ○ A. lack of productivity
   ○ B. substandard office equipment
   ○ C. difficulties with the boss's temper
   ○ D. individualism in the workplace

   Part B: Which line from the excerpt best supports the satirical message in Part A?

   ○ A. "I was well persuaded that whatever might be his faults in other respects, he was, at least, a temperate young man"
   ○ B. "nature herself seemed to have been his vintner, and at his birth charged him so thoroughly with an irritable, brandy-like disposition"
   ○ C. "I plainly perceive that for Nippers, brandy and water were altogether superfluous."
   ○ D. "When Nippers' was on, Turkey's was off; and *vice versa*."

2. Which line from the excerpt supports this satirical message by explanation: "Their fits relieved each other like guards"?

   ○ A. "for Nippers, brandy and water were altogether superfluous"
   ○ B. "When Nippers' was on, Turkey's was off; and vice versa."
   ○ C. "This was a good natural arrangement under the circumstances."
   ○ D. "I never had to do with their eccentricities at one time."

Reading & Writing
Companion

Skill:
Figurative Language

Use the Checklist to analyze Figurative Language in "Bartleby, the Scrivener: A Story of Wall Street." Refer to the sample student annotations about Figurative Language in the text.

••• CHECKLIST FOR FIGURATIVE LANGUAGE

In order to determine the meaning of a figure of speech in context, note the following:

- ✓ words and phrases that mean one thing literally and suggest something else

- ✓ similes, metaphors, or personification

- ✓ figures of speech, including

  - paradoxes, or a seemingly contradictory statement that when further investigated or explained proves to be true, such as

    > a character described as "a wise fool"

    > a character stating "I must be cruel to be kind"

  - hyperbole, or exaggerated statements not meant to be taken literally, such as

    > a child saying "I'll be doing this homework until I'm 100!"

    > a claim such as, "I'm so hungry I could eat a horse!"

In order to interpret a figure of speech in context and analyze its role in the text, consider the following questions:

- ✓ Where is there figurative language in the text, and what seems to be the author's purpose in using it?

- ✓ Why does the author use a figure of speech rather than literal language?

- ✓ What impact does exaggeration or hyperbole have on your understanding of the text?

- ✓ Where are there examples of paradoxes, and how do they affect the meaning in the text?

- ✓ Where are contradictory words and phrases used to enhance the reader's understanding of the character, object, or idea?

- ✓ How does the figurative language develop the message or themes of the literary work?

Skill:
Figurative Language

Reread paragraph 53 from "Bartleby, the Scrivener: A Story of Wall Street." Then, using the Checklist on the previous page, answer the multiple-choice questions below.

⟳ YOUR TURN

1. Which of the following sentences from the paragraph contains an an example of paradox?

   ○ A. Nothing so aggravates an earnest person as a passive resistance.

   ○ B. Even so, for the most part, I regarded Bartleby and his ways.

   ○ C. If I turn him away, the chances are he will fall in with some less indulgent employer, and then he will be rudely treated, and perhaps driven forth miserably to starve.

   ○ D. The passiveness of Bartleby sometimes irritated me.

2. How does the use of paradox from Question 1 serve to enhance the reader's understanding of Bartleby's character?

   ○ A. It demonstrates the strong relationship between the narrator and Bartleby.

   ○ B. It helps the reader to see him in a more favorable light.

   ○ C. It highlights his strangeness and the narrator's confusion towards him.

   ○ D. It helps the reader to see what motivates his actions as a character.

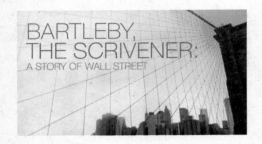

Close Read

Reread "Bartleby, the Scrivener: A Story of Wall Street." As you reread, complete the Skills Focus questions below. Then use your answers and annotations from the questions to help you complete the Write activity.

◎ SKILLS FOCUS

1. Satire is a literary technique for criticizing people's foolishness or vices through humor, to inspire improvement. Find an example of satire in the story and explain its impact on the reader.

2. Identify details from paragraph 17 that help readers visualize the arrangement of the law office. Explain how theme emerges in the arrangement of rooms and desks.

3. The author uses figurative language throughout the story. Find an example and explain the effect of your example on the reader.

4. Determine how the narrator's information about Bartleby's past in paragraph 246 helps develop the themes in this story.

5. How do different characters react to Bartleby when his behavior breaks away from expected office behavior? Identify evidence from the text to support your answer. What do these reactions suggest about how humans respond to those who don't fit the norm?

✎ WRITE

LITERARY ANALYSIS: How does Melville use a satirical point of view as well as figurative language to develop the themes in the story? Determine at least one satirical critique in the story and one use of figurative language, and explain how these literary devices help develop the story's themes. Use evidence from the text to support your response.

The Namesake

FICTION
Jhumpa Lahiri
2003

Introduction

The works of contemporary Indian American writer Jhumpa Lahiri (b. 1967), a
Pulitzer Prize winner, span two disparate cultures just like their author does,
and the struggles of incorporating and inhabiting two very different identities
are richly evoked in her works. *The Namesake* tells the story of an Indian couple who
have immigrated to the United States and struggle with cultural differences. In this
excerpt from early in the novel, Ashima recalls the moment she first met her husband,

"... Ashima, unable to resist a sudden and overwhelming urge, stepped into the shoes at her feet."

NOTES

from Chapter 1: 1968

1   It had been after tutoring one day that Ashima's mother had met her at the door, told her to go straight to the bedroom and prepare herself; a man was waiting to see her. He was the third in as many months. The first had been a widower with four children. The second, a newspaper cartoonist who knew her father, had been hit by a bus in Esplanade and lost his left arm. To her great relief they had both rejected her. She was nineteen, in the middle of her studies, in no rush to be a bride. And so, obediently but without expectation, she had untangled and rebraided her hair, wiped away the kohl that had smudged below her eyes, patted some Cuticura powder from a velvet puff onto her skin. The sheer parrot green sari[1] she pleated and tucked into her petticoat had been laid out for her on the bed by her mother.

2   Before entering the sitting room, Ashima had paused in the corridor. She could hear her mother saying, "She is fond of cooking, and she can knit extremely well. Within a week she finished this cardigan I am wearing." Ashima smiled, amused by her mother's salesmanship; it had taken her the better part of a year to finish the cardigan, and still her mother had had to do the sleeves. Glancing at the floor where visitors customarily removed their slippers, she noticed, beside two sets of chappals, a pair of men's shoes that were not like any she'd ever seen on the streets and trams and buses of Calcutta, or even in the windows of Bata. They were brown shoes with black heels and off-white laces and stitching. There was a band of lentil-sized holes embossed on either side of each shoe, and at the tips was a pretty pattern pricked into the leather as if with a needle. Looking more closely, she saw the shoemaker's name written on the insides, in gold lettering that had all but faded: something and sons, it said. She saw the size, eight and a half, and the initials U.S.A. And as her mother continued to sing her praises, Ashima, unable to resist a sudden and overwhelming urge, stepped into the shoes at her feet. Lingering sweat from the owner's feet mingled with hers, causing her heart to race; it was the closest thing she had ever experienced to the touch of a man. The leather was creased, heavy, and still warm. On the left shoe she

---

1. **sari** a long garment traditionally worn by women in South Asia

NOTES

had noticed that one of the crisscrossing laces had missed a hole, and this oversight set her at ease.

3   She extracted her feet, entered the room. The man was sitting in a rattan chair, his parents perched on the edge of the twin bed where her brother slept at night. He was slightly plump, scholarly-looking but still youthful, with black thick-framed glasses and a sharp, prominent nose. A neatly trimmed mustache connected to a beard that covered only his chin lent him an elegant, vaguely aristocratic air. He wore brown socks and brown trousers and a green-and-white-striped shirt and was staring glumly at his knees.

4   He did not look up when she appeared. Though she was aware of his gaze as she crossed the room, by the time she managed to steal another look at him he was once again indifferent, focused on his knees. He cleared his throat as if to speak but then said nothing. Instead it was his father who did the talking, saying that the man had gone to St. Xavier's, and then B.E. College, graduating first-class-first from both institutions. Ashima took her seat and smoothed the pleats of her sari. She sensed the mother eyeing her with approval. Ashima was five feet four inches, tall for a Bengali woman, ninety-nine pounds. Her complexion was on the dark side of fair, but she had been compared on more than one occasion to the actress Madhabi Mukherjee. Her nails were admirably long, her fingers, like her father's, artistically slim. They inquired after her studies and she was asked to recite a few stanzas from "The Daffodils." The man's family lived in Alipore. The father was a labor officer for the customs department of a shipping company. "My son has been living abroad for two years," the man's father said, "earning a Ph.D. in Boston, researching in the field of fiber optics."

5   Ashima had never heard of Boston, or of fiber optics. She was asked whether she was willing to fly on a plane and then if she was capable of living in a city characterized by severe, snowy winters, alone.

6   "Won't he be there?" she'd asked, pointing to the man whose shoes she'd briefly occupied, but who had yet to say a word to her. It was only after the **betrothal** that she'd learned his name. One week later the invitations were printed, and two weeks after that she was adorned and adjusted by countless aunts, countless cousins hovering around her. These were her last moments as Ashima Bhaduri, before becoming Ashima Ganguli. Her lips were darkened, her brow and cheeks dotted with sandalwood paste, her hair wound up, bound with flowers, held in place by a hundred wire pins that would take an hour to remove once the wedding was finally over. Her head was draped with scarlet netting. The air was damp, and in spite of the pins Ashima's hair, thickest of all the cousins', would not lie flat. She wore all the necklaces and chokers and bracelets that were destined to live most of their lives in an extra-large safety deposit box in a bank vault in New England. At the

NOTES

designated hour she was seated on a piri that her father had decorated, hoisted five feet off the ground, carried out to meet the groom. She had hidden her face with a heart-shaped betel leaf, kept her head bent low until she had circled him seven times. Eight thousand miles away in Cambridge, she has come to know him. In the evenings she cooks for him, hoping to please, with the unrationed, remarkably **unblemished** sugar, flour, rice, and salt she had written about to her mother in her very first letter home. By now she has learned that her husband likes his food on the salty side, that his favorite thing about lamb curry is the potatoes, and that he likes to finish his dinner with a small final helping of rice and **dal**. At night, lying beside her in bed, he listens to her describe the events of her day: her walks along Massachusetts Avenue, the shops she visits, the Hare Krishnas[2] who pester her with their leaflets, the pistachio ice cream cones she treats herself to in Harvard Square. In spite of his meager graduate student wages he sets aside money to send every few months to his father to help put an extension on his parents' house. He is **fastidious** about his clothing; their first argument had been over a sweater she'd shrunk in the washing machine. As soon as he comes home from the university the first thing he does is hang up his shirt and trousers, donning a pair of drawstring pajamas and a pullover if it's cold.

7   On Sundays he spends an hour occupied with his tins of shoe polishes and his three pairs of shoes, two black and one brown. The brown ones are the ones he'd been wearing when he'd first come to see her. The sight of him cross-legged on newspapers spread on the floor, intently whisking a brush over the leather, always reminds her of her **indiscretion** in her parents' corridor. It is a moment that shocks her still, and that she prefers, in spite of all she tells him at night about the life they now share, to keep to herself.

Excerpted from *The Namesake* by Jhumpa Lahiri by Mariner Books.

 WRITE

DISCUSSION: Jhumpa Lahiri once said, "That's the thing about books. They let you travel without moving your feet." Defend or challenge her claim about books using textual evidence from this excerpt of *The Namesake*. Prepare for a discussion with your peers by writing down your stance about this claim as well as your reasoning.

2. **Hare Krishnas** members of a monastic Hindu religious sect often known for proselytizing in public spaces

Extended Writing Project and Grammar

EXTENDED WRITING PROJECT

NARRATIVE WRITING

Narrative Writing Process: Plan

| PLAN | DRAFT | REVISE | EDIT AND PUBLISH |

The story of America is built on the concept of liberty—that we have the right to act and speak as we choose. This belief led to our independence and has continued to influence the course of events in the centuries that have followed, shaping us into the country—and the people—that we are today.

WRITING PROMPT

How does the desire for independence affect our choices?

Write about a character, real or imagined, who feels trapped by circumstance and who wishes to become more independent. Using the skills you have learned in this unit, write a narrative in which a character moves from dependence to independence. Be sure to describe how the character feels limited at the beginning, the decisions the character makes to become independent, and the consequences and responsibilities of this newfound independence. If you choose to write a personal narrative, use the same outline to write about how you or someone you know has achieved independence. Remember to include the following in your narrative:

- a plot with a beginning, middle, and end
- a clear setting
- characters and dialogue
- descriptive details
- a clear theme

Introduction to Narrative Writing

Narrative writing tells a story of experiences or events that have been imagined by a writer or that have happened in real life. Good narrative writing effectively uses genre characteristics and craft, such as relevant descriptive details and a purposeful structure with a series of events that includes a beginning, middle, and end. The characteristics of narrative writing include:

- setting
- theme/ reflection
- characters
- point of view
- plot

In addition to these characteristics, narrative writers carefully craft their work through their use of dialogue, details, word choice, and figurative language. These choices help to shape the tone, mood, and overall style of the text. Effective narratives combine these genre characteristics and craft to engage the reader.

As you continue with this Extended Writing Project, you'll receive more instruction and practice in crafting each of the characteristics of narrative writing to create your own personal or fictional narrative.

Before you get started on your own fictional or personal narrative, read this narrative that one student, Daniel, wrote in response to the writing prompt. As you read the Model, highlight and annotate the features of narrative writing that Daniel included in his narrative.

NOTES

☰ STUDENT MODEL

The Price of Freedom

1   Nora firmly presses her phone between her ear and shoulder. "I can't believe this is our last summer at camp," she says as she digs through her dirty laundry hamper. "Simone, I have to put you on speaker phone." She sets her phone on the carpet. "Did you borrow my wool socks? I can't find them anywhere."

2   "Nope," Simone replies. Nora sighs. Wool socks are a must-have for cold nights camping in the mountains. Camp doesn't start until a month from now, but she's already packing.

3   "We must make the most out of camp this year. This is our last summer before our senior year! Then comes college, marriage, kids . . . ," Simone hesitates. "Who knows if we'll ever be free of responsibility again?"

4   "No!" Nora cries. "Please don't get serious again. We are still kids! This summer will be the best yet."

5   "You're right. I need to stay positive. We'll be out in the open air before we know it, and everything is going to be great. Don't forget that the application and fee are due in a week, okay? Bye!"

6   Every July, Evergreen High School hosts a two-week camping trip for students. The trip is an opportunity to learn about the outdoors and build a community before the school year starts. Nora has made her most cherished memories in the great outdoors. She especially loves camp because it reminds her of when she used to go to state parks with her grandpa to bird-watch. It's because of him that she loves nature. Since he passed away five years ago, Nora has made it a point to get outside as much as possible. She even takes his old binoculars with her to camp so that she can observe the birds and other wildlife.

7 Nora gives up searching for her socks and lies on the floor. Her mom shouts for her to come downstairs to talk. *What is it this time?* she thinks. *Did I forget to take out the trash? Was I supposed to clean the bathroom?* She closes her eyes, takes a deep breath, and imagines she is back at camp lying in the grass by the lake. She feels the mellow breeze glide across her bare arms and face. The pine trees dance in the wind as tiny rays of sunlight peek out through their branches. A blue jay swoops through the sky and lands in its nest. Nora wishes she could be free from worries, like the wildlife in the forest. She wants to rid herself of stress from family, school, and money. For now, summer camp is the closest she can get to independence. She opens her eyes. They take a moment to adjust to the artificial glare of her ceiling light. *I must get out of this house,* she thinks.

8 When Nora finally makes her way downstairs, she finds her mom sitting in the living room. She looks more tired than usual and wears a gloomy expression. "Why the sad face, Mom?" Nora jests.

9 "Honey, sit down. We need to talk." Nora sits on the couch across from her. "You are old enough now, so I'm going to jump straight to the point. I was laid off from my job at the nursing home this morning. Until I find a new job, I need you to pitch in and help with the bills." Her mother exhales and looks down at the floor. Nora is shocked. However, she isn't frightened the way she knows some of her friends would be. Nora and her mom have fallen on hard times in the past, but they have always come out on top.

10 "I'm sorry, Mom. I will help in any way I can," Nora says sincerely.

11 "Really? Thank you." Her mom's mood lightens.

12 "Of course. We need to stick together!" Nora exclaims. "I was going to get a summer job to keep me busy until camp anyway. Speaking of camp, I need to turn in my signed application and $250 fee soon. Do you have it ready?"

13 "Well, Nora, that's the problem. Money is tight now, so we can't afford to pay the fee."

14 Nora wants to yell and protest, but she knows that won't help the situation. *But you promised I could go,* she thinks. Instead, she says,

"I understand. We'll figure something out." Nora smiles faintly, but tears begin to well in her eyes. She excuses herself from the room.

15   Back in her bedroom, Nora's thoughts race. *I can't believe this is happening. I deserve to go to camp just as much as my friends do. So much for one summer of freedom before adult responsibilities kick in. This summer is going to be the worst!*

16   Nora picks up her duffle bag and dumps its contents onto the floor. Amid the pile of sweatpants and t-shirts, she spots her grandpa's antique binoculars. *This isn't fair. Grandpa would want me to go to camp,* she thinks. Suddenly, she knows exactly what she has to do.

17   Nora puts the binoculars in her backpack, throws on her tennis shoes, and races downtown on her bike. She parks outside the local pawn shop. Then, clutching her backpack, she takes a deep breath and enters the shop. Nora glances around the room and notices the plethora of jewelry, electronics, and musical instruments. She imagines the histories of the abandoned items and their forgotten owners. *Will the memory of Grandpa and his love for nature be lost as well?*

18   A man emerges from the back of the store and asks if he can help her. Nora places her backpack on the counter and carefully removes the binoculars. She sees her reflection in the lens and realizes that selling the binoculars is wrong. Her grandfather's memory is worth much more than a quick payout and a summer away from home. Plus, if she went away, she'd abandon her mother, who needs her help.

19   "Uh, never mind," Nora stammers as she puts the binoculars away. On her way out the door, she sees a bulletin board covered with posts for job openings. A poster catches her eye. The local community center is looking for someone to lead nature walks and weekly birding outings. She takes the flyer and stuffs it in her backpack. As she bikes home, Nora cannot believe what she almost did. She realizes that a summer job is a much better solution to her problems. She might not be able to go to camp, but she will be free to be outside and share her love for the great outdoors.

WRITE

Writers often take notes about story ideas before they sit down to write. Think about what you've learned so far about organizing narrative writing to help you begin prewriting.

- **Audience:** Who is your audience, and what message do you want to express to your audience?

- **Purpose:** What kind of independence do you want to write about, and why is it desired?

- **Characters:** What types of characters would you like to write about in your narrative?

- **Setting:** Where and when will your story be set? How might the setting of your story affect the characters and problem?

- **Plot:** What challenges might these characters face? What events will lead to the resolution of the conflict while keeping a reader engaged?

- **Point of View:** From which point of view should your story be told, and why?

- **Theme/Reflection:** If you are writing an imagined narrative, what general message about life do you want to express? If you are writing a real narrative, what careful thoughts about the significance of your experience will you include?

Response Instructions

Use the questions in the bulleted list to write a one-paragraph summary. Your summary should describe what will happen in your narrative.

Don't worry about including all of the details now; focus only on the most essential and important elements. You will refer to this short summary as you continue through the steps of the writing process.

Please note that excerpts and passages in the StudySync® library and this workbook are intended as touchstones to generate interest in an author's work. The excerpts and passages do not substitute for the reading of entire texts, and StudySync® strongly recommends that students seek out and purchase the whole literary or informational work in order to experience it as the author intended. Links to online resellers are available in our digital library. In addition, complete works may be ordered through an authorized reseller by filling out and returning to StudySync® the order form enclosed in this workbook.

Reading & Writing Companion   **125**

Skill:
Organizing Narrative Writing

••• CHECKLIST FOR ORGANIZING NARRATIVE WRITING

As you consider how to organize your writing for your narrative, use the following questions as a guide:

- Who is the narrator, and who are the characters in the story?

- Where will the story take place?

- Have I created a problem that characters will have to face and resolve, while noting its significance to the characters?

- Have I created a smooth progression of experiences or plot events?

Here are some strategies to help you create a smooth progression of experiences or events in your narrative:

- Establish a context

  > choose a setting and a problem that characters will have to face and resolve, noting its significance to the characters

  > decide how the conflict will be resolved

    o the problem often builds to a climax, when the characters are forced to take action

- Introduce a narrator and/or characters

  > characters can be introduced all at once or over the course of the narrative

  > choose the role each character will play in the story

Copyright © BookheadEd Learning, LLC

YOUR TURN

Place each event, listed under Event Options, in the correct position in the narrative sequence by writing the corresponding letter in the chart below.

	Event Options
A	Sophie is going on a trip to California to visit her aunt. She is supposed to fly from Washington, D.C., to San Diego. Sophie is fifteen years old, and she has never traveled by plane. She is nervous about navigating the airport and flying alone.
B	There is little time left before her plane's departure. Sophie starts to think that her mom, dad, and aunt were wrong to believe she could do this alone. Then, she sees an airport employee. She takes a deep breath.
C	Sophie's parents explain the process of checking in, getting through security, and finding the gate. They drop her off and hug her goodbye. Sophie is nervous but knows that her parents can't go with her beyond the security checkpoint anyway, so she has to do this herself.
D	Sophie passes through security and is immediately intimidated by the hordes of people in the terminal. Everyone seems to know exactly what to do and where to go. She asks a stranger for directions and ends up going the wrong way. Sophie gets lost in the airport with little time to board her flight. She is certain she is going to miss her flight to San Diego. She panics and frantically searches for a map.
E	Sophie relaxes. She asks the airport employee how to find her flight's gate. The employee gives her directions, and she makes it to the gate just in time. She realizes she has the ability to fly on her own after all.

Narrative Sequence	Event
Exposition	
Rising Action	
Climax	
Falling Action	
Resolution	

YOUR TURN

Complete the chart below by writing a short summary of what will happen in each section of your narrative.

Narrative Sequence	Event
Exposition	
Rising Action	
Climax	
Falling Action	
Resolution	

Narrative Writing Process: Draft

PLAN	DRAFT	REVISE	EDIT AND PUBLISH

You have already made progress toward writing your personal or fictional narrative. Now it is time to draft your personal or fictional narrative.

 WRITE

Use your plan and other responses in your Binder to draft your narrative. You may also have new ideas as you begin drafting. Feel free to explore those new ideas as you have them. You can also ask yourself these questions to ensure that your writing is focused, organized, and detailed:

Draft Checklist:

☐ **Purpose and Focus:** Have I made the conflict clear to readers? Have I included only relevant information and details and nothing extraneous that might confuse my readers?

☐ **Organization:** Does the sequence of events in my story make sense? Will readers be engaged by the organization and want to keep reading to find out what happens next?

☐ **Ideas and Details:** Does my writing include engaging ideas and details? Will my readers be able to easily follow and understand descriptions of characters, settings, or events?

Before you submit your draft, read it over carefully. You want to be sure that you've responded to all aspects of the prompt.

Please note that excerpts and passages in the StudySync® library and this workbook are intended as touchstones to generate interest in an author's work. The excerpts and passages do not substitute for the reading of entire texts, and StudySync® strongly recommends that students seek out and purchase the whole literary or informational work in order to experience it as the author intended. Links to online resellers are available in our digital library. In addition, complete works may be ordered through an authorized reseller by filling out and returning to StudySync® the order form enclosed in this workbook.

Reading & Writing
Companion

129

Here is Daniel's narrative draft. As you read, notice how Daniel develops his draft to be focused, organized, and detailed. As he continues to revise and edit his narrative, he will find and improve weak spots in his writing, as well as correct any language or punctuation mistakes.

☰ STUDENT MODEL: FIRST DRAFT

The Price of Freedom

~~Nora is on the phone with her best friend, Simone.~~ Nora firmly presses her phone between her ear and shoulder. "I can't beleive this is our last summer at camp," she says as she digs through her dirty laundry hamper. "Simone, I have to put you on speaker phone." She sets her phone on the carpet. "Did you borrow my wool socks? I can't find them anywhere."

"Nope," she replies. Nora sighs. Wool socks are a must have for cold nights camping in the mountains. Camp doesn't start until a month from now, but already packing.

~~"We must make the most out of camp this year. This is our last summer. Then comes college, marriage, kids…"~~

~~"Please don't get serious again. This summer will be the best yet."~~

"We must make the most out of camp this year. This is our last summer before our senior year! Then comes college, marriage, kids . . . ," Simone hesitates. "Who knows if we'll ever be free of responsibility again?"

"No!" Nora cries. "Please don't get serious again. We are still kids! This summer will be the best yet."

"You're right. I need to stay positive. We'll be out in the open air before we know it, and everything is going to be great. Don't forget that the application and fee are due in a week, okay? Bye!"

Every july, Evergreen high school hosts a two-week camping trip for students. The trip is an opportunity to learn about the outdoors. The trip is also an opportunity to build a community before the school year starts. Nora has made her most cherished memories in the great outdoors. She especially loves camp because it reminds her of

Skill:
Story Beginnings

After reviewing the checklist for story beginnings, Daniel decides he could use techniques that are more creative to interest readers in his story. He starts the story in a more engaging way and uses dialogue to help set up the conflict.

when she used to go to state parks with her Grandpa to bird-watch. It's because of him that she loved nature. Since he passed away five years ago, Nora had made it a point to get outside at much as possible. She even takes his old binoculars with her to camp so that she can observe the Birds and other Wildlife.

~~Nora gives up searching for her socks and lies on the floor. Her mom shouts for her to come downstairs to talk. *What is it this time?* she thinks. *Did I forget to take out the trash? Was I supposed to clean the bathroom?* She closes her eyes, takes a deep breath, and imagines she is back at camp lying in the grass by the lake. She feels the breeze on her arms and face. The pine trees sway in the wind and the sun shines. A blue jay flies through the sky and lands in its nest. Nora wishes she could be free from worries like the wildlife in the forest. She wants to rid herself of stress from family, school, and money. For now, summer camp is the closest she can get to independence. She opens her eyes. They take a moment to adjust to her ceiling light. I must get out of this house, she thinks.~~

Nora gives up searching for her socks and lies on the floor. Her mom shouts for her to come downstairs to talk. *What is it this time?* she thinks. *Did I forget to take out the trash? Was I supposed to clean the bathroom?* She closes her eyes, takes a deep breath, and imagines she is back at camp lying in the grass by the lake. She feels the mellow breeze glide across her bare arms and face. The pine trees dance in the wind as tiny rays of sunlight peek out through their branches. A blue jay swoops through the sky and lands in its nest. Nora wishes she could be free from worries, like the wildlife in the forest. She wants to rid herself of stress from family, school, and money. For now, summer camp is the closest she can get to independence. She opens her eyes. They take a moment to adjust to the artificial glare of her ceiling light. *I must get out of this house,* she thinks.

When Nora finally makes her way downstairs, her mom sitting in the liveing room. She looks more tired than usual and wore a gloomy expression. "Why the sad face, Mom?" nora jests.

~~"Honey, sit down. We need to talk." Nora sits on the couch across from her. "You are old enough now, so I'm going to jump straight to the point. I was laid off from my job at the nurseing home this morning. Until I find~~

Skill:
Descriptive Details

Daniel adds more descriptive language to enhance the sensory appeal of Nora's imagined scene. Touch details, such as "the mellow breeze," contribute to the mood of the scene. They help readers understand that Nora feels relaxed and free at camp.

**Skill:
Transitions**

Daniel realizes he hasn't used the correct transition to show the relationship between ideas in two sentences. He has used *in addition,* as if he were just adding information. He replaces that transition with *however* to set the ideas in opposition and stress that Nora's surprise is not accompanied by fear.

**Skill:
Narrative Techniques**

Daniel replaces his explanation of Nora's thoughts, after she learns that her mom can't afford to pay the camp fee, with her actual thoughts. He uses italics to show that these thoughts are a break from the conventional narration.

~~a new job, I need you to pitch in and help with the bills." Her mother exhales and looks down at the floor. Nora is shocked. In addition, she isn't frightened the way she knows some of her friends would be.~~

"Honey, sit down. We need to talk." Nora sits on the couch across from her. "You are old enough now, so I'm going to jump straight to the point. I was laid off from my job at the nursing home this morning. Until I find a new job, I need you to pitch in and help with the bills." Her mother exhales and looks down at the floor. Nora is shocked. However, she isn't frightened the way she knows some of her friends would be. Nora and her mom have fallen on hard times in the past, but they have always come out on top.

"I'm sorry, Mom. I will help in any way I can," Nora says sincerely.

"Really? Thank you." Her mom's mood lightens.

"Of course. We need to stick together!" Nora exclaims. "I was going to get a summer job to keep me busy until camp anyway and speaking of camp I need to turn in my signed application and $250 fee soon. Do you have it ready?"

"Well, Nora, that's the problem. Money is tight now, so we can't afford to pay the fee."

~~Nora wants to yell and protest, but she knows that won't help the situation. She wants to remind her mom that she promised to sign the application and pay the fee. Instead, she says, "I understand. We'll figure something out." Nora smiles faintly, but tears begin to well in her eyes.~~

~~Nora's thoughts race. She can't believe this is happening to her. She deserves to go to camp just as much as her friends do. Nora was looking forward to one summer of freedom before adult responsibilities kick in. She decides that without camp, this summer is going to be the worst.~~

Nora wants to yell and protest, but she knows that won't help the situation. *But you promised I could go,* she thinks. Instead, she says, "I understand. We'll figure something out." Nora smiles faintly, but tears begin to well in her eyes. She excuses herself from the room.

Back in her bedroom, Nora's thoughts race. *I can't believe this is happening. I deserve to go to camp just as much as my friends do. So much for one summer of freedom before adult responsibilities kick in. This summer is going to be the worst!*

Nora picks up her duffle bag and dumps its contents onto the floor. Amid the pile of sweatpants and t-shirts, she spots her Grandpa's antique binoculars. Suddenly, she knows exactly what she has to do.

Nora puts the binoculars in her the backpack. She parks outside the local pawn shop. Then, clutching her backpack, she takes a deep breath and enters the shop. Nora glances around the room and notices a bunch of jewelry, electronics, and musical instruments. *Will the memory of Grandpa and his love for nature be lost as well?*

A man emerges from the back of the store and asks if he can help her. Nora places her backpack on the counter and carefuly removes the binoculars. Her grandfather's memory is worth much more than a quick payout and a summer away from home. Plus, if she went away, she'd leave her mother who needs her help. She sees her reflection in the lens and realizes that selling the binoculars is wrong.

~~"Uh, never mind," Nora says as she puts the binoculars away. A poster catches her eye. On her way out the door, she sees a bulletin board covered with posts for job openings. The local community center is looking for someone to lead nature walks and weekly birding outings. She takes the flyer and stuffs it in her backpack. As she bikes home, Nora cannot believe what she almost did. She will realize that a summer job is a much better solution to her problems.~~

"Uh, never mind," Nora stammers as she puts the binoculars away. On her way out the door, she sees a bulletin board covered with posts for job openings. A poster catches her eye. The local community center is looking for someone to lead nature walks and weekly birding outings. She takes the flyer and stuffs it in her backpack. As she bikes home, Nora cannot believe what she almost did. She realizes that a summer job is a much better solution to her problems. She might not be able to go to camp, but she will be free to be outside and share her love for the great outdoors.

 Skill:
Conclusions

Daniel thinks about how to summarize his narrative's message in his conclusion. He adds a final sentence to provide a sense of closure and conclusion for readers.

Skill:
Story Beginnings

••• CHECKLIST FOR STORY BEGINNINGS

Before you write the beginning of your narrative, ask yourself the following questions:

- What information does my reader need to know at the beginning of the story about the narrator, main character, setting, and the character's conflict?
- What will happen to my character in the story?

There are many ways to help you engage and orient your reader. Here are some questions to help you set out a problem, situation, or observation as well as its significance and introduce a narrator and/or characters:

- Action

  > What action could help reveal information about my character or conflict?

  > How might an exciting moment or observation and its significance grab my reader's attention?

  > How could a character's reaction help set the mood?

- Description

  > Does my story take place in a special location or specific time period?

  > How can describing a location or character grab my reader's attention? What powerful emotions can I use?

- Dialogue

  > What dialogue would help my reader understand the setting or the conflict?

  > How could a character's internal thoughts provide information for my reader?

- Information

  > Would a surprising statement grab the reader's attention?

  > What details will help my reader understand the character, conflict, or setting?

YOUR TURN

Below is the revised beginning of Daniel's narrative. Choose the best answer to each question about his story beginning.

> Nora firmly presses her phone between her ear and shoulder. "I can't believe this is our last summer at camp," she says as she digs through her dirty laundry hamper. "Simone, I have to put you on speaker phone." She sets her phone on the carpet. "Did you borrow my wool socks? I can't find them anywhere."
>
> "Nope," Simone replies. Nora sighs. Wool socks are a must have for cold nights camping in the mountains. Camp doesn't start until a month from now, but she's already packing.

1. Which line could you add to the first paragraph to better show the contrast between the initial setting and camp?

   ○ A. Nora's ear aches as she struggles to hear Simone through the worn-out phone receiver.
   ○ B. Nora perks up when she realizes that maybe the socks are in the basement.
   ○ C. Nora smiles as she thinks of the fresh air of camp and holds her breath, digging deeper into the hamper.
   ○ D. Nora is distracted from her search for wool socks as her stomach growls for a snack.

2. In the second paragraph, how does the detail "Camp doesn't start until a month from now, but she's already packing." help the reader better understand the main character?

   ○ A. It illustrates Nora's level of excitement about camp.
   ○ B. It shows that Nora is a very disorganized person and packing will take her a long time.
   ○ C. It characterizes Nora as anxious.
   ○ D. It shows that Nora does not want to go to camp.

✎ **WRITE**

Use the questions in the checklist to revise the beginning of your narrative.

Skill:
Narrative Techniques

••• CHECKLIST FOR NARRATIVE TECHNIQUES

As you begin to develop the techniques you will use in your narrative, ask yourself the following questions:

- Is it clear which character is talking in a dialogue?

- Is the pacing of events suitable and effective?

- Which literary devices can strengthen descriptions of the characters or plot events? How can I use personal reflection to develop my narrative?

- What additional characters and/or events might help to develop the narrative?

Here are some methods that can help you use dialogue, description, pacing, reflection, and multiple plot lines to develop experiences, events, and/or characters in your narrative:

- use character dialogue to explain events or actions

  > use quotation marks correctly

  > include identifying names as needed before or after quotation marks

- use description so the reader can visualize the characters, setting, and other elements

  > descriptions should contribute to the reader's understanding of the element being described

- use pacing effectively

  > for a quick pace, use limited description, short paragraphs, brief dialogue, and simpler sentences

  > for a slower pace, use detailed description, longer paragraphs, and complex sentence structures

- use reflection to comment on the overall message

  > include a character's or personal inner thoughts or insights

- create multiple plot lines that further develop the narrative's message

  > include characters, events, or other elements that will further develop the plot

- use any combination of the techniques above

YOUR TURN

Choose the best answer to each question.

1. Below is a section from a previous draft of Daniel's story, in which he wants to include Nora's thoughts to enhance the narration. How should he rewrite the underlined sentence to accurately show Nora's thoughts in this moment?

> Nora catches the pawn shop owner eyeing her grandpa's binoculars. His face lights up. She wonders how much he is willing to pay for them. <u>Nora wishes she researched how much they are worth before hastily riding her bike downtown to the shop.</u> Nora hopes he doesn't try to sell her short.
>
> "How did you manage to get your hands on that pair of binoculars, Miss?" he says curiously.

- A. If only Nora knew how much the binoculars were worth.
- B. *I should have researched the value of the binoculars before coming here,* she thinks.
- C. She thinks about how she should have researched how much the binoculars are worth.
- D. *What if the binoculars aren't worth as much as I thought?*

2. Daniel wants to add details to a previous draft to develop the relationship between characters. Which sentence should he add between sentences 1 and 2 below to further describe how the characters relate to one another?

> (1) Nora and Simone have known each other since kindergarten, but they did not become friends until their first summer at camp. (2) Since then, they have been inseparable.

- A. They shared a cabin with seven other girls and a counselor.
- B. They took swimming lessons and practiced archery.
- C. They were fourteen years old.
- D. They instantly clicked because they share an appreciation for the great outdoors.

✎ **WRITE**

Use the questions in the checklist for narrative techniques to revise a section of your fictional or personal narrative.

Skill:
Transitions

••• CHECKLIST FOR TRANSITIONS

Before you revise your current draft to include transitions, think about:

- the order of plot events
- how events build to create a unified story, build a specific mood, and work toward a particular outcome

Next, reread your current draft and note areas in your narrative where:

- the order of events is unclear or illogical
- changes in time or setting are confusing or unclear. Look for:

  > sudden jumps

  > missing or illogical plot events or outcome(s)

  > moments where the mood does not connect to the development of plot events

Revise your draft to use a variety of techniques to sequence events so that they build on one another to create a coherent whole and build toward a particular mood and outcome, using the following questions as a guide:

- What other techniques could I use so that events in my story build on one another, creating a coherent whole?
- Does the sequence of events in my story build toward a particular mood and outcome?

  > For example, you can build the mood of your story by creating a sense of mystery or suspense.

  > For example, you can build toward a particular outcome by showing character growth or by developing a resolution.

- Are there better transitional words, phrases, or clauses that I can use to show shifts in time or setting and relationships between experiences and events?

YOUR TURN

Choose the best answer to each question about Daniel's final draft of his narrative (see the Plan lesson).

1. Which of the following sentences from Daniel's story best illustrates a transition that helps Daniel build toward a consistent theme throughout the narrative?

    ○ A. *"I must get out of this house*, she thinks."
    ○ B. "'I'm sorry, Mom. I will help in any way I can,' Nora says sincerely."
    ○ C. "Camp doesn't start until a month from now, but she's already packing."
    ○ D. "She might not be able to go to camp, but she will be free to be outside and share her love for the great outdoors."

2. What effect does the use of the transition word *then* have in this sentence from paragraph 17 of Daniel's story: "Then, clutching her backpack, she takes a deep breath and enters the shop."

    ○ A. It lets the reader know that Nora is having second thoughts about the pawn shop.
    ○ B. It shows how much Nora does not want to go into the pawn shop.
    ○ C. It pivots the reader toward Nora's decision to go to the pawn shop, emphasizing a major event or moment in the plot.
    ○ D. It reinforces the theme of Nora's making tough decisions.

 WRITE

Use the questions in the checklist to revise the transitions in your narrative.

Skill:
Descriptive Details

••• CHECKLIST FOR DESCRIPTIVE DETAILS

First, reread the draft of your narrative and identify the following:

- places where descriptive details are needed to convey experiences and events
- vague, general, or overused words and phrases
- places where you want to tell how something looks, sounds, feels, smells, or tastes, such as:

  > experiences

  > events

  > settings

  > characters

Use telling details, sensory language, and precise words and phrases to convey a vivid picture of the experiences, events, setting, and/or characters, using the following questions as a guide:

- What experiences and events do I want to convey in my writing?
- Have I included telling details that help reveal the experiences and events in the story?
- How do I want the characters and setting portrayed?
- How can I use sensory language—or words that appeal to the sense of sight, sound, touch, smell, or taste—so that readers can clearly visualize the experiences, events, setting, and/or characters in my story?
- What can I refine or revise in my word choice to make sure the reader can picture what is taking place?

YOUR TURN

Choose the best answer to each question.

1. Daniel would like to add a descriptive smell detail to this sentence from a previous draft. Which sentence best adds a smell detail to his sentence?

> Nora enters the pawn shop.

- ○ A. Nora tries to enter the pawn shop, but the door is locked.
- ○ B. Nora feels a sticky substance on the door handle as she enters the pawn shop.
- ○ C. As Nora enters the pawn shop, she is overwhelmed by the distinct aroma of mothballs.
- ○ D. Nora enters the pawn shop only to find her mom crying as she talks to the owner.

2. Daniel wants to add a sensory detail to this passage from a previous draft to better establish the mood of the scene. What sentence can he add to help communicate an uplifting mood?

> *This job is perfect for me!* she thinks. Nora hastily stuffs the job posting into her backpack and hops on her bike. She rides home to deliver the news to her mom.

- ○ A. The sun burns brightly, guiding Nora on her way.
- ○ B. Nora is startled by a car horn and nearly falls.
- ○ C. Nora splashes through a pothole full of dirty water.
- ○ D. Nora feels the heat from the sun radiate off the asphalt.

 WRITE

Use the questions in the checklist for descriptive details to revise a section of your fictional or personal narrative.

Please note that excerpts and passages in the StudySync® library and this workbook are intended as touchstones to generate interest in an author's work. The excerpts and passages do not substitute for the reading of entire texts, and StudySync® strongly recommends that students seek out and purchase the whole literary or informational work in order to experience it as the author intended. Links to online resellers are available in our digital library. In addition, complete works may be ordered through an authorized reseller by filling out and returning to StudySync® the order form enclosed in this workbook.

Reading & Writing Companion   141

Skill:
Conclusions

sync•skills

••• CHECKLIST FOR CONCLUSIONS

Before you write your conclusion, ask yourself the following questions:

- What important details should I include in the summary in my conclusion?

- What other thoughts and feelings could the characters share with readers in the conclusion?

- Should I express the importance of the events in my narrative through dialogue or a character's actions?

Below are two strategies to help you provide a conclusion that follows from and reflects on what is experienced, observed, or resolved over the course of the narrative:

- Peer Discussion

  > After you have written your introduction and body paragraphs, talk with a partner about possible endings for your narrative.

  > Review your notes, and think about how you want to end your story.

  > Briefly summarize the events in the narrative through the narrator or one of the characters.

  > Describe the narrator's observations about events in the narrative.

  > Reveal to readers why the experiences in the narrative matter through a character's reflections or resolutions.

  > Write your conclusion.

- Freewriting

  > Freewrite for 10 minutes about what you might include in your conclusion.

  > Review your notes, and think about how you want to end your story.

  > Briefly summarize the events in the narrative through the narrator or one of the characters.

  > Describe the narrator's observations about events in the narrative.

  > Reveal to readers why the experiences in the narrative matter through a character's reflections or resolutions.

  > Write your conclusion.

YOUR TURN

Below is the revised conclusion of Daniel's narrative. Choose the best answer to each question about his concluding paragraphs.

> A man emerges from the back of the store and asks if he can help her. Nora places her backpack on the counter and carefully removes the binoculars. She sees her reflection in the lens and realizes that selling the binoculars is wrong. Her grandfather's memory is worth much more than a quick payout and a summer away from home. Plus, if she went away, she'd abandon her mother, who needs her help.
>
> "Uh, never mind," Nora stammers as she puts the binoculars away. On her way out the door, she sees a bulletin board covered with posts for job openings. A poster catches her eye. The local community center is looking for someone to lead nature walks and weekly birding outings. She takes the flyer and stuffs it in her backpack. As she bikes home, Nora cannot believe what she almost did. She realizes that a summer job is a much better solution to her problems. She might not be able to go to camp, but she will be free to be outside and share her love for the great outdoors.

1. What is the effect of mentioning Nora's grandfather in the conclusion of the story?

   ○ A. It shows that Nora really misses her grandfather and thinks of him often.
   ○ B. It conveys to the reader how desperate Nora is to get to camp.
   ○ C. It illustrates the theme that family is more important than camp by showing why Nora makes an important decision.
   ○ D. It reinforces the value Nora's family places on the outdoors.

2. Which sentence from the revised conclusion best shows what Nora learned?

   ○ A. "She realizes that a summer job is a much better solution to her problems."
   ○ B. "She might not be able to go to camp, but she will be free to be outside and share her love for the great outdoors."
   ○ C. "She sees her reflection in the lens and realizes that selling the binoculars is wrong."
   ○ D. "Plus, if she went away, she'd abandon her mother, who needs her help."

✏ WRITE

Use the questions in the checklist for conclusions to revise the ending of your narrative.

Narrative Writing Process: Revise

| PLAN | DRAFT | REVISE | EDIT AND PUBLISH |

You have written a draft of your fictional or personal narrative. You have also received input from your peers about how to improve it. Now you are going to revise your draft.

⬅ REVISION GUIDE

Examine your draft to find areas for revision. Keep in mind your purpose and audience as you revise for clarity, development, organization, and style. Use the guide below to help you review:

Review	Revise	Example
Clarity		
Label parts of the narration that signal the characters' locations or movement between locations.	Insert words or phrases to better establish the setting and the transition between settings.	Nora puts the binoculars in her backpack, throws on her tennis shoes, and races downtown on her bike. She parks outside the local pawn shop. Then, clutching her backpack, she takes a deep breath and enters the shop.
Development		
Identify moments in which your characters respond to conflict. Annotate moments where a character's reaction is confusing or unclear.	Focus on a single event and add details that show the motivation behind the character's reaction.	Nora is shocked. ~~In addition,~~ However, she isn't frightened the way she knows some of her friends would be. Nora and her mom have fallen on hard times in the past, but they have always come out on top. "I'm sorry, Mom. I will help in any way I can," Nora says sincerely.

Review	Revise	Example
Organization		
Explain your story in one or two sentences. Reread and annotate any places that don't match your explanation.	Rewrite the events in the correct sequence. Delete events and details that are not essential to the story, including any redundant description.	~~Nora is on the phone with her best friend, Simone.~~ Nora firmly presses her phone between her ear and shoulder. "I can't believe this is our last summer at camp," she says as she digs through her dirty laundry hamper. "Simone, I have to put you on speaker phone."
Style: Word Choice		
Identify each piece of dialogue that uses the word *says*.	Select pieces of dialogue to rewrite using action verbs.	"Uh, never mind," Nora ~~says~~ stammers as she puts the binoculars away.
Style: Sentence Fluency		
Read aloud your writing and listen to the way the text sounds. Does it sound choppy? Or does it flow smoothly with rhythm, movement, and emphasis on important details and events?	Rewrite a key event, making your sentences longer or shorter to achieve a better flow of writing and the emotion you want your reader to feel.	"This is our last ~~summer.~~ summer before our senior year! Then comes college, marriage, kids. . . ," Simone hesitates. "Who knows if we'll ever be free of responsibility again?" "No!" Nora cries. "Please don't get serious again. We are still kids! This summer will be the best yet."

✏ WRITE

Use the revision guide, as well as your peer reviews, to help you evaluate your fictional or personal narrative to determine areas that should be revised.

Grammar: Capitalization

Proper nouns should always be capitalized. If the noun is composed of several words, do not capitalize articles (*a, an, the*), coordinating conjunctions (*and, but, for, or, nor, yet*), or prepositions of fewer than five letters. Capitalize a title showing family relationship when used with or in place of a proper noun. Do not capitalize it when preceded by an article or a possessive noun or pronoun.

Susanna Walcott's here from **Doctor Griggs.** The Crucible	The grass-plot before the jail, in **Prison Lane**, on a certain summer morning, not less than two centuries ago, was occupied by a pretty large number of the inhabitants of **Boston**, … The Scarlet Letter	Because her leg did not improve but swelled more and more, the doctors at the school bound it with crude splints and took her by car, on September 9th, to the **Red Cross Hospital** in Hiroshima. Hiroshima

Salutations and closings require capitalization as well. Capitalize the first word of the salutation and the recipient's first and last names. Additionally, capitalize the first word of the closing of a letter.

Dear **M**iss **B**reed, **G**reetings from far-off Poston, Arizona! Dear Miss Breed	**Y**ours very truly, Einstein's Letter to the President	**T**o the Editor of the New York Times: The Case of Susan B. Anthony

Direct quotations appear in quotation marks. If a quotation is a complete sentence, the first word of the quotation should be capitalized even if the quotation appears in the middle of a sentence, but do not capitalize the first word of a quotation that cannot stand as a complete sentence.

As Bacon said of manners, "To obtain them, it only needs not to despise them," so we say of animal spirits, that they are the spontaneous product of health and of a social habit. Society and Solitude	This common response to unfulfilled expectations is known as the "frustration-aggression hypothesis." Dumped!

YOUR TURN

1. How should this sentence be changed?

   > My Sister told me that Richard joined the peace corps and would be going to Ghana.

   ○ A. Lowercase **sister.**
   ○ B. Capitalize **peace corps.**
   ○ C. Lowercase **Ghana.**
   ○ D. Answers A and B are correct.

2. How should this closing be changed?

   > With Great Admiration,

   ○ A. Change the word **Great** to **great.**
   ○ B. Change the words **Great Admiration** to **great admiration.**
   ○ C. Change the word **With** to **with.**
   ○ D. No change needs to be made to this closing.

3. How should this sentence be changed?

   > Muir remembers his journey to America in 1849 with his brothers and father as "The first grand adventure of my life."

   ○ A. Capitalize **journey.**
   ○ B. Capitalize **brothers** and **father.**
   ○ C. Do not capitalize **The.**
   ○ D. No change needs to be made to this sentence.

4. How should this sentence be changed?

   > *Metamorphoses,* the Roman poet Ovid's fascinating retelling of the daphne and Phoebus myth, is based on earlier Greek tales.

   ○ A. Make **Roman** lowercase.
   ○ B. Capitalize **fascinating.**
   ○ C. Capitalize **daphne.**
   ○ D. No change needs to be made to this sentence.

Grammar: Consistent Verb Tenses

The tense of a verb should remain consistently in the past, present, or future, as the action is placed.

When writing about two or more events that occur at the same time, do not shift, or change, tenses. If verb tenses are inconsistent, it is difficult for the reader to know when something happened.

Correct	Incorrect
We planned a picnic, but the rain forced us to postpone it.	We planned a picnic, but the rain forces us to postpone it.

It is possible to have more than one tense in a sentence, but it must be clear why there is a difference.

Rule	Text
It is possible to have different tenses in a sentence, if the shift in tenses shows that one event precedes or follows another in time.	She did not hear the story as many women have heard the same, with a paralyzed inability to accept its significance. The Story of an Hour
A present tense verb can express a general truth even if the rest of the sentence is not in the present.	We hold these truths to be self-evident, that all men are created equal, that they are endowed by their Creator with certain unalienable Rights, that among these are Life, Liberty, and the pursuit of Happiness. The Declaration of Independence
Even when there are several verbs in a long sentence, the verb tenses need to remain consistent if they are showing action over a consistent period of time.	When Lee came to the sentence about the officers' side-arms, private horses, and baggage, he showed for the first time during the reading of the letter a slight change of countenance, and was evidently touched by this act of generosity. Lee Surrenders to Grant, April 9th, 1865

↻ YOUR TURN

1. Decide whether the verb tenses are consistent. If not, pick the change that will make the sentence correct.

   > Lou Gehrig was a legendary baseball player in the 1930s; he hits four home runs in one game.

   ○ A. Change *was* to *is*.
   ○ B. Change *hits* to *hit*.
   ○ C. Change *hits* to *will hit*.
   ○ D. No change needs to be made to this sentence.

2. Decide whether the verb tenses are consistent. If not, pick the change that will make the sentence correct.

   > Sadly, a terrible neurological disease would cut his career short, and his name would become associated with the disease: Lou Gehrig's disease.

   ○ A. Change *would cut* to *cuts*.
   ○ B. Change *would become* to *becomes*.
   ○ C. Change *would become* to *will become*.
   ○ D. No change needs to be made to this sentence.

3. Decide whether the verb tenses are consistent. If not, pick the change that will make the sentence correct.

   > Gehrig gives a famous speech on July 4, 1939, and said good-bye to all his fans and called himself the luckiest man in the world.

   ○ A. Change *gives* to *gave*.
   ○ B. Change *said* to *says*.
   ○ C. Change *called* to *will call*.
   ○ D. No change needs to be made to this sentence.

Please note that excerpts and passages in the StudySync® library and this workbook are intended as touchstones to generate interest in an author's work. The excerpts and passages do not substitute for the reading of entire texts, and StudySync® strongly recommends that students seek out and purchase the whole literary or informational work in order to experience it as the author intended. Links to online resellers are available in our digital library. In addition, complete works may be ordered through an authorized reseller by filling out and returning to StudySync® the order form enclosed in this workbook.

Reading & Writing
Companion

149

Grammar: Basic Spelling Rules

Rule	Text
When adding a suffix that begins with a vowel to a word that ends with a silent **e**, usually drop the **e**. When adding a suffix that begins with a vowel to a word that ends in **ee** or **oe,** keep the **e**.	Lee now looked greatly relieved, and though anything but a **demonstrative** man, he gave every evidence of his **appreciation** of this concession, and said, "This will have the best possible effect upon the men. It will be very gratifying and will do much toward **conciliating** our people." Lee Surrenders to Grant, April 9th, 1865
When a word ends in a consonant + **y**, change the **y** to **i** before adding a suffix.	America is rapidly losing its position as leader of the world simply because the Democratic Administration has **pitifully** failed to provide effective leadership. Remarks to the Senate in Support of a Declaration of Conscience
When adding **-ly** to a word that ends in a single **l**, keep the **l**. When adding **-ly** to a word that ends in a consonant + **le,** drop the **le**.	I looked around and up at Mr. Cunningham, whose face was **equally** impassive. To Kill a Mockingbird
Generally, double the final consonant if the last syllable of the word is accented or if the word ends in a single consonant preceded by a single vowel, and the accent does not move after the suffix is added.	The effect of this separation on their educational opportunities was well stated by a finding in the Kansas case by a court which nevertheless felt **compelled** to rule against the Negro plaintiffs. Brown v. Board of Education

↻ YOUR TURN

1. How should this sentence be changed?

> Despite David's efforts at being careful, he dropped his eyeglasses and the lenses shatterred.

- ○ A. Change **dropped** to **droped.**
- ○ B. Change **eyeglasses** to **eye glasses.**
- ○ C. Change **shatterred** to **shattered.**
- ○ D. No change needs to be made to this sentence.

2. How should this sentence be changed?

> The largest assemblely of competitors gathered in Munich, Germany, which showcased ten thousand athletes in 1972.

- ○ A. Change **gathered** to **gatherred.**
- ○ B. Change **assemblely** to **assembly.**
- ○ C. Change **showcased** to **showcaseed.**
- ○ D. No change needs to be made to this sentence.

3. How should this sentence be changed?

> The valueable lessons to be learned from studying any historical event are made more meaningful by comparing and contrasting varyous historyans' interpretations of the same event.

- ○ A. Change **valueable** to **valuable.**
- ○ B. Change **historyans'** to **historians'.**
- ○ C. Change **varyous** to **various.**
- ○ D. Choices A, B, and C are all correct.

4. How should this sentence be changed?

> The representative of the crown was busy decreing this and that and did not notice the fulminating fury of the burgeoning crowd beneath the balcony.

- ○ A. Change **representative** to **representetive.**
- ○ B. Change **decreing** to **decreeing.**
- ○ C. Change **fulminating** to **fulminateing.**
- ○ D. No change needs to be made to this sentence.

Narrative Writing Process: Edit and Publish

PLAN	DRAFT	REVISE	EDIT AND PUBLISH

You have revised your fictional or personal narrative based on your peer feedback and your own examination.

Now, it is time to edit your narrative. When you revised, you focused on the content of your narrative. You probably looked at your story's beginning, descriptive details, and conclusion. When you edit, you focus on the mechanics of your story, paying close attention to things like grammar and punctuation.

Use the checklist below to guide you as you edit:

☐ Have I correctly capitalized words?

☐ Have I used a consistent verb tense throughout the story?

☐ Do I have any sentence fragments or run-on sentences?

☐ Have I spelled everything correctly?

Notice some edits Daniel has made:

- Added a subject and verb to correct a sentence fragment

- Corrected the spelling of a word ending in silent e when adding a suffix that begins with a vowel

- Changed a verb's tense to maintain consistency

- Capitalized a proper noun

> When Nora finally makes her way downstairs, **she finds** her mom sitting in the ~~liveing~~ **living** room. She looks more tired than usual and ~~wore~~ **wears** a gloomy expression. "Why the sad face, Mom?" ~~nora~~ **Nora** jests.

WRITE

Use the questions on the previous page, as well as your peer reviews, to help you evaluate your personal or fictional narrative to determine areas that need editing. Then, edit your narrative to correct those errors.

Once you have made all your corrections, you are ready to publish your work. You can distribute your writing to family and friends, hang it on a bulletin board, or post it on your blog. If you publish online, share the link with your family, friends, and classmates.

At the Foot of the Gallows

FICTION

Introduction

"At the Foot of the Gallows" tells the story of Ann Hibbins, a Puritan woman who was tried and hanged for witchcraft in Boston in 1656 despite a lack of evidence against her. This work of historical fiction is told from the perspective of a fictional Puritan woman who protests the verdict but is powerless under the same patriarchal, or male-controlled, society that convicted Hibbins.

 VOCABULARY

jostle

push against or collide with someone

affrighted

frightened (archaic)

boon

advantage; benefit

indictment

a formal accusation of a crime

benevolence

goodwill; acts of kindness

≡ READ

NOTES

1   The air outside the courthouse hangs thick and heavy. Despite the heat of the oppressive midday sun, the people of Boston **jostle** for position at the foot of the wooden platform. The gallows stand imposingly. A gentle breeze, a **boon** on any other day, makes the noose sway menacingly. Today, Ann Hibbins will hang for her crimes.

2   Among those present at this show of justice are Susana Blackstone and her daughter, Abigail. Goody Blackstone does not want to witness the day's events, nor does she want Abigail to see them. She would have rathered they visited the church to pray for Goody Hibbins's soul. She was there at the trial. She knows there is no real evidence to support the case against Goody Hibbins. But she also knows that innocence is not enough to stop the hangman. She wants to scream or leave quietly, but something stops her. Her husband works as a carpenter. She knows his business would likely suffer if she were not there to show her support. Mr. Blackstone flashes a warning look as he joins them in the crowd, subtly reminding her that her behavior

reflects on him. He also wants their daughter to see what happens if a woman steps out of line.

3   The trouble started sixteen years ago, in 1640. Goody Hibbins hired several carpenters, well-respected men not unlike Mr. Blackstone, to do some work on her house. Everyone knew that Mr. William Hibbins was wealthy and influential. He was an assistant to Governor John Endicott. The carpenters figured that Goody Hibbins could afford to pay well, so they took advantage and overcharged her. Savvy and assertive, Goody Hibbins filed a lawsuit against them. She won, but her problems were just beginning. The community agreed that Goody Hibbins had been wronged. But they also believed it was too forward of a Puritan woman to pursue legal action. Her husband should have taken care of such business. After the trial, church authorities demanded that Goody Hibbins apologize. She refused. As a result, she was excommunicated. Her fellow colonists lost respect for her, but they still respected Mr. Hibbins enough to let the matter rest—for a time.

4   Last year, Mr. Hibbins died, and any **benevolence** the people of Boston had for Goody Hibbins died along with him. No more than a few months passed before Goody Hibbins found herself back in the courtroom. She was accused and convicted of witchcraft.

5   Goody Blackstone does not know why Goody Hibbins was not hanged immediately. Perhaps her husband's memory still held value. Perhaps the legal system was hesitant to hang a woman of high social standing. Or perhaps they were reluctant to take a human life without hard evidence that she was guilty. The case passed to a higher court. This past month, Goody Hibbins again stood trial for witchcraft. Goody Blackstone observed the trial from the rear of the courthouse.

6   Goody Blackstone had expected the defendant to appear **affrighted**. If she were the one on trial, she should be too scared to breathe. Instead, Goody Hibbins stood tall and spoke with confidence. The **indictment** against her was read aloud, and the charge remained as flimsy as it had always been. Goody Hibbins's voice rang out as she swore her innocence. Goody Blackstone's fear that Goody Hibbins's strength might work against her was confirmed when Governor Endicott himself pronounced her guilty of a made-up crime. He sentenced her to hang.

7   The door to the courthouse creaks open. Ann Hibbins is led out, defiant as ever. She does not bow her head until the noose is fastened around her neck. Whispers flow through the crowd. Goody Blackstone recognizes a minister's hushed, sympathetic voice as he says that Goody Hibbins's only crime was having more wit than her neighbors. Goody Blackstone closes her eyes to hold back brimming tears, and she hears the gallows' trapdoor fall.

First Read

Read the story. After you read, complete the Think Questions below.

1. Where and when does the story take place?

   The story takes place in _____

   _____.

2. Write two or three sentences describing the plot of the story.

   The story opens with _____

   _____.

3. Why do readers know that Ann Hibbins is innocent?

   Readers know Ann Hibbins is innocent because _____

   _____.

4. Use context to confirm the meaning of the word *benevolence* as it is used in "At the Foot of the Gallows." Write your definition of *benevolence* here.

   Benevolence means _____

   A context clue is _____

5. What is another way to say that a person feels *affrighted*?

   A person feels _____

   _____

Please note that excerpts and passages in the StudySync® library and this workbook are intended as touchstones to generate interest in an author's work. The excerpts and passages do not substitute for the reading of entire texts, and StudySync® strongly recommends that students seek out and purchase the whole literary or informational work in order to experience it as the author intended. Links to online resellers are available in our digital library. In addition, complete works may be ordered through an authorized reseller by filling out and returning to StudySync® the order form enclosed in this workbook.

Reading & Writing
Companion   157

Skill:
Analyzing Expressions

★ DEFINE

When you read, you may find English expressions that you do not know. An **expression** is a group of words that communicates an idea. Three types of expressions are idioms, sayings, and figurative language. They can be difficult to understand because the meanings of the words are different from their **literal**, or usual, meanings.

An **idiom** is an expression that is commonly known among a group of people. For example, "It's raining cats and dogs" means it is raining heavily. **Sayings** are short expressions that contain advice or wisdom. For instance, "Don't count your chickens before they hatch" means do not plan on something good happening before it happens. **Figurative** language is when you describe something by comparing it with something else, either directly (using the words *like* or *as*) or indirectly. For example, "I'm as hungry as a horse" means I'm very hungry. None of the expressions are about actual animals.

••• CHECKLIST FOR ANALYZING EXPRESSIONS

To determine the meaning of an expression, remember the following:

✓ If you find a confusing group of words, it may be an expression. The meaning of words in expressions may not be their literal meaning.

- Ask yourself: Is this confusing because the words are new? Or because the words do not make sense together?

✓ Determining the overall meaning may require that you use one or more of the following:

- context clues
- a dictionary or other resource
- teacher or peer support

✓ Highlight important information before and after the expression to look for clues.

YOUR TURN

Notice the sentences that have literal meanings and those that do not have literal meanings. Write the letter of each sentence in the correct column.

	Sentences
A	The sun shines brightly.
B	Collecting pennies is a good way to save money.
C	The traffic after the concert was a nightmare.
D	The biology test was a piece of cake.
E	The sun shines like a diamond in the sky.
F	There was a lot of traffic after the concert.
G	A penny saved is a penny earned.
H	The biology test was easy.

Has Literal Meaning	Does Not Have Literal Meaning

Skill:
Conveying Ideas

★ DEFINE

Conveying ideas means communicating a **message** to another person. When speaking, you might not know what word to use to convey your ideas. When you do not know the exact English word, you can try different strategies. For example, you can ask for help from classmates or your teacher. You may use gestures and physical movements to act out the word. You can also try using **synonyms** or **defining** and describing the meaning you are trying to express.

••• CHECKLIST FOR CONVEYING IDEAS

To convey ideas for words you do not know when speaking, use the following learning strategies:

- ✓ Request help.

- ✓ Use gestures or physical movements.

- ✓ Use a synonym for the word.

- ✓ Describe what the word means using other words.

- ✓ Give an example of the word you want to use.

YOUR TURN

Match each example with its correct strategy for conveying the meaning of the word *witness*.

Example Options	
A	The person uses the similar word *see*.
B	The person explains that the word means "watching something happen."
C	The person says it is like when you go to a wedding and watch two people get married.
D	The person mimes a reaction to seeing something surprising.

Strategies	Examples
Use gestures or physical movements.	
Use a synonym for the word.	
Describe what the word means using other words.	
Give examples of the word you want to use.	

Close Read

✏ WRITE

LITERARY ANALYSIS: At the end of "At the Foot of the Gallows," Goody Blackstone cries when Ann Hibbins is hanged. But is she crying only because Ann is dead? Describe another reason why Goody Blackstone may be crying. Explain your reason using specific details from the story. Pay attention to and edit for spelling patterns.

Use the checklist below to guide you as you write.

☐ Why do you think Goody Blackstone cries at the end of the story?

☐ Does Goody Blackstone think Ann Hibbins' punishment is fair?

☐ How do you know?

Use the sentence frames to organize and write your literary analysis.

Goody Blackstone cries because she feels _____.

She knows that Ann Hibbins is _____.

She thinks the punishment is _____.

There was no real _____. There is only one reason Ann Hibbins was hanged.

She stepped _____.

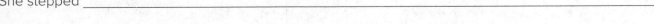

Repeal the Stamp Act!

ARGUMENTATIVE TEXT

Introduction

In 1765, the British Parliament passed the Stamp Act, a law that imposed a tax on all documents in the American colonies. The revenue from the tax was intended to pay debts from the recent French and Indian War fought on American soil. Many American colonists, however, were not willing to accept a direct tax from a government across the ocean. In this newspaper editorial, a fictional member of the Sons of Liberty protest group explains why he won't pay the tax.

Ⅴ VOCABULARY

levy
to use legal authority to demand payment of a tax or fine

odious
causing or deserving of hatred or disgust

excise
a tax charged on the manufacture or sale of a product

jurisdiction
an area in which a government has power or a set of laws is used

petition
to formally ask a person or organization for something

NOTES

☰ READ

Readers:

1   Recently, our dear friends in Parliament passed a law known as the Stamp Act. This is the first direct tax that the government in London has tried to **levy** on the colonies. This wide-ranging tax affects all printed products. This includes legal documents, newspapers, pamphlets, playing cards, and even college diplomas.

2   I am not against paying taxes. I pay property taxes on my home and business. I pay **excise** taxes on the products I buy. However, those taxes are different. They were created by a legislative body that represents me. This infernal Act was passed by a sovereign body that does not represent us colonists. Common law has long held that British subjects are not taxed without representation. As such, the Stamp Act must be repealed not because it is unjust, but because it is illegal.

NOTES

3 For many years, British subjects have not had taxes imposed on them without their consent. They have the opportunity to **petition** their member of Parliament and argue against the new tax. However, we colonists are not represented in Parliament. We have no one to petition. Besides, the law was passed without debate. Who spoke for us? The Crown would contend that we have virtual representation in Parliament because we are British citizens. I shall accept that the colonists have fair representation in Parliament when this imaginary member of Parliament reads and responds to my letters. Until that time, I will only pay taxes levied by my elected colonial assembly.

4 There is also the matter of the reason this tax was levied. Revenue from this **odious** Act will support the British army in North America. Yet, the war against the French is over. Still the Crown insists on having a standing army upon our shores. In addition, this money for soldiers comes on top of the recent Quartering Act. That Act requires us to provide housing for soldiers, even giving them free rooms in our inns and on our private property. What more does the army want from us? Shall I remove the boots from my feet and hand them to the nearest soldier? Will they bleed us dry in the name of defense?

5 But the most egregious line in the Stamp Act concerns those who refuse to pay the tax. The law permits violators to be tried without a jury in Vice-Admiralty Court. That is a maritime law court. Trial by jury is a right of all British people. Any court that does not have a jury is invalid. Worst of all, Vice-Admiralty Court can be held anywhere, even far from one's local **jurisdiction**. I will not be sent to Nova Scotia to defend myself. We have courts here that would be happy to try these violators, with the help of a jury. Some members of Parliament believe that jurors are too sympathetic to their fellow colonists. To me, that is the way that the courts are designed to work. A jury can be sympathetic to a man who steals bread to feed his children. Why should they not have the chance to be sympathetic to a publisher who avoids the stamp to avoid destitution?

6 A law that requires taxation without representation to support an unnecessary standing army, enforced by an illegal court—we cannot let this law stand. To amend the situation, we must first refuse to pay any taxes levied by Parliament until we have fair representation. In the meantime, dockworkers, refuse to unload ships that come with these stamps. Lawyers, continue to draw up contracts as you have always done. Publishers, continue printing your newspapers. As a city, we should stall the commissioners who try to collect this tax. We must convince them to resign! Together, we can stop this illegal Act. Help me stop future attempts at tyranny!

Yours in protest,
A Son of Liberty

First Read

Read the text. After you read, complete the Think Questions below.

☁ THINK QUESTIONS

1. Who passed the Stamp Act? What is the Stamp Act?

   The Stamp Act was passed by _____.

   The Stamp Act is _____.

2. Write two or three sentences telling why the Stamp Act must be repealed.

   The Stamp Act must be repealed because _____

   _____.

3. What kind of trial is a right of all British people?

   All British people have the right to _____

   _____.

4. Use context to confirm the meaning of the word *petition* as it is used in "Repeal the Stamp Act!" Write your definition of *petition* here.

   Petition means _____

   A context clue is _____.

5. What is another way to say that a law is *odious*?

   Another way to say a law is odious is _____

   _____.

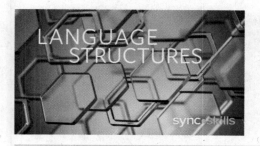

Skill:
Language Structures

★ DEFINE

In every language, there are rules that tell how to **structure** sentences. These rules define the correct order of words. In the English language, for example, a **basic** structure for sentences is subject, verb, and object. Some sentences have more **complicated** structures.

You will encounter both basic and complicated **language structures** in the classroom materials you read. Being familiar with language structures will help you better understand the text.

••• CHECKLIST FOR LANGUAGE STRUCTURES

To improve your comprehension of language structures, do the following:

✓ Monitor your understanding.

- Ask yourself: Why do I not understand this sentence? Is it because I do not understand some of the words? Or is it because I do not understand the way the words are ordered in the sentence?

✓ Break down the sentence into its parts.

- In English, many sentences share this basic pattern: subject + verb + object.

  > The **subject** names who or what is doing the action.

  > The **verb** names the action or state of being.

  > The **object** answers questions such as Who?, What?, Where?, and When?

- Ask yourself: What is the action? Who or what is doing the action? What details do the other words provide?

✓ Confirm your understanding with a peer or teacher.

Please note that excerpts and passages in the StudySync® library and this workbook are intended as touchstones to generate interest in an author's work. The excerpts and passages do not substitute for the reading of entire texts, and StudySync® strongly recommends that students seek out and purchase the whole literary or informational work in order to experience it as the author intended. Links to online resellers are available in our digital library. In addition, complete works may be ordered through an authorized reseller by filling out and returning to StudySync® the order form enclosed in this workbook.

Reading & Writing Companion   **167**

⟳ YOUR TURN

Read each sentence below. Then, complete the chart by identifying the subject, verb, and object of each sentence.

Subject, Verb, and Object Options			
smartphones	reheated	I	pizza
order	Terry	sells	have
Kylie	ate	soup	We

Sentence	Subject	Verb	Object
For dinner, I ate a pepperoni pizza.			
Terry sells smartphones at a store on Central Street.			
Kylie reheated some of the soup from yesterday's lunch.			
We'll have an order of breadsticks.			

Skill:
Retelling and Summarizing

★ DEFINE

You can retell and summarize a text after reading to show your understanding. **Retelling** is telling a story again in your own words. **Summarizing** is giving a short explanation of the most important ideas in a text.

Keep your retelling or summary **concise**. Only include important information and key words from the text. By summarizing and retelling a text, you can improve your comprehension of the text's ideas.

••• CHECKLIST FOR RETELLING AND SUMMARIZING

In order to retell or summarize a text, note the following:

✓ Identify the main events of the text.

- Ask yourself: What happens in this text? What are the main events that happen at the beginning, the middle, and the end of the text?

✓ Identify the main ideas in a text.

- Ask yourself: What are the most important ideas in the text?

✓ Determine the answers to the six WH questions.

- Ask yourself: After reading this text, can I answer Who?, What?, Where?, When?, Why?, and How? questions?

↻ YOUR TURN

Reread the following excerpt from "Repeal the Stamp Act!" Then, sort the details into those that would help you write a summary and those that would not help.

---

from "Repeal the Stamp Act!"

There is also the matter of the reason this tax was levied. Revenue from this odious Act will support the British army in North America. Yet, the war against the French is over. Still the Crown insists on having a standing army upon our shores. In addition, this money for soldiers comes on top of the recent Quartering Act. That Act requires us to provide housing for soldiers, even giving them free rooms in our inns and on our private property. What more does the army want from us? Shall I remove the boots from my feet and hand them to the nearest soldier? Will they bleed us dry in the name of defense?

	Details
A	"Revenue from this odious Act will support the British army in North America."
B	"What more does the army want from us?"
C	"Shall I remove the boots from my feet and hand them to the nearest soldier?"
D	"Yet, the war against the French is over."
E	"Will they bleed us dry in the name of defense?"
F	"Still the Crown insists on having a standing army upon our shores."

Details That Help in a Summary	Details That Do Not Help in a Summary

Close Read

✏ WRITE

LITERARY ANALYSIS: "Repeal the Stamp Act!" is a letter of protest. How do the arguments in the letter help persuade readers to take the side of the writer? State your opinion in response to this question. Support your opinion with evidence from the text. Pay attention to and edit for subject-verb agreement.

Use the checklist below to guide you as you write.

☐ What arguments does the writer provide?

☐ What does the writer want the reader to think and do?

☐ What is your opinion? Do you think the writer is persuasive?

Use the sentence frames to organize and write your literary analysis.

The writer of the letter presents three main arguments against the Stamp Act. First, the act is _____

because there is no _____. Second, the act is _____

because the British already have _____. Finally, the act is enforced by courts without juries,

and these courts are far away from the colonists' _____.

The writer persuades readers that the Stamp Act is totally _____.

Any one of those reasons should have stopped the Stamp Act from being passed.

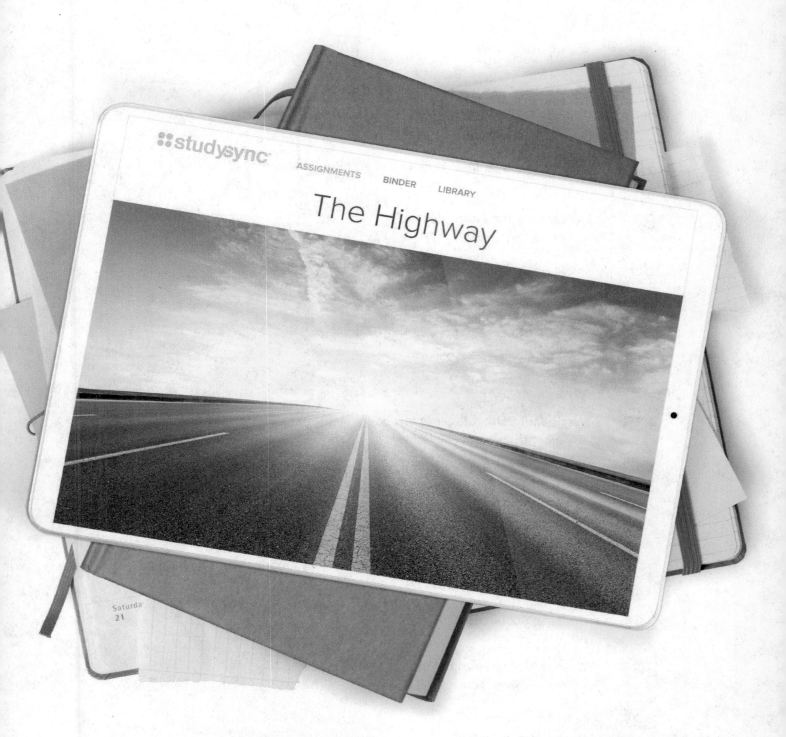

studysync

ASSIGNMENTS   BINDER   LIBRARY

The Highway

UNIT 2

The Highway

How do journeys influence perspective?

Genre Focus: **INFORMATIONAL**

Texts

Paired Readings

Extended Writing Project and Grammar

English Language Learner Resources

Unit 2: The Highway
How do journeys influence perspective?

MANAL AL-SHARIF

Saudi Arabian native Manal al-Sharif (b. 1979) is best known as a leader for women's rights, who came to fame after a video was posted online of her being detained for driving a car in her home country in 2011. A graduate of King Abdulaziz University, she studied computer science, and wrote a book, *Daring to Drive: A Saudi Woman's Awakening* which was published in 2017. *Foreign Policy* magazine named her as one of the Top 100 Global Thinkers of 2011, and *Time* magazine has since named her one of the world's most influential people.

MICHAEL ARNDT

American screenwriter Michael Arndt is best known for his Academy Award-winning screenplay *Little Miss Sunshine*, but he was also nominated for Best Adapted Screenplay for *Toy Story 3*, which made him the first screenwriter to be nominated for these awards for his first two scripts. He graduated from New York University and worked as a personal assistant to actor Matthew Broderick (*Ferris Bueller's Day Off, Glory, The Producers*) until he focused on writing full-time. Arndt wrote the original script for *Little Miss Sunshine* in just three days.

EMILY DICKINSON

Emily Dickinson (1830–1886) was born in Amherst, Massachusetts. Known for living in near total isolation from the outside world, her verse went unrecognized during her lifetime. After she died in 1886, forty volumes containing nearly 1,800 poems were found by her family, and published in a style that eliminated her now-trademark use of dashes. It wasn't until 1998 that her poems were published with full fidelity to their original style.

EDDY L. HARRIS

A native of St. Louis, Missouri, Eddy L. Harris (b. 1956) has been on the move since he was a teenager and first traveled across America by bus. He wrote his first book, a memoir, after he canoed the entire length of the Mississippi River. He graduated from Stanford University and works as a screenwriter and journalist in St. Louis, Missouri. About his nomadic life, he has said "it would perhaps be better to live and travel like the tortoise, who spends the 150 years of its life moving slowly, learning intimately every inch of ground it covers."

LYNDON B. JOHNSON

The 36th president of the United States, Lyndon Baines Johnson (1908–1973) took the office after President Kennedy was assassinated. Born in Stonewall, Texas, Johnson worked as a school teacher before joining the House of Representatives in 1937. He is best known for championing the expansion of civil rights and a "War on Poverty." He helped pass the Voting Rights Act, and also escalated US involvement in the Vietnam War. He did not seek re-election, left office in 1969, and died of a heart attack four years later at his ranch in Texas.

FLANNERY O'CONNOR

Flannery O'Connor (1925–1964) was born in Savannah, Georgia. She graduated from the Georgia State College for Women in three years, and in 1946 she was accepted into the Iowa Writers' Workshop. Known for her short stories, she published *A Good Man is Hard to Find* in 1955, and *Everything That Rises Must Converge* in 1965. O'Connor often wrote in the Southern Gothic style, and stated "anything that comes out of the South is going to be called grotesque by the Northern reader, unless it is grotesque, in which case it is going to be called realistic."

HENRY DAVID THOREAU

Henry David Thoreau (1817–1862) was born in Concord, Massachusetts. He is widely known for his work *Walden: or, Life in the Woods*, a memoir detailing his transcendental reflections on living a simple life in nature and being self-reliant. Of his time there, he wrote "I went to the woods because I wished to live deliberately." His essay "Civil Disobedience" inspired many key figures years later, including Mahatma Gandhi and Martin Luther King Jr. Thoreau was a lifelong abolitionist and a graduate of Harvard College.

MARK TWAIN

Born Samuel Langhorne Clemens (1835–1910) and raised in Hannibal, Missouri, the author is best known as Mark Twain. His childhood growing up along the Mississippi River inspired his most famous works including *The Adventures of Tom Sawyer* and *Adventures of Huckleberry Finn*. He dreamed of being a steamboat captain, and eventually piloted ships down the Mississippi, an experience that inspired his pen name. He was born under Halley's Comet in 1835, and predicted he'd die when it returned. He did, in 1910, one day after the comet's closest approach to Earth.

ISABEL WILKERSON

Pulitzer Prize–winning author Isabel Wilkerson (b. 1961) interviewed over 1,200 people over the course of fifteen years for her book *The Warmth of Other Suns*, a book that charts the course of three people searching for a better life after fleeing oppression and violence in the South. She was the first black woman to win the Pulitzer Prize for Journalism for her work in 1994 as the Chicago Bureau Chief of *The New York Times*. Toni Morrison called the *The Warmth of Other Suns*, a *New York Times* Best Seller, "profound, necessary, and a delight to read."

VICTOR H. GREEN

The Green Book, a guide for African Americans to travel safely through the Jim Crow South, was borne of Victor H. Green's (1892–1960) desire to allow black Americans to partake in a burgeoning car culture despite ongoing racial segregation and violence. To that effect, Green, a postal employee from Harlem, New York, created a publishing office and travel agency to publish his guide and book reservations at black-owned establishments. Published for the first time in 1936, roughly 15,000 copies a year were printed until 1966.

LITERARY FOCUS:
Transcendentalism and Romanticism

Introduction

This informational text provides readers with insight into the history and culture behind the Romantic and Transcendentalist movements, offering a portrait of the society and social climate that gave rise to some of the most well-respected authors of American literature. In a society increasingly dominated by industrialism, these literary and philosophical movements rebelliously celebrated nature and the individual. This text demonstrates how Romantic and Transcendentalist writers provided a strong, inspiring new literary foundation for an America that was attempting to show the world just who and what it was. Soon, Henry David Thoreau had breathed fresh life into the essay, and Walt Whitman pioneered a new form of poetry that would come to be the preferred form for great poets from Emily Dickinson to Nikki Giovanni.

"According to Emerson, the highest form of language was the language of nature."

1   When you think of the word **Romanticism**, what movies come to mind? *Titanic*, perhaps? *Love & Basketball*? *The Notebook* or *The Fault in Our Stars*? You wouldn't be wrong to think that Romanticism has a lot to do with emotion. But you might be surprised to learn that movies like *Star Wars: Rogue One*, Wes Anderson's *Moonrise Kingdom*, *Princess Mononoke*, and the independent film *Captain Fantastic* exemplify the qualities of "big R" Romanticism more than the "little r" romance movies that may have first come to mind. It's true that *Titanic* has some elements of Romanticism and romance, and the same goes for *Moonrise Kingdom*. So how can we differentiate Romanticism from romanticism?

Romanticism

2   "Big R" Romanticism—as opposed to "little r" romanticism—dealt with big emotions and ideas. Beginning in the late eighteenth century in Europe, Romanticism was a philosophical, artistic, and literary movement that developed partly as a reaction to the Enlightenment. Romantics prized individualism and rejected rapidly expanding **industrialism** in favor of a renewed reverence for nature. Romantic artists and poets often regarded the formalism—adherence to traditional structures and forms—of the Enlightenment as confining and artificial. European Romantic authors included Stendhal, Goethe, Lord Byron, Coleridge, Wordsworth, and Mary Shelley.

The Oxbow (The Connecticut River at Northampton) by Thomas Cole

NOTES

3 When Romantic ideals reached America in the early nineteenth century, the nation was caught up in a massive westward expansion and was simultaneously trying to define what it was to be American, both to itself and to the world. As American cities and towns grew, people had more time for philosophical and creative endeavors and began to write original works of fiction and poetry, as well as contemplative essays. Spanning from 1820 until the end of the Civil War in 1865, American Romanticism was highly concerned with the individual and this was reflected in the literature of the era. American Romantics placed a high value on nature, seeing it as something that brought one closer to one's true self. Renouncing blind obedience to the customs of the past, American artists and writers of the period embraced emotion, imagination, liberation, free expression, and a fascination with mysticism and the supernatural. American Romantic authors included Washington Irving, James Fenimore Cooper, Nathaniel Hawthorne, Herman Melville, Walt Whitman, and Edgar Allan Poe. American Romanticism made the world sit up and take notice of American literature.

Transcendentalism

4 **Transcendentalism** developed in the lates 1820s and 1830s and was influenced by American Romanticism and a religious movement known as Unitarianism. During the nineteenth century, New Englanders began moving away from the Puritanism of their colonial past and toward Unitarianism, which perceived God as a singular being and had an optimistic view of human nature. Ralph Waldo Emerson, who is now regarded as the father of Transcendentalism, was an ordained Unitarian minister, but eventually resigned because he came to feel that Unitarianism was too restrictive and did not sufficiently recognize what he characterized as "the universal soul," or the divine, within each person. He felt that a church or religious authority only served to impede one's direct personal connection to God, causing "the withdrawal of the soul."

5 In 1836, Emerson began a discussion group, along with three other disaffected Unitarian clergy members, that became known as the **Transcendental Club**. It was through this forum that Emerson and other Transcendentalists formulated and explored the ideas that they would later publish in books of essays, as well as the literary magazine *The Dial* (1840–1844). Transcendentalism held that there was a part of the self that transcended the physical senses and logic, was highly in tune with nature, and brought individuals a kind of direct, divine knowledge. Transcendentalism was marked by optimism, idealism, and intuition. Transcendentalists criticized materialism, which they viewed as a corrupting influence, and championed social reform. Other well-known Transcendentalists include Henry David Thoreau, who wrote *Walden; or, Life in the Woods*, and Margaret Fuller, who was a writer and early feminist.

6   Transcendentalism, despite being a relatively short-lived movement, had a definitive impact on American culture. Transcendentalist literature and philosophy influenced Walt Whitman, Emily Dickinson, and Frederick Douglass. Transcendentalist ideas about social improvement contributed to the Age of Reform (1830–1850) and Thoreau's essay "Civil Disobedience" informed the thinking of leaders such as Martin Luther King Jr.

Romanticism and Transcendentalism in Art

7   In Romanticism and Transcendentalism, creativity was highly esteemed. Painters used **symbolism** and **allegory** in their attempts to capture the essence of the sublime, or the essence of greatness. American Romantic painters from the Hudson River School looked to the vast and breathtaking American wilderness for inspiration and elevated landscape painting to the level of high art.

8   **Major Concepts**

- **Optimism and Individualism** — Romantics and Transcendentalists advocated individualism, but that didn't mean that they were selfish. They were also fiercely optimistic, and, for them, individualism and optimism went hand-in-hand. They believed that every individual possessed a natural inclination toward truth and spiritual enlightenment and that every person had the ability to rise above the material and emotional clutter of life in order to reflect on their lives and take individual action toward a greater good.

- **Kinship with Nature** — Both American Romantics and Transcendentalists believed that a close connection between humanity and nature brought humans closer to their true selves. This belief was complimented by a concern that the spread of industry not only threatened the natural world, but also isolated people from it. Furthermore, Transcendentalists felt that when individuals were detached from nature they also risked disconnection from the divine.

- **The Power of Darkness** — The Romantic fascination with emotion and the supernatural led to darker themes, as well. The Gothic and Horror genres took an interest in fear, madness, death, evil, and the destructive aspects of nature. The Dark Romantics, such as Nathaniel Hawthorne, Edgar Allan Poe, and Herman Melville, also contemplated sin, the nature of human fallibility, and the intrinsic challenges of social reform.

Frankenstein and his Creature

Style and Form

9 **Essays**

- Transcendentalism was more than a genre; it was a philosophy. Transcendentalists were critical thinkers who explored many of their ideas through essays, short pieces of writing that attempted to grapple with an idea, explain something, or argue a point.

- The essay "Nature" (1836) by Ralph Waldo Emerson was the first essay to expound on the ideals of Transcendentalism. In the essay, Emerson set out to address one of Transcendentalism's defining concepts: the individual's relationship to nature. Emerson's abundant natural imagery and deeply felt personal connection to nature infused the otherwise serious philosophical tone of the piece with beauty, color, and life.

- The primary subject of Henry David Thoreau's work was the natural world. Many of his essays and books were structured as a literal or metaphorical journey. Essays such as "A Winter Walk" or "A Walk to Wachusett" were structured as small travelogues based on walks Thoreau had taken. Others, such as "Autumn Tints," "Wild Apples," or "A Succession of Forest Trees," journeyed through the cycles of nature. In his writings, Thoreau made scientific observations about nature, but also used natural imagery metaphorically and poetically. His sentences tended to be long and digressive. Thoreau was also a passionate abolitionist. His persuasive essays on the subject, including "Civil Disobedience," are still influential today.

10 **Poet-Prophet**

- The idea of the poet-prophet during the American Romantic period was defined by Emerson in his 1844 essay, "The Poet." Emerson saw poets as spiritual visionaries and "liberating gods." The poet, he said, interpreted nature—the thing that brought an individual closest to the divine—for society. According to Emerson, the highest form of language was the language of nature, which incorporated symbols related to the natural world as well as *synecdoche*, or the use of a part to represent the whole or vice versa. Emerson felt that the American literary landscape lacked such a visionary and ended "The Poet" with an impassioned call for a uniquely American poet-prophet.

- In 1855, the first edition of *Leaves of Grass* was published and Walt Whitman became America's own poetic visionary. Whitman's personal beliefs most closely resembled Transcendentalism and he was well versed in the work of Emerson, but he also had a broad understanding of American and European religious traditions, language, and symbolism, which he used stylistically in his poetry. He employed traditional symbols such as the stars, moon, and earth, but also created his own symbology, which included lilacs, the calamus plant, and, of course, grass. Whitman's tone was exuberant and his diction, or word choice, is notable for its eccentricities; he used colloquial words, foreign words, technical words, and sometimes even made up his own words. Whitman thought poetry should be read aloud and he was particularly attentive to sound imagery. Whitman's poetry did not rhyme and did not fit into any formal category, it followed the free and energetic path of Whitman's own mind and emotions. Today we call this informal structure **free verse**.

Leaves of Grass by Walt Whitman

11 Free Verse

- It is not surprising that free-verse poetry rose to popularity during the American Romantic period when artists sought to reject the restrictive customs of the past in order to embrace liberation, individualism, imagination, intuition, and spiritual transcendence. Free verse is a non-metrical, non-rhyming form of poetry that tends to follow the natural cadence of speech. While a pattern of sound or rhythm may form within a free-verse poem, giving the poem its own unique structure, the poet does not plan or write the poem with any specific, preset poetic form in mind.

- Walt Whitman popularized the use of free verse, which has become one of the most frequently used forms of poetry in American literature and has been practiced, either on the whole or in part, by many American poets, including Emily Dickinson, Langston Hughes, Marianne Moore, Wallace Stevens, William Carlos Williams, Gwendolyn Brooks, Allen Ginsberg, Luis Omar Salinas, Pat Mora, and Nikki Giovanni, among many others.

12 Nature

- Romanticism and Transcendentalism are centered on a reverence for nature. The literature of these movements used abundant natural imagery and symbolism as well as sensory imagery, which endeavored to bring the sounds, sights, and feelings of nature to the reader. Nature not only served as a necessary counterbalance to the sweep of industrialization, urbanization, and materialism, but the Transcendentalists believed that nature, above all else, connected man to the divine within himself.

- The Dark Romantics used the weather, the tempestuous sea, nocturnal or menacing animals, and the frightening mysteries of the natural world in their imagery and settings. Poe's poem "The Raven" used the bird as a prophet of darkness, which drove the narrator to madness. Herman Melville's *Moby-Dick* takes place on a whaling ship in the lonely isolation of a vast seascape and the white whale is a complex symbol used to represent the nature of good and evil.

13 So where's the romance? American Romanticism and Transcendentalism are not about romance, per se, but they do have something to do with love—the love of truth, the love of beauty, and the love of nature. Like romantic love, Romanticism is characterized by optimism, idealism, and intuition. Romanticism and Transcendentalism, however, direct all of this love and optimism not toward another person, but toward the natural world and the divine within ourselves. The ideals of "big R" Romanticism, as well as Transcendentalism, are woven into the fabric of the American psyche. We can see their effects in movies about people who retreat to nature to become closer to themselves or reassess their life's purpose. We see these themes played out in stories about rugged individualists.

14 Which of your favorite books or stories incorporate ideas from the American Romantic period? Is there someone in your life who you think embodies some facet of American Romanticism or Transcendentalism? How do you disconnect from technology, the material world, and the distractions of everyday life?

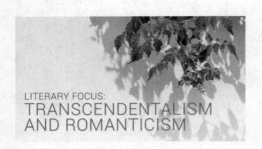

LITERARY FOCUS:
TRANSCENDENTALISM
AND ROMANTICISM

Literary Focus

Read "Literary Focus: Transcendentalism and Romanticism." After you read, complete the Think Questions below.

☁ THINK QUESTIONS

1. How are Romanticism and Transcendentalism connected? What do the two periods or philosophies have in common? Be sure to use evidence from the text to support your response.

2. Which major concepts of Romanticism and Transcendentalism continue to be influential or important in the culture and art of today? Give specific examples.

3. "Transcendentalism was more than a genre; it was a philosophy." Explain how the ideals of the Transcendentalist movement connected to the writing forms that gained popularity during that period. Use evidence from this informational piece to back up your explanation.

4. What is the meaning of **Romanticism** as it used in this text? Write your own definition of the word, along with a brief explanation of how you came to that conclusion.

5. The word **allegory** comes from the Greek word *allēgorein*, which means to speak figuratively. With this information in mind and using context from the text, write your best definition of *allegory*, along with any words or phrases that were helpful in determining its meaning. Finally, check a dictionary to confirm your understanding.

I never hear the word "Escape"

POETRY
Emily Dickinson
1860

Introduction

Emily Dickinson (1830–1886), one of the most influential voices of American poetry, was quieter in real life than she was on the page. She is known for keeping mostly to herself in her adult years, in which she rarely left her room and never stepped foot off of her family's Amherst, Massachusetts, estate. Her unconventional poetry, in many ways, mirrored her unconventional life. In this poem, Dickinson uses the meter of church hymns to create a work that goes beyond the personal "I" of the narrator and expands into the communal experience.

"I never hear the word 'Escape' Without a quicker blood"

NOTES

Emily Dickinson

1　I never hear the word **"Escape"**
2　Without a quicker blood,
3　A sudden **expectation** –
4　A flying **attitude**!

5　I never hear of prisons **broad**
6　By soldiers **battered** down,
7　But I tug childish at my bars
8　Only to fail again!

✏ **WRITE**

PERSONAL RESPONSE: What do you think the speaker of the poem means by the idea of "escape"? Think about a scenario when you wanted to "escape." How did your feelings compare to the speaker's? Include details from the poem and your own experiences in your response.

Adventures of Huckleberry Finn

FICTION
Mark Twain
1885

Introduction

Ernest Hemingway claimed that Mark Twain's *Adventures of Huckleberry Finn* is the one book from which all modern American literature springs. While capturing cultural changes of the times, Mark Twain (1835–1910) weaves a memorable tale as told by the spirited Huck. In Chapter 1, Huck considers settling

"We got six thousand dollars apiece— all gold. It was an awful sight of money when it was piled up."

> Note: The text you are about to read contains offensive language. Remember to be mindful of the thoughts and feelings of your peers as you read and discuss this text. Please consult your teacher for additional guidance and support.

CHAPTER I

Steamboat Race on the Mississippi by Weingartner's Lith

Skill: Language, Style, and Audience

The author's informal language and untraditional syntax include contractions, slang, simple words, and colloquialisms. The language helps shape Huck's youthful voice and creates a light, carefree style.

Skill: Summarizing

Huck Finn struggles with living a more traditional life in Widow Douglas's home but needing the freedom to live on his own.

1   You don't know about me without you have read a book by the name of Adventures of Tom Sawyer; but that ain't no matter. That book was made by Mr. Mark Twain, and he told the truth, mainly. There was things which he stretched, but mainly he told the truth. That is nothing. I never seen anybody but lied one time or another, without it was Aunt Polly, or the widow, or maybe Mary. Aunt Polly— Tom's Aunt Polly, she is—and Mary, and the Widow Douglas is all told about in that book, which is mostly a true book, with some stretchers, as I said before.

2   Now the way that the book winds up is this: Tom and me found the money that the robbers hid in the cave, and it made us rich. We got six thousand dollars apiece—all gold. It was an awful sight of money when it was piled up. Well, Judge Thatcher he took it and put it out at interest, and it fetched us a dollar a day apiece all the year round—more than a body could tell what to do with. The Widow Douglas she took me for her son, and allowed she would sivilize me; but it was rough living in the house all the time, considering how **dismal** regular and decent the widow was in all her ways; and so when I couldn't stand it no longer I lit out. I got into my old rags and my sugar-hogshead again, and was free and satisfied. But Tom Sawyer he hunted me up and said he was going to start a band of robbers, and I might join if I would go back to the widow and be respectable. So I went back.

3   The widow she cried over me, and called me a poor lost lamb, and she called me a lot of other names, too, but she never meant no harm by it. She put me

in them new clothes again, and I couldn't do nothing but sweat and sweat, and feel all cramped up. Well, then, the old thing **commenced** again. The widow rung a bell for supper, and you had to come to time. When you got to the table you couldn't go right to eating, but you had to wait for the widow to tuck down her head and **grumble** a little over the victuals, though there warn't really anything the matter with them,—that is, nothing only everything was cooked by itself. In a barrel of odds and ends it is different; things get mixed up, and the juice kind of swaps around, and the things go better.

4 After supper she got out her book and learned me about Moses and the Bulrushers,[1] and I was in a sweat to find out all about him; but by and by she let it out that Moses had been dead a **considerable** long time; so then I didn't care no more about him, because I don't take no stock in dead people.

5 Pretty soon I wanted to smoke, and asked the widow to let me. But she wouldn't. She said it was a mean practice and wasn't clean, and I must try to not do it any more. That is just the way with some people. They get down on a thing when they don't know nothing about it. Here she was a-bothering about Moses, which was no kin to her, and no use to anybody, being gone, you see, yet finding a power of fault with me for doing a thing that had some good in it. And she took snuff, too; of course that was all right, because she done it herself.

6 Her sister, Miss Watson, a tolerable slim old maid, with goggles on, had just come to live with her, and took a set at me now with a spelling-book. She worked me middling hard for about an hour, and then the widow made her ease up. I couldn't stood it much longer. Then for an hour it was deadly dull, and I was fidgety. Miss Watson would say, "Don't put your feet up there, Huckleberry;" and "Don't scrunch up like that, Huckleberry—set up straight;" and pretty soon she would say, "Don't gap and stretch like that, Huckleberry— why don't you try to behave?" Then she told me all about the bad place, and I said I wished I was there. She got mad then, but I didn't mean no harm. All I wanted was to go somewheres; all I wanted was a change, I warn't particular. She said it was wicked to say what I said; said she wouldn't say it for the whole world; she was going to live so as to go to the good place. Well, I couldn't see no advantage in going where she was going, so I made up my mind I wouldn't try for it. But I never said so, because it would only make trouble, and wouldn't do no good.

7 Now she had got a start, and she went on and told me all about the good place. She said all a body would have to do there was to go around all day long with a harp and sing, forever and ever. So I didn't think much of it. But I

Skill:
Summarizing

Huck Finn points out the hypocrisy of the Widow's ways.

---

1. **Moses and the Bulrushers** Huck's mispronunciation of *bulrushes*, the river plants among which the baby Moses was found floating in a basket

NOTES

never said so. I asked her if she **reckoned** Tom Sawyer would go there, and she said not by a considerable sight. I was glad about that, because I wanted him and me to be together.

8   Miss Watson she kept pecking at me, and it got tiresome and lonesome. By and by they fetched the n-----s in and had prayers, and then everybody was off to bed. I went up to my room with a piece of candle, and put it on the table. Then I set down in a chair by the window and tried to think of something cheerful, but it warn't no use. I felt so lonesome I most wished I was dead. The stars were shining, and the leaves rustled in the woods ever so mournful; and I heard an owl, away off, who-whooing about somebody that was dead, and a whippowill and a dog crying about somebody that was going to die; and the wind was trying to whisper something to me, and I couldn't make out what it was, and so it made the cold shivers run over me. Then away out in the woods I heard that kind of a sound that a ghost makes when it wants to tell about something that's on its mind and can't make itself understood, and so can't rest easy in its grave, and has to go about that way every night grieving. I got so down-hearted and scared I did wish I had some company. Pretty soon a spider went crawling up my shoulder, and I flipped it off and it lit in the candle; and before I could budge it was all shriveled up. I didn't need anybody to tell me that that was an awful bad sign and would fetch me some bad luck, so I was scared and most shook the clothes off of me. I got up and turned around in my tracks three times and crossed my breast every time; and then I tied up a little lock of my hair with a thread to keep witches away. But I hadn't no confidence. You do that when you've lost a horseshoe that you've found, instead of nailing it up over the door, but I hadn't ever heard anybody say it was any way to keep off bad luck when you'd killed a spider.

9   I set down again, a-shaking all over, and got out my pipe for a smoke; for the house was all as still as death now, and so the widow wouldn't know. Well, after a long time I heard the clock away off in the town go boom—boom—boom—twelve licks; and all still again—stiller than ever. Pretty soon I heard a twig snap down in the dark amongst the trees—something was a stirring. I set still and listened. Directly I could just barely hear a "me-yow! me-yow!" down there. That was good! Says I, "me-yow! me-yow!" as soft as I could, and then I put out the light and **scrambled** out of the window on to the shed. Then I slipped down to the ground and crawled in among the trees, and, sure enough, there was Tom Sawyer waiting for me.

First Read

Read *Adventures of Huckleberry Finn*. After you read, complete the Think Questions below.

 THINK QUESTIONS

1. How does Huck describe living with the Widow Douglas? What does Huck's view of the widow reveal about himself? Cite evidence from the text to support your response.

2. What is the conflict between Huck Finn and Miss Watson? How does this conflict reveal that the two characters do not fully understand each other? Cite evidence from the text to support your response.

3. In the eighth paragraph, how does Huck feel? How does Huck's description of the evening reflect his own mood? Cite evidence from the text to support your response.

4. Read the following dictionary entry:

   reckon
   reck•on \ ˈrekən \ verb

   1. to estimate
   2. to determine based on referencing
   3. to count or calculate
   4. to think or regard

   Decide which definition best matches **reckon** as it is used in *Adventures of Huckleberry Finn*. Write that definition of *reckon* here as well as the clues from the text that helped you determine the meaning.

5. Use context clues to determine the meaning of the word **scrambled**. Write your best definition here, along with the words and phrases that were most helpful in coming to your conclusion. Then, check a dictionary to confirm your understanding.

Skill:
Summarizing

Use the Checklist to analyze Summarizing in *Adventures of Huckleberry Finn*. Refer to the sample student annotations about Summarizing in the text.

••• CHECKLIST FOR SUMMARIZING

In order to determine how to write an objective summary of a text, consider the following:

✓ find details that answer the basic questions *who, what, where, when, why,* and *how*

✓ identify key details that support theme, plot, and other major story elements

✓ exclude from summaries minor details that don't contribute to the theme or plot

✓ exclude from summaries personal thoughts, judgments, or opinions to ensure that the summaries are objective

To provide an objective summary of a text, consider the following questions:

✓ What are the answers to the basic *who, what, where, when, why,* and *how* questions?

✓ Have I included major details that support story elements?

✓ Have I avoided including minor details that don't contribute to the theme or plot?

✓ Is my summary objective, or have I added my own thoughts, judgments, and personal opinions?

Skill:
Summarizing

Reread paragraphs 8 and 9 of *Adventures of Huckleberry Finn*. Then, using the Checklist on the previous page, answer the multiple-choice questions below.

⟳ YOUR TURN

1. Which statement provides the most objective summary of the information from paragraph 8?

   ○ A. Huck is a coward; he is afraid of everything.
   ○ B. Huck is afraid as he thinks about the darkness and loneliness of the night.
   ○ C. Huck is deeply superstitious, but his fears of darkness and loneliness are real.
   ○ D. Huck has a right to be afraid because the frontier was full of dangers.

2. Which statement provides the most objective summary of the information from paragraph 9?

   ○ A. Late at night, Huck likes to smoke behind the Widow's back.
   ○ B. After midnight, Huck's smoking is interrupted by Tom's meow signal.
   ○ C. Tom Sawyer signals Huck at the Widow Douglas's.
   ○ D. Huck tries to calm himself down after the spider scare.

Skill: Language, Style, and Audience

Use the Checklist to analyze Language, Style, and Audience in *Adventures of Huckleberry Finn*. Refer to the sample student annotations about Language, Style, and Audience in the text.

••• CHECKLIST FOR LANGUAGE, STYLE, AND AUDIENCE

In order to determine an author's style and possible intended audience, do the following:

✓ identify and define any unfamiliar words or phrases that have multiple meanings

✓ identify language that is particularly fresh, engaging, or beautiful

✓ analyze the surrounding words and phrases as well as the context in which the specific words are being used

✓ determine if syntax is simple or complex, traditional or nontraditional, and its effects on mood, voice, and tone

✓ determine style of language and connections to the voice(s) of characters

✓ determine audience—both intended and unintended—and possible reactions to the author's word choice and style, considering period of publication

✓ examine your reaction to the author's word choice and how the author's choice affected your reaction

To analyze the impact of a specific word choice on meaning, including words with multiple meanings or language that is particularly fresh, engaging, or beautiful, consider the following questions:

✓ How does the author's use of vernacular enhance or change what is being described?

✓ How does the author's use of vernacular relate to the syntax used in the text?

✓ How would a specific phrase or sentence sound different or shift in meaning if standard English were used?

✓ How would the text be different if another type of technique or standard English words were used?

✓ How does the author's choice of language help reveal a character's tone toward a situation or another character?

LANGUAGE,
STYLE, AND
AUDIENCE

sync•skills

Skill: Language, Style, and Audience

Reread paragraph 6 of *Adventures of Huckleberry Finn*. Then, using the Checklist on the previous page, answer the multiple-choice questions below.

↻ YOUR TURN

1. How does the author's use of specific word choices suggest Huck's attitude toward the sister?

   ○ A. Huck's use of "tolerable" to describe her weight suggests that he accepts her as she is.
   ○ B. His repetition of "All I wanted" indicates Huck's need for independence.
   ○ C. Phrases like "old maid" and "deadly dull" suggest that he dislikes her.
   ○ D. The phrase "never said so" reveals Huck's fear that he cannot meet her expectations.

2. What effect do Miss Watson's repetitious commands to Huck have on the reader?

   ○ A. Her "Don't" commands create sympathy for Huck.
   ○ B. They create compassion for Miss Watson who is tirelessly trying to help Huck.
   ○ C. The reader understands that Miss Watson is an unhappy person who does not understand children.
   ○ D. The reader understands Miss Watson's frustration and failure to help Huck.

3. What effect does the author's varied syntax have on the narrator's voice and style?

   ○ A. It helps create a formal, melancholy voice.
   ○ B. It helps shape the voice of a likable, well-educated young man.
   ○ C. It helps shape an uneven voice that is sometimes playful and sometimes defiant.
   ○ D. It helps create the voice of a young boy who is carefree.

Close Read

Reread *Adventures of Huckleberry Finn*. As you reread, complete the Skills Focus questions below. Then use your answers and annotations from the questions to help you complete the Write activity.

◎ SKILLS FOCUS

1. What details does the author include to help develop the setting of the novel? What influence does the setting have on characters and plot so far?

2. Summarize the tone Huck uses when he speaks to the Widow Douglas. Which word choices suggest this tone, and how?

3. What word choices does the author make towards the end of this chapter to create a specific feeling or mood? Describe this mood.

4. Find an example of syntax that is different from what you would use. How does the author use this syntax to better help the reader understand the characters or tone of the novel?

5. How do Huck's former experiences described at the beginning of this chapter influence his attitude towards living with the widow? Which style of life is he most suited for, and why?

✎ WRITE

LITERARY ANALYSIS: Summarize the main character's tone towards traditional society. Then, analyze how Mark Twain's choices regarding words and syntax help develop the main character's tone towards traditional society. Support your response with textual evidence.

The Negro Motorist Green Book

INFORMATIONAL TEXT
Victor H. Green
1937, 1950, 1954

Introduction

Victor Hugo Green (1892–1960), a postal carrier in the 1930s, wanted to use his knowledge of local businesses to help black travelers navigate safely in this era of racial discrimination. Relying on his own expertise, he first published *The Negro Motorist Green Book* in 1936. Although his first edition covered only the New York area, the success and depth of the guide book expanded as he was able to collect input from colleagues and readers themselves. Publication continued, as did segregation and discrimination, but the guide book was not deterred by business owners who refused to serve black patrons. Green and his publishing staff found ways to list welcoming accommodations across the country, sometimes relying on private homes. Ultimately, the publishers hoped for the day when the guide would be unnecessary but in the meantime were determined to empower African Americans to enjoy both safe and exciting travel. What follows are several excerpts from different editions that span many years of the guide's

"There will be a day sometime in the near future when this guide will not have to be published."

1937 Edition:

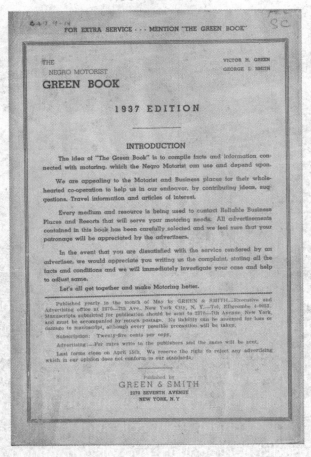

Transcript:

FOR EXTRA SERVICE. . .MENTION "THE GREEN BOOK"

THE NEGRO MOTORIST **GREEN BOOK**

VICTOR H. GREEN
GEORGE L. SMITH

1937 EDITION

INTRODUCTION

1 The idea of "The Green Book" is to compile facts and information connected with motoring, which the Negro Motorist can use and depend on.

2 We are appealing to the Motorist and Business places for their whole hearted co-operation to help us in our endeavor, by contributing ideas, suggestions, Travel information and articles of interest.

3 Every medium and **resource** is being used to contact Reliable Business Places and Resorts that will serve your motoring needs. All advertisements contained in this book has been carefully selected and we feel sure that your patronage will be appreciated by the advertisers.

4 In the event that you are dissatisfied by the service **rendered** by an advertiser, we would appreciate you writing us the complaint, stating all the facts and conditions and we will immediately investigate your case and help to adjust same.

5 Let's all get together and make Motoring better.

Published yearly in the month of May by GREEN & SMITH—Executive and Advertising office at 2370—7th Ave. New York City, N.Y.—Tel. EDgecombe 4-0053. Manuscripts submitted for publication should be sent to 2370—7th Avenue, New York, and must be accompanied by return postage. No liability can be assumed for loss or damage to manuscript, although every possible precaution will be taken.

Subscription: Twenty-five cents per copy.
Advertising: —For rates write to the publishers and the same will be sent.

Last forms close on April 15th. We reserve the right to reject any advertising which in our opinion does not conform to our standards.

Published by
GREEN & SMITH
2370 SEVENTH AVENUE
NEW YORK, N.Y

1950 Edition:

ESTABLISHED 1936

The *Negro Motorist* Green Book

INTRODUCTION

6 With the introduction of this travel guide in 1936, it has been our idea to give the Negro traveler information that will keep him from running into difficulties, embarrassments and to make his trips more enjoyable.

7 The Jewish press has long published information about places that are restricted and there are numerous publications that give the gentile whites all kinds of information. But during these long years of discrimination, before 1936 other guides have been published for the Negro, some are still published, but the majority have gone out of business for various reasons.

8 In 1936 the Green Book was only a local publication for Metropolitan New York, the response for copies was so great it was turned into a national issue in 1937 to cover the United States. This guide while lacking in many respects was accepted by thousands of travelers. Through the courtesy of the United States Travel Bureau of which Mr. Chas. A. R. McDowell was the collaborator on Negro Affairs, more valuable information was secured. With the two working together, this guide contained the best ideas for the Negro traveler. Year after year it grew until 1941 "PM"[1] one of New York's great white newspapers found out about it. Wrote an article about the guide and praised it highly. At the present time the guide contains 80 pages and lists numerous business places, including whites which cater to the Negro trade.

9 There are thousands of first class business places that we don't know about and can't list, which would be glad to serve the traveler, but it is hard to secure listings of these places since we can't secure enough agents to send us the information. Each year before we go to press the new information is included in the new edition.

10 When you are traveling please mention the Green Book, in order that they might know how you found their place of business, as they can see that you are strangers. If they haven't heard about this guide, ask them to get in touch with us so that we might list their place.

11 If this guide has proved useful to you on your trips, let us know. If not, tell us also as we appreciate your criticisms and ideas in the improvement of this guide from which you benefit.

12 There will be a day sometime in the near future when this guide will not have to be published. That is when we as a race will have equal opportunities and privileges in the United States. It will be a great day for us to suspend this

Skill:
Word Meaning

What does secure mean here? I know the term is used as a verb in this sentence. I know it refers to business listings. I need to find out more information.

---

1. **"PM"** a liberal New York daily newspaper from 1940–48 that published without advertisements in order to remain free from private business interests

publication for then we can go wherever we please, and without embarrassment. But until that time comes we shall continue to publish this information for your convenience each year.

The Green Book is the Guide to Every Traveler's Dream

The title says that this is every traveler's dream. Then there is a bold quote that mentions the pleasures of travel. This page is trying to persuade all people to travel. The idyllic photo of Denver helps achieve this purpose.

13   Sometime in everyone's life, there are dreams of traveling either to distant lands, or to see their own land. Some dream of travel by air, some by boat, railway or motor.

14   Today beautiful highways with conveniently situated stations, bus lines, air-lines and fast trains, make it possible to realize these dreams.

15   There is much to be seen and more to learn, of this our land which offers everything of beauty, wonder and history.

"MAKE TRAVELLING A REAL PLEASURE"

SEE —

16   Denver, Colorado — the scenic "City of Churches." Partially encircled by the beautiful and dramatic Rocky Mountains, Mt. Evans to the west; Longs Peak and Rocky Mountain National Park to the north; while to the south, Pikes Peak holds its snow-capped crest above the clouds. The Capitol Building dominates the city and the Valley of Platte. From the tower, beneath a golden dome, visitors may view the panorama of a great city whose parks stretch into the distance for miles. Mesa Verde National Park, Denver's state museum, facing the state house, has one of the most complete collections of artifacts of Pueblo culture in the nation. The Indian collection is exhibited mainly in the

Central room, depicting Indian life in minute detail. The Park of the Red Rocks, an amphitheatre, seating 10,000, is one of Denver's most outstanding mountain parks. Another interesting and picturesque spot is the old Mining Camp of Central City, famous for its annual Play Festival, held three weeks each summer in its historic old opera house. (Central City was the center of what was once declared the "richest square mile on earth.")

17 Visitors from everywhere make use of the scenic trails and highways leading from Denver into the surrounding regions of unsurpassed scenery and recreation.

18 Colorado's "mile-high city" extends the "Arms of Welcome" to all visitors.

[Photo of Denver's Civic Center building surrounded by sprawling lawns and trees]

LOOKING ACROSS DENVER'S FAMOUS CIVIC CENTER, WITH THE CITY HALL IN THE BACKGROUND. IN THE DISTANCE IS THE CONTINENTAL DIVIDE OF THE ROCKY MOUNTAINS, WITH MT. EVANS, 14,260 FEET, THE SUMMIT OF WHICH IS REACHED BY THE HIGHEST AUTOMOBILE ROAD ON THE CONTINENT, DOMINATING THE SCENE.

BOSTON —

19 The city that offers so much of interest to those who visit for here you find history preserved in the natural settings and surroundings. Its Beacon Hill, with its cobblestoned, aristocratic Lonisburg Square, its famous State House, and its Charles Street, where the antique shops can be found —and there are the colorful Public Gardens with their perennial "Swan Boats"—and the Christian Science "Mother Church."

20 No trip to Boston would be complete until the picturesque T. Wharf is visited, with its **quaint** artists' studios and the sea food restaurants that overlook the busy harbor and colorful fishing craft.

21 Up-town Boston boasts the beautiful Fenway with its Rose Gardens and the world-renowned Boston museum. One of the foremost cities of America touching Boston proper is Cambridge, the seat of the famous Institute of Technology and Harvard University, with their numerous libraries and museums. Here also are the famous edifices of Radcliffe College, Christ Church, Mt. Auburn — "The Cemetery of Poets" — containing the graves of Henry Wadsworth Longfellow, Oliver Wendell Holmes, Philips Brooks and Mary Baker Eddy.

22 Other places of interest touching Boston are Lexington, Concord — famous for the historic ride of Paul Revere and the Minute Men. The "First Town of America" — Plymouth, where the famous Plymouth Rock can be seen. Duxberg, where the statue of Miles Standish stands atop Captains' Hill, and the house where John Alden took Priscilla as his bride. Gloucester is the true New England fishing village, with its traditional fishing nets hanging over the wharves, and where is the bronze statue dedicated to "those who go down to the sea in ships."

[Photo of the statue of Paul Revere on horseback]

STATUE OF PAUL REVERE

[Photo of Boston's State House building]

STATE HOUSE

Skill:
Media

This page shows a glamorous place and travelers enjoying it. I think the publisher was trying to show how enjoyable traveling can be. The descriptive text and appealing images of interesting places make people want to go there.

23 These little villages and towns can be reached conveniently by bus or motor. A few days spent covering these areas should be time well spent and most enlightening.

[Photo of a row of homes on Beacon Street]

GRILL WORK ON BEACON STREET COR. OF JOY, OPP. BOSTON COMMON. FORMER HOME OF FRANCIS PARKMAN WHO FINANCED BUILDING OF COMMON.

NIAGARA FALLS —

24 New York State's greatest natural attraction for honeymooning couples and other visitors, offers also the great American and Horseshoe Falls, the upper and lower Rapids, the Whirlpool, the Great Gorge and Honeymoon Bridge.

25 Fort Niagara, built by the French to prevent the control of the "gateway to the west" by the English, is open to visitors. **Adjacent** to the great Falls is the city of Niagara Falls, center of the world's electro-chemical and electro-metallurgical industries. The city has fine recreational facilities. Nearest cities —Buffalo and Chautauqa[2] [sic], which is famous for its symphony concerts and cultural movements and summer school.

[Photo of a man looking up at Niagara Falls from a boat at the bottom]

2. **Chautauqua** a small town in New York, most famous for The Chautauqua Institution—a non-profit summer resort that hosts intellectual and educational activities and artistic forums

**NIAGARA FALLS
AS VIEWED FROM BOAT**

[Photo of a man and woman viewing Niagara Falls from a set of steps]

NIAGARA FALLS

Studebaker Cars

26 Studebaker,[3] the car that set the post-war styling pace for the automobile industry, has done it again.

27 Details of the company's line of 1950 model passenger cars were disclosed today by H.S. Vance, chairman of the board and president, with a prediction that this latest Studebaker will be acclaimed the most distinctive looking car on the road.

28 In these new cars the company's designers, Raymond Loewy[4] Associates, have achieved an automotive style pattern as revolutionary today as were the first Studebakers of postwar design three years ago. A complete change in frontal appearance and fender treatment gives the 1950 models sleek, new lines which make them appear in motion even when they're standing still.

29 Both ride and handling ease have been considerably bettered by engineering innovations complementing the use of an improved self-stabilizing coil spring front suspension.

---

3. **Studebaker** Family-owned wagon business founded in 1852 that moved into the automotive business in 1902, but eventually closed as it couldn't compete with the massive production of Ford and General Motors
4. **Raymond Loewy** French American industrial designer responsible for some of the most iconic American products and machines, he designed the most memorable models of Studebaker cars before the company's collapse

30 The front of the 1950 Studebaker is particularly striking. It embodies an airplane fuselage-type hood, flanked by air-foil front fenders and set off by a chrome "spinner." In addition to providing an ornamental touch, the "spinner" augments four frontal openings which direct air to the engine for maximum cooling. The largest of these air passages consists of two oval-shaped honeycomb grille scoops located below the two smaller air channels which flank the "spinner." Chrome moldings over these small twin channels contribute to the unusual decorative effect.

[Photo of a woman smiling and waving while standing next to a 1950 Studebaker car]

FRONT END DESIGN OF THE NEW 1950 STUDEBAKER MODELS IS PARTICULARLY STRIKING. THE "SPINNER," IN ADDITION TO PROVIDING A HANDSOME ORNAMENTAL TOUCH, AUGUMENTS [sic] FOUR FRONTAL OPENINGS WHICH DIRECT AIR TO THE ENGINE. THE LARGEST OF THESE AIR PASSAGES CONSISTS OF TWO OVAL-SHAPED HONEYCOMB GRILLE SCOOPS LOCATED BELOW TWO SMALLER AIR CHANNELS WHICH FLANK THE "SPINNER."

31 In harmony with a styling that expresses power, speed and sleekness are the heavy wrap-around bumpers. In front they are held by supports enclosed within tubular housings which are painted to match the automobile.

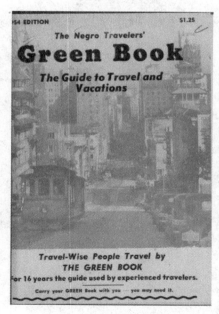

The Negro Travelers'
Green Book
The Guide to Travel and Vacations

**For 16 years the guide used by experienced travelers.
Carry your GREEN Book with you — you may need it.**

A Chat With The Editor

32   Traveling is one of the large industries of this era. Millions of people hit the road as soon as the warm weather sets in. They want to get away from their old surroundings: to see—to learn how people live—to meet old and new friends.

33   In this era of the automobile, trains, buses, boats and fast flying air liners, we have an assortment of transportation which will take one to any place that they might wish to go. With all of these transportation facilities at hand, modern travel has brought thousands of people out of their homes to view the wonders of the world.

34   Thousands and thousands of dollars are spent each year in the various modes of transportation. Money spent like this brings added revenue to trades people throughout the country.

35   The white traveler for years has had no difficulty in getting accomodations [sic], but with the Negro it has been different. He before the advent of Negro Travel Guides has had to depend on word of mouth and then sometimes **accommodations** weren't available. But now a days things are different—he has his own travel guide, that he can depend on for all the information that he wants and with a selection. Hence these guides have made traveling more popular and without running into embarrassing situations.

36 Since 1936, THE GREEN BOOK has been published yearly. A few years after its publication, THE GREEN BOOK was recognized as the official Negro Travel Guide by the United States Travel Bureau, a part of the Department of Commerce, which bureau has been closed, due to the lack of funds. By being such an important piece of literature, white business has also recognized its value and it is now in use by the Esso Standard Oil Co.,[5] The American Automobile Assn. and its affiliate automobile clubs throughout the country, other automobile clubs, air lines, travel bureaus, travelers aid, libraries and thousands of subscribers.

37 Hence we have filled one of our life's ambitions, to give the Negro a travel guide that will be of service to him, by this method we have established ourselves in the minds of the traveling public. THE GREEN BOOK is known from coast to coast as the source of information for travel and vacations.

Victor H. Green,
Editor & Publisher

Skill: Informational
Text Elements

Green explains the developments since the first publication and uses examples to show how far the guidebook has come. He then connects that to having filled his life ambition. This makes me realize that it had a great impact.

---

5. **Esso Standard Oil Co.** Now ExxonMobile, Esso was a huge supporter of *The Negro Motorist Green Book*, distributing the "Green Book" at gas stations and African American-owned franchises.

First Read

Read *The Negro Motorist Green Book*. After you read, complete the Think Questions below.

☁ THINK QUESTIONS

1. According to the introduction to the 1937 Edition, what is the purpose of *The Negro Motorist Green Book*? What kind of information can the reader expect the guide to offer? Use evidence from the text to support your response.

2. Why might the information provided about Studebaker automobiles have been important to readers? Cite evidence from the text that supports your response.

3. What does this guide book tell you about the people that put it together? Explain, citing evidence from the text to support your inferences.

4. Read the following dictionary entry:

   render

   ren•der \ 'ren-dər

   verb

   1. to represent, depict, or describe in words
   2. to cause to become
   3. to give or provide

   noun

   1. a protective coating of plaster applied to an outdoor surface

Decide which definition best matches **render** as it is used in *The Negro Motorist Green Book*. Write that definition here, and indicate which clues from the text helped you determine its meaning.

5. Read the following dictionary entry:

   accommodation

   ac·com·mo·da·tion \ ə-'kä-mə-'dā-shən \ *noun*

   1. an arrangement or understanding
   2. the process of adjusting or adapting to something
   3. a room or building in which one may live

Decide which definition best matches the word **accommodation** as it is used in *The Negro Motorist Green Book*. Write that definition here along with any context clues from the text that helped you arrive at your conclusion.

Skill: Informational Text Elements

Use the Checklist to analyze Informational Text Elements in *The Negro Motorist Green Book*. Refer to the sample student annotations about Informational Text Elements in the text.

••• CHECKLIST FOR INFORMATIONAL TEXT ELEMENTS

In order to identify a complex set of ideas or sequence of events, note the following:

- ✓ key details in the text that provide information about individuals, events, and ideas

- ✓ interactions between specific individuals, ideas, or events

- ✓ important developments of ideas over the course of the text

- ✓ transition words and phrases that signal interactions between individuals, events, and ideas, such as *because, as a consequence,* or *as a result*

- ✓ similarities and differences of types of information in a text

- ✓ visual text elements such as photos, graphs, or charts, that support ideas in the text or that enhance the reader's understanding

To analyze a complex set of ideas or sequence of events and to explain how specific individuals, ideas, or events interact and develop over the course of the text, consider the following questions:

- ✓ How does the author present the information as a sequence of events?

- ✓ How does the order in which ideas or events are presented affect the connections between them?

- ✓ How do specific individuals, ideas, or events interact and develop over the course of the text?

- ✓ What other features, if any, help readers to analyze the events, ideas, or individuals in the text?

Skill: Informational Text Elements

sync•skills

Reread *The Negro Motorist Green Book*. Then, using the Checklist on the previous page, answer the multiple-choice questions below.

↻ YOUR TURN

1. The guidebook provides multiple pieces of background information about Boston. Which sequence of ideas below represents the progression of information in the passage about Boston?

    ○ A. Boston is an interesting city; Cambridge is one of the most famous cities and is where many colleges, libraries, and museums are; Boston is famous for the ride of Paul Revere; the cities of Plymouth, Duxberg, and Gloucester, are places that share the history and traditions of Boston.

    ○ B. The natural surroundings of the city have preserved its history; The beautiful harbor offers restaurants and fishing; Cambridge is one of the most famous cities and is where many colleges, libraries, and museums are located; The cities of Plymouth, Duxberg, and Gloucester, are places that share the history and traditions of Boston.

    ○ C. The city offers many interesting things to do; The beautiful harbor offers restaurants and fishing; Harvard and other colleges are in Boston; Boston is famous for the ride of Paul Revere.

    ○ D. The natural surroundings of the city have preserved its history; T. Wharf is a great place to visit; Cambridge is one of the most famous cities and is where many colleges, libraries, and museums are located; Boston is famous for the ride of Paul Revere.

2. Which clause or phrase from the passage above indicates a transition between different pieces of information about Boston?

    ○ A. "No trip to Boston would be complete until the picturesque T. Wharf is visited"

    ○ B. "and the house where John Alden took Priscilla as his bride"

    ○ C. "Other places of interest touching Boston are Lexington, Concord"

    ○ D. "A few days spent covering these areas should be time well spent and most enlightening."

3. What features of this passage best help the reader connect to real people, places, and ideas?

○ A. The clear, sequential presentation of Boston's history explains to the reader why Boston would be a great place to visit.

○ B. The clear, sequential presentation of important key details helps the reader to better understand Boston.

○ C. The clear, sequential presentation of important key details about the city, its people, and its history helps the reader better understand why Boston would be a great place to visit.

○ D. The chronological presentation of historic events helps readers visualize how Boston is today.

Skill:
Media

Use the Checklist to analyze Media in *The Negro Motorist Green Book*. Refer to the sample student annotations about Media in the text.

••• CHECKLIST FOR MEDIA

In order to determine how to integrate and evaluate multiple sources of information presented in different media or formats, note the following:

- ✓ the key elements in each source of information

- ✓ the various elements of a particular medium and how the parts are put together

- ✓ how each medium or format, such as visual or quantitative, presents the sources of information

- ✓ what information is included or excluded in each media presentation

- ✓ how different sources of media enhance the reader's understanding of an idea or argument

- ✓ the audience of each media presentation and the author's purpose

- ✓ the reliability and credibility of each presentation

To integrate and evaluate multiple sources of information presented in different media or formats as well as in words in order to address a question or solve a problem, consider the following questions:

- ✓ How is each media presentation reliable or credible?

- ✓ How can you use each media presentation?

- ✓ How can you integrate multiple sources of information presented in different media or formats to address a question or solve a problem?

Skill:
Media

Reread paragraphs 26–30 of *The Negro Motorist Green Book*. Then, using the Checklist on the previous page, answer the multiple-choice questions below.

🔄 YOUR TURN

1. Based on the title, information, and image on this page, what is most likely the purpose of including this page in the guidebook?

    - ○ A. The author wanted to share the history of Studebaker cars with his audience.
    - ○ B. This is most likely an advertisement intended to convince travelers to purchase Studebaker Cars.
    - ○ C. The author wanted to highlight Studebaker cars since it is a corporation that was friendly to African Americans.
    - ○ D. This is most likely intended to educate readers about the importance of buying a reliable car to avoid hassles on the road.

2. How does the photo included on this page support the purpose you identified in Question 1?

    - ○ A. The photo shows an older model of the car so that readers can compare it to the newest version.
    - ○ B. The photo helps readers understand what to look for in a new car.
    - ○ C. The photo shows that the maker of Studebaker cars is friendly to African Americans.
    - ○ D. The photo shows a happy and carefree looking woman, which would have helped convince readers to purchase this car.

Skill:
Word Meaning

Use the Checklist to analyze Word Meaning in *The Negro Motorist Green Book*. Refer to the sample student annotations about Word Meaning in the text.

••• CHECKLIST FOR WORD MEANING

In order to find the pronunciation of a word or to determine or clarify its precise meaning, do the following:

- ✓ determine the word's part of speech

- ✓ use context clues to make an inferred meaning of the word or phrase

- ✓ consult a dictionary to verify your preliminary determination of the meaning of a word or phrase

- ✓ read all definitions, and decide which definition makes sense within the context of the text

In order to determine or to clarify a word's part of speech, do the following:

- ✓ determine what the word is describing

- ✓ identify how the word is being used in the phrase or sentence

In order to determine the etymology of a word, or its origin or standard usage, do the following:

- ✓ use reference materials, such as a dictionary, to determine the word's origin and history

- ✓ consider how the historical context of the word clarifies its usage

To determine or to clarify the etymology or standard usage of a word, considering the following questions:

- ✓ How formal or informal is this word?

- ✓ What is the word describing? What inferred meanings can I make?

- ✓ In what context is the word being used?

- ✓ Is this slang? An example of vernacular? In what other contexts might this word be used?

Skill:
Word Meaning

Reread paragraph 16 of *The Negro Motorist Green Book*. Then, using the Checklist on the previous page, answer the multiple-choice questions below.

YOUR TURN

From *The Negro Motorist Green Book* by Victor H. Green

Mesa Verde National Park, Denver's state museum, facing the state house, has one of the most complete collections of artifacts of Pueblo culture in the nation. The Indian collection is exhibited mainly in the Central room, depicting Indian life in **minute** detail.

minute /mī-'nüt/ *adjective*
1. extremely small
2. too small to be significant
3. careful and precise

1. Which of the following parts of the dictionary entry provides the pronunciation of the word?

   ○ A. **minute**   C. adjective
   ○ B. /mī-'nut/   D. 1. extremely small

2. This question has two parts. First, answer Part A. Then, answer Part B.

Part A: Which definition best fits the way the word *minute* is used in paragraph 16?

   ○ A. Definition 1   C. Definition 3
   ○ B. Definition 2   D. None of the above

Part B: Which of the following phrases provides context that best explains the meaning of *minute* as identified in Part A?

   ○ A. "facing the state house"   C. "in the Central room"
   ○ B. "one of the most complete collections"   D. "artifacts of Pueblo culture"

Close Read

Reread *The Negro Motorist Green Book*. As you reread, complete the Skills Focus questions below. Then use your answers and annotations from the questions to help you complete the Write activity.

◎ SKILLS FOCUS

1. Reread the introduction to the 1950 edition of *The Negro Motorist Green Book,* and look at the image of the cover of the book. Then, analyze how effectively the two modes work together to convey the purpose of the guide. Cite evidence to support your answer.

2. Reread the passage about visiting Denver, and evaluate how effectively the photograph helps support the information in the passage. Cite evidence to support your answer.

3. Identify examples of where the author uses headings in the text. What purpose does the author's use of headings serve in the text? How do the headings serve the author's purpose?

4. Look up the meaning of the word **compile,** and determine which meaning from the dictionary is intended in paragraph 1 of the text. Highlight contextual evidence to support your choice, and explain how you chose the correct definition.

5. How did *The Negro Motorist Green Book* change the experience of traveling for African Americans? Cite evidence to support your answer.

✎ WRITE

EXPLANATORY: How do the media features of *The Negro Motorist Green Book* along with the text elements of the book create a profound new meaning about the relationship between travel and identity? Analyze the effect of viewing the images alongside reading the book, using textual evidence and original commentary to support your response.

Walden

ARGUMENTATIVE TEXT
Henry David Thoreau
1854

Introduction

studysync tv

Henry David Thoreau (1817–1862) was a prominent transcendentalist writer and philosopher from the 19th century. He spent two years in solitude on Walden Pond to escape the chaos and distractions of civilization and his busy life. There, Thoreau observed nature and called himself an "inspector of snow-storms and rainstorms." Thoreau's goal was to live simply and self-sufficiently. In this excerpt from the second chapter of *Walden*, Thoreau explains "Where I Lived and What I Lived For." This text is accompanied by the 1849 oil-on-canvas painting *Kindred Spirits* by the New York artist Asher B. Durand.

"Why should we live with such hurry and waste of life?"

Kindred Spirits by Asher B. Durand, 1849

1   I went to the woods because I wished to live deliberately, to front only the essential facts of life, and see if I could not learn what it had to teach, and not, when I came to die, discover that I had not lived. I did not wish to live what was not life, living is so dear; nor did I wish to practise resignation, unless it was quite necessary. I wanted to live deep and suck out all the marrow of life, to live so sturdily and Spartan-like[1] as to put to rout all that was not life, to cut a broad swath and shave close, to drive life into a corner, and reduce it to its lowest terms, and, if it proved to be mean, why then to get the whole and genuine meanness of it, and publish its meanness to the world; or if it were sublime, to know it by experience, and be able to give a true account of it in my next **excursion**. For most men, it appears to me, are in a strange uncertainty about it, whether it is of the devil or of God, and have *somewhat hastily* concluded that it is the chief end of man here to "glorify God and enjoy him forever."

1. **Spartan-like** uncaring toward comfort or luxury, as exemplified by ancient Sparta

2   Still we live meanly, like ants; though the fable tells us that we were long ago changed into men; like pygmies² we fight with cranes; it is error upon error, and clout upon clout, and our best virtue has for its occasion a superfluous and **evitable** wretchedness. Our life is frittered away by detail. An honest man has hardly need to count more than his ten fingers, or in extreme cases he may add his ten toes, and lump the rest. Simplicity, simplicity, simplicity! I say, let your affairs be as two or three, and not a hundred or a thousand; instead of a million count half a dozen, and keep your accounts on your thumb-nail. In the midst of this chopping sea of civilized life, such are the clouds and storms and quicksands and thousand-and-one items to be allowed for, that a man has to live, if he would not **founder** and go to the bottom and not make his port at all, by dead reckoning, and he must be a great calculator indeed who succeeds. Simplify, simplify. Instead of three meals a day, if it be necessary eat but one; instead of a hundred dishes, five; and reduce other things in proportion. Our life is like a German Confederacy, made up of petty states, with its boundary forever fluctuating, so that even a German cannot tell you how it is bounded at any moment. The nation itself, with all its so-called internal improvements, which, by the way are all external and superficial, is just such an unwieldy and overgrown establishment, cluttered with furniture and tripped up by its own traps, ruined by luxury and heedless expense, by want of calculation and a worthy aim, as the million households in the land; and the only cure for it, as for them, is in a rigid economy, a stern and more than Spartan simplicity of life and elevation of purpose. It lives too fast. Men think that it is essential that the Nation have commerce, and export ice, and talk through a telegraph, and ride thirty miles an hour, without a doubt, whether they do or not; but whether we should live like baboons or like men, is a little uncertain. If we do not get out sleepers, and forge rails, and devote days and nights to the work, but go to tinkering upon our lives to improve them, who will build railroads? And if railroads are not built, how shall we get to heaven in season? But if we stay at home and mind our business, who will want railroads? We do not ride on the railroad; it rides upon us. Did you ever think what those sleepers are that underlie the railroad? Each one is a man, an Irishman, or a Yankee man. The rails are laid on them, and they are covered with sand, and the cars run smoothly over them. They are sound sleepers, I assure you. And every few years a new lot is laid down and run over; so that, if some have the pleasure of riding on a rail, others have the misfortune to be ridden upon. And when they run over a man that is walking in his sleep, a supernumerary sleeper in the wrong position, and wake him up, they suddenly stop the cars, and make a hue and cry about it, as if this were an exception. I am glad to know that it takes a gang of men for every five miles to keep the sleepers down and level in their beds as it is, for this is a sign that they may sometime get up again.

---

2. **pygmies** referring to tribal ethnic groups whose average height is especially short

NOTES

Carnegie Steel Company, 'Lucy' Furnace, Pittsburgh, Pennsylvania, USA, circa 1910

3   Why should we live with such hurry and waste of life? We are determined to be starved before we are hungry. Men say that a stitch in time saves nine, and so they take a thousand stitches today to save nine tomorrow. As for work, we haven't any of any **consequence**. We have the Saint Vitus' dance,[3] and cannot possibly keep our heads still. If I should only give a few pulls at the parish bell-rope, as for a fire, that is, without setting the bell, there is hardly a man on his farm in the outskirts of Concord, notwithstanding that press of engagements which was his excuse so many times this morning, nor a boy, nor a woman, I might almost say, but would forsake all and follow that sound, not mainly to save property from the flames, but, if we will confess the truth, much more to see it burn, since burn it must, and we, be it known, did not set it on fire—or to see it put out, and have a hand in it, if that is done as handsomely; yes, even if it were the parish church itself. Hardly a man takes a half-hour's nap after dinner, but when he wakes he holds up his head and asks, "What's the news?" as if the rest of mankind had stood his sentinels. Some give directions to be waked every half-hour, doubtless for no other purpose; and then, to pay for it, they tell what they have dreamed. After a night's sleep the news is as indispensable as the breakfast. "Pray tell me anything new that has happened to a man anywhere on this globe"—and he reads it over his coffee and rolls, that a man has had his eyes gouged out this morning on the Wachito River; never dreaming the while that he lives in the dark unfathomed mammoth cave of this world, and has but the **rudiment** of an eye himself.

✏ WRITE

PERSONAL RESPONSE: Thoreau writes that "I went into the woods because I wished to live deliberately." He then goes on to describe what living deliberately means to him—a life away from society and the establishment. After reading this excerpt, do you agree or disagree with his philosophy? Using evidence from the text, as well as your own experiences, write a personal essay in which you explain how you "live deliberately."

---

3. **Saint Vitus' dance**   layman's term for Sydenham's chorea, a disorder marked by uncontrolled movements in the head, face, and limbs

Mississippi Solo: A River Quest

INFORMATIONAL TEXT
Eddy L. Harris
1988

Introduction

Eddy L. Harris (b. 1956) is a filmmaker and an author, but first and foremost a traveler. Most of Harris's books have been inspired by extended stays in places that fascinated him. This excerpt comes from his memoir *Mississippi Solo: A River Quest* which chronicles his solo trip down the length of the Mississippi River in a canoe. Harris embarked on the journey armed with little camping or canoeing experience but filled with a lifetime of intrigue about the river itself. This particular excerpt gives the reader background about why Harris decided to begin his adventure despite protests from virtually everyone he knew.

"I decided to canoe down the Mississippi River and to find out what I was made of."

1.

1   The Mississippi River is laden with the burdens of a nation. Wide at St. Louis where I grew up, the river in my memory flows brown and heavy and slow, seemingly lazy but always busy with barges and tugs, always working—like my father—always traveling, always awesome and intimidating. I have watched this river since I was small, too young to realize that the burdens the Mississippi carries are more than barges loaded with grain and coal, that the river carries as well sins and salvation, dreams and adventure and destiny. As a child I feared this river and respected it more than I feared God. As an adult now I fear it even more.

2   I used to have nightmares filled with screams whenever I knew my family planned some excursion across the river and I'd have to go along. That old Veteran's Bridge seemed so weak and rickety. My imagination constructed a **dilapidated** and shaky span of old wooden slats, rotted and narrow and weak with no concrete support anywhere. The iron girders that held the poor thing up were ancient and rusty, orange and bumpy with oxidation where they should have been shiny and black. The bridge wavered in the wind and was ready to collapse as the car with my family in it approached, and then we would plunge through the air after crashing the brittle wooden guardrail and we'd dive toward the river. Everyone screamed at me. I held my ears every time and waited for the splash. It never came. I always awoke, always lived to dream the dream again and again, not only when asleep but even as we crossed the river.

3   The river was full of giant catfish and alligators, ice floes and trees that the often enraged and monster-like river had ripped from the shores along its path.

4   The Mississippi. Mighty, muddy, dangerous, rebellious, and yet a strong, fathering kind of river. The river captured my imagination when I was young and has never let go. Since I can remember I have wanted to be somehow a part of the river as much as I wanted to be a hero, strong and brave and relentless like the river, looming so large in the life and world around me that

I could not be ignored or forgotten. I used to sit on the levee and watch the murkiness lumber down to the sea and I'd dream of the cities and towns the river had passed, the farms and fields and bridges, the magic in the debris picked up here, deposited there, and the other rivers along the way: Ohio, Illinois, Arkansas, taking all on a beautiful voyage to the Gulf of Mexico and beyond. I wanted to go too. I wanted to dip my toes in the water to test, then all of me, hanging onto whatever and floating along with it, letting the river drop me off wherever and pick me up later and take me on again. I didn't care where I just wanted to go. But my parents wouldn't let me.

5   But now I am a man and my parents can't stop me. I stand at that magical age, thirty, when a man stops to take stock of his life and he reflects on all the young-man's dreams that won't come true. No climbs up Everest, no try-out with the Yankees, no great American novel. Instead, reality: wives and babies and mortgages, pensions, security and the far-away future. No great risks. No more falling down. No more skinned knees. No great failures. I wondered: is all this **inevitable**?

6   I've never minded looking stupid and I have no fear of failure. I decided to canoe down the Mississippi River and to find out what I was made of.

2.

7   Once they have reached a certain age, dreamers are no longer held in high esteem. They are ridiculed instead, called loony and lazy, even by their friends. Especially by their friends!

8   Dreams are delicate and made of **gossamer**. They hang lightly on breezes and suspend as if from nothing. The slightest wind can tear them apart. My dream was **buffeted** by my friends. What the hell for? they asked me. What are you trying to prove? Why don't you just go over Niagara Falls in a barrel?

9   And this was from my friends. God, how that hurt. One friend even told me to take a bus, for God's sake. Instead of helping me fly, my friends were pulling me down, and laughing at me.

10   Putting a canoe into the headwaters of the Mississippi and aiming it for New Orleans is not something a man is supposed to do. It is not considered normal or sane. Perhaps it is the danger involved, perhaps it is too much an act of desire and determination, an act of passion and **volition**, or simply too out of the ordinary.

11   For whatever reasons, my idea met with disapproval, and instead of childish **jubilation** I approached canoeing the river with doubt and sorrow—sorrow because the glory with which I first came upon this adventure was dashed by

NOTES

friends. Like Galileo[1] before the Church, I was ready to relinquish my radical approaches to be normal.

12 But this dream of mine, still suspended on the breeze and delicate as ever, was just as real as those flimsy summer spider webs hanging in the air, and just as clinging. Once the webs attach themselves to you they are hard to get rid of. And so it was with my desire to ride the river.

Excerpted from Mississippi Solo: A River Quest *by Eddy L. Harris, published by Henry Holt & Company.*

✏ WRITE

DISCUSSION: Thoreau and Harris each weigh the pros and cons of undergoing a journey versus settling down. Have a discussion in which you compare and contrast the reason(s) each person decides to leave or stay. To prepare for your discussion, write the decision each made, as well as the underlying or implicit motivations and reasons behind that decision. Use textual evidence and original commentary to support your ideas.

---

1. **Galileo** a 17th-century astronomer who was famously convicted of heresy and imprisoned by the Catholic Church for saying that Earth revolves around the sun

Remarks at the Signing of the Highway Beautification Act

INFORMATIONAL TEXT
Lyndon B. Johnson
1965

Introduction

Lyndon Baines Johnson (1908-1973) was the 36th president of the United States. Serving as vice president to John F. Kennedy, Johnson assumed the presidency immediately following Kennedy's assassination in 1963. The Civil Rights Movement and the Vietnam War came to be defining factors of Johnson's term, and his legacy was shaped by decisions made amidst this tumultuous backdrop. Striving to honor Kennedy's memory and to continue the legacy of Franklin Delano Roosevelt's "New Deal," Johnson's ambition gave birth to the concept of "The Great Society," a series of federally funded social reforms in education, health care, employment, civil rights, and the environment. At the same time, his administration presided over the escalation of an increasingly unpopular war in Vietnam, complicating Johnson's legacy. The Highway Beautification Act of 1965, initially proposed by First Lady Claudia Alta "Lady Bird" Johnson, called for stricter regulations protecting the scenery and cleanliness of the nation's highways, notably calling for the removal of nonconforming advertisements and providing funding for landscaping projects. In "Remarks at the Signing of the Highway Beautification Act," Johnson celebrates one small victory toward protecting the nation's heritage and resolves to lead the restoration of "national greatness."

"Beauty belongs to all the people."

1 Secretary Gardner, distinguished Members of the leadership of the Congress and Members of the Congress, and all other lovers of beauty:

President Lyndon B. Johnson and Lady Bird Johnson

2 America likes to think of itself as a strong and stalwart and expanding Nation. It identifies itself gladly with the products of its own hands. We frequently point with pride and with confidence to the products of our great free enterprise system—management and labor.

Skill: Arguments and Claims

At first, Johnson is making a claim that American industry is very important. This helps establish a relationship with his audience. His second claim is that America is more than just material success.

3 These are and these should be a source of pride to every American. They are certainly the source of American strength. They are truly the fountainhead of American wealth. They are actually a part of America's soul.

4 But there is more to America than raw **industrial** might. And when you go through what I have gone through the last two weeks you constantly think of things like that. You no longer get your computers in and try to count your riches.

5 There is a part of America which was here long before we arrived, and will be here, if we preserve it, long after we depart: the forests and the flowers, the open prairies and the slope of the hills, the tall mountains, the granite, the limestone, the caliche, the unmarked trails, the winding little streams—well, this is the America that no amount of science or skill can ever recreate or actually ever duplicate.

6 This America is the source of America's greatness. It is another part of America's soul as well.

7 When I was growing up, the land itself was life. And when the day seemed particularly harsh and bitter, the land was always there just as nature had left it—wild, rugged, beautiful, and changing, always changing.

8   And really, how do you measure the excitement and the happiness that comes to a boy from the old swimming hole in the happy days of yore, when I used to lean above it; the old sycamore, the baiting of a hook that is tossed into the stream to catch a wily fish, or looking at a graceful deer that leaps with hardly a quiver over a rock fence that was put down by some settler a hundred years or more ago?

9   How do you really put a value on the view of the night that is caught in a boy's eyes while he is stretched out in the thick grass watching the million stars that we never see in these crowded cities, breathing the sounds of the night and the birds and the pure, fresh air while in his ears are the crickets and the wind?

10 Well, in recent years I think America has sadly neglected this part of America's national heritage. We have placed a wall of civilization between us and between the beauty of our land and of our countryside. In our eagerness to expand and to improve, we have **relegated** nature to a weekend role, and we have banished it from our daily lives.

11 Well, I think that we are a poorer Nation because of it, and it is something I am not proud of.

12 And it is something I am going to do something about. Because as long as I am your President, by choice of your people, I do not choose to preside over the destiny of this country and to hide from view what God has gladly given it.

13 And that is why today there is a great deal of real joy within me, and within my family, as we meet here in this historic East Room to sign the Highway Beautification Act of 1965.

14 Now, this bill does more than control advertising and junkyards along the billions of dollars of highways that the people have built with their money— public money, not private money. It does more than give us the tools just to landscape some of those highways.

15 This bill will bring the wonders of nature back into our daily lives.

16 This bill will enrich our spirits and restore a small measure of our national greatness.

17 As I rode the George Washington Memorial Parkway back to the White House only yesterday afternoon, I saw nature at its purest. And I thought of the honor roll of names—a good many of you are sitting here in the front row today—that made this possible. And as I thought of you who had helped and stood up against private greed for public good, I looked at those dogwoods that had turned red,

Skill: Arguments and Claims

Johnson makes a case for the future progress brought by the Highway Beautification Act. He uses detailed imagery about nature, which invites the audience to identify with the emotional impact of his central claim.

Skill:
Context Clues

I am unsure what the verb marred means. In the surrounding sentences, Johnson says that construction and advertisements ruin nature. This makes me think that marred means "to make worse or ugly."

and the maple trees that were scarlet and gold. In a pattern of brown and yellow, God's finery was at its finest. And not one single foot of it was marred by a single, unsightly, man-made construction or obstruction—no advertising signs, no old, **dilapidated** trucks, no junkyards. Well, doctors could prescribe no better medicine for me, and that is what I said to my surgeon as we drove along.

18 This bill does not represent everything that we wanted. It does not represent what we need. It does not represent what the national interest requires. But it is a first step, and there will be other steps. For though we must crawl before we walk, we are going to walk.

19 I remember the fierce resolve of a man that I admired greatly, a great leader of a great people, Franklin D. Roosevelt. He fought a pitched battle in 1936 with private interests whose target was private gain. And I shall long remember the words that I believe he echoed at Madison Square Garden, when he declared to the Nation that the forces of selfishness had not only met their match, but these forces had met their master.

20 Well, I have not asked you to come here today to tell you that I have a desire to master anyone. But until the clock strikes the last hour of the time allotted to me as President by vote of all the people of this country, I will never turn away from the duty that my office demands or the **vigilance** that my oath of office requires.

21 And this administration has no desire to punish or to penalize any private industry, or any private company, or any group, or any organization of complex associations in this Nation. But we are not going to allow them to intrude their own specialized private **objective** on the larger public trust. Beauty belongs to all the people. And so long as I am President, what has been divinely given to nature will not be taken recklessly away by man.

22 This Congress is to be thanked for the bill that you have given us. I wish it could have been more, but I realize, too, that there are other views to be considered in our system of checks and balances.

23 The grandchildren of those of you in this country that may have mocked and ridiculed us today, someday will point with pride to the public servants who are here in this room, who cast their lot with the people.

24 And unless I miss my guess, history will remember on its honor roll those of you whom the camera brings into focus in this room today, who stood up and were counted when that roll was called that said we are going to preserve at least a part of what God gave us.

25 Thank you very much.

First Read

Read "Remarks at the Signing of the Highway Beautification Act." After you read, complete the Think Questions below.

☁ THINK QUESTIONS

1. According to Johnson, what makes up the "soul" of America? What does he mean when he says these are part of the nation's "soul"? Explain in your own words why he believes this and what this particular word encapsulates, citing evidence from the text.

2. Why does President Johnson believe that the Highway Beautification Act will help restore "national greatness"? How will it achieve this goal? Cite specific examples from the text to support your answer.

3. What does Johnson believe his responsibilities are as leader of the United States? In his opinion, how is he meeting these obligations? Explain, using evidence from the text to support your answer.

4. Based on the context clues found in paragraph 10, what do you think is the meaning of **relegated**? Compose your own definition, citing how you came to this meaning.

5. The Latin word *vigilantia* means "watchfulness" or "wakefulness." Using this information, in addition to context clues, consider what the word **vigilance** in paragraph 20 is meant to convey. In your own words, create a definition for *vigilance*.

Copyright © BookheadEd Learning, LLC

Please note that excerpts and passages in the StudySync® library and this workbook are intended as touchstones to generate interest in an author's work. The excerpts and passages do not substitute for the reading of entire texts, and StudySync® strongly recommends that students seek out and purchase the whole literary or informational work in order to experience it as the author intended. Links to online resellers are available in our digital library. In addition, complete works may be ordered through an authorized reseller by filling out and returning to StudySync® the order form enclosed in this workbook.

Reading & Writing Companion 233

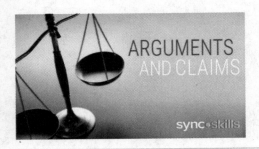

Skill:
Arguments and Claims

Use the Checklist to analyze Arguments and Claims in "Remarks at the Signing of the Highway Beautification Act." Refer to the sample student annotations about Arguments and Claims in the text.

••• CHECKLIST FOR ARGUMENTS AND CLAIMS

In order to delineate the premises, purposes, and arguments in works of public advocacy, note the following:

- ✓ the use of legal reasoning, which includes the thinking processes and strategies used by lawyers and judges when arguing and deciding legal cases, and is based on constitutional principles, or laws written down in the U.S. Constitution

- ✓ whether or not the premise, or the basis of the proposal the individual or group makes, is based on logical reasoning and factual evidence

- ✓ the purpose of the text and the position, or stance, the speaker takes

- ✓ how a speaker uses evidence and reasoning to support his or her claim

- ✓ language that makes a rhetorical or emotional appeal to the reader or audience including the words a speaker uses, what points the speaker emphasizes, and the speaker's tone towards the subject

To evaluate the premises, purposes, and arguments in works of public advocacy, consider the following questions:

- ✓ What position, or stance, does the speaker take?

- ✓ How does the speaker use legal reasoning to support his or her position?

- ✓ How does the speaker use evidence and reasoning to support his or her claim?

- ✓ How does the speaker try to influence or support a cause or policy?

- ✓ What points does the speaker choose to emphasize?

- ✓ How does the speaker's choice of words affect his or her tone?

Skill:
Arguments and Claims

Reread paragraphs 13–17 of "Remarks at the Signing of the Highway Beautification Act." Then, using the Checklist on the previous page, answer the multiple-choice questions below.

↻ YOUR TURN

1. Why does Johnson clarify the use of "public money" in paragraph 14 to help support his argument?

   ○ A. To reinforce that all Americans contributed to the beautification of the highway.
   ○ B. To restate that Johnson believes everyone should pay their taxes.
   ○ C. To emphasize that the highways belong to the people.
   ○ D. To show that it is the people's job to keep nature in tact.

2. How does Johnson's mention of nature as medicine help contribute to his claim in this speech?

   ○ A. It highlights that the natural world is an important part of human wellbeing and should be protected.
   ○ B. It builds credibility with the audience because it is a personal anecdote.
   ○ C. It shows that nature has been important to Johnson his entire life.
   ○ D. It emphasizes that the natural world has magical properties.

Skill:
Context Clues

Use the Checklist to analyze Context Clues in "Remarks at the Signing of the Highway Beautification Act." Refer to the sample student annotations about Context Clues in the text.

••• CHECKLIST FOR CONTEXT CLUES

In order to use context as a clue to the meaning of a word or phrase, note the following:

- ✓ clues about the word's part of speech

- ✓ clues in the surrounding text about the word's meaning

- ✓ words with similar denotations that seem to differ slightly in meaning

- ✓ signal words that cue a type of context clue, such as:

  - *comparably*, *related to*, or *similarly* to signal a comparison context clue

  - *on the other hand*, *however*, or *in contrast* to signal a contrast context clue

  - *by reason of*, *because*, or *as a result* to signal a cause-and-effect context clue

To determine the meaning of a word or phrase as it is used in a text, consider the following questions:

- ✓ What is the meaning of the overall sentence, paragraph, or text?

- ✓ How does the position of the word in the sentence help me define it?

- ✓ How does the word function in the sentence? What clues help identify the word's part of speech?

- ✓ What clues in the text suggest the word's definition?

- ✓ What do I think the word means?

To verify the preliminary determination of the meaning of the word or phrase based on context, consider the following questions:

- ✓ Does the definition I inferred make sense within the context of the sentence?

- ✓ Which of the dictionary's definitions makes sense within the context of the sentence?

Skill:
Context Clues

Reread paragraphs 19–20 of "Remarks at the Signing of the Highway Beautification Act." Then, using the Checklist on the previous page, answer the multiple-choice questions below.

⟳ YOUR TURN

1. This question has two parts. First, answer Part A. Then, answer Part B.

Part A: Using context clues, determine the meaning of the word *pitched* in paragraph 19.

- ○ A. Threw a baseball
- ○ B. Mild
- ○ C. Intense
- ○ D. Aggressive

Part B: What words in this excerpt provide a clue to the meaning of this word?

- ○ A. "fierce resolve"
- ○ B. "private interests"
- ○ C. "admired greatly"
- ○ D. "met their master"

REMARKS AT THE
SIGNING OF
THE HIGHWAY
BEAUTIFICATION ACT

Close Read

Reread "Remarks at the Signing of the Highway Beautification Act." As you reread, complete the Skills Focus questions below. Then use your answers and annotations from the questions to help you complete the Write activity.

◎ SKILLS FOCUS

1. Locate a passage from paragraphs 3–6 that clearly states President Johnson's argument. According to Johnson, what is the source of America's greatness? What is part of America's soul?

2. Identify details that support Johnson's belief that our preservation of nature is important. Explain how these details help develop his argument.

3. Analyze context to infer the meaning of the word *might* in paragraph 4. Explain how you used evidence from the text to arrive at your definition of the word *might*.

4. Identify Johnson's closing statements. What is Johnson's purpose in giving this speech?

5. Find instances where Johnson mentions his own relationship with nature throughout his life. How does Johnson draw upon this relationship to strengthen his argument?

✎ WRITE

ARGUMENTATIVE: President Johnson includes brief, yet detailed snapshots of his experience with nature as a young boy to help his audience digest his message. Consider the function of these anecdotes. How do Johnson's descriptions of his own relationships with nature work to support his claim? Analyze the effectiveness of Johnson's personal accounts to support his argument, using evidence from the text and original commentary to support your conclusions.

Driving My Own Destiny

INFORMATIONAL TEXT
Manal al-Sharif
2012

Introduction

M anal al-Sharif (b. 1979) is a women's rights activist who was named one of the 100 Most Influential People of 2012 by *Time* magazine. In this essay, al-Sharif details her experience growing up in extremist Saudi Arabia. She also explains what inspired her to start a social media campaign called "Drive Your Own Life" and why women's rights in Saudi Arabia are so important.

"We were voiceless. We were faceless. We were nameless."

Skill: Informational Text Structure

The author says the essay will be about her life in Saudi Arabia. Memoirs are often organized by date, so this is probably a sequential text structure. The author's purpose is to inform how historical events affected her life.

1   My name is Manal al-Sharif. I'm from Saudi Arabia. I want to tell you about two separate chapters of my life. Chapter one is the story of my generation; it begins the year I was born, 1979.

2   On November 20 of that year, there was a siege of Mecca, the holiest shrine in the world for Muslims. It was seized by Juhayman al-Otaybi, a militant Islamist, and some 400 of his men. The occupation lasted for two weeks. Saudi authorities had to use force—heavily armed force—to eject the occupiers and end the violation. They beheaded Juhayman and his men publicly.

3   Nevertheless, the authorities became very anxious. They feared another uprising. Saudi Arabia was newly formed, rapidly changing, and had been adopting a new civil way of life. For rebel militants, such changes were against their beliefs, against Islam, and they wanted to stop them.

4   So, although the Saudi government had executed Juhayman, it began to **abide** by his doctrine. In order to prevent another uprising, extremists in power quickly moved to roll back liberties that had been tolerated in previous years. Like Juhayman, some ruling Saudis had long been upset over the gradual loosening of restrictions for women. In the weeks after the Mecca uprising, female announcers were removed from television. Pictures of women were banned. All possible female employment was narrowed to two fields: education or healthcare.

5   Activities that encouraged male-female contact were curbed: Music was banned; cinemas were closed; the separation between genders was strictly enforced everywhere. That separation became law, from public places to government offices, to banks, schools, even to our own houses. In time, each house in Saudi Arabia ended up having two entrances: one for men, one for women.

6   There was another sea change: Petrodollars began to pour into those extremists' pockets. They used that money to spread missionary teachers

14   My face was *awra*, my voice was *awra*. Even my name was *awra*. Women cannot be called by name, so they are called "daughter of" a man's name, "wife of" a husband, or "mother of" one of her sons.

15   There were no sports for women, no engineering schools. There was also, of course, no driving. And how could there be? We weren't even allowed to have identity cards with pictures, except for passports, which were only necessary to leave the country.

16   We were voiceless. We were faceless. We were nameless. And we were completely invisible.

17   Our lives had been stolen with a lie: We are doing this to protect you from the prying eyes of men, they told us. You deserve to be treated like a queen.

Skill: Textual Evidence

I notice that the author cites a specific historical event to justify her understanding of her society. The importance of this event is evidenced in the text by the inclusion of her response to the news at the time.

18   But during that time, something happened to show that not everyone was going along with this. On November 6, 1990, forty-seven courageous women emerged to challenge the ban on women driving. They went out into the streets of Riyadh and drove. The women were detained, banned from leaving the country, and dismissed from their jobs. I remember receiving that news when I was a kid. We were told that those women were really bad. Afterwards, there was a fatwa. The Grand Mufti of Saudi Arabia said that a woman driving was *haram*, forbidden in Islam. A television announcer came on to say that the Minister of the Interior had warned that women were not allowed to drive in the Kingdom of Saudi Arabia.

Al-Sharif delivering her historic speech in May 2012 at the Oslo Freedom Forum. She was honored at the event with the Vaclav Havel Prize for Creative Dissent. (Oslo Freedom Forum)

19   For the next twenty-two years, we were not even supposed to talk about women driving, whether on television and news broadcasts, or in magazines and newspapers.

20   So, yet another taboo was created.

21 The first had prevented us from talking about Juhayman; the second prevented us from talking about women driving.

22 But something else happened in that first chapter of my young life: the attack on Khobar Towers, a housing complex for foreign military personnel. The Towers were bombed on June 25, 1996, and, according to the Saudi government, the attack had been carried out by Saudi Islamic militants, including many veterans of the Afghan War. Nineteen US Air Force personnel had been killed and 372 more people of various nationalities injured.

23 I remember my mother gasping when she saw the pictures. "Juhayman is back," she said.

24 I was only seventeen, and it surprises me now to recall it, but I had no sympathy for the dead. I was brainwashed, I had been brought up in a particular time; I was the product of a terrorist culture.

25 The change in my life started four years later, in 2000. That year, the Internet was introduced in Saudi Arabia. It was the first time I went online. Now, let me give you a picture of myself: as an extremist, I covered myself from head to toe. I had always followed that custom strictly. I also loved drawing, but one day when they told us in school that it was sinful to draw portraits of animals or people, I felt I had to comply. I dutifully took all my paintings and drawings and burned them. Meanwhile, I found myself burning inside. This was not fair. I had learned as much from a computer. The Internet, you see, was the first door for Arab youth to venture into the outside world. I was young, thirsty to learn about other people and other religions. I started communicating with people who held different opinions, and soon those conversations raised questions in my head. I began to realize how very small was the box I was living in. It looked all the smaller once I stepped out of it. Slowly, I started to lose my phobia of having my pure beliefs polluted.

26 Let me tell you another story. Do you remember the first time you listened to music? Do you remember your very first song? I do. I was twenty-one years old. It was the first I had ever allowed myself to listen to music. I remember the song: It was "Show Me the Meaning of Being Lonely," by the Backstreet Boys.

27 Maybe it will help you to understand if I tell you that I used to burn my brother's cassettes in the oven. I was that extreme. And then I listened to that song.

28 They had told us that music was Satan's flute, a path to adultery, a door to sin. But the song I heard sounded so pure, so beautiful, so angelic. It could be anything but evil to me. It was then that I realized how lonely I was in my isolated little world.

NOTES

Skill: Word Patterns and Relationships

The words *military* and *militant* have the same root, but *military* is functioning as an adjective in the text, whereas *militant* is a noun. I can infer that the *militants* are the people carrying out the attack.

NOTES

29 Another important moment for me was 9/11, a turning point for so many people in my generation. When the events of 9/11 happened, the extremists said it was God's punishment to Americans for what they had done to us over the years.

30 I was confused about which side to take. I had been brought up to hate any non-Muslims or anyone who didn't practice Islam as we viewed it. But when I watched the breaking news that night, I saw a man throwing himself from one of the World Trade Center towers. He was falling, straight down, escaping the fire.

31 That night I couldn't sleep. The picture was in my head, and it was ringing a bell. Something is wrong, it was telling me. No religion on Earth can be this bloody, this cruel, this merciless.

32 Al Qaeda later announced their responsibility for the attacks. My heroes were no more than horrifying, bloody monsters. It was the turning point of my life.

33 After 9/11, Saudi Arabia faced a sweep of terrorist attacks on our own land. The interesting outcome? A few months later, for the first time, authorities started issuing women identification papers. Even though an appointed male needed to give the permission, we were finally being recognized as citizens in our own country.

34 Which brings me to chapter two: driving for freedom. In this chapter, the inspiration was the Arab Spring—for me as for so many of my generation. I had been leaving my doctor's clinic at nine o'clock one night, and couldn't find a ride home. A car kept following me and the men in it almost kidnapped me. The next day at work I complained to my colleague how frustrating it was that I have a driver's license from traveling overseas, but at home I'm not allowed to drive because I'm a woman. He said the simplest thing: "But there is no law banning you from driving." A fatwa was a fatwa. Not a law. That plain truth ignited everything. It was June 2011, and a group of women, Saudis all, decided to start a movement, "Drive Your Own Life."

35 It was to be a very straightforward campaign, using social media and calling women to come out and drive on one single day, June 17. We encouraged women with international drivers' licenses only to participate, as we didn't want to cause accidents.

36 That day, I recorded a video of myself driving. I used my face, my voice, my real name. I was determined to speak for myself. I had once been ashamed of who I was, a mere woman, but not anymore. When I posted that video on YouTube, it got 700,000 views on the first day.

37   Clearly, I was not alone. On June 17, when we called for women to come forward, some 100 brave women drove. The streets of Riyadh were packed with police cars and religious police SUVs were posted in every corner of the city. But of the 100 who drove, not one was arrested. We had broken the taboo on driving.

38   The next day, I was arrested and sent to jail. A riot broke out around Saudi Arabia, and people were divided in two camps: one called for my trial and a flogging in a public place. They called me a whore, an outcast, **licentious**, immoral, rebellious, disobedient, Westernized, a traitor and double agent to boot. Pages sprang up on Facebook to **denounce** me, claiming that men would take their igals, cords Arab men wear on their heads, and thrash any woman who dared break the taboo and drive. Women shot back, "We will throw shoes at you." So it was a full fight between genders.

39   I didn't realize until after I was released from prison how many people had been inspired by a simple act that many women do every single day. The support that was rallied around the world led to my release nine days later.

40   This is not about driving a car. It is about being in the driver's seat of our destiny. I now say that I can measure the impact we made by how harsh the attacks were. It's this simple: We've started a movement in Saudi Arabia. We call it the Saudi Woman's Spring.

41   We believe in full citizenship for women, because a child cannot be free if his mother is not free. A husband cannot be free if his wife is not free. Parents are not free if their daughters are not free. Society is nothing if its women are nothing.

42   Freedom starts from within.

43   I am free. But I have to admit that when I go home to Saudi Arabia, it's not the same for everyone. The struggle has just begun.

44   I don't know how long it will last, and I don't know how it will end. But I do know that a drenching rain begins with a single drop. And eventually there are flowers.

By Manal al-Sharif, 2012. Used by permission of Manal al-Sharif. Image used by permission of Oslo Freedom Forum, oslofreedomforum.com.

 Skill: Informational Text Structure

This passage is still organized sequentially but also uses a cause-and-effect structure. The author's use of a cause-and-effect structure shows the impact of the "Drive Your Own Destiny" campaign.

Please note that excerpts and passages in the StudySync® library and this workbook are intended as touchstones to generate interest in an author's work. The excerpts and passages do not substitute for the reading of entire texts, and StudySync® strongly recommends that students seek out and purchase the whole literary or informational work in order to experience it as the author intended. Links to online resellers are available in our digital library. In addition, complete works may be ordered through an authorized reseller by filling out and returning to StudySync® the order form enclosed in this workbook.

Reading & Writing Companion   **245**

First Read

Read "Driving My Own Destiny." After you read, complete the Think Questions below.

 THINK QUESTIONS

1. In the essay, al-Sharif claims that she was brainwashed as a child and that her life was stolen with a lie. What lie was she told growing up in Saudi Arabia? How does this lie suppress the rights and freedoms of women? Cite evidence from the text to support your answer.

2. What impact did the Internet have on al-Sharif as a young woman? Support your answer with evidence from the text.

3. In June 2011, al-Sharif helped to start a campaign called "Drive Your Own Life." Was this campaign successful? Support your answer with evidence from the text.

4. What is the meaning of the word **distribute** as it is used in the text? Write your best definition here, along with a brief explanation of how you arrived at its meaning.

5. The Latin verb *licere* means "to be permitted." *Licere* is the root of the words *licence*, *licit*, *illicit*, and *leisure*. Keeping this in mind and using context from the passage, what do you think the word **licentious** means in the context of this text? Explain.

Skill:
Textual Evidence

Use the Checklist to analyze Textual Evidence in "Driving My Own Destiny." Refer to the sample student annotations about Textual Evidence in the text.

In order to support an analysis by citing evidence that is explicitly stated in the text, do the following:

✓ read the text closely and critically

✓ identify what the text says explicitly

✓ find the most relevant textual evidence that supports your analysis

✓ consider why an author explicitly states specific details and information

✓ cite the specific words, phrases, sentences, or paragraphs from the text that support your analysis

✓ determine where evidence in the text still leaves certain matters uncertain or unresolved

In order to interpret implicit meanings in a text by making inferences, do the following:

✓ combine information directly stated in the text with your own knowledge, experiences, and observations

✓ cite the specific words, phrases, sentences, or paragraphs from the text that led to and support this inference

In order to cite textual evidence to support an analysis of what the text says explicitly as well as inferences drawn from the text, consider the following questions:

✓ Have I read the text closely and critically?

✓ What inferences am I making about the text?

Please note that excerpts and passages in the StudySync® library and this workbook are intended as touchstones to generate interest in an author's work. The excerpts and passages do not substitute for the reading of entire texts, and StudySync® strongly recommends that students seek out and purchase the whole literary or informational work in order to experience it as the author intended. Links to online resellers are available in our digital library. In addition, complete works may be ordered through an authorized reseller by filling out and returning to StudySync® the order form enclosed in this workbook.

Reading & Writing Companion

247

✓ What textual evidence am I using to support these inferences?

✓ Am I quoting the evidence from the text correctly?

✓ Does my textual evidence logically relate to my analysis or the inference I am making?

✓ Does evidence in the text still leave certain matters unanswered or unresolved? In what ways?

Skill:
Textual Evidence

Reread paragraphs 2–4 of "Driving My Own Destiny." Then, using the Checklist on the previous page, answer the multiple-choice questions below.

⟳ YOUR TURN

1. This question has two parts. First, answer Part A. Then, answer Part B.

Part A: What can be inferred about the removal of women from public life and prominent positions in Saudi Arabia?

- ○ A. The government is sending the message that women's rights will again be severely restricted.
- ○ B. The government believes that women in public positions promote Westernization and therefore are dangerous.
- ○ C. The government is trying to change the role of women in society to be more focused on raising families and maintaining a home.
- ○ D. The government is trying to send a message to young women that they are not fit for public life.

Part B: Which of the sentences below best supports the inference from Part A?

- ○ A. "Like Juhayman, some ruling Saudis had long been upset over the gradual loosening of restrictions for women."
- ○ B. "For rebel militants, such changes were against their beliefs, against Islam, and they wanted to stop them."
- ○ C. "In order to prevent another uprising, extremists in power quickly moved to roll back liberties that had been tolerated in previous years."
- ○ D. "Pictures of women were banned."

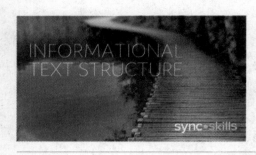

Skill:
Informational Text Structure

Use the Checklist to analyze Informational Text Structure in "Driving My Own Destiny." Refer to the sample student annotations about Informational Text Structure in the text.

••• CHECKLIST FOR INFORMATIONAL TEXT STRUCTURE

In order to determine the structure an author uses in his or her writing, note the following:

- ✓ where the author introduces and clarifies his or her argument

- ✓ sentences and paragraphs that reveal the text structure the author uses to frame the argument

- ✓ whether the text structure is effective in presenting all sides of the argument, and makes the author's points clear, convincing and engaging

- ✓ whether the author uses one text structure throughout the text, or multiple text structures

To analyze and evaluate the effectiveness of the structure an author uses in his or her writing, including whether the structure makes points clear, convincing, and engaging, consider the following questions:

- ✓ Did I have to read a particular sentence or paragraph over again? Where?

- ✓ Did I find myself distracted or uninterested while reading the text? When?

- ✓ Did the structure the author used make his or her points clear, convincing, and engaging? Why or why not?

- ✓ In what ways did the structure of the text enhance my understanding of the argument and its development?

- ✓ Does the author use one text structure throughout, or multiple text structures? How might these different text structures help the author achieve his or her purpose?

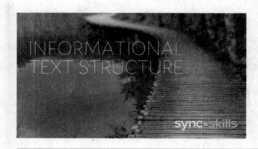

Skill:
Informational Text Structure

Reread paragraphs 29–33 of "Driving My Own Destiny." Then, using the Checklist on the previous page, answer the multiple-choice questions below.

↻ YOUR TURN

1. The information in this passage that best helps the reader identify the text structure is—

   ○ A. a description of Islam through a comparison of world religions.

   ○ B. procedural information about how to get identification papers.

   ○ C. a description of how the author and society both change in response to a historical event.

   ○ D. the critical examination of the problems presented by religious extremism and some possible solutions.

2. Given your answer to Question 1, what is the primary text structure used in this portion of the essay?

   ○ A. compare-and-contrast

   ○ B. sequential

   ○ C. problem-and-solution

   ○ D. cause-and-effect

3. The characteristics that you identified about this passage in Question 1 and the structures you identified in Question 2 convey the author's specific purpose of—

   ○ A. explaining why the 9/11 attacks were God's judgment on the United States.

   ○ B. describing the relationship between women's rights and being allowed to drive.

   ○ C. explaining why 9/11 was the turning point of her life.

   ○ D. suggesting ways that her country should change after 9/11.

Skill: Word Patterns and Relationships

Use the Checklist to analyze Word Patterns and Relationships in "Driving My Own Destiny." Refer to the sample student annotations about Word Patterns and Relationships in the text.

••• CHECKLIST FOR WORD PATTERNS AND RELATIONSHIPS

In order to identify patterns of word changes to indicate different meanings or parts of speech, do the following:

✓ determine the word's part of speech

✓ use context clues to make a preliminary determination of the meaning of the word

✓ use knowledge of common roots words, prefixes, and suffixes to determine a word's part of speech or meaning

✓ when writing a response to a text, check that you understand the meaning and part of speech and that it makes sense in your sentence

✓ consult a dictionary to verify your preliminary determination of the meanings and parts of speech

✓ be sure to read all the definitions, and then decide which definition, form, and part of speech makes sense within the context of the text

To identify and correctly use patterns of word changes that indicate different meanings or parts of speech, consider the following questions:

✓ What is the intended meaning of the word?

✓ How does this meaning relate to the meaning of other words in the text with the same root or base word?

✓ What prefixes or suffixes do I see, and how might they change the meaning of the word?

✓ When I consult a dictionary, can I confirm that the meaning I have determined for this word is correct? Do I know how to use it correctly?

Copyright © BookheadEd Learning, LLC

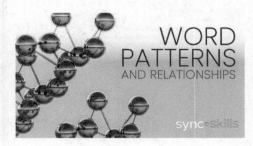

Skill: Word Patterns and Relationships

Reread paragraphs 26–31 of "Driving My Own Destiny." Then, using the Checklist on the previous page, answer the multiple-choice questions below.

↻ YOUR TURN

1. What is the relationship between the words *extreme* and *extremists*?

   ○ A. They have the same root word, and they are both used as nouns in the sentence.
   ○ B. They have the same root word, but *extreme* is an adjective and *extremist* is a noun.
   ○ C. They have the same root word and are both adjectives.
   ○ D. They are both nouns but have different root words.

2. Consider the word *merciless*. If *mercy* means "kindness," then how does the addition of the suffix *-less* change the meaning?

   ○ A. It changes the meaning to "being only somewhat kind."
   ○ B. It changes the meaning to "being aggressive."
   ○ C. It changes the meaning to "a lack of kindness or compassion."
   ○ D. It does not change the meaning.

Close Read

Reread "Driving My Own Destiny." As you reread, complete the Skills Focus questions below. Then use your answers and annotations from the questions to help you complete the Write activity.

◎ SKILLS FOCUS

1. Identify a passage in which the author describes the bans and restrictions on the interaction between genders in Saudi Arabia. Evaluate how the author's word choice and syntax contribute to the feel of the passage.

2. Locate a passage that describes events after the 1980s, and analyze the informational text elements for clues that suggest the structure/s of that text. Explain whether the structure/s you identified make/s the author's argument more effective or not.

3. Locate where in paragraphs 19–21 al-Sharif talks about the taboos surrounding the idea of women driving after forty-seven women protested the

driving ban in 1990. Analyze how the author structures the passage to fulfill her purpose, and cite textual evidence to support the analysis of your claims.

4. Identify the word *Petrodollars* in paragraph 6. Using your knowledge of word patterns and relationships as well as the context of the passage, tell what you think *Petrodollars* means, and explain how you arrived at your answer.

5. Highlight a passage from "chapter two," which begins at paragraph 34 and in which al-Sharif connects driving and personal freedom. How did her perspective on what is just change?

✎ WRITE

EXPLANATORY: Manal al-Sharif uses text structure in order to convey a message about driving and what it represents to her. Identify the text structure/s she uses, then analyze how the chosen structure/s relate/s to her purpose for writing "Driving My Own Destiny." Use textual evidence and original commentary to support your response.

The Warmth of Other Suns:
The Epic Story of America's Great Migration

INFORMATIONAL TEXT
Isabel Wilkerson
2013

Introduction

Between 1915 and 1970, over six million African Americans migrated from the rural southern United States to the Northeast, Midwest, and West to escape racial oppression and pursue economic and social opportunities. One of the largest migrations ever to take place on national soil, the Great Migration changed the food, music, culture, and social fabric of American cities. In *The Warmth of Other Suns*, Pulitzer-Prize winning journalist Isabel Wilkerson (b. 1961) tells the history, intertwining the personal stories of three young African Americans who left family and home to participate in this epic migration.

"He wasn't going to lose his life over them. He had come close enough as it was."

NOTES

1.

Chickasaw County, Mississippi, Late October 1937

Ida Mae Brandon Gladney

1   The night clouds were closing in on the salt licks east of the oxbow lakes along the folds in the earth beyond the Yalobusha River. The cotton was at last cleared from the field. Ida Mae tried now to get the children ready and to gather the clothes and quilts and somehow keep her mind off the churning within her. She had sold off the turkeys and **doled** out in secret the old stools, the wash pots, the tin tub, the bed pallets. Her husband was settling with Mr. Edd over the worth of a year's labor, and she did not know what would come of it. None of them had been on a train before—not unless you counted the clattering local from Bacon Switch to Okolona, where, "by the time you sit down, you there," as Ida Mae put it. None of them had been out of Mississippi. Or Chickasaw County, for that matter.

2   There was no explaining to little James and Velma the stuffed bags and chaos and all that was at stake or why they had to put on their shoes and not cry and bring undue attention from anyone who might happen to see them leaving. Things had to look normal, like any other time they might ride into town, which was rare enough to begin with.

3   Velma was six. She sat with her ankles crossed and three braids in her hair and did what she was told. James was too little to understand. He was three. He was upset at the commotion. Hold still now, James. Lemme put your shoes on, Ida Mae told him. James wriggled and kicked. He did not like shoes. He ran free in the field. What were these things? He did not like them on his feet. So Ida Mae let him go barefoot.

4   Miss Theenie stood watching. One by one, her children had left her and gone up north. Sam and Cleve to Ohio. Josie to Syracuse. Irene to Milwaukee. Now the man Miss Theenie had tried to keep Ida Mae from marrying in the first place was taking her away, too. Miss Theenie had no choice but to accept it and let Ida Mae and the grandchildren go for good. Miss Theenie drew them close to her, as she always did whenever anyone was leaving. She had them

bow their heads. She whispered a prayer that her daughter and her daughter's family be protected on the long journey ahead in the Jim Crow car.

5   "May the Lord be the first in the car," she prayed, "and the last out."

6   When the time had come, Ida Mae and little James and Velma and all that they could carry were loaded into a brother-in-law's truck, and the three of them went to meet Ida Mae's husband at the train depot in Okolona for the night ride out of the bottomland.

2.

Wildwood, Florida, April 14, 1945

George Swanson Starling

7   A man named Roscoe Colton gave Lil George Starling a ride in his pickup truck to the train station in Wildwood through the fruit-bearing scrubland of central Florida. And Schoolboy, as the toothless orange pickers mockingly called him, boarded the Silver Meteor pointing north.

8   A railing divided the stairs onto the train, one side of the railing for white passengers, the other for colored, so the soles of their shoes would not touch the same stair. He boarded on the colored side of the railing, a final reminder from the place of his birth of the **absurdity** of the world he was leaving.

9   He was getting out alive. So he didn't let it bother him. "I got on the car where they told me to get on," he said years later.

10 He hadn't had time to bid farewell to everyone he wanted to. He stopped to say good-bye to Rachel Jackson, who owned a little café up on what they called the Avenue and the few others he could safely get to in the little time he had. He figured everybody in Egypt town, the colored section of Eustis, probably knew he was leaving before he had climbed onto the train, small as the town was and as much as people talked.

11 It was a clear afternoon in the middle of April. He folded his tall frame into the hard surface of the seat, his knees knocking against the seat back in front of him. He was packed into the Jim Crow car, where the railroad stored the luggage, when the train pulled away at last. He was on the run, and he wouldn't rest easy until he was out of range of Lake County, beyond the reach of the grove owners whose invisible laws he had broken.

12 The train rumbled past the forest of citrus trees that he had climbed since he was a boy and that he had tried to wrestle some **dignity** out of and, for a time, had. They could have their trees. He wasn't going to lose his life over them. He had come close enough as it was.

13 He had lived up to his family's accidental **surname**. Starling. Distant cousin to the mockingbird. He had spoken up about what he had seen in the world he was born into, like the **starling** that sang Mozart's own music back to him or the starling out of Shakespeare that tormented the king by speaking the name of Mortimer. Only, George was paying the price for tormenting the ruling class that owned the citrus groves. There was no place in the Jim Crow South[1] for a colored starling like him.

14 He didn't know what he would do once he got to New York or what his life would be. He didn't know how long it would take before he could send for Inez. His wife was mad right now, but she'd get over it once he got her there. At least that's what he told himself. He turned his face to the North and sat with his back to Florida.

15 Leaving as he did, he figured he would never set foot in Eustis again for as long as he lived. And as he settled in for the twenty-three-hour train ride up the coast of the Atlantic, he had no desire to have anything to do with the town he grew up in, the state of Florida, or the South as a whole, for that matter.

Excerpted from *The Warmth of Other Suns: The Epic Story of America's Great Migration* by Isabel Wilkerson, published by Vintage Books.

✏ WRITE

RESEARCH: In "The Warmth of Other Suns," Wilkerson relates the tale of young African Americans who left family and home to participate in the Great Migration. Research the events that helped to launch the Great Migration, and then write a response in which you explain how the two perspectives in the selected text reflect your research.

---

1. **Jim Crow South** refers to the areas and times of the American South which there were mandated segregation laws

Because I could not stop for Death

POETRY
Emily Dickinson
1890

Introduction

Beloved American poet Emily Dickinson (1830–1886) composed nearly 1,800 poems, but less than a dozen were published during her lifetime. The famously private Dickinson lived an untraditional lifestyle but held a deep understanding of the human condition. It shines through in "Because I could not stop for Death," her flawlessly written lyrical poem about death and what might follow.

"We slowly drove – He knew no haste"

1 Because I could not stop for Death –
2 He kindly stopped for me –
3 The Carriage held but just Ourselves –
4 And **Immortality**.

5 We slowly drove – He knew no haste
6 And I had put away
7 My labor and my leisure too,
8 For His **Civility** –

9 We passed the School, where Children strove
10 At Recess – in the Ring –
11 We passed the Fields of Gazing Grain –
12 We passed the Setting Sun –

13 Or rather – He passed us –
14 The Dews drew quivering and chill –
15 For only **Gossamer**, my Gown –
16 My Tippet[1] – only Tulle[2] –

17 We paused before a House that seemed
18 A Swelling of the Ground –
19 The Roof was scarcely visible –
20 The Cornice[3] – in the Ground –

21 Since then – 'tis Centuries – and yet
22 Feels shorter than the Day
23 I first **surmised** the Horses' Heads
24 Were toward **Eternity** –

Emily Elizabeth Dickinson, c. 1846

---

1. **Tippet** (old-fashioned) a shawl or cape
2. **Tulle** a soft, silk-like fabric
3. **Cornice** a horizontal beam that crowns a room

WRITE

LITERARY ANALYSIS: Dickinson uses a variety of images to give insight and convey an idea about mortality. Select one image that stands out to you and interpret how it contributes to the poem's overall meaning. Use textual evidence and original commentary to support your response.

A Good Man Is Hard to Find

FICTION
Flannery O'Connor
1953

Introduction

Flannery O'Connor (1925–1964) was one of a kind. A lifelong resident of Milledgeville, Georgia, and a devout Catholic, she produced in her short career some of the best American writing of the postwar period. Her style of Southern Gothic writing was characterized by elements of religion, morality, violence, and redemption. In this, her most famous story, a disgruntled family on a grudging trip to Florida takes a detour with devastating consequences. Have they met the Devil himself? Or merely wandered into a predestined fate?

"Why you're one of my babies. You're one of my own children!"

> Note: The text you are about to read contains offensive language. Remember to be mindful of the thoughts and feelings of your peers as you read and discuss this text. Please consult your teacher for additional guidance and support.

1   THE GRANDMOTHER didn't want to go to Florida. She wanted to visit some of her connections in east Tennessee and she was seizing at every chance to change Bailey's mind. Bailey was the son she lived with, her only boy. He was sitting on the edge of his chair at the table, bent over the orange sports section of the Journal. "Now look here, Bailey," she said, "see here, read this," and she stood with one hand on her thin hip and the other rattling the newspaper at his bald head. "Here this fellow that calls himself The Misfit is aloose from the Federal Pen and headed toward Florida and you read here what it says he did to these people. Just you read it. I wouldn't take my children in any direction with a criminal like that aloose in it. I couldn't answer to my conscience if I did."

2   Bailey didn't look up from his reading so she wheeled around then and faced the children's mother, a young woman in slacks, whose face was as broad and innocent as a cabbage and was tied around with a green head-kerchief that had two points on the top like rabbit's ears. She was sitting on the sofa, feeding the baby his apricots out of a jar. "The children have been to Florida before," the old lady said. "You all ought to take them somewhere else for a change so they would see different parts of the world and be broad. They never have been to east Tennessee."

3   The children's mother didn't seem to hear her but the eight-year-old boy, John Wesley, a stocky child with glasses, said, "If you don't want to go to Florida, why dontcha stay at home?" He and the little girl, June Star, were reading the funny papers on the floor.

4   "She wouldn't stay at home to be queen for a day," June Star said without raising her yellow head.

5   "Yes and what would you do if this fellow, The Misfit, caught you?" the grandmother asked.

Skill:
Story Structure

The grandmother is determined to get what she wants. She points out that a criminal has escaped in Florida to manipulate her son. She even brings up her conscience. This creates tension and foreshadows the ending of the story.

6   "I'd smack his face," John Wesley said.

7   "She wouldn't stay at home for a million bucks," June Star said. "Afraid she'd miss something. She has to go everywhere we go."

8   "All right, Miss," the grandmother said. "Just remember that the next time you want me to curl your hair."

9   June Star said her hair was naturally curly.

10 The next morning the grandmother was the first one in the car, ready to go. She had her big black valise that looked like the head of a hippopotamus in one corner, and underneath it she was hiding a basket with Pitty Sing, the cat, in it. She didn't intend for the cat to be left alone in the house for three days because he would miss her too much and she was afraid he might brush against one of the gas burners and accidentally asphyxiate himself. Her son, Bailey, didn't like to arrive at a motel with a cat.

11 She sat in the middle of the back seat with John Wesley and June Star on either side of her. Bailey and the children's mother and the baby sat in front and they left Atlanta at eight forty-five with the mileage on the car at 55890. The grandmother wrote this down because she thought it would be interesting to say how many miles they had been when they got back. It took them twenty minutes to reach the outskirts of the city.

12 The old lady settled herself comfortably, removing her white cotton gloves and putting them up with her purse on the shelf in front of the back window. The children's mother still had on slacks and still had her head tied up in a green kerchief, but the grandmother had on a navy blue straw sailor hat with a bunch of white violets on the brim and a navy blue dress with a small white dot in the print. Her collars and cuffs were white organdy trimmed with lace and at her neckline she had pinned a purple spray of cloth violets containing a sachet. In case of an accident, anyone seeing her dead on the highway would know at once that she was a lady.

13 She said she thought it was going to be a good day for driving, neither too hot nor too cold, and she cautioned Bailey that the speed limit was fifty-five miles an hour and that the patrolmen hid themselves behind billboards and small clumps of trees and sped out after you before you had a chance to slow down. She pointed out interesting details of the scenery: Stone Mountain; the blue granite that in some places came up to both sides of the highway; the brilliant red clay banks slightly streaked with purple; and the various crops that made rows of green lace-work on the ground. The trees were full of silver-white sunlight and the meanest of them sparkled. The children were reading comic magazines and their mother had gone back to sleep.

14 "Let's go through Georgia fast so we won't have to look at it much," John Wesley said.

15 "If I were a little boy," said the grandmother, "I wouldn't talk about my native state that way. Tennessee has the mountains and Georgia has the hills."

16 "Tennessee is just a hillbilly dumping ground," John Wesley said, "and Georgia is a lousy state too."

17 "You said it," June Star said.

18 "In my time," said the grandmother, folding her thin veined fingers, "children were more respectful of their native states and their parents and everything else. People did right then. Oh look at the cute little pickaninny!"[1] she said and pointed to a Negro child standing in the door of a shack. "Wouldn't that make a picture, now?" she asked and they all turned and looked at the little Negro out of the back window. He waved.

19 "He didn't have any britches on," June Star said.

20 "He probably didn't have any," the grandmother explained. "Little n-----s in the country don't have things like we do. If I could paint, I'd paint that picture," she said.

21 The children exchanged comic books.

22 The grandmother offered to hold the baby and the children's mother passed him over the front seat to her. She set him on her knee and bounced him and told him about the things they were passing. She rolled her eyes and screwed up her mouth and stuck her leathery thin face into his smooth bland one. Occasionally he gave her a faraway smile. They passed a large cotton field with five or six graves fenced in the middle of it, like a small island. "Look at the graveyard!" the grandmother said, pointing it out. "That was the old family burying ground. That belonged to the plantation."

23 "Where's the plantation?" John Wesley asked.

24 "Gone With the Wind," said the grandmother. "Ha. Ha."

25 When the children finished all the comic books they had brought, they opened the lunch and ate it. The grandmother ate a peanut butter sandwich and an olive and would not let the children throw the box and the paper napkins out the window. When there was nothing else to do they played a game by choosing a cloud and making the other two guess what shape it suggested. John Wesley took one the shape of a cow and June Star guessed a cow and John Wesley said, no, an automobile, and June Star said he didn't play fair, and they began to slap each other over the grandmother.

1. **pickaninny** term used to refer to an African American child, considered a slur

NOTES

26   The grandmother said she would tell them a story if they would keep quiet. When she told a story, she rolled her eyes and waved her head and was very dramatic. She said once when she was a maiden lady she had been courted by a Mr. Edgar Atkins Teagarden from Jasper, Georgia. She said he was a very good-looking man and a gentleman and that he brought her a watermelon every Saturday afternoon with his initials cut in it, E. A. T. Well, one Saturday, she said, Mr. Teagarden brought the watermelon and there was nobody at home and he left it on the front porch and returned in his buggy to Jasper, but she never got the watermelon, she said, because a n----- boy ate it when he saw the initials, E. A. T.! This story tickled John Wesley's funny bone and he giggled and giggled but June Star didn't think it was any good. She said she wouldn't marry a man that just brought her a watermelon on Saturday. The grandmother said she would have done well to marry Mr. Teagarden because he was a gentleman and had bought Coca-Cola stock when it first came out and that he had died only a few years ago, a very wealthy man.

27   They stopped at The Tower for barbecued sandwiches. The Tower was a part stucco and part wood filling station and dance hall set in a clearing outside of Timothy. A fat man named Red Sammy Butts ran it and there were signs stuck here and there on the building and for miles up and down the highway saying, TRY RED SAMMY'S FAMOUS BARBECUE. NONE LIKE FAMOUS RED SAMMY'S! RED SAM! THE FAT BOY WITH THE HAPPY LAUGH. A VETERAN! RED SAMMY'S YOUR MAN!

28   Red Sammy was lying on the bare ground outside The Tower with his head under a truck while a gray monkey about a foot high, chained to a small chinaberry tree, chattered nearby. The monkey sprang back into the tree and got on the highest limb as soon as he saw the children jump out of the car and run toward him.

29   Inside, The Tower was a long dark room with a counter at one end and tables at the other and dancing space in the middle. They all sat down at a board table next to the nickelodeon and Red Sam's wife, a tall burnt-brown woman with hair and eyes lighter than her skin, came and took their order. The children's mother put a dime in the machine and played "The Tennessee Waltz," and the grandmother said that tune always made her want to dance. She asked Bailey if he would like to dance but he only glared at her. He didn't have a naturally sunny **disposition** like she did and trips made him nervous. The grandmother's brown eyes were very bright. She swayed her head from side to side and pretended she was dancing in her chair. June Star said play something she could tap to so the children's mother put in another dime and played a fast number and June Star stepped out onto the dance floor and did her tap routine.

30   "Ain't she cute?" Red Sam's wife said, leaning over the counter. "Would you like to come be my little girl?"

Skill: Connotation and Denotation

The word glared has a negative connotation and is in contrast with the words sunny and bright. I think Bailey is annoyed by the grandmother, and she seems to be pretending everything is cheerful.

---

31 "No I certainly wouldn't," June Star said. "I wouldn't live in a broken-down place like this for a minion bucks!" and she ran back to the table.

32 "Ain't she cute?" the woman repeated, stretching her mouth politely.

33 "Arn't you ashamed?" hissed the grandmother.

34 Red Sam came in and told his wife to quit lounging on the counter and hurry up with these people's order. His khaki trousers reached just to his hip bones and his stomach hung over them like a sack of meal swaying under his shirt. He came over and sat down at a table nearby and let out a combination sigh and yodel. "You can't win," he said. "You can't win," and he wiped his sweating red face off with a gray handkerchief. "These days you don't know who to trust," he said. "Ain't that the truth?"

35 "People are certainly not nice like they used to be," said the grandmother.

36 "Two fellers come in here last week," Red Sammy said, "driving a Chrysler. It was a old beat-up car but it was a good one and these boys looked all right to me. Said they worked at the mill and you know I let them fellers charge the gas they bought? Now why did I do that?"

37 "Because you're a good man!" the grandmother said at once.

38 "Yes'm, I suppose so," Red Sam said as if he were struck with this answer.

39 His wife brought the orders, carrying the five plates all at once without a tray, two in each hand and one balanced on her arm. "It isn't a soul in this green world of God's that you can trust," she said. "And I don't count nobody out of that, not nobody," she repeated, looking at Red Sammy.

40 "Did you read about that criminal, The Misfit, that's escaped?" asked the grandmother.

41 "I wouldn't be a bit surprised if he didn't attack this place right here," said the woman. "If he hears about it being here, I wouldn't be none surprised to see him. If he hears it's two cent in the cash register, I wouldn't be a tall surprised if he . . ."

42 "That'll do," Red Sam said. "Go bring these people their Co'-Colas," and the woman went off to get the rest of the order.

43 "A good man is hard to find," Red Sammy said. "Everything is getting terrible. I remember the day you could go off and leave your screen door unlatched. Not no more."

44 He and the grandmother discussed better times. The old lady said that in her opinion Europe was entirely to blame for the way things were now. She said the way Europe acted you would think we were made of money and Red

Skill:
Story Structure

The Misfit is mentioned again, and the wife says that he would "attack" them. Red Sam feels that there are few good men and that the world is terrible. This is a dark view of humanity, which is sad and scary.

Sam said it was no use talking about it, she was exactly right. The children ran outside into the white sunlight and looked at the monkey in the lacy chinaberry tree. He was busy catching fleas on himself and biting each one carefully between his teeth as if it were a **delicacy**.

45 They drove off again into the hot afternoon. The grandmother took cat naps and woke up every few minutes with her own snoring. Outside of Toombsboro she woke up and recalled an old plantation that she had visited in this neighborhood once when she was a young lady. She said the house had six white columns across the front and that there was an avenue of oaks leading up to it and two little wooden trellis arbors on either side in front where you sat down with your suitor after a stroll in the garden. She recalled exactly which road to turn off to get to it. She knew that Bailey would not be willing to lose any time looking at an old house, but the more she talked about it, the more she wanted to see it once again and find out if the little twin arbors were still standing. "There was a secret panel in this house," she said craftily, not telling the truth but wishing that she were, "and the story went that all the family silver was hidden in it when Sherman came through but it was never found . . ."

46 "Hey!" John Wesley said. "Let's go see it! We'll find it! We'll poke all the woodwork and find it! Who lives there? Where do you turn off at? Hey Pop, can't we turn off there?"

47 "We never have seen a house with a secret panel!" June Star shrieked. "Let's go to the house with the secret panel! Hey Pop, can't we go see the house with the secret panel!"

48 "It's not far from here, I know," the grandmother said. "It wouldn't take over twenty minutes."

49 Bailey was looking straight ahead. His jaw was as rigid as a horseshoe. "No," he said.

50 The children began to yell and scream that they wanted to see the house with the secret panel. John Wesley kicked the back of the front seat and June Star hung over her mother's shoulder and whined desperately into her ear that they never had any fun even on their vacation, that they could never do what THEY wanted to do. The baby began to scream and John Wesley kicked the back of the seat so hard that his father could feel the blows in his kidney.

51 "All right!" he shouted and drew the car to a stop at the side of the road. "Will you all shut up? Will you all just shut up for one second? If you don't shut up, we won't go anywhere."

52 "It would be very educational for them," the grandmother murmured.

53 "All right," Bailey said, "but get this: this is the only time we're going to stop for anything like this. This is the one and only time."

54 "The dirt road that you have to turn down is about a mile back," the grandmother directed. "I marked it when we passed."

55 "A dirt road," Bailey groaned.

56 After they had turned around and were headed toward the dirt road, the grandmother recalled other points about the house, the beautiful glass over the front doorway and the candle-lamp in the hall. John Wesley said that the secret panel was probably in the fireplace.

57 "You can't go inside this house," Bailey said. "You don't know who lives there."

58 "While you all talk to the people in front, I'll run around behind and get in a window," John Wesley suggested.

59 "We'll all stay in the car," his mother said. They turned onto the dirt road and the car raced roughly along in a swirl of pink dust. The grandmother recalled the times when there were no paved roads and thirty miles was a day's journey. The dirt road was hilly and there were sudden washes in it and sharp curves on dangerous embankments. All at once they would be on a hill, looking down over the blue tops of trees for miles around, then the next minute, they would be in a red depression with the dust-coated trees looking down on them.

60 "This place had better turn up in a minute," Bailey said, "or I'm going to turn around."

61 The road looked as if no one had traveled on it in months.

62 "It's not much farther," the grandmother said and just as she said it, a horrible thought came to her. The thought was so embarrassing that she turned red in the face and her eyes dilated and her feet jumped up, upsetting her valise in the corner. The instant the valise moved, the newspaper top she had over the basket under it rose with a snarl and Pitty Sing, the cat, sprang onto Bailey's shoulder.

63 The children were thrown to the floor and their mother, clutching the baby, was thrown out the door onto the ground; the old lady was thrown into the front seat. The car turned over once and landed right-side-up in a gulch off the side of the road. Bailey remained in the driver's seat with the cat—gray-striped with a broad white face and an orange nose—clinging to his neck like a caterpillar.

64 As soon as the children saw they could move their arms and legs, they scrambled out of the car, shouting, "We've had an ACCIDENT!" The

Please note that excerpts and passages in the StudySync® library and this workbook are intended as touchstones to generate interest in an author's work. The excerpts and passages do not substitute for the reading of entire texts, and StudySync® strongly recommends that students seek out and purchase the whole literary or informational work in order to experience it as the author intended. Links to online resellers are available in our digital library. In addition, complete works may be ordered through an authorized reseller by filling out and returning to StudySync® the order form enclosed in this workbook.

Reading & Writing Companion 269

grandmother was curled up under the dashboard, hoping she was injured so that Bailey's wrath would not come down on her all at once. The horrible thought she had had before the accident was that the house she had remembered so vividly was not in Georgia but in Tennessee.

65   Bailey removed the cat from his neck with both hands and flung it out the window against the side of a pine tree. Then he got out of the car and started looking for the children's mother. She was sitting against the side of the red gutted ditch, holding the screaming baby, but she only had a cut down her face and a broken shoulder. "We've had an ACCIDENT!" the children screamed in a frenzy of delight.

66   "But nobody's killed," June Star said with disappointment as the grandmother limped out of the car, her hat still pinned to her head but the broken front brim standing up at a **jaunty** angle and the violet spray hanging off the side. They all sat down in the ditch, except the children, to recover from the shock. They were all shaking.

67   "Maybe a car will come along," said the children's mother hoarsely.

68   "I believe I have injured an organ," said the grandmother, pressing her side, but no one answered her. Bailey's teeth were clattering. He had on a yellow sport shirt with bright blue parrots designed in it and his face was as yellow as the shirt. The grandmother decided that she would not mention that the house was in Tennessee.

69   The road was about ten feet above and they could see only the tops of the trees on the other side of it. Behind the ditch they were sitting in there were more woods, tall and dark and deep. In a few minutes they saw a car some distance away on top of a hill, coming slowly as if the occupants were watching them. The grandmother stood up and waved both arms dramatically to attract their attention. The car continued to come on slowly, disappeared around a bend and appeared again, moving even slower, on top of the hill they had gone over. It was a big black battered hearse-like automobile. There were three men in it.

70   It came to a stop just over them and for some minutes, the driver looked down with a steady expressionless gaze to where they were sitting, and didn't speak. Then he turned his head and muttered something to the other two and they got out. One was a fat boy in black trousers and a red sweat shirt with a silver stallion embossed on the front of it. He moved around on the right side of them and stood staring, his mouth partly open in a kind of loose grin. The other had on khaki pants and a blue striped coat and a gray hat pulled down very low, hiding most of his face. He came around slowly on the left side. Neither spoke.

71 The driver got out of the car and stood by the side of it, looking down at them. He was an older man than the other two. His hair was just beginning to gray and he wore silver-rimmed spectacles that gave him a scholarly look. He had a long creased face and didn't have on any shirt or undershirt. He had on blue jeans that were too tight for him and was holding a black hat and a gun. The two boys also had guns.

72 "We've had an ACCIDENT!" the children screamed.

73 The grandmother had the peculiar feeling that the bespectacled man was someone she knew. His face was as familiar to her as if she had known him all her life but she could not recall who he was. He moved away from the car and began to come down the embankment, placing his feet carefully so that he wouldn't slip. He had on tan and white shoes and no socks, and his ankles were red and thin. "Good afternoon," he said. "I see you all had you a little spill."

74 "We turned over twice!" said the grandmother.

75 "Oncet," he corrected. "We seen it happen. Try their car and see will it run, Hiram," he said quietly to the boy with the gray hat.

76 "What you got that gun for?" John Wesley asked. "Whatcha gonna do with that gun?"

77 "Lady," the man said to the children's mother, "would you mind calling them children to sit down by you? Children make me nervous. I want all you all to sit down right together there where you're at."

78 "What are you telling US what to do for?" June Star asked.

79 Behind them the line of woods gaped like a dark open mouth. "Come here," said their mother.

80 "Look here now," Bailey began suddenly, "we're in a predicament! We're in . . ."

81 The grandmother shrieked. She scrambled to her feet and stood staring. "You're The Misfit!" she said. "I recognized you at once!"

82 "Yes'm," the man said, smiling slightly as if he were pleased in spite of himself to be known, "but it would have been better for all of you, lady, if you hadn't of reckernized me."

83 Bailey turned his head sharply and said something to his mother that shocked even the children. The old lady began to cry and The Misfit reddened.

84 "Lady," he said, "don't you get upset. Sometimes a man says things he don't mean. I don't reckon he meant to talk to you thataway."

85   "You wouldn't shoot a lady, would you?" the grandmother said and removed a clean handkerchief from her cuff and began to slap at her eyes with it.

86   The Misfit pointed the toe of his shoe into the ground and made a little hole and then covered it up again. "I would hate to have to," he said.

87   "Listen," the grandmother almost screamed, "I know you're a good man. You don't look a bit like you have common blood. I know you must come from nice people!"

88   "Yes mam," he said, "finest people in the world." When he smiled he showed a row of strong white teeth. "God never made a finer woman than my mother and my daddy's heart was pure gold," he said. The boy with the red sweat shirt had come around behind them and was standing with his gun at his hip. The Misfit squatted down on the ground. "Watch them children, Bobby Lee," he said. "You know they make me nervous." He looked at the six of them huddled together in front of him and he seemed to be embarrassed as if he couldn't think of anything to say. "Ain't a cloud in the sky," he remarked, looking up at it. "Don't see no sun but don't see no cloud neither."

89   "Yes, it's a beautiful day," said the grandmother. "Listen," she said, "you shouldn't call yourself The Misfit because I know you're a good man at heart. I can just look at you and tell."

90   "Hush!" Bailey yelled. "Hush! Everybody shut up and let me handle this!" He was squatting in the position of a runner about to sprint forward but he didn't move.

91   "I prechate that, lady," The Misfit said and drew a little circle in the ground with the butt of his gun.

92   "It'll take a half a hour to fix this here car," Hiram called, looking over the raised hood of it.

93   "Well, first you and Bobby Lee get him and that little boy to step over yonder with you," The Misfit said, pointing to Bailey and John Wesley. "The boys want to ast you some-thing," he said to Bailey. "Would you mind stepping back in them woods there with them?"

94   "Listen," Bailey began, "we're in a terrible predicament! Nobody realizes what this is," and his voice cracked. His eyes were as blue and intense as the parrots in his shirt and he remained perfectly still.

95   The grandmother reached up to adjust her hat brim as if she were going to the woods with him but it came off in her hand. She stood staring at it and after a second she let it fall on the ground. Hiram pulled Bailey up by the arm as if he were assisting an old man. John Wesley caught hold of his father's

hand and Bobby Lee followed. They went off toward the woods and just as they reached the dark edge, Bailey turned and supporting himself against a gray naked pine trunk, he shouted, "I'll be back in a minute, Mamma, wait on me!"

96 "Come back this instant!" his mother shrilled but they all disappeared into the woods.

97 "Bailey Boy!" the grandmother called in a tragic voice but she found she was looking at The Misfit squatting on the ground in front of her. "I just know you're a good man," she said desperately. "You're not a bit common!"

98 "Nome, I ain't a good man," The Misfit said after a second as if he had considered her statement carefully, "but I ain't the worst in the world neither. My daddy said I was a different breed of dog from my brothers and sisters. 'You know,' Daddy said, 'it's some that can live their whole life out without asking about it and it's others has to know why it is, and this boy is one of the latters. He's going to be into every-thing!'" He put on his black hat and looked up suddenly and then away deep into the woods as if he were embarrassed again. "I'm sorry I don't have on a shirt before you ladies," he said, hunching his shoulders slightly. "We buried our clothes that we had on when we escaped and we're just making do until we can get better. We borrowed these from some folks we met," he explained.

99 "That's perfectly all right," the grandmother said. "Maybe Bailey has an extra shirt in his suitcase."

100 "I'll look and see terrectly," The Misfit said.

101 "Where are they taking him?" the children's mother screamed.

102 "Daddy was a card himself," The Misfit said. "You couldn't put anything over on him. He never got in trouble with the Authorities though. Just had the knack of handling them."

103 "You could be honest too if you'd only try," said the grandmother. "Think how wonderful it would be to settle down and live a comfortable life and not have to think about some-body chasing you all the time."

104 The Misfit kept scratching in the ground with the butt of his gun as if he were thinking about it. "Yes'm, somebody is always after you," he murmured.

105 The grandmother noticed how thin his shoulder blades were just behind his hat because she was standing up looking down on him. "Do you ever pray?" she asked.

106 He shook his head. All she saw was the black hat wiggle between his shoulder blades. "Nome," he said.

107 There was a pistol shot from the woods, followed closely by another. Then silence. The old lady's head jerked around. She could hear the wind move through the tree tops like a long satisfied insuck of breath. "Bailey Boy!" she called.

108 "I was a gospel singer for a while," The Misfit said. "I been most everything. Been in the arm service, both land and sea, at home and abroad, been twict married, been an undertaker, been with the railroads, plowed Mother Earth, been in a tornado, seen a man burnt alive oncet," and he looked up at the children's mother and the little girl who were sitting close together, their faces white and their eyes glassy; "I even seen a woman flogged," he said.

109 "Pray, pray," the grandmother began, "pray, pray . . ."

110 "I never was a bad boy that I remember of," The Misfit said in an almost dreamy voice, "but somewheres along the line I done something wrong and got sent to the **penitentiary.** I was buried alive," and he looked up and held her attention to him by a steady stare.

111 "That's when you should have started to pray," she said. "What did you do to get sent to the penitentiary that first time?"

112 "Turn to the right, it was a wall," The Misfit said, looking up again at the cloudless sky. "Turn to the left, it was a wall. Look up it was a ceiling, look down it was a floor. I forget what I done, lady. I set there and set there, trying to remember what it was I done and I ain't recalled it to this day. Oncet in a while, I would think it was coming to me, but it never come."

113 "Maybe they put you in by mistake," the old lady said vaguely.

114 "Nome," he said. "It wasn't no mistake. They had the papers on me."

115 "You must have stolen something," she said.

116 The Misfit sneered slightly. "Nobody had nothing I wanted," he said. "It was a head-doctor at the penitentiary said what I had done was kill my daddy but I known that for a lie. My daddy died in nineteen ought nineteen of the epidemic flu and I never had a thing to do with it. He was buried in the Mount Hopewell Baptist churchyard and you can go there and see for yourself."

117 "If you would pray," the old lady said, "Jesus would help you."

118 "That's right," The Misfit said.

119 "Well then, why don't you pray?" she asked trembling with delight suddenly.

120 "I don't want no hep," he said. "I'm doing all right by myself."

121 Bobby Lee and Hiram came **ambling** back from the woods. Bobby Lee was dragging a yellow shirt with bright blue parrots in it.

122 "Thow me that shirt, Bobby Lee," The Misfit said. The shirt came flying at him and landed on his shoulder and he put it on. The grandmother couldn't name what the shirt reminded her of. "No, lady," The Misfit said while he was buttoning it up, "I found out the crime don't matter. You can do one thing or you can do another, kill a man or take a tire off his car, because sooner or later you're going to forget what it was you done and just be punished for it."

123 The children's mother had begun to make heaving noises as if she couldn't get her breath. "Lady," he asked, "would you and that little girl like to step off yonder with Bobby Lee and Hiram and join your husband?"

124 "Yes, thank you," the mother said faintly. Her left arm dangled helplessly and she was holding the baby, who had gone to sleep, in the other. "Hep that lady up, Hiram," The Misfit said as she struggled to climb out of the ditch, "and Bobby Lee, you hold onto that little girl's hand."

125 "I don't want to hold hands with him," June Star said. "He reminds me of a pig."

126 The fat boy blushed and laughed and caught her by the arm and pulled her off into the woods after Hiram and her mother.

127 Alone with The Misfit, the grandmother found that she had lost her voice. There was not a cloud in the sky nor any sun. There was nothing around her but woods. She wanted to tell him that he must pray. She opened and closed her mouth several times before anything came out. Finally she found herself saying, "Jesus. Jesus," meaning, Jesus will help you, but the way she was saying it, it sounded as if she might be cursing.

128 "Yes'm," The Misfit said as if he agreed. "Jesus thown everything off balance. It was the same case with Him as with me except He hadn't committed any crime and they could prove I had committed one because they had the papers on me. Of course," he said, "they never shown me my papers. That's why I sign myself now. I said long ago, you get you a signature and sign everything you do and keep a copy of it. Then you'll know what you done and you can hold up the crime to the punishment and see do they match and in the end you'll have something to prove you ain't been treated right. I call myself The Misfit," he said, "because I can't make what all I done wrong fit what all I gone through in punishment."

129 There was a piercing scream from the woods, followed closely by a pistol report. "Does it seem right to you, lady, that one is punished a heap and another ain't punished at all?"

Reading & Writing Companion **275**

130　"Jesus!" the old lady cried. "You've got good blood! I know you wouldn't shoot a lady! I know you come from nice people! Pray! Jesus, you ought not to shoot a lady. I'll give you all the money I've got!"

131　"Lady," The Misfit said, looking beyond her far into the woods, "there never was a body that give the undertaker a tip."

132　There were two more pistol reports and the grandmother raised her head like a parched old turkey hen crying for water and called, "Bailey Boy, Bailey Boy!" as if her heart would break.

133　"Jesus was the only One that ever raised the dead," The Misfit continued, "and He shouldn't have done it. He thown everything off balance. If He did what He said, then it's nothing for you to do but thow away everything and follow Him, and if He didn't, then it's nothing for you to do but enjoy the few minutes you got left the best way you can—by killing somebody or burning down his house or doing some other meanness to him. No pleasure but meanness," he said and his voice had become almost a snarl.

134　"Maybe He didn't raise the dead," the old lady mumbled, not knowing what she was saying and feeling so dizzy that she sank down in the ditch with her legs twisted under her.

135　"I wasn't there so I can't say He didn't," The Misfit said. "I wisht I had of been there," he said, hitting the ground with his fist. "It ain't right I wasn't there because if I had of been there I would of known. Listen lady," he said in a high voice, "if I had of been there I would of known and I wouldn't be like I am now." His voice seemed about to crack and the grandmother's head cleared for an instant. She saw the man's face twisted close to her own as if he were going to cry and she murmured, "Why you're one of my babies. You're one of my own children!" She reached out and touched him on the shoulder. The Misfit sprang back as if a snake had bitten him and shot her three times through the chest. Then he put his gun down on the ground and took off his glasses and began to clean them.

136　Hiram and Bobby Lee returned from the woods and stood over the ditch, looking down at the grandmother who half sat and half lay in a puddle of blood with her legs crossed under her like a child's and her face smiling up at the cloudless sky.

137　Without his glasses, The Misfit's eyes were red-rimmed and pale and defenseless-looking. "Take her off and thow her where you thown the others," he said, picking up the cat that was rubbing itself against his leg.

138　"She was a talker, wasn't she?" Bobby Lee said, sliding down the ditch with a yodel.

139 "She would of been a good woman," The Misfit said, "if it had been somebody there to shoot her every minute of her life."

140 "Some fun!" Bobby Lee said.

141 "Shut up, Bobby Lee," The Misfit said. "It's no real pleasure in life."

Please note that excerpts and passages in the StudySync® library and this workbook are intended as touchstones to generate interest in an author's work. The excerpts and passages do not substitute for the reading of entire texts, and StudySync® strongly recommends that students seek out and purchase the whole literary or informational work in order to experience it as the author intended. Links to online resellers are available in our digital library. In addition, complete works may be ordered through an authorized reseller by filling out and returning to StudySync® the order form enclosed in this workbook.

Reading & Writing Companion   277

First Read

Read "A Good Man Is Hard to Find." After you read, complete the Think Questions below.

☁ THINK QUESTIONS

1. How would you describe the grandmother's general outlook on the world? How does she think and act differently from her son, Bailey, and her grandchildren, John Wesley and June Star?

2. Why does the grandmother recognize the driver of the car? Explain the events in the story leading up to this moment that foreshadow the man's arrival.

3. What is The Misfit's philosophy? How does he see things differently from the grandmother?

4. Based on its context, what do you think the word **jaunty** means? Write your best definition of *jaunty* here, explaining how you determined its meaning.

5. What do you think the word **ambling** means? Look at the context in which the word is used in the story, and write your own definition of *ambling* here.

Skill:
Story Structure

Use the Checklist to analyze Story Structure in "A Good Man Is Hard to Find." Refer to the sample student annotations about Story Structure in the text.

••• CHECKLIST FOR STORY STRUCTURE

In order to identify the choices an author makes when structuring specific parts of a text, note the following:

- ✓ the choices an author makes to organize specific parts of a text such as where to begin and end a story, or whether the ending should be tragic, comic, or inconclusive

- ✓ the author's use of any literary devices, such as:

  - foreshadowing: a way of hinting at what will come later
  - flashback: a part of a story that shows something that happened in the past
  - pacing: how quickly or slowly the events of a story unfold

- ✓ how the overall structure of the text contributes to its meaning as well as to its aesthetic impact

  - the effect structure has on the reader, such as the creation of suspense through the use of pacing
  - the use of flashback to reveal hidden dimensions of a character that affect the theme

To analyze how an author's choices concerning how to structure specific parts of a text contribute to its overall structure and meaning as well as its aesthetic impact, consider the following questions:

- ✓ How does the author structure the text overall? How does the author structure specific parts of the text?

- ✓ Does the author incorporate literary elements such as flashback or foreshadowing?

- ✓ How do these elements affect the overall text structure and the aesthetic impact of the text?

Copyright © BookheadEd Learning, LLC

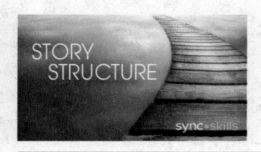

Skill:
Story Structure

Reread paragraphs 66–73 of "A Good Man Is Hard to Find." Then, using the Checklist on the previous page, answer the multiple-choice questions below.

⟳ YOUR TURN

1. What impact does the author's narration of this scene have on the reader?

   ○ A. It creates comfort, anticipation, and excitement in the reader and sets up the reader for the story's surprise ending.

   ○ B. It creates discomfort, anticipation, and fear in the reader and sets up the reader for the story's eerie, tragic ending.

   ○ C. It creates discomfort, anticipation, and fear in the reader and sets up the reader for the story's happy ending.

   ○ D. It creates comfort, anticipation, and excitement in the reader and sets up the reader for the story's eerie, tragic ending.

2. In this scene, the reader encounters The Misfit. How does the revelation about who he is contribute to the suspense of this scene?

   ○ A. To create suspense, the driver of the car is portrayed with vivid, descriptive details and the grandmother is described as having a feeling that he is someone she knows, which gives the reader subtle hints about who he is.

   ○ B. To create suspense, the driver of the car is portrayed as a man with glasses that make him look like a scholar, which gives the reader subtle hints about who he is.

   ○ C. To create suspense, the driver of the car is described as getting out of the car and standing by it as the grandmother is screaming that they have had an accident, which gives the reader subtle hints about who he is.

   ○ D. To create suspense, the driver of the car is described as having a gun and no shirt. The grandmother is described as noting that the driver's face is very familiar to her, which gives the reader subtle hints about who he is.

3. The grandmother has a feeling that she recognizes the driver. How does this realization lead to the story's climax?

○ A. The grandmother realizes that she is mistaken and begins to try to persuade the driver not to kill her and this leads up to the story's climax.

○ B. The grandmother's recognition of the driver makes the reader wonder if he is The Misfit. She then realizes that the man whom she is looking to for help is The Misfit, which is the conflict in the story that leads to the climax.

○ C. The grandmother's recognition of the driver makes the reader wonder if he is The Misfit. She then realizes that the man whom she is looking to for help is The Misfit, and this leads up to the story's climax.

○ D. The grandmother's recognition of the driver makes the reader wonder if the man is related to her. She then realizes that the man whom she is looking to for help is her estranged nephew, and this leads up to the story's climax.

Skill:
Connotation and Denotation

Use the Checklist to analyze Connotation and Denotation in "A Good Man Is Hard to Find." Refer to the sample student annotations about Connotation and Denotation in the text.

••• CHECKLIST FOR CONNOTATION AND DENOTATION

In order to identify the denotative meanings of words, use the following steps:

- ✓ first, note unfamiliar words and phrases, key words used to describe important characters, events, and ideas, or words that inspire an emotional reaction

- ✓ next, determine and note the denotative meaning of words by consulting a reference material such as a dictionary, glossary, or thesaurus

- ✓ finally, analyze nuances in the meaning of words with similar denotations

To better understand the meaning of words and phrases as they are used in a text, including connotative meanings, use the following questions as a guide:

- ✓ What is the genre or subject of the text? Based on context, what do you think the meaning of the word is intended to be?

- ✓ Is your inference the same as or different from the dictionary definition?

- ✓ Does the word create a positive, negative, or neutral emotion? .

- ✓ What synonyms or alternative phrasings help you describe the connotative meaning of the word?

To determine the meaning of words and phrases as they are used in a text, including connotative meanings, use the following questions as a guide:

- ✓ What is the denotative meaning of the word? Is that denotative meaning correct in context?

- ✓ What possible positive, neutral, or negative connotations might the word have, depending on context?

- ✓ What textual details signal a particular connotation for the word?

Skill:
Connotation and Denotation

Reread paragraphs 49–53 of "A Good Man Is Hard to Find." Then, using the Checklist on the previous page, answer the multiple-choice questions below.

↻ YOUR TURN

1. How does the description of Bailey's jaw as "rigid as a horseshoe" in paragraph 49 affect the reader's understanding of this part of the story?

   ○ A. The description of Bailey's jaw suggests that he is a rigid person but that he is also willing to do things to make his children and mother happy.

   ○ B. The description of Bailey's jaw suggests that he is determined not to stray off course and implies a lack of flexibility and unwillingness to be swayed.

   ○ C. The description of Bailey's jaw suggests that he is determined not to stray off course and implies that he has opinions that he is unwilling to change.

   ○ D. The description of Bailey's jaw suggests that he is determined to stray off course and implies that although he is flexible, he does not want to be told what to do.

2. Which word does not have a negative connotation as used in this excerpt of the text?

   ○ A. desperately
   ○ B. scream
   ○ C. blows
   ○ D. educational

Please note that excerpts and passages in the StudySync® library and this workbook are intended as touchstones to generate interest in an author's work. The excerpts and passages do not substitute for the reading of entire texts, and StudySync® strongly recommends that students seek out and purchase the whole literary or informational work in order to experience it as the author intended. Links to online resellers are available in our digital library. In addition, complete works may be ordered through an authorized reseller by filling out and returning to StudySync® the order form enclosed in this workbook.

Reading & Writing
Companion

283

Close Read

Reread "A Good Man Is Hard to Find." As you reread, complete the Skills Focus questions below. Then use your answers and annotations from the questions to help you complete the Write activity.

◎ SKILLS FOCUS

1. Identify the attitude the children have towards their grandmother. Find examples of words with negative connotations that reveal the kids' tone.

2. In what ways does the grandmother manipulate her family members? How do her manipulations contribute to the story's tragic ending?

3. How does the scene with Red Sam and his wife contribute to the overall structure of the story?

Identify evidence from the text to support your answer.

4. How does the ending of the story contribute to its overall meaning? Identify evidence from the text to support your answer.

5. How does the grandmother's perspective change over the course of the story? Find evidence to support your answer.

✏ WRITE

COMPARE AND CONTRAST: Compare and contrast the way the short story "A Good Man Is Hard to Find" and the poem "Because I could not stop for Death" use text structure to express and contribute to each text's overall meaning about death. Provide analysis and textual evidence from both the poem and the short story to support your response.

Little Miss Sunshine

DRAMA
Michael Arndt
2006

Introduction

*L*ittle Miss Sunshine is a 2006 screenplay by Michael Arndt about a family from Albuquerque, New Mexico—the Hoovers—who set off to California in order for their youngest daughter, Olive, to compete in the "Little Miss Sunshine" beauty pageant. In the scene excerpted here, Olive and her grandfather play games in the back seat of their now-broken-down Volkswagen bus while the mother and father, Sheryl and Richard strategize with a mechanic. Outside the car, Sheryl's brother Frank and her oldest son, Dwayne, look on.

"Dwayne watches bitterly—this is just one more fiasco he's been dragged into."

INT. VW BUS - PARKED - DAY

1   Sheryl is trying to back up the bus. She's grinding gears.

RICHARD
2   Push the stick down hard!

SHERYL
3   I'm pushing hard!

RICHARD
4   Put the clutch in all the way!

SHERYL
5   It's on the floor!

JUMP CUT TO:

6   Richard tries. He keeps grinding gears as well. It's a horrible sound.

INT. SERVICE STATION GARAGE - DAY

7   Richard and Sheryl talk to a MECHANIC.

8   Behind them, Olive and Grandpa are playing that game where you try to slap the other person's wrists. When Grandpa gets hit, he reacts with cries of pain—much to Olive's delight.

9   In the background, across the lot, Dwayne and Frank sit on a cinderblock wall, waiting for the situation to **resolve** itself.

MECHANIC
10   Well, you got a problem. Your clutch
     is shot.

RICHARD
11   Can we get a new one?

MECHANIC

12 Well, I tell you what: These old buses?
We'd have to order it.

RICHARD

13 How long'd that take?

MECHANIC

14 Well, it's the weekend, so . . .
Maybe Thursday?

15 Richard and Sheryl react.

EXT. SERVICE STATION - DAY

16 Frank and Dwayne sit silently. Dwayne watches bitterly--this is just one more **fiasco** he's been dragged into.

17 Frank looks on **wistfully** as Sheryl--thirty yards away--glances worriedly between Richard and the Mechanic. Frank notices Dwayne's stare. He speaks without looking at Dwayne.

FRANK

18 I don't know if you know this, but growing up? Your Mom was the cool one. She turned me on to Proust. She could've done anything.

19 Dwayne looks at Frank—he can't quite believe this. He takes out his pad, half-smirking, and writes:

20 "What happened?"

21 Frank looks at the pad, then at Dwayne.

FRANK (cont'd)

22 She had you, Dwayne.

23 He pats Dwayne on the leg, gets up, and walks back towards Richard and Sheryl. Dwayne is left alone, taking this in.

INT. SERVICE STATION GARAGE - DAY

24 Frank wanders in as Richard presses the Mechanic. Grandpa and Olive stop their game and join the conversation.

RICHARD

25 Okay, look: we've come two hundred miles . . . Is there a dealership around here?

NOTES

MECHANIC

26   Well, you could call over to Clarksville, but they're probably closed. Y'know, it's the weekend.

RICHARD

27   Yeah, we're all aware of that.

28   Silence. The Mechanic feels bad for them. Dwayne re-enters.

MECHANIC

29   Well, I tell you what: these old buses? You don't need a clutch to shift from third to fourth. You just ease up on the gas. You only really need the clutch for first and second.

30   Richard doesn't understand what he's getting at.

MECHANIC (cont'd)

31   What I'm sayin' is: as long as you keep parkin' on a hill, you get yourself goin' fifteen, twenty miles an hour, and you just start up in third. Then you shift between third and fourth.

RICHARD

32   And you can drive like that?

MECHANIC

33   Oh, yeah. The problem's just getting that speed up. As long as you keep parkin' it on a hill, you're fine. My brother and I once drove from here to Canada . . .

RICHARD

34   What if you're not on a hill?

MECHANIC

35   What?

RICHARD

36   I mean, it's sitting here right now. There's no hill. How do we . . . ?

37   The Mechanic considers this. He squints his eyes and runs his tongue back and forth across his teeth.

MECHANIC

38   Well, I tell you what: You get enough people—you just get behind there and push. Just push it up to ten, fifteen miles an hour, and you just go. Everybody jump inside, and you just go!

39   They all stare at him.

EXT. PARKING LOT - DAY

40 Richard's at the wheel of the bus. Everyone else, including the Mechanic, is behind the bus. The sliding door is open.

RICHARD
41 Okay, ready?! Olive, Dad: I want you in the car first.

OLIVE
42 I know. We know.

RICHARD
43 Okay, is everyone ready?

SHERYL
44 Yes! Let's go!

45 Richard starts up the bus. Frank turns to the others.

FRANK
46 I just want everyone here to know I'm the **preeminent** Proust scholar in the United States.

RICHARD
47 Okay, go! Push!

48 They all push. The van starts rolling, slow at first, then faster and faster. Finally, they're all running behind it.

RICHARD (cont'd)
49 Olive, Dad, get in! Sheryl!

50 Olive, Grandpa, and Sheryl jump in the side door. The Mechanic fades. Frank and Dwayne keep pushing faster.

RICHARD (cont'd)
51 Okay, I'm puttin' it into gear! Get
    ready!

52 He guns the engine and shifts from neutral to third. The bus is REVVING low but is powering itself nonetheless.

SHERYL
53 Okay, get in! Get in!
    (to Richard)
54 Slow down! You're losing them!

RICHARD
55 I can't! I can't slow down!

56 Dwayne runs up to the door. He sees Frank is fading.

57 He runs back to Frank, gets behind him, and pushes him up alongside the bus. Frank dives in. Dwayne dives after him.

INT. VW BUS - ON THE ROAD - DAY

58 Everyone cheers. Frank is panting. Dwayne shuts the door.

RICHARD

59 Is that it? Are we in?

FRANK
(to Dwayne)

60 "No one gets left behind! No one gets left behind!" Outstanding, soldier! Outstanding!

61 Frank salutes him. Dwayne smiles, embarrassed.

Excerpted from *Little Miss Sunshine* by Michael Arndt, published by Newmarket Press.

 WRITE

NARRATIVE: Write an account about a time, real or imagined, when something broke down. What was that experience like? How did those involved respond? Incorporate characteristics of literary texts such as characterization, point of view, setting, plot, and descriptive details in your narrative.

Extended
Writing
Project and
Grammar

EXTENDED
WRITING
PROJECT
INFORMATIVE
WRITING

Informative Writing Process: Plan

| PLAN | DRAFT | REVISE | EDIT AND PUBLISH |

Americans have been travelers since indigenous peoples arrived here many millennia ago. Though modes of travel have changed, movement from one location to another has been a constant aspect of our identity. We have become who we are not just from the destinations we have reached, but also from what we have learned in the many years we have spent "on the road."

WRITING PROMPT

What do we learn along the way?

From non-fiction selections in this unit (including research links in the Blasts), select two or three texts that connect to the idea of being on a journey. Write an informative essay in which you describe the road or the route of the journey in each text, who travels it, and what he or she learns, or might learn, along the way. Be sure to include the personal and cultural importance this journey has and any risks the traveler may have to take. Your informative essay should also include the following:

- an introduction
- a thesis statement
- a clear text structure
- supporting evidence and details
- a conclusion

Writing to Sources

As you gather ideas and information from the texts in the unit, be sure to

- use evidence from multiple sources,
- avoid overly relying on one source.

Introduction to Informative Writing

Informative writing examines a topic and conveys ideas and information through comparisons, description, and explanation. Strong informative writing includes a main idea or thesis statement supported by evidence, such as definitions, quotations, examples, and facts. The characteristics of informative writing include:

- an introduction with a clear thesis statement

- evidence and details that support the thesis

- a clear and logical text structure

- a formal style

- a conclusion that wraps up your ideas

In addition to these characteristics, informative writers also carefully craft their work through word choice and an objective point of view. These choices help to shape the tone and overall style of the text. Effective informative essays combine these genre characteristics and craft to engage the reader.

As you continue with this Extended Writing Project, you'll receive more instruction and practice in crafting each of the characteristics of informative writing to create your own informative essay.

Please note that excerpts and passages in the StudySync® library and this workbook are intended as touchstones to generate interest in an author's work. The excerpts and passages do not substitute for the reading of entire texts, and StudySync® strongly recommends that students seek out and purchase the whole literary or informational work in order to experience it as the author intended. Links to online resellers are available in our digital library. In addition, complete works may be ordered through an authorized reseller by filling out and returning to StudySync® the order form enclosed in this workbook.

Reading & Writing
Companion

293

Before you get started on your own informative essay, read this essay that one student, Juliana, wrote in response to the writing prompt. As you read the Model, highlight and annotate the features of informative writing that Juliana included in her informative essay.

NOTES

☰ STUDENT MODEL

Journeys Lead to Liberation

1 Beginning with the indigenous people who first inhabited this land, Americans have time and again demonstrated the self-determination it takes to journey into the unknown. Whether the goal is the expansion of the nation's boundaries or personal growth, journeys have guided curious travelers through a range of transformations. Eddy L. Harris and Henry David Thoreau published firsthand accounts of their ambitious adventures into the American wilderness. Their journeys took place at different periods in our nation's history. Yet, they both show a desire to seize the opportunity to defy expectations and prove their self-reliance. Harris's and Thoreau's personal accounts serve as a roadmap that shows where courage can take you in life.

2 In *Mississippi Solo: A River Quest,* Eddy L. Harris describes growing up in St. Louis, Missouri, near the Mississippi River. Since he was a child, the Mississippi has dominated Harris's imagination. He fantasized yielding to the river's power by "hanging onto whatever and floating along with it, letting the river drop me off wherever and pick me up later and take me on again." At thirty years old, Harris fears that he is no longer free to go on adventures and that he must give in to mundane responsibilities. Instead of allowing his anxieties to take over, he commits to making his dream a reality. Harris chooses the Mississippi River as his route to independence because, to him, it is more than just a body of water. On the one hand, he appreciates its function as a means of transportation. He acknowledges the roles it has played as a physical landmark in the history of America's "sins and salvation, dreams and adventure and destiny." On the other hand, Harris fears the river. He compares it to authoritative figures in his life, such as his father and God. By going up against the historically and intimately significant river, Harris hopes to test his resilience and become a part of the river's complex legacy.

3   Harris takes dreams, like his desire to travel down the Mississippi River, very seriously. He is willing to do whatever he can to accomplish them. He states, "Dreams are delicate and made of gossamer," which suggests that he believes they must be treated carefully. Therefore, Harris is hurt when his friends respond to his journey down the Mississippi River with skepticism. They don't understand the purpose of his journey or why he must put himself in harm's way. The river is hazardous due to unpredictable weather, wind, and water conditions as well as the large boats transporting goods and people. Even Harris himself admits canoeing down the entire river isn't safe. Nevertheless, he is determined to live his dream.

4   Similarly, Henry David Thoreau decided to prove his own abilities by facing nature head-on. Thoreau was a prolific writer and prominent figure in the transcendentalist movement in the nineteenth century. Transcendentalism was an intellectual and religious movement that prioritized self-reliance and the natural world in response to industrialization. In *Walden,* Thoreau discusses how he participated in a noteworthy experiment that required him to put transcendentalist values into practice. At the age of twenty-seven, he built a cabin at Walden Pond near Concord, Massachusetts. He lived there for over two years, fully immersing himself in the natural world to better understand the negative effects of the Industrial Revolution.

5   Although industrialization had positive effects, such as more efficient transportation, in *Walden* Thoreau disputes the benefits of the rapid growth of civilization in America. For example, life began to move at a faster pace than ever before. Thoreau believes this led people to live hectic lives constantly occupied by non-essential factors. A passionate naturalist, he aimed to use his own journey at Walden Pond to advocate for a lifestyle grounded in simplicity. He famously states, "I went to the woods because I wished to live deliberately, to front only the essential facts of life." In other words, Thoreau believes a life that is not wasteful is better for people and the environment. Life in the woods, away from the constant buzz of civilization, allowed him to engage more deeply with what is essential: nature and his own spirit.

6   Thoreau's adventure at Walden Pond was a personal journey as well as a campaign against the new obsession with building capital. Thoreau criticizes people's preoccupation with money, suggesting

that the nation was so concerned with accruing wealth that people were no longer invested in internally bettering themselves. To emphasize this point, he asks, "Why should we live with such hurry and waste of life? We are determined to be starved before we are hungry." Here he uses a metaphor of hunger to demonstrate that people had developed a habit of both producing and consuming in excess to a point that they were no longer in touch with their most basic needs. Thoreau does not believe financial success is a progressive or admirable goal. Instead, he proposes that people free themselves from this mindset by emulating his minimalist and nature-based lifestyle.

7   Both Eddy L. Harris and Henry David Thoreau learned a lot about themselves through their journeys in nature. Harris planned an overdue solo adventure to see how his life would change if he joined forces with the river he so loved and feared. Thoreau spent two years alone in the woods to fully engage in the natural world so that he might report on the best way to live life. Neither knew exactly what he would encounter. Both men were willing to risk their lives because they feared missing out on the chance to liberate themselves. Their reward was learning that they were strong enough to survive on their own.

WRITE

Writers often take notes about their ideas before they sit down to write. Think about what you've learned so far about informative writing to help you begin prewriting.

- **Purpose:** What texts do you want to write about? How do the texts connect to each other as well as to the idea of being on a journey?

- **Audience:** Who is your audience, and what is their connection to the topic of your essay? How will you engage them in your point of view?

- **Introduction:** How will you clearly introduce the topic and thesis of your essay? What language can you use that is both precise and intriguing?

- **Thesis Statement:** What is your unique claim or observation about the texts? Why is your opinion relevant and significant?

- **Text Structure:** What strategies will you use to organize your response to the prompt? How can you ensure that the progression of your ideas is logical and well developed?

- **Supporting Evidence and Details:** What textual evidence might you use to add substance to your essay? Where did you find this information? Which details are essential, and which details can you leave out?

- **Conclusion:** How does the information in the body of your essay relate to your thesis? How can you connect the ideas presented in your essay to a greater concept or to society in a thoughtful way?

Response Instructions

Use the questions in the bulleted list to write a one-paragraph summary. Your summary should describe what you will explain in your essay.

Don't worry about including all of the details now; focus only on the most essential and important elements. You will refer to this short summary as you continue through the steps of the writing process.

Skill:
Organizing Informative Writing

••• CHECKLIST FOR ORGANIZING INFORMATIVE WRITING

As you begin to organize your writing for your informative essay, use the following questions as a guide:

- What is a brief summary of my topic?
- How can I organize my ideas so that each new element builds on previous material?
- Can I use visual elements such as headings, graphics, or multimedia?

Here are steps you can use to organize complex ideas, concepts, and information so that each new element builds on that which precedes it to create a unified whole:

- definitions
  > first, define a subject or concept
  > second, define the qualities of the subject or concept
  > third, provide examples, focusing on showing different aspects of the subject or concept

- classifications
  > first, identify the main idea or topic
  > second, divide the main idea or topic into categories, focusing on how you want to explain your ideas
  > third, use the categories to provide descriptive details and deepen understanding

- comparisons
  > first, identify two texts about similar topics to compare
  > second, identify the similarities and differences between the texts
  > third, determine how those comparisons reveal larger ideas about the topic of the texts

- cause and effect
  > first, determine what happened in a text, including the order of events
  > second, identify the reasons that something happened
  > third, connect what happened and the reasons for it to the main idea or claim

⟳ YOUR TURN

Read each sentence from an informative essay below. Then, complete the chart by writing the organizational structure that would be most appropriate for the purpose, topic, and context of the informative essay, as well as its audience.

Organizational Structure Options			
comparisons	cause and effect	definitions	classifications

Informative Essay Sentence	Organizational Structure
Understanding the idea of democracy begins with understanding the meaning of the word.	
The second category of caffeinated beverages that were popular in ancient civilizations is tea.	
Not everyone thinks it is a wise decision to buy a home.	
Every fall, monarch butterflies migrate south to Southern California and Mexico to escape the cold weather.	

Please note that excerpts and passages in the StudySync® library and this workbook are intended as touchstones to generate interest in an author's work. The excerpts and passages do not substitute for the reading of entire texts, and StudySync® strongly recommends that students seek out and purchase the whole literary or informational work in order to experience it as the author intended. Links to online resellers are available in our digital library. In addition, complete works may be ordered through an authorized reseller by filling out and returning to StudySync® the order form enclosed in this workbook.

Reading & Writing Companion 299

YOUR TURN

Complete the chart below by writing a short summary of what you will focus on in each paragraph of your essay.

Outline	Summary
Introduction	
Body Paragraph 1	
Body Paragraph 2	
Body Paragraph 3	
Conclusion	

Skill:
Thesis Statement

Before you begin writing your thesis statement, ask yourself the following questions:

- What is the prompt asking me to write about?
- What claim do I want to make about the topic of this essay?
- Is my claim precise and informative?
- Does my thesis statement introduce the body of my essay?
- Where should I place my thesis statement?

Here are some methods to introduce and develop a topic as well as a precise and informative claim:

- think about your central claim of your essay
  - > identify a clear claim you want to introduce, thinking about:
    - how closely your claim is related to your topic and how specific it is to your supporting details
    - how your claim includes necessary information to guide the reader through the topic
  - > identify as many claims as you intend to prove

- your thesis statement should:
  - > let the reader anticipate the content of your essay
  - > help you begin your essay in an organized manner
  - > present your opinion clearly
  - > respond completely to the writing prompt

- consider the best placement for your thesis statement
  - > if your response is short, you may want to get right to the point and present your thesis statement in the first sentence of the essay
  - > if your response is longer (as in a formal essay), you can build up to your thesis statement and place it at the end of your introductory paragraph

Please note that excerpts and passages in the StudySync® library and this workbook are intended as touchstones to generate interest in an author's work. The excerpts and passages do not substitute for the reading of entire texts, and StudySync® strongly recommends that students seek out and purchase the whole literary or informational work in order to experience it as the author intended. Links to online resellers are available in our digital library. In addition, complete works may be ordered through an authorized reseller by filling out and returning to StudySync® the order form enclosed in this workbook.

Reading & Writing Companion   **301**

⟳ YOUR TURN

Read the sentences below. Then, complete the chart by sorting the sentences into two categories: thesis statements and statements of fact. Write the corresponding letter for each sentence in the appropriate column.

	Sentence Options
A	Harris feared that he was too old to pursue his childhood dream of journeying along the Mississippi River.
B	Henry David Thoreau's determination to put his own beliefs and abilities to the test proves that people are often stronger than they think they are.
C	Eddy L. Harris's journey teaches readers that it is never too late to follow their dreams.
D	Striking out on your own may be dangerous, but Harris's and Thoreau's reflections on their journeys show that it is worth the risk.
E	Although Harris's and Thoreau's accounts were published more than 100 years apart, their memoirs are similar because they discuss the risks each man took.
F	One of the most fundamental tenets of transcendentalism is the close connection between humanity and the natural world.

Thesis Statement	Statement of Fact

✎ WRITE

Use the checklist to draft a thesis statement for your informative essay.

SUPPORTING DETAILS

sync•skills

Skill:
Supporting Details

Copyright © BookheadEd Learning, LLC

••• CHECKLIST FOR SUPPORTING DETAILS

As you look for supporting details to develop your topic, claim, or thesis statement, ask yourself the following questions:

- What is my main idea about this topic?
- What does a reader need to know about the topic in order to understand the main idea?
- What details will support my thesis?
- Is this information necessary to the reader's understanding of the topic?
- Does this information help to develop and refine my main idea?

Here are some suggestions for how you can develop your topic:

- review your thesis or claim
- consider what your audience knows about the topic
- note what the audience will need to know to understand the topic
- develop your topic thoroughly and accurately, taking into consideration all of its aspects
- be sure to consult credible sources
- use different types of supporting details, such as:
  - > the most significant and relevant facts that are specific to your topic, make an impact in your discussion, and fully support your thesis or claim
  - > extended definitions to explain difficult concepts, terms, or ideas
  - > concrete details that will add descriptive material about your topic
  - > quotations to directly connect your thesis statement or claim to the text
  - > examples and other information to deepen the audience's knowledge

↻ YOUR TURN

Read the thesis statement and detail options below. Then, complete the chart by sorting the details into two categories: concrete details and not concrete details. Write the corresponding letter for each detail in the appropriate column.

THESIS: In their memoirs, both Eddy L. Harris and Henry David Thoreau show a determination to defy the expectations of others and prove their self-reliance in nature.

	Details Options
A	Both Eddy L. Harris and Henry David Thoreau learned a lot about themselves through their journeys in nature.
B	Harris states, "Dreams are delicate and made of gossamer," which suggests that he believes they must be treated carefully.
C	Eddy L. Harris and Henry David Thoreau published firsthand accounts of their ambitious adventures into the American wilderness.
D	Thoreau's adventure at Walden Pond was a personal journey that brought him satisfaction.
E	Thoreau was a prolific writer and prominent figure in the transcendentalist movement in the nineteenth century.
F	By traveling the river, Harris hopes to get closer to nature and the river's legacy.

Concrete Detail	Not Concrete Detail

WRITE

Use the checklist to create a two-column chart. Write your thesis statement at the top of the chart. Then, in the first column, list supporting details for at least one of the texts you have chosen to discuss in your informative essay. In the second column, list your reasons for including the details.

Informative Writing Process: Draft

PLAN	DRAFT	REVISE	EDIT AND PUBLISH

You have already made progress toward writing your informative essay. Now it is time to draft your informative essay.

✎ WRITE

Use your plan and other responses in your Binder to draft your informative essay. You may also have new ideas as you begin drafting. Feel free to explore those new ideas as you have them. You can also ask yourself these questions to ensure that your writing is focused, organized, and supported by details:

Draft Checklist:

☐ **Focused:** Have I made my thesis clear to readers?

☐ **Organized:** Does the organizational structure in my essay make sense? Will readers be engaged by the organization and interested in the way I present my information and evidence?

☐ **Supported by Details:** Have I included only relevant supporting evidence and nothing extraneous that might confuse my readers?

Before you submit your draft, read it over carefully. You want to be sure that you've responded to all aspects of the prompt.

Here is Juliana's informative essay draft. As you read, notice how Juliana develops her draft to be focused, organized, and supported by details. As she continues to revise and edit her essay, she will find and improve weak spots in her writing, as well as correct any language or punctuation mistakes.

~~Journeys have guided curious travelers through a range of transformations. Eddy L. Harris and Henry David Thoreau published memoirs about their adventures into the great outdoors. Their journeys took place at different places and times. Yet, Harris and Thoreau both show a determination to seize the opportunity to defy expectations and prove their self-reliance. Harris's and Thoreau's stories show where courage can take you in life.~~

Beginning with the indigenous people who first inhabited this land, Americans have time and again demonstrated the self-determination it takes to journey into the unknown. Whether the goal is the expansion of the nation's boundaries or personal growth, journeys have guided curious travelers through a range of transformations. Eddy L. Harris and Henry David Thoreau published firsthand accounts of their ambitious adventures into the American wilderness. Their journeys took place at different periods in our nation's history. Yet, they both show a desire to seize the opportunity to defy expectations and prove their self-reliance. Harris's and Thoreau's personal accounts serve as a roadmap that shows where courage can take you in life.

~~Harris takes dreams way too seriously. He is willing to do whatever he can to accomplish them. He states "dreams are made of gossamer," which suggests that he believes they must be treated delicately. That's why Harris is really sore when his friends respond to his journey down the Mississippi River with skepticism. I would be too. They don't understand the purpose of his journey or why he must put himself in harms way. The river is hazardous due to unpredictable weather, wind, and water conditions as well as the large boats transporting goods and people. Even Harris himself admits canoeing down the entire river is a dumb idea. Nevertheless, he is determined to live his dream.~~

Skill:
Introductions

Juliana decides to create a more engaging, complex introduction to hook her readers' interest. She provides more context about the history of American journeys and includes inspiring and more descriptive language.

In *Mississippi Solo: A River Quest*, Eddy L. Harris describes growing up in St. Louis, Missouri, near the Mississippi River. Since he was growing up, the Mississippi has dominated Harris's imagination. He fantasized yielding to the rivers power by hanging onto whatever and floating along with it, letting the river drop me off wherever and pick me up later and take me on again. Harris fears that he is no longer free to go on adventures and that he must give in to mundain responsibilities. Instead of allowing his anxieties to take over, he commits to making his dream a reality. Harris chooses the Mississippi River as his route to independence because, to him, it is more than just a body of water. On the one hand, he appreciates its function as a means of transportation and the roles it has played as a physical landmark in the history of America's, "sins and salvation, dreams and adventure and destiny." On the other hand, Harris fears the river. He compares it to authoritative figures in his life. He makes connections to his father and God. By going up against the historically and intimately significant river Harris hopes to test his resilience and become a part of the river's complex legacy.

In *Mississippi Solo: A River Quest*, Eddy L. Harris describes growing up in St. Louis, Missouri, near the Mississippi River. Since he was a child, the Mississippi has dominated Harris's imagination. He fantasized yielding to the river's power by "hanging onto whatever and floating along with it, letting the river drop me off wherever and pick me up later and take me on again." At thirty years old, Harris fears that he is no longer free to go on adventures and that he must give in to mundane responsibilities. Instead of allowing his anxieties to take over, he commits to making his dream a reality. Harris chooses the Mississippi River as his route to independence because, to him, it is more than just a body of water. On the one hand, he appreciates its function as a means of transportation. He acknowledges the roles it has played as a physical landmark in the history of America's "sins and salvation, dreams and adventure and destiny." On the other hand, Harris fears the river. He compares it to authoritative figures in his life, such as his father and God. By going up against the historically and intimately significant river, Harris hopes to test his resilience and become a part of the river's complex legacy.

NOTES

Skill:
Transitions

Juliana notices that her two paragraphs about Harris's journey are not in a logical order, so she reverses them. Then she realizes she needs to connect the paragraphs. So she adds a transition to the beginning of the second one.

Harris takes dreams, like his desire to travel down the Mississippi River, very seriously. He is willing to do whatever he can to accomplish them. He states, "Dreams are delicate and made of gossamer," which suggests that he believes they must be treated carefully. Therefore, Harris is hurt when his friends respond to his journey down the Mississippi River with skepticism. They don't understand the purpose of his journey or why he must put himself in harm's way. The river is hazardous due to unpredictable weather, wind, and water conditions as well as the large boats transporting goods and people. Even Harris himself admits canoeing down the entire river isn't safe. Nevertheless, he is determined to live his dream.

Henry David Thoreau also decided to prove his own abilities by facing nature head-on. Thoreau was a prolific writer and prominent figure in the transcendentalist movement in the 19th century. In *Walden*, Thoreau discusses how he participated in a noteworthy experiment that required him to put transcendentalist values into practice. He lived there for over too years, fully immersing himself in the natural world to better understand the negative effects of the Industrial Revolution. At the age of 27, he built a cabin at Walden Pond near Concord, Massachussetts.

Thoreau disputes the benefits of the rapid growth of civilization in America even though industrialization had positive effects, such as more efficient transportation. For example, life began to move at a faster pace than ever before. Thoreau believes this led people to live hectic lives constantly occupied by non-essential things. A passionate Naturalist, he aimed to use his own journey at Walden Pond to advocate for a lifestyle grounded by simplicity. "I went to the woods because I wished to live deliberately, to front only the essential facts of life," In other words, Thoreau believes a life that is not wasteful is better for people and the environment. Life in the woods, away from the constant buzz of civilization, allowed him to engage more deeply with what is essential. Nature and his own spirit.

~~Thoreaus adventure at Walden Pond was a personal journey as well as a campaign against the new obsession with building capital. Thoreau criticizes peoples preoccupation with money, suggesting that the nation was so concerned with accruing wealth that people were no longer invested in internally bettering themselves. To~~

emphasize this point, he asks "Why should we live with such hungry waste of life? We are determined to be starved before we are hungry." I tried to imagine what it means, "to be starved before we are hungry." I typically interpret starvation as the effect of long term hunger. Hunger is usually temporary, but starvation is life-threatening. I once had to skip breakfast because I was late for school. I had to wait until lunch time for my first meal of the day. In the hours leading up to lunch time, I was hungry. However, that hunger went away when I ate lunch. If I were to go days with eating a meal, I would begin to starve. That being said, how can someone starve before experiencing hunger? That does not make sense logically. I think Thoreau is using hunger and starvation as metaphors. I think he is saying that people had developed a habit of both producing and consuming in excess to a point that they were no longer in touch with their most basic needs. Thoreau does not believe financial success is a progressive or admirable goal. Instead, he proposes that people free themselves from this mindset by emulating his minimalist and nature-based lifestyle.

Thoreau's adventure at Walden Pond was a personal journey as well as a campaign against the new obsession with building capital. Thoreau criticizes people's preoccupation with money, suggesting that the nation was so concerned with accruing wealth that people were no longer invested in internally bettering themselves. To emphasize this point, he asks, "Why should we live with such hurry and waste of life? We are determined to be starved before we are hungry." Here he uses a metaphor of hunger to demonstrate that people had developed a habit of both producing and consuming in excess to a point that they were no longer in touch with their most basic needs. Thoreau does not believe financial success is a progressive or admirable goal. Instead, he proposes that people free themselves from this mindset by emulating his minimalist and nature-based lifestyle.

Both Eddy L. Harris and Henry David Thoreau learned a lot about themselves through their journeys in nature. Harris planned an overdue solo adventure to see how his life would change if he joined forces with the river he so loved and feared. Thoreau spent two years alone in the woods to fully engage in the natural world so that he might report on the best way to live life. Both authors show a

Skill:
Precise Language

Juliana revises her paragraph to make her point more direct and precise. She cuts unnecessary sentences as well as the phrase I think, which makes her point seem tentative. By saying, "Here he uses a metaphor of hunger to demonstrate . . ." instead, she expresses her point much more strongly.

~~determination to seize the opportunity to defy expectations and prove their self-reliance.~~

Both Eddy L. Harris and Henry David Thoreau learned a lot about themselves through their journeys in nature. Harris planned an overdue solo adventure to see how his life would change if he joined forces with the river he so loved and feared. Thoreau spent two years alone in the woods to fully engage in the natural world so that he might report on the best way to live life. Neither knew exactly what he would encounter. Both men were willing to risk their lives because they feared missing out on the chance to liberate themselves. Their reward was learning that they were strong enough to survive on their own.

Skill:
Conclusions

Juliana revises her conclusion by rephrasing her thesis in a thoughtful way and adding a memorable final observation. Her last two sentences reveal the depth of her thinking about both texts.

Skill:
Introductions

••• CHECKLIST FOR INTRODUCTIONS

Before you write your introduction, ask yourself the following questions:

- What is my claim? In addition:

  > How can I make it more precise and informative?

  > Have I included why my claim is significant to discuss?

  > How can I distinguish my claim from alternate or opposing claims?

- Have I organized complex ideas, concepts, and information so that each new element builds on the previous element and creates a unified whole?

- How will I "hook" my reader's interest? I might:

  > start with an attention-grabbing statement

  > begin with an intriguing question

Below are two strategies to help you introduce your precise claim and topic clearly in your introduction:

- Peer Discussion

  > Talk about your topic with a partner, explaining what you already know and your ideas about your topic.

  > Write notes about the ideas you have discussed and any new questions you may have.

  > Review your notes, and think about what your claim or controlling idea will be.

  > Write a possible "hook."

- Freewriting

  > Freewrite for 10 minutes about your topic. Don't worry about grammar, punctuation, or having fully formed ideas. The point of freewriting is to discover ideas.

  > Review your notes, and think about what your claim or controlling idea will be.

  > Write a possible "hook."

YOUR TURN

Choose the best answer to each question.

1. The following introduction is from a previous draft of Juliana's essay. Juliana needs to add a hook to grab her audience's attention and introduce her topic. Which sentence could she add to achieve this goal?

> Eddy L. Harris and Henry David Thoreau were both travelers. These men published memoirs about the journeys they took. These adventurous souls both relied on determination to prove themselves in nature. Harris's and Thoreau's stories show that you can learn a lot about yourself on a journey.

- ○ A. Have you ever heard of Henry David Thoreau?
- ○ B. Henry David Thoreau was born in 1817.
- ○ C. Transcendentalism was a nineteenth-century philosophical movement.
- ○ D. For good or for bad, journeys often take people to unexpected places.

2. The following is Juliana's revised introduction. Which of the following sentences is the thesis?

> (1) Beginning with the indigenous people who first inhabited this land, Americans have time and again demonstrated the self-determination it takes to journey into the unknown. (2) Whether the goal is the expansion of the nation's boundaries or personal growth, journeys have guided curious travelers through a range of transformations. (3) Eddy L. Harris and Henry David Thoreau published firsthand accounts of their ambitious adventures into the American wilderness. (4) Their journeys took place at different periods in our nation's history. (5) Yet, they both show a desire to seize the opportunity to defy expectations and prove their self-reliance. (6) Harris's and Thoreau's personal accounts serve as a roadmap that shows where courage can take you in life.

- ○ A. Sentence 1
- ○ B. Sentence 2
- ○ C. Sentences 3 and 4
- ○ D. Sentence 5

 WRITE

Use the checklist to revise the introduction of your informative essay.

Skill:
Transitions

••• CHECKLIST FOR TRANSITIONS

Before you revise your current draft to include transitions, think about:

- the key ideas you discuss
- the major sections of your essay
- the organizational structure of your essay
- the relationships between complex ideas and concepts

Next, reread your current draft and note areas in your essay where:

- the organizational structure is not yet apparent
  - > For example, if you are comparing and contrasting two texts, your explanations about how the two texts are similar and different should be clearly stated
- the relationship between ideas from one paragraph to the next is unclear
  - > For example, when you describe a process in sequential order, you should clarify the order of steps using transitional words like *first*, *then*, *next*, and *finally*
- your ideas do not create cohesion, or a united whole
- your transition and/or syntax is inappropriate

Revise your draft to use appropriate and varied transitions to link the major sections of your essay, create cohesion, and clarify the relationships between complex ideas and concepts, using the following questions as a guide:

- What kind of transitions should I use to make the organizational structure clear to readers?
- Are my transitions linking the major sections of my essay?
- What transitions create cohesion between complex ideas and concepts?
- Are my transitions varied and appropriate?
- Have my transitions clarified the relationships between complex ideas and concepts?

YOUR TURN

Choose the best answer to each question.

1. Below is a section of a previous draft of Juliana's essay. The connection between the ideas in the underlined sentences is unclear. What transition should Juliana add to the beginning of the second sentence to make her writing more coherent and appropriate for the purpose, topic, and context of her essay, as well as her audience?

> Not all journeys require traveling across long distances. Henry David Thoreau separates himself from society and lives in a cabin at Walden Pond for the entirety of his journey. This goes to show that a journey can be interpreted more broadly as a divergence from one's usual way of life.

- ○ A. Eventually
- ○ B. For example
- ○ C. On balance
- ○ D. On the other hand

2. Below is a section of a previous draft of Juliana's essay. Juliana did not use an appropriate transition to show the relationship between paragraphs. Which of the following transitions is the best replacement for the word *yet*? Choose the transition that makes her writing more coherent and is the most appropriate for the purpose, topic, and context of her essay, as well as her audience.

> Thoreau knows he may encounter danger or difficulties, but he is still willing to immerse himself in living in the woods.
>
> Yet, Harris is familiar with the Mississippi River's reputation for being hazardous. He acts against the wishes of his friends and family and continues on his canoeing journey.

- ○ A. Similarly
- ○ B. With attention to
- ○ C. Whereas
- ○ D. As a result

 WRITE

Use the questions in the checklist to revise your use of transitions in a section of your informative essay.

Skill:
Precise Language

••• CHECKLIST FOR PRECISE LANGUAGE

As you consider precise language, domain-specific vocabulary, and techniques related to a complicated subject or topic, use the following questions as a guide:

- What information am I trying to explain to my audience?

- What domain-specific vocabulary is relevant to my topic?

- Have I determined the complexity of the subject matter and whether any words or domain-specific vocabulary needs additional explanation?

- How can I use techniques such as metaphors, similes, or analogies to help explain difficult concepts?

- Where can I use more precise vocabulary in my explanation?

Here are some suggestions for using precise language, domain-specific vocabulary, and techniques such as metaphor, simile, and analogy to help make complex topics clear:

- determine your topic or area of study

- determine the complexity of the subject matter and whether any words or domain-specific vocabulary needs additional explanation in order to make concepts clear

- replace vague, general, or overused words and phrases with more precise, descriptive, and domain-specific language

- try to use metaphors, similes, or analogies to make information easier to understand

  > an example of an analogy for a scientific concept is *a cell membrane is similar to the bricks that make up the outside of a building*

  > a metaphor such as *there is an endless battle between thermodynamics and gravity* can help readers begin to understand the meaning of thermodynamics

YOUR TURN

Below is a passage from a previous draft of Juliana's essay. Choose the best answer to each question about using precise language.

(1) Thoreau disputes the benefits of the rapid growth of civilization in America even though industrialization had positive effects, such as more efficient transportation. (2) For example, life began to move at a faster pace than ever before. (3) Thoreau believes this led people to live hectic lives constantly occupied by non-essential <u>things</u>. (4) A passionate Naturalist, he aimed to use his own journey at Walden Pond to advocate for a lifestyle grounded by simplicity. (5) "I went to the woods because I wished to live deliberately, to front only the essential facts of life." (6) In other words, Thoreau believes a life that is not wasteful is better for people and the environment. (7) Life in the woods, away from the constant buzz of civilization, <u>allowed him to do what matters.</u>

1. Which of the choices would be a more precise phrase for *things* in sentence 3?

   ○ A. nature and camping
   ○ B. interests and pursuits
   ○ C. philosophies and religions
   ○ D. family and the home

2. What would be a more precise replacement for the underlined phrase in sentence 7?

   ○ A. allowed him to better understand the meaning of life.
   ○ B. allowed him to engage more deeply with nature.
   ○ C. allowed him to have some peace.
   ○ D. allowed him to be alone.

 WRITE

Choose a portion of your draft where you would like to include more precise language. Use the checklist to revise your draft.

Skill:
Conclusions

Before you write your conclusion, ask yourself the following questions:

- How can I rephrase the thesis or main idea?
- How can I write my conclusion so that it supports and follows from the information I presented?
- How can I communicate the importance of my topic? What information do I need?

Below are two strategies to help you provide a concluding statement or section that follows from and supports the information or explanation presented:

- Peer Discussion
  - > After you have written your introduction and body paragraphs, talk with a partner about what you want readers to remember, writing notes about your discussion.
  - > Think about how you can articulate, or express, the significance of your topic in the conclusion.
  - > Rephrase your main idea to show the depth of your knowledge and support for the information you presented.
  - > Write your conclusion.
- Freewriting
  - > Freewrite for 10 minutes about what you might include in your conclusion. Don't worry about grammar, punctuation, or having fully formed ideas. The point of freewriting is to discover ideas.
  - > Think about how you can articulate, or express, the significance of your topic in the conclusion.
  - > Rephrase your main idea to show the depth of your knowledge and support for the information you presented.
  - > Write your conclusion.

YOUR TURN

Choose the best answer to each question.

1. The following conclusion is from a previous draft of Juliana's essay. Juliana would like to add a sentence to encourage readers to apply the main idea of the essay to their own lives. Which sentence could she add after the last sentence to achieve this goal?

> Both Eddy L. Harris and Henry David Thoreau took journeys to learn how nature shapes the world around them. What they didn't expect to learn was a lesson about themselves. Harris decided to chase a childhood dream down the Mississippi River. Thoreau wanted to test the fundamental ideals of transcendentalism. Yet, both men discovered something unexpected. They both learned about courage and self-reliance.

- A. These are both examples of great American journeys.
- B. I would like to go on a journey with Eddy L. Harris or Henry David Thoreau!
- C. Both men defied society's expectations and sought to fulfill the essential human need to step outside one's personal comfort zone.
- D. The ideas in this essay can also be applied to other texts.

2. Which sentence in Juliana's final concluding paragraph below best summarizes her thesis?

> (1) Both Eddy L. Harris and Henry David Thoreau learned a lot about themselves through their journeys in nature. (2) Harris planned an overdue solo adventure to see how his life would change if he joined forces with the river he so loved and feared. (3) Thoreau spent two years alone in the woods to fully engage in the natural world so that he might report on the best way to live life. (4) Neither knew exactly what he would encounter. (5) Both men were willing to risk their lives because they feared missing out on the chance to liberate themselves. (6) Their reward was learning that they were strong enough to survive on their own.

- A. Sentence 1
- B. Sentence 2
- C. Sentence 4
- D. Sentence 5

WRITE

Use the checklist to revise the conclusion of your informative essay.

Informative Writing Process: Revise

PLAN	DRAFT	REVISE	EDIT AND PUBLISH

You have written a draft of your informative essay. You have also received input from your peers about how to improve it. Now you are going to revise your draft.

← REVISION GUIDE

Examine your draft to find areas for revision. Use the guide below to help you review:

Review	Revise	Example
Clarity		
Identify places in your writing where adding a transition word or phrase will make your writing clearer. Pay close attention to how you transition between explanations and quotations.	Transition into a quotation in the text by adding "He/She states," or "According to [author's name]," before inserting the quotation.	A passionate Naturalist, he aimed to use his own journey at Walden Pond to advocate for a lifestyle grounded by simplicity. He famously states, "I went to the woods because I wished to live deliberately, to front only the essential facts of life."
Development		
Identify places where your audience may not have background knowledge about your topic. What supporting details could you add to make the content clearer?	Add supporting details to enhance the reader's understanding of words or ideas in your essay.	Thoreau was a prolific writer and prominent figure in the transcendentalist movement in the 19th century. Transcendentalism was an intellectual and religious movement that prioritized self-reliance and the natural world in response to industrialization.

Review	Revise	Example
Organization		
Review your body paragraphs. Are they coherent? Identify and annotate any sentences within and across paragraphs that don't flow in a clear and logical way.	Rewrite the sentences so they appear in a clear and logical order.	He lived there for over too years, fully immersing himself in the natural world to better understand the negative effects of the Industrial Revolution. ~~At the age of 27, he built a cabin at Walden Pond near Concord, Massachussetts.~~ Although industrialization had positive effects, such as more efficient transportation, in *Walden* Thoreau disputes the benefits of the rapid growth of civilization in America ~~even though industrialization had positive effects, such as more efficient transportation.~~
Style: Word Choice		
Identify repetitive words or phrases that do not clearly express your ideas to the reader.	Replace weak and repetitive words and phrases with more descriptive ones that better convey your ideas.	In *Mississippi Solo: A River Quest,* Eddy L. Harris describes growing up in St. Louis, Missouri, near the Mississippi River. Since he was ~~growing up~~ a child, the Mississippi has dominated Harris's imagination.
Style: Sentence Fluency		
Read aloud your writing and listen to the way the text sounds. Does it sound choppy? Or does it flow smoothly with rhythm, movement, and emphasis on important details and events?	Rewrite a key passage, making your sentences longer or shorter to achieve a better flow of writing and the effect you want your reader to feel.	Harris chooses the Mississippi River as his route to independence because, to him, it is more than just a body of water. On the one hand, he appreciates its function as a means of transportation ~~and~~. He acknowledges the roles it has played as a physical landmark in the history of America's, "sins and salvation, dreams and adventure and destiny." On the other hand, Harris fears the river. He compares it to authoritative figures in his life.~~, He makes connections to~~ such as his father and God.

WRITE

Use the revision guide, as well as your peer reviews, to help you evaluate your informative essay to determine areas that should be revised.

Please note that excerpts and passages in the StudySync® library and this workbook are intended as touchstones to generate interest in an author's work. The excerpts and passages do not substitute for the reading of entire texts, and StudySync® strongly recommends that students seek out and purchase the whole literary or informational work in order to experience it as the author intended. Links to online resellers are available in our digital library. In addition, complete works may be ordered through an authorized reseller by filling out and returning to StudySync® the order form enclosed in this workbook.

Reading & Writing Companion   **323**

Skill:
Style

••• CHECKLIST FOR STYLE

First, reread the draft of your informative essay and identify the following:

- slang, colloquialisms, contractions, abbreviations, or a conversational tone
- places where you could use academic language in order to help persuade or inform your readers
- the use of the first person (*I*) or the second person (*you*)
- statements that express judgment or emotion, rather than objective statements that rely on facts and evidence
- places where you could vary sentence structure and length by using compound, complex, and compound-complex sentences
  - > for guidance on effective ways of varying syntax, use a style guide
- incorrect uses of the conventions of standard English for grammar, spelling, capitalization, and punctuation

Establish and maintain a formal style in your essay, using the following questions as a guide:

- Have I avoided slang in favor of academic language?
- Did I consistently use a third-person perspective, using third-person pronouns (*he, she, they*)?
- Have I maintained an objective tone without expressing my own judgments and emotions?
- Have I used varied sentence lengths and different sentence structures? Did I consider using style guides to learn about effective ways of varying syntax?
  - > Where should I make some sentences longer by using conjunctions to connect independent clauses, dependent clauses, and phrases?
  - > Where should I make some sentences shorter by separating independent clauses?
- Have I followed the conventions of standard English?

YOUR TURN

Choose the best answer to each question.

1. Which type of stylistic error did Juliana make in this sentence from a previous draft?

> I think naturalism is a very interesting philosophy and it makes Thoreau's journey at Walden Pond all the more powerful.

- ○ A. The sentence contains an incorrect use of capitalization.
- ○ B. The sentence is too complex.
- ○ C. Juliana uses the pronoun *I* and makes a statement based on her feelings.
- ○ D. Juliana uses slang.

2. How should this sentence be rewritten to address stylistic errors?

> Thoreau was totally into naturalism, and so he aimed to use his own journey at Walden Pond to get other people really into nature and living a life with less stuff.

- ○ A. I think Thoreau was a passionate naturalist and he wanted people to live a more simplistic lifestyle.
- ○ B. A passionate naturalist, he aimed to use his own journey at walden pond to advocate for a lifestyle grounded by simplicity.
- ○ C. Thoreau was a naturalist. Being a naturalist was very important to Thoreau. He thought people should live simpler lives.
- ○ D. A passionate naturalist, Thoreau aimed to use his own journey at Walden Pond to advocate for a lifestyle grounded in simplicity.

 WRITE

Use the checklist to revise a paragraph of your informative essay to improve the style.

Grammar:
Quotation Marks

Quotation marks are used to enclose direct quotations and dialogue. They are always used in pairs.

Rule	Text
Use quotation marks before and after a direct quotation or piece of dialogue.	"What do we talk of marks and brands, whether on the bodice of her gown or the flesh of her forehead?" cried another female, the ugliest as well as the most pitiless of these self-constituted judges. The Scarlet Letter
Use quotation marks before and after each part of an interrupted quotation.	"Whenever you feel like criticizing any one," he told me, "just remember that all the people in this world haven't had the advantages that you've had." The Great Gatsby
Use single quotation marks around a quotation within a quotation.	Just before the anniversary, Mr. Tanimoto wrote in a letter to an American some words which expressed this feeling: "What a heartbreaking scene this was the first night! About midnight I landed on the riverbank. So many injured people lied on the ground that I made my way by striding over them. Repeating 'Excuse me,' I forwarded and carried a tub of water with me and gave a cup of water to each of them." Hiroshima
Do not use quotation marks in an indirect quotation. An indirect quotation is a description of a quotation rather than the quotation itself.	But he bid me tell you, that you might look to unnatural things for the cause of it. The Crucible

⟳ YOUR TURN

1. How should this sentence be changed?

> Miss Carson's science cannot be questioned," said oceanographer William Beebe.

- ○ A. Delete the quotation mark after **questioned**.
- ○ B. Insert a quotation mark before **Miss**.
- ○ C. Insert a quotation mark before **science**.
- ○ D. No change needs to be made to this sentence.

2. How should this sentence be changed?

> Carson's mother taught her daughter that intelligence and personal worth were more valuable than money or success."

- ○ A. Place a quotation mark after **daughter**.
- ○ B. Place a quotation mark after **her**.
- ○ C. Delete the quotation mark after the period.
- ○ D. No change needs to be made to this sentence.

3. How should these sentences be changed?

> "It was a spring without voices," she wrote. On the mornings that had once throbbed with the dawn chorus of robins, catbirds, doves, jays, wrens, and scores of other bird voices there was now no sound; only silence lay over the fields and woods and marsh."

- ○ A. Delete the quotation mark after the last period.
- ○ B. Insert a quotation mark before **On**.
- ○ C. Delete the quotation mark before **It**.
- ○ D. No change needs to be made to these sentences.

4. How should this sentence be changed?

> "Did you know that when Rachel Carson wrote her classic *Silent Spring*, *Time* magazine called it "an emotional and inaccurate outburst"?" Simone asked in disbelief.

- ○ A. Delete the first and last quotation marks.
- ○ B. Delete the quotation marks around **an emotional and inaccurate outburst.**
- ○ C. Remove the double quotation marks around **an emotional and inaccurate outburst** and replace them with single quotation marks around the same phrase.
- ○ D. No change needs to be made to this sentence.

Please note that excerpts and passages in the StudySync® library and this workbook are intended as touchstones to generate interest in an author's work. The excerpts and passages do not substitute for the reading of entire texts, and StudySync® strongly recommends that students seek out and purchase the whole literary or informational work in order to experience it as the author intended. Links to online resellers are available in our digital library. In addition, complete works may be ordered through an authorized reseller by filling out and returning to StudySync® the order form enclosed in this workbook.

Grammar: Commas with Direct Quotes

Commas separate explanatory text, such as *he said* or *she wrote,* from the words inside quotation marks.

- If the explanatory text comes before the direct quote, the comma follows it.

- If the explanatory text interrupts the direct quote and neither part of the quote is a complete sentence, then the explanatory text is set off with two commas. The first comma follows the final word of the first part of the quote. It stays inside the closing quotation mark. The second comma follows the explanatory text.

- If the explanatory text comes after the direct quote, the comma follows the final word of the quote. It remains inside the closing quotation mark.

Rule	Text
Use a comma between explanatory text and an opening quotation mark.	Lee now looked greatly relieved, and though anything but a demonstrative man, he gave every evidence of his appreciation of this concession, and said, "This will have the best possible effect upon the men." Lee Surrenders to Grant, April 9th, 1865
When the direct quote comes before the explanatory text, use a comma between the final word of the quote and the closing quotation mark.	"Anyhow he gives large parties," said Jordan, changing the subject with an urbane distaste for the concrete. The Great Gatsby
Use a comma both before and after explanatory text if the explanatory text interrupts the direct quote and neither part of the quote is a complete sentence.	"The Montresors," I replied, "were a great and numerous family." The Cask of Amontillado
When explanatory text interrupts a direct quote in which the second part is a complete sentence, end the first part of the quote with a comma inside the closing quotation mark. Put a period after the explanatory text and begin the second part of the quote with a capital letter.	"One of those shot by the carabinieri is from my town," Passini said. "He was a big smart tall boy to be in the granatieri." A Farewell to Arms

⟳ YOUR TURN

1. How should this sentence be changed?

   > The young Rachel Carson wrote poems and stories, and when a story was accepted by a magazine, she wrote "The pay, I believe, was a cent a word."

   ○ A. Delete the comma after **stories.**
   ○ B. Delete the comma after **magazine.**
   ○ C. Insert a comma after **wrote.**
   ○ D. No change needs to be made to this sentence.

2. How should this sentence be changed?

   > John Muir, renowned American explorer and conservationist, said of his school days "We were simply driven point blank against our books like soldiers against an enemy,"

   ○ A. Insert a comma after **days** and place the comma outside the closing quotation mark.
   ○ B. Place a period outside the closing quotation mark.
   ○ C. Insert a comma after **days** and replace the comma after **enemy** with a period.
   ○ D. No change needs to be made to this sentence.

3. How should this sentence be changed?

   > "I'll acquaint myself with glaciers and wild gardens," Muir wrote "and get as near the heart of the world as I can."

   ○ A. Insert a comma after **wrote.**
   ○ B. Delete the comma after **gardens.**
   ○ C. Insert a period after **wrote.**
   ○ D. No change needs to be made to this sentence.

4. How should this sentence be changed?

   > "Many silent film stars could not make the transition to sound," Angelo told the class, "because they did not have good speaking voices."

   ○ A. Delete the comma after **sound.**
   ○ B. Reverse the comma and closing quotation mark after **sound.**
   ○ C. Delete the comma after **class.**
   ○ D. No change needs to be made to this sentence.

APOSTROPHES

sync•skills

Grammar: Apostrophes

Rule	Text
Use an apostrophe and an *s* to form the possessive of a singular noun.	In the nights in their thousands to dream the dreams of a child**'s** imaginings, worlds rich or fearful such as might offer themselves but never the one to be. The Road
Use an apostrophe and an *s* to form the possessive of a plural noun that does not end in *s*.	These are the times that try men**'s** souls. The Crisis
Use an apostrophe alone to form the possessive of a plural noun that ends in *s*.	I am Dekanawidah and with the Five Nation**s'** Confederate Lords I plant the Tree of Great Peace. The Constitution of the Iroquois Nations
Put only the last word of a compound noun in the possessive form.	The attorney general**'s** schedule was completely full that afternoon.
If two or more people possess something jointly, use the possessive form for the last person named.	All About Pie is the name of Tess and Bev**'s** new pie cafe.
If two or more people possess something individually, put each one's name in the possessive form.	Sarah**'s** and Bobby**'s** SAT scores were excellent.
Use an apostrophe to replace a letter or letters that have been omitted in a contraction.	"I don't know," she insisted, "I just don't think he went there." The Great Gatsby
Use an apostrophe in place of the omitted numerals of a particular year, but not with the plural of full dates.	In the 1900s, Soraya was named the homecoming queen of the Class of '39.

⟳ YOUR TURN

1. How should this sentence be changed?

> The publisher of Miamis morning newspaper criticized both developers proposed plans for the Everglades.

- ○ A. Insert an apostrophe after the *s* in **Miamis** and **Everglades**.
- ○ B. Delete the *s* in **Miamis** and insert an apostrophe before the *s* in **developers**.
- ○ C. Insert an apostrophe before the *s* in **Miamis** and after the *s* in **developers**.
- ○ D. No change needs to be made to this sentence.

2. How should this sentence be changed?

> Marjory Stoneman Douglas and her friends would visit the Everglades to observe herons nests, spoonbills flights, and egrets at rest.

- ○ A. Add apostrophes before the *s* in **friends** and **egrets**.
- ○ B. Add an apostrophe after the *s* in **herons** and **spoonbills**.
- ○ C. Add an apostrophe and *s* after **Douglas**.
- ○ D. No change needs to be made to this sentence.

3. How should this sentence be changed?

> The Miami newspapers editorial didnt stop the governor from making an assault on the Everglades.

- ○ A. Insert an apostrophe after the *s* in **newspapers** and **Everglades**.
- ○ B. Insert an apostrophe before the *s* in **newspapers** and between the *n* and the *t* in **didnt**.
- ○ C. Insert an apostrophe before the *s* in **Everglades**.
- ○ D. No change needs to be made to this sentence.

4. How should this sentence be changed?

> Marjory met Ernest Coe, who wanted to protect the Everglades' unique characteristics.

- ○ A. Delete the apostrophe in **Everglades'**.
- ○ B. Insert an apostrophe between the *c* and the *s* at the end of **characteristics**.
- ○ C. Insert an apostrophe after the *s* in **characteristics**.
- ○ D. No change needs to be made to this sentence.

Informative Writing Process: Edit and Publish

| PLAN | DRAFT | REVISE | EDIT AND PUBLISH |

You have revised your informative essay based on your peer feedback and your own examination.

Now, it is time to edit your informative essay. When you revised, you focused on the content of your essay. You probably looked at how to write an introduction, incorporate transitions, use precise language, and craft a memorable conclusion. When you edit, you focus on the mechanics of your essay, paying close attention to things like grammar and punctuation.

Use the checklist below to guide you as you edit:

☐ Have I followed all the rules for using quotation marks?

☐ Have I used commas with direct quotes correctly throughout the essay?

☐ Have I used apostrophes correctly throughout the essay?

☐ Have I spelled everything correctly?

Notice some edits Juliana has made:

- Added an apostrophe to show possession

- Added quotation marks to a quotation from a text

- Corrected a spelling mistake

He fantasized yielding to the ~~rivers~~ river's power by "hanging onto whatever and floating along with it, letting the river drop me off wherever and pick me up later and take me on again." At thirty years old, Harris fears that he is no longer free to go on adventures and that he must give in to ~~mundain~~ mundane responsibilities. Instead of allowing his anxieties to take over, he commits to making his dream a reality.

✏ WRITE

Use the questions on the previous page, as well as your peer reviews, to help you evaluate your informative essay to determine areas that need editing. Then, edit your essay to correct those errors.

Once you have made all your corrections, you are ready to publish your work. You can distribute your writing to family and friends, hang it on a bulletin board, or post it on your blog. If you publish online, share the link with your family, friends, and classmates.

A New Beginning

FICTION

Introduction

This work of historical fiction tells the story of a young man who must leave his home in the wake of the Irish Potato Famine and move to New York City to become his uncle's apprentice. Overwhelmed by his first impressions of the big city, he feels homesick and anxious, but the promise of a new friendship gives

V VOCABULARY

clambered

climbed in a quick and
awkward way

throng

a dense crowd

cobbler

a person who makes or fixes
shoes for a living

harried

very nervous or anxious due to
difficulties

disembarked

got off a plane or boat

☰ READ

NOTES

1   My stomach was doing somersaults as I **clambered** off the boat in New York Harbor. I had been looking forward to a new life as my uncle's apprentice. But now that I had set foot in this strange city, I yearned for the quiet hills of my native Ireland. Life had been difficult since the Great Famine took hold. Our potato crops began to fail. When my uncle suggested that I come live with him and learn his trade, my parents put me on the next boat. I'd had no real desire to become a **cobbler**. But as a growing twelve-year-old boy, I did maintain a desire to eat regular meals. I left home without a fight.

2   From the moment I spotted New York City, I knew that my life would never be the same. I had heard stories about the city. But even in my wildest dreams, I never imagined anything like what I was seeing with my own two eyes. There were more buildings than I could count. I thought back to the dozen buildings that made up our small town square. I shook my head in disbelief.

3 I **disembarked** from the ship, and I found myself pushed along with the ebb and flow of the city. I barely felt my feet touch the ground as I was carried away from the harbor. I had never seen so many people. Everywhere I turned there were bodies. I quickly lost sight of the corner where I was supposed to meet my uncle. I couldn't breathe as chaos swirled around me. A hand reached out from the **throng** and grasped my shoulder roughly. I started to scream, but then I recognized my uncle's **harried** face.

4 The foot traffic thinned out as we made our way into the city. I summoned the courage to look up. I tipped my head back and gasped with astonishment at the clotheslines stretched between buildings. What looked like hundreds of shirts and pants swayed gently in the breeze above the street. I thought we'd had a lot of laundry at home between my parents and five siblings, but it was nothing like this. I suddenly realized that each item of clothing represented a person that I might never meet in this vast city. At the same time, I thought of everyone at home that I might never see again. Homesickness gripped my heart. I was surrounded by hundreds of thousands of people, but I had never felt so alone.

5 We arrived at the tenement. I grabbed onto the railing so I wouldn't trip as I made my way up the steep stairway toward our apartment. A boy about my age appeared on the landing. He nodded a silent greeting, and I returned the gesture. I wondered who the boy was. Since my uncle did not stop to say hello, I kept climbing the stairs. With a frown, I almost said, "Back home, we would have stopped to chat with our neighbors." But I caught myself. This city was where I lived now. I needed to make a home here.

6 Later, I sat down to write a letter to my parents. I did not know what to say. New York was supposed to be better than Ireland, but so far, it was not. Just then, I heard a burst of laughter coming from the other side of the wall. My mind flashed back to the boy I met on the stairs. Eager to make a new friend, I hurried to the door just in time to see the same boy walk out of the next apartment. He flashed me a quick smile and continued on his way, laughing with each step. As the sounds of his laughter bounced off the walls around me, I came to realize something important. If he was so happy here, then I could be too. We were not friends yet, but I could not wait to see what tomorrow would bring.

First Read

Read "A New Beginning." After you read, complete the Think Questions below.

☁ THINK QUESTIONS

1. Where is the narrator from in the story? Why did he leave?

    The narrator is from _____.

    He left because _____.

2. With whom is the narrator living in New York City?

    The narrator is living with _____.

3. What feelings does the narrator experience in the story?

    The narrator feels _____.

4. Use context to confirm the meaning of the word *disembarked* as it is used in "A New Beginning." Write your definition of *disembarked* here.

    Disembarked means _____.

    A context clue is _____.

5. What is another way to say that the narrator got lost in the *throng*?

    The narrator got lost _____.

Please note that excerpts and passages in the StudySync® library and this workbook are intended as touchstones to generate interest in an author's work. The excerpts and passages do not substitute for the reading of entire texts, and StudySync® strongly recommends that students seek out and purchase the whole literary or informational work in order to experience it as the author intended. Links to online resellers are available in our digital library. In addition, complete works may be ordered through an authorized reseller by filling out and returning to StudySync® the order form enclosed in this workbook.

Reading & Writing Companion   337

Skill: Analyzing Expressions

★ DEFINE

When you read, you may find English expressions that you do not know. An **expression** is a group of words that communicates an idea. Three types of expressions are idioms, sayings, and figurative language. They can be difficult to understand because the meanings of the words are different from their **literal,** or usual, meanings.

An **idiom** is an expression that is commonly known among a group of people. For example, "It's raining cats and dogs" means "It is raining heavily." **Sayings** are short expressions that contain advice or wisdom. For instance, "Don't count your chickens before they hatch" means "Do not plan on something good happening before it happens." **Figurative** language is when you describe something by comparing it with something else, either directly (using the word *like* or *as*) or indirectly. For example, "I'm as hungry as a horse" means "I'm very hungry." None of the expressions are about actual animals.

••• CHECKLIST FOR ANALYZING EXPRESSIONS

To determine the meaning of an expression, remember the following:

✓ If you find a confusing group of words, it may be an expression. The meaning of words in expressions may not be their literal meaning.

- Ask yourself: Is this confusing because the words are new? Or because the words do not make sense together?

✓ Determining the overall meaning may require that you use one or more of the following:

- context clues
- a dictionary or other resource
- teacher or peer support

✓ Highlight important information before and after the expression to look for clues.

YOUR TURN

Read the following excerpt from "A New Beginning." Then, answer the multiple-choice questions below.

---

from **"A New Beginning"**

I disembarked from the ship, and I found myself pushed along with the ebb and flow of the city. I barely felt my feet touch the ground as I was carried away from the harbor. I had never seen so many people. Everywhere I turned there were bodies. I quickly lost sight of the corner where I was supposed to meet my uncle. I couldn't breathe as chaos swirled around me. A hand reached out from the throng and grasped my shoulder roughly. I started to scream, but then I recognized my uncle's harried face.

---

1. **At the start of the paragraph, the expression "the ebb and flow of the city" means:**
   - ○ A. the tide of the ocean near New York City
   - ○ B. the noise of the city that sounds like ocean waves
   - ○ C. the unreliable electrical current that powers the city's street lights
   - ○ D. the continuous movement of people in the city

2. **Which context clues helped you determine the meaning of "the ebb and flow of the city"?**
   - ○ A. disembarked from the ship
   - ○ B. barely felt feet touch ground, carried away, so many people
   - ○ C. everywhere turned, there were bodies
   - ○ D. quickly lost sight of corner, couldn't breathe, chaos swirled

Skill: Sharing Information

★ DEFINE

Sharing information involves asking for and giving information. The process of sharing information with other students can help all students learn more and better understand a text or a topic. You can share information when you participate in **brief** discussions or **extended** speaking assignments.

••• CHECKLIST FOR SHARING INFORMATION

When you have to speak for an extended period of time, as in a discussion, you ask for and share information. To ask for and share information, you may use the following sentence frames:

✓ To ask for information:

- What do you think about _____?

- Do you agree that _____?

- What is your understanding of _____?

✓ To give information:

- I think _____.

- I agree because _____.

- My understanding is _____.

⟳ YOUR TURN

Watch the "The Railway Train" Sharing Information SkillsTV episode and listen for the following quotes. Decide if the students are asking for information, giving information, or both. Choose the correct answer.

1. David: "It's crazy if you think about it. Once trains exist, you can actually move mountains."

   ○ A. Asking for Information
   ○ B. Giving Information
   ○ C. Both

2. Sophia: "What year was this poem written?"

   ○ A. Asking for Information
   ○ B. Giving Information
   ○ C. Both

3. Alicia: "I was worried about the train losing control, but really, it's the meter we should be concerned about."

   ○ A. Asking for Information
   ○ B. Giving Information
   ○ C. Both

4. Sophia: "So Dickinson uses images and technical tricks to affect the way the poem makes us feel. So, how do we feel?"

   ○ A. Asking for Information
   ○ B. Giving Information
   ○ C. Both

Please note that excerpts and passages in the StudySync® library and this workbook are intended as touchstones to generate interest in an author's work. The excerpts and passages do not substitute for the reading of entire texts, and StudySync® strongly recommends that students seek out and purchase the whole literary or informational work in order to experience it as the author intended. Links to online resellers are available in our digital library. In addition, complete works may be ordered through an authorized reseller by filling out and returning to StudySync® the order form enclosed in this workbook.

Reading & Writing Companion   341

Close Read

✏ WRITE

NARRATIVE: Think about the events the narrator experiences in "A New Beginning." Write a paragraph that describes what you think happens the next day. Use specific details from the story and add some of your own. Pay attention to and edit for negatives and contractions.

Use the checklist below to guide you as you write.

☐ How does the narrator feel on his second day in New York?

☐ What are some activities the narrator will do after he wakes up?

☐ What happens with the boy who lives next door to the narrator?

Use the sentence frames to organize and write your narrative.

The next day, the narrator feels _____ .

He goes to his new _____ with his uncle.

Later, he meets _____ .

The two boys explore _____ . At the end of the day,

he has a new _____ and a new home.

Holding On for Dear Life

INFORMATIONAL TEXT

Introduction

Before the year 1929, a typical American teenager would go to school, do chores, and spend time with friends. However, when the stock market crashed and unemployment in America hit an all-time high, families became poor and desperate for money. Since many families didn't have enough food to feed their families, children as young as thirteen years old left home, jumped on a train, and found a job. In many ways, childhood was over for these "boxcar boys and girls" who set out for a new life.

VOCABULARY

abandon

to leave or give up something

income

money received from a job

desperate

feeling hopeless, like something is impossible to achieve

option

a choice or the right to choose something

burden

an annoying responsibility or duty that causes stress

NOTES

≡ READ

1   The story of a teenager sneaking away from home is not very unique. However, when about 250,000 teenagers left home during the Great Depression, this event told a much greater story. In 1933, children as young as thirteen years old left home in search of a better life. These teenagers are known as the "boxcar boys and girls." They got this name because they would jump onto the

Young people jump onto the boxcars of a freight train.

boxcars of freight trains. The trains would take the children far away from their problems. What would drive such a large number of young people to **abandon** their childhood for a life on the road? The reasons behind this movement are as unique as the boxcar kids themselves.

NOTES

2   The stock market crashed in 1929, and American families were **desperate** for money. To help their families, many children began working. It was easier for teenagers to find jobs than adults because they received a much lower wage. Plus, there were no child labor laws in the 1930s. Teenagers would find jobs at factories far away from home. They would return once they had earned enough money to support their families.

Teenagers work in a textile factory before the child labor laws of the 1930s.

3   Other teenagers left home because they believed they were a **burden** to their families. "Riding the rails," or living on trains until finding work, was a relief to some families. It meant one less mouth to feed. The Great Depression lasted from 1929–1939. By the mid-1930s, about 25% of families had no **income**. Families were starving. Many teenagers felt like it was better to disappear than take food away from family members.

A family gathers in their house during the Great Depression.

4   Many young people abandoned their homes in search of a life with meaning. The lives they previously knew were gone. Before the Great Depression, children were expected to go to school and graduate from high school. However, schools were affected by the Great Depression. They lacked materials, heat, and food. Many schools closed in rural areas. Since school was no longer a priority for many American children, dropping out to find work was the only **option**.

5   No matter the reason for leaving home, all of these "boxcar boys and girls" took risks that made their childhood very brief. Teenagers during the Great Depression had to grow up quickly. They took on adult responsibilities in order to survive. Some received jobs. Some children provided for their parents. Others were looking for a new life. The boxcar kids were holding on for dear life as they rode the rails. They were holding on for hope of a better future.

First Read

Read "Holding On for Dear Life." After you read, complete the Think Questions below.

☁ **THINK QUESTIONS**

1. How many teenagers left home during the Great Depression?

   During the Great Depression, _____

2. Why were these teenagers called "boxcar boys and girls"?

   These teenagers were called "boxcar boys and girls" because _____

   _____.

3. Why did so many teenagers leave their homes during the Great Depression?

   Many teenagers left their homes because _____

   _____.

4. Use context to confirm the meaning of the word *burden* as it is used in "Holding On for Dear Life." Write your definition of *burden* here.

   Burden means _____.

   A context clue is _____.

5. What is another way to say that families were *desperate* for food?

   Families were _____.

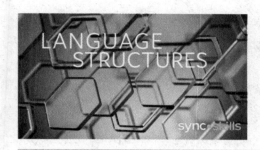

Skill: Language Structures

★ DEFINE

In every language, there are rules that tell how to **structure** sentences. These rules define the correct order of words. In the English language, for example, a **basic** structure for sentences is subject, verb, and object. Some sentences have more **complicated** structures.

You will encounter both basic and complicated **language structures** in the classroom materials you read. Being familiar with language structures will help you better understand the text.

••• CHECKLIST FOR LANGUAGE STRUCTURES

To improve your comprehension of language structures, do the following:

✓ Monitor your understanding.

- Ask yourself: Why do I not understand this sentence? Is it because I do not understand some of the words? Or is it because I do not understand the way the words are ordered in the sentence?

✓ Pay attention to verbs followed by prepositions.

- A **verb** names an action.

  > Example: I **sit** on my chair.

  > This tells the reader what the subject of the sentence is doing (sitting).

- A **preposition** defines the relationship between two or more nouns or verbs in a sentence.

  > Example: I sit **on** my chair.

  > This tells the reader where the subject is doing the action (on a chair).

- Sometimes the preposition comes directly after the verb, but it can also be separated by another word.

  > Example: I **took** it **to** school with me.

- Sometimes the preposition changes the meaning of the verb. This is called a **phrasal verb**.

  > Example: The teacher liked to **call on** the students in the front of the class.

  > The phrasal verb *call on* means "to select someone to share information."

✓ Break down the sentence into its parts.

- Ask yourself: What words make up the verbs in this sentence? Is the verb followed by a preposition? How does this affect the meaning of the sentence?

✓ Confirm your understanding with a peer or teacher.

⟳ YOUR TURN

Read each sentence and notice the verb and preposition pairs. Then, sort each sentence into the correct category by writing the letter in the phrasal or non-phrasal verb column.

	Sentence Options
A	They took on adult responsibilities in order to survive.
B	Many schools closed in rural areas.
C	They were holding on for hope of a better future.
D	Before the Great Depression, children were expected to go to school and graduate from high school.

Phrasal Verb	Non-Phrasal Verb

Please note that excerpts and passages in the StudySync® library and this workbook are intended as touchstones to generate interest in an author's work. The excerpts and passages do not substitute for the reading of entire texts, and StudySync® strongly recommends that students seek out and purchase the whole literary or informational work in order to experience it as the author intended. Links to online resellers are available in our digital library. In addition, complete works may be ordered through an authorized reseller by filling out and returning to StudySync® the order form enclosed in this workbook.

Reading & Writing Companion   **349**

Skill: Visual and Contextual Support

★ DEFINE

Visual support is an image or an object that helps you understand a text. **Contextual support** is a **feature** that helps you understand a text. By using visual and contextual supports, you can develop your vocabulary so you can better understand a variety of texts.

First, preview the text to identify any visual supports. These might include illustrations, graphics, charts, or other objects in a text. Then, identify any contextual supports. Examples of contextual supports are titles, headers, captions, and boldface terms. Write down your **observations**.

Then, write down what those visual and contextual supports tell you about the meaning of the text. Note any new vocabulary that you see in those supports. Ask your peers and your teacher to **confirm** your understanding of the text.

••• CHECKLIST FOR VISUAL AND CONTEXTUAL SUPPORT

To use visual and contextual support to understand texts, do the following:

✓ Preview the text. Read the title, headers, and other features. Look at any images and graphics.

✓ Write down the visual and contextual supports in the text.

✓ Write down what those supports tell you about the text.

✓ Note any new vocabulary that you see in those supports.

✓ Create an illustration for the reading and write a descriptive caption.

✓ Confirm your observations with your peers and teacher.

⟳ YOUR TURN

Read the following excerpt from "Holding On for Dear Life." Then, using the Checklist on the previous page, answer the multiple-choice questions below.

---

from **"Holding On for Dear Life"**

Other teenagers left home because they believed they were a burden to their families. "Riding the rails," or living on trains until finding work, was a relief to some families. It meant one less mouth to feed. The Great Depression lasted from 1929 to 1939. By the mid-1930s, about 25% of families had no income. Families were starving. Many teenagers felt like it was better to disappear than take food away from family members.

---

1. **The paragraph is mostly about —**

   ○ A. living on trains

   ○ B. the dates of the Great Depression

   ○ C. the size of families during the Great Depression

   ○ D. teenagers leaving home to help their families during the Great Depression

2. **The visual support helps readers to —**

   ○ A. see what families did for fun in the 1930s

   ○ B. imagine the condition of a family during the Great Depression

   ○ C. see children fighting each other during the Great Drepression

   ○ D. see a neighborhood from the 1930s

HOLDING
ON FOR
DEAR LIFE

Close Read

 WRITE

INFORMATIONAL: Imagine you are a student during the Great Depression. Write text for a flyer to inform students about the desperate situation of boxcar boys and girls in the U.S. and why it is bad for everyone. Use information from the selection to explain your ideas. Pay attention to and edit for correct spelling of words with the letters *ei* and *ie*.

Use the checklist below to guide you as you write.

☐ What is the situation of boxcar boys and girls?

☐ Why is it bad for everyone?

☐ What information in the text supports your ideas?

Use the sentence frames to organize and write your informational text.

Their families are starving and have no _____.

They have to leave home to find _____.

They think their lives have no _____.

They are the _____.

Help boxcar boys and girls stay _____.

studysync®

ASSIGNMENTS   BINDER   LIBRARY

No Strangers Here

UNIT 3

No Strangers Here

How does place shape the individual?

Genre Focus: **POETRY**

Texts

Extended Writing Project and Grammar

English Language Learner Resources

Reading & Writing Companion

How does place shape the individual?

WILLIAM BARTRAM

American naturalist and writer William Bartram (1739–1823) was born in Pennsylvania, and is known for surveying and documenting his travels across the American Southeast. His eponymous work detailed the region's peoples, flora, fauna, and wildlife with evocative descriptions and popularized Florida for prospective settlers. Of Lake George and its biodiversity, he wrote, "Here the trout swims by the very nose of the alligator and laughs in his face, and the bream swims by the trout." He died in his home state of Pennsylvania at the age of eighty-four.

RICHARD BLANCO

The first immigrant, Latino, openly gay, and the youngest person to be the U.S. presidential inaugural poet, Ricardo Blanco (b. 1968) was born in Madrid, Spain, to a family of Cuban expatriates. Shortly after, his family moved to the United States and settled in Miami. Blanco earned a BS degree in civil engineering and an MFA degree in creative writing. At President Obama's inauguration in 2013, Blanco read his poem "One Today," which he wrote for the occasion. Currently, he is a Distinguished Visiting Professor at his alma mater, Florida International University and lives in Bethel, Maine.

JERICHO BROWN

Jericho Brown (b. 1976) is an American poet and professor of creative writing at Emory University. He has published two highly regarded poetry collections, "Please" and *The New Testament*. A Louisiana native, Brown worked as a speechwriter for the mayor of New Orleans before his career as a poet took off. In his poetry, Brown often explores issues related to his own identity—such as race, sexuality, and faith. He has described his writing as grappling with the question: "What is it to be a citizen of a country that does not want you as its citizen?"

FREDERICK DOUGLASS

A vital leader in the abolitionist movement, Frederick Douglass (1818–1895) was the first African American to serve as a United States official and was nominated for vice president of the United States. He was well-regarded in his time as a brilliant and eloquent speaker. Douglass's autobiographical writings, including *Narrative of the Life of Frederick Douglass, An American Slave*, offer a portrait of slavery from the point of view of the enslaved, a much-needed contribution to literature that continues to be widely read.

WILLIAM FAULKNER

As a young man, it seemed unlikely that William Faulkner (1897–1962) was destined to become one of the most celebrated voices in American fiction. After failing to graduate from high school, Faulkner enrolled in courses at the University of Mississippi—and dropped out after earning a D in English. Years later, while working at a local power plant, Faulkner penned *As I Lay Dying*, considered by many to be his masterpiece. The novel, like most of his work, is set in the fictional county of Yoknapatawpha, Mississippi, and was inspired by his hometown.

LAUREN GROFF

Lauren Groff (b. 1978) is the author of three novels and two collections of short stories. Born in New York, she attended Amherst College before earning her MFA degree at the University of Wisconsin–Madison. Her first novel, *The Monsters of Templeton*, debuted on *The New York Times* Best Seller list, and her third novel, *Fates and Furies*, was nominated for many "best of 2015" lists and was named by then-president Barack Obama as his favorite novel of the year. Her latest collection of stories, *Florida*, was released in 2018. She lives in Gainesville, Florida.

ZORA NEALE HURSTON

Born in Alabama, Zora Neale Hurston (1891–1960), who grew up just outside Orlando, called Florida home. In 1928, she graduated from Barnard College in New York City, and was involved in the Harlem Renaissance, working alongside Langston Hughes and Wallace Thurman. She is best known for her 1937 novel *Their Eyes Were Watching God*, which *The New York Times* Book Review called "beautiful" and a "perfect story." A revival in interest in her work occurred after Alice Walker published "In Search of Zora Neale Hurston" in a 1975 issue of *Ms. Magazine*.

KATHERINE A. PORTER

Born in Indian Creek, Texas, Katherine A. Porter (1890–1980) was a journalist, short story writer, and novelist who went on to win the National Book Award and the Pulitzer Prize for Fiction. Porter nearly died in Denver during the 1918 flu pandemic. Shortly thereafter, she moved to New York City, and traveled as a journalist between the U.S. and Mexico. There she became acquainted with Mexican revolutionaries, including Diego Rivera. She was nominated for the Nobel Prize in Literature three times. She died in Silver Spring, Maryland at the age of ninety.

NATASHA TRETHEWAY

Being born black and biracial in Gulfport, Mississippi, is one of the two "existential wounds" poet Natasha Trethewey (b. 1966) says she's been writing with her whole adult life. The other was losing her mother at the age of nineteen. In poetry collections like *Native Guard, Bellocq's Ophelia*, and *Domestic Work*, she explores how her personal history is tied to larger historical narratives and the way private recollection often diverges from collective memory.

JESMYN WARD

A native of the Mississippi Gulf Coast, Jesmyn Ward (b. 1977) experienced Hurricane Katrina first hand. This devastating event features prominently in her work, especially her 2011 novel, *Salvage the Bones*, as a focal point for broader inquiries into race and class struggles. Her complex characters and poetic language reflect the depth of experience that constitutes life along the Gulf Coast.

VIEVEE FRANCIS

Born in West Texas, Vievee Francis is currently an associate professor of English and creative writing at Dartmouth College. Francis graduated from Fisk University and earned her MFA degree from the University of Michigan in 2009. She's the author of three collections of poetry: *Forest Primeval, Horse in the Dark*, and *Blue-Tail Fly*. About the study of poetry, Francis has said she is interested in "how poetry acts as a foundational art, both catalyst and girder for other genres of literature."

Realism, Naturalism, and Regionalism

Introduction

This informational text provides readers with cultural and historical background information about the society that inspired the literary movements of realism, naturalism, and regionalism. These movements arose from the aftermath of the American Civil War, in a society whose economy and urban populations were rapidly expanding. Many functions of American government and social structure were ill-prepared for the new challenges that Reconstruction and industrialization would bring. Writers, however, responded to these injustices and struggles by creating written works of both fiction and nonfiction that engaged with these changes. Realists, naturalists, and regionalists were determined to create a new period of literature in which the realities of everyday life were exposed, for better or for worse, at all levels of society.

"Artists tried to hold up a mirror to America and truthfully reflect people's common experiences."

1   Is reality TV realistic? When we secretly binge-watch *The Bachelor* or *Big Brother,* is it real, realistic, an interpretation of reality, or a staged fiction parading around as reality? The question of how to create a true depiction of human experience in literature and art is one that Americans have been grappling with for over 150 years. Can art authentically and accurately reflect the concerns, conflicts, trials, and triumphs of human life? Is it possible to observe and interpret reality in a scientific and artistic manner at the same time? Whose reality is being depicted? Can fiction—by definition, something that is made up—be realistic?

A Complex Reality: The Aftermath of the Civil War

2   The Civil War marked a turning point in American history and in the American imagination. After such a violent and turbulent test of the nation's soul, Americans viewed their experience in a more complex, unvarnished light and began to question their ideas about religion, society, and what it meant to rebuild the country. American writers and artists rejected the idealism and lofty symbolism of the Romantic and Transcendentalist movements because they failed to address the realities of rapid socio-economic change in post-war American life. Instead, artists tried to hold up a mirror to America and truthfully reflect people's common experiences. The result was an artistic movement known as **realism**, which emerged in the latter half of the nineteenth century and attempted to create a representation of reality in the arts by authentically depicting everyday life in comprehensive detail. American realist writers took a down-to-earth approach as they explored ethical and psychological conflicts involving the individual's relationship to nature, society, and the past.

Civil War Soldiers and Sailors Memorial in Philadelphia

3 One example of realism in fiction is Stephen Crane's *The Red Badge of Courage* (1895). Though it was written 30 years after the Civil War and the 24-year-old author had only read about the war in magazines, the book is thought to be one of the most realistic and affecting portraits of the Civil War ever written. Other American realists include Edith Wharton, William Dean Howells, Henry James, and Mark Twain.

4 In the latter part of the nineteenth century and early part of the twentieth century, African American writers and intellectuals, like W. E. B. Du Bois, Booker T. Washington, Paul Laurence Dunbar, Alice Dunbar Nelson, and Charles Chesnutt, began to establish a body of realist literature—both fiction and nonfiction—about black life in America. In 1910, Du Bois co-founded and served as the editor of *The Crisis*, the magazine of the NAACP, which published essays, history, fiction, and poetry by and about African Americans.

A Changing Reality: The Post-War South, Industrialization, and Urbanization

5 In the years following the Civil War, America underwent rapid political, social, and economic change.

6 The South emerged from the war into a period known as Reconstruction. African American men had been granted the right to vote and began running for and serving in public office. By the end of this short period, however, politics began to swing decidedly back toward discrimination and maltreatment of African Americans as segregationist laws—known as Jim Crow laws—began to be passed and enforced all over the South. Economically, white Southerners tried to rebuild their economy without slavery but soon subjected African Americans to other exploitative systems of labor, including peonage and prisoner leasing.

Copyright © BookheadEd Learning, LLC

7   In the North, industrialization was quickly altering the social and economic fabric of the cities. Scientific innovation made mass production possible and factories became central to urban economies. Cities grew as rural Americans migrated to the North in search of factory jobs. At the same time, more than 9 million immigrants entered the United States and settled primarily in the cities of the North.

Boy standing near workers inside a glass factory. Photograph by Lewis Hine, 1911

8   Industrialization and urbanization had significant benefits, such as providing both mass transit and a massive boost to the northern economy. However, these movements also had a dark side. Very few laws were in place to protect workers. There were no laws against child labor, for example. Furthermore, low pay, long hours, as well as poor, even dangerous, working conditions kept families in a vicious cycle of poverty. Political corruption was rampant. Pollution from factories was unregulated. Massive population growth caused overcrowding as well as sanitation and health problems. City governments could not keep pace with how quickly their populations were expanding and were unable to extend clean-water services, garbage collection, and up-to-date sewage systems in all areas.

9   Realities like these became the subject of two related forms of writing in the mid-to-late nineteenth century: **Naturalism** (1865–1900) and a form of investigative journalism called "muckraking." Naturalism was a literary movement that branched from realism. Naturalists often depicted the circumstances of middle- and working-class urban life in a detached and deterministic manner. They did not believe in free will and thought humans were powerless to overcome social, natural, and **hereditary**—or, genetically

inherited—forces. For authors working during this period, it was not unusual for some works to be considered realist and others naturalist. This is the case with Edith Wharton, whose classic novel *Ethan Frome* (1911) is considered to be naturalist, while many of her other novels are in the realist vein, and with Stephen Crane, whose *Maggie: A Girl of the Streets* (1893) also qualifies as a naturalist novel. Perhaps the most well-known American naturalist writer was Frank Norris, whose works include *The Pit: A Story of Chicago* and *A Deal in Wheat and Other Stories of the New and Old West*.

10 Investigative journalists during this period worked to expose social injustice, including the harsh labor practices, dangerous housing conditions, corporate greed, and political corruption. Their work was less deterministic and detached than that of the naturalists. They saw journalism as a way to raise awareness and bring about change. "Muckrakers" wrote mostly nonfiction, although a small number also wrote fiction. Some well-known muckrakers included Ida Tarbell, Lincoln Steffens, Ida B. Wells, and Upton Sinclair, who wrote *The Jungle* (1905), an exposé of the unfair labor practices and unsanitary conditions in the meat-packing industry. In addition, photojournalists Jacob Riis and Lewis Hine exposed the gritty realities of factory and tenement life in remarkable documentary photographs. Riis's photographs were collected in a book entitled *How the Other Half Lives: Studies among the Tenements of New York* (1890), which brought attention to the poor conditions of working-class housing. The book began to inspire reforms almost immediately after being published.

Whose Reality?: Life Outside the Cities

11 Of course, the experiences of people in the large eastern and midwestern cities were not the same as those of people in other parts of the country. **American literary regionalism**, or local color, was influenced by realism and depicted the unique characteristics, dialects, and landscapes of particular regions. While works of realism and naturalism were written predominantly by urban, white males, regionalist literature tended to include a more diverse range of voices. Northeastern regionalists included Sarah Orne Jewett and Mary E. Wilkins Freeman. Hamlin Garland wrote about the Midwest. Zitkála-Šá, a Dakota Sioux writer, portrayed life in the plains. Bret Harte and Mary Austin were Western regionalist writers. Southern regionalist writers included Mary N. Munfree, Kate Chopin, Grace King, Alice Dunbar Nelson, and Charles Chesnutt, an African American writer who satirized the tradition of plantation literature in his collection of stories *The Conjure Woman* (1899).

NOTES

Zitkála-Šá, a Yankton Dakota Sioux writer, musician, and political activist, in 1901

12 Major Concepts

- **Realism**—Realist literature focused primarily on the lives of the middle class. Realist authors intended their novels to be carefully detailed representations of the complexities of everyday life. They believed that the author should be objective and refrain from idealizing or romanticizing life. Realists thought that individuals had free will, or the ability to act on their environment and improve their circumstances.

- **Naturalism**—Naturalism was a branch of realism. Naturalism did differ from realism, however. Naturalists believed that human behavior was determined by heredity and environment, that people had no recourse to supernatural forces, and that the laws of nature were beyond human control.

- **Regionalism**—Regionalists, or local color writers, created vivid portraits of their own regions. Regionalism was particularly concerned with issues of place. The local landscape was often of central importance. Regionalists also emphasized local culture and community rituals. Local color, or regional, stories tended to contain more nostalgia and sentimentality than other realist writing.

New York by George Bellows, 1911

Style and Form

13 **Focus on Character and Setting over Plot**

- Realists were primarily focused on character. They prioritized the portrayal of their characters' relationships—to one another, to nature, to their past, to their social class—and their ethical, moral, and psychological dilemmas over the action of the plot. Realists frequently used **literary techniques**, such as imagery, ironic twists, and internal dialogue—as opposed to figurative language and symbolism—to detail their characters' inner lives. The conflicts in realist works often turned on changes of mood, perspective, opinion, or belief. For example, "The Cactus" by O. Henry focuses on Trysdale, who experiences a dilemma brought on by his girlfriend's sudden and inexplicable change of heart and eventual marriage to another man. The author uses an ironic twist at the end to explain the real reason for the demise of their relationship.

- Naturalist stories also focused on character over plot, but mainly to show the futility of the individual's actions against the forces of nature, society, and heredity. The tone of naturalist works was often detached and **amoral**, meaning they did not take any kind of moral stand and existed outside the realm of moral judgement. The events and conflicts in these stories tended to be more dramatic, though naturalists did not engage in any authorial commentary or interpretation. A good example of a character who is powerless to act upon the outside forces that influence her life is Laura in Katherine Anne Porter's short story "Flowering Judas." Laura finds herself among revolutionaries in Mexico working for a cause she feels ambivalent about, with people from whom she feels alienated. Though she tries to respond stoically to her circumstances, she is unable to act in her own interest at all, and her life devolves into tragedy.

- Setting and a sense of place were the most significant elements of regionalist writing, followed closely by characterization. Landscape, as well as the cultural, economic, and historical context of the location, played an important role in regionalist fiction. In fact, in some stories the setting itself became a character. Characters in regionalist literature often spoke in dialect and adhered to local customs and ideas. Just as with realism and naturalism, plot often took a backseat in regionalist literature. An example of a regional poem in which the setting is inextricably linked to the speaker's dilemma is "The Poetical Farmwife" by Bernice Love Wiggins, which provides details describing the speaker's life on the farm and her conflict between doing what she loves—writing—and what her environment demands of her—working on and maintaining the farm.

14 **Application of Scientific Ideas**

- Naturalists, in particular, tried to approach their material in a scientific manner. They called their style of description "observations." They believed in social and hereditary determinism. In other words, they subscribed to the idea that an individual could not escape the social and environmental circumstances that they had been born into or had inherited.

15 Against the tumult of rapid change, realists, naturalists, and regionalists portrayed the complexities of the average American's everyday life. If our continued fascination with consuming realistic art, literature, movies, and television is any indication, the realist experiment was a successful one. Works of realism have depicted relatable, authentic scenarios that help us consider deep and abiding questions, such as the extent to which we can control the influence of outside forces on our lives. When we read regionalist literature, we realize that there is no one, dominant narrative about American reality. Though the long-term value of reality TV is still debatable, realist literature and other forms of artistic realism have become an enduring form of representation, keeping their audience engaged in a constantly changing world and helping build an ever-growing document of national identity. Why do you think realism continues to appeal to audiences today? If you were to write a realist, regionalist, or naturalist story, which details and characters from your everyday life would you choose to write about?

Please note that excerpts and passages in the StudySync® library and this workbook are intended as touchstones to generate interest in an author's work. The excerpts and passages do not substitute for the reading of entire texts, and StudySync® strongly recommends that students seek out and purchase the whole literary or informational work in order to experience it as the author intended. Links to online resellers are available in our digital library. In addition, complete works may be ordered through an authorized reseller by filling out and returning to StudySync® the order form enclosed in this workbook.

Reading & Writing Companion   365

Literary Focus

Read "Literary Focus: Realism, Naturalism, and Regionalism." After you read, complete the Think Questions below.

 THINK QUESTIONS

1. Why did Americans lose interest in Romanticism and Transcendentalism?

2. What were some of the benefits of industrialization and urbanization? What were some of the drawbacks?

3. What style characteristics do Regionalists, Naturalists, and Realists have in common?

4. Use context clues to determine the meaning of the word **hereditary**. Write your best definition here, along with the words and phrases that were most helpful in determining the word's meaning. Then, check a dictionary to confirm your understanding.

5. Use context clues to determine the meaning of the word **amoral**. Write your best definition here, along with the words and phrases that were most helpful in determining the word's meaning. Then, use the word in a sentence about the literary movement.

My True South:
Why I Decided To Return Home

INFORMATIONAL TEXT
Jesmyn Ward
2018

Introduction

J esmyn Ward (b. 1977) is a highly acclaimed contemporary writer and professor. She followed her successful 2008 debut novel *Where the Line Bleeds* with 2011's *Salvage the Bones* and 2017's *Sing, Unburied, Sing*, both of which won a National Book Award for Fiction. In 2017, Ward was awarded a highly prestigious MacArthur "Genius" Fellowship. Much of her work centers on themes of race and identity, which feature prominently in this short autobiographical piece.

"I fantasize about living in that fabled America."

Skill:
Figurative
Language

The author uses personification to describe the dry desert air. This contrasts with the humidity she encounters closer to home. The moisture in the air once she gets to the South frees her.

Skill:
Connotation and
Denotation

The word "notorious" has a negative connotation. The white men who grew rich by slavery were "notorious" for their brutality, a word that has a very strong negative connotation. I think "notorious" means "known for something bad."

1   When I moved home in 2010, I packed my two-door car nearly to the roof and drove for three days from California's Bay Area to the Mississippi Gulf Coast. I took my preferred route, avoiding long, blistered I–10 through Phoenix and the very bottom of New Mexico and Texas in favor of I–40 across northern Arizona and New Mexico and into Dallas. Except for the bright puncture of pinwheeling stars across the night sky, I despised the desert. The dry air, suffused with heat, felt as if it were flaying me. The plants, so sparse and scraggly, offered no shade, no succor. When I crossed the 100th meridian west of Dallas, with moisture settling in the air and plants crowding the sides of the highway, tall pines and verdant vines and lush shrubs, it was as if the very water in the air buoyed me up so I could float through the heat.

2   When I crossed the Louisiana-Texas state line, I exhaled. And I exhaled again when I crossed the Mississippi state line over the swampy expanse of Pearl River. When I turned right on Kiln DeLisle Road, driving past my grandmother's house, my grandaunt's house, my uncles' houses and my sister's house, where my uncles were fixing the roof on the pump shed and my aunt waved from her porch, another exhalation. When I pulled into my mother's rocky driveway and cut my car off, another; and then a deep breath to steady myself and gain my **bearings**.

3   When people ask me why I returned home to Mississippi after years of living in the West, the East and the Midwest, I simply say this: I moved home because I love the beauty of the place, and I love the people. But this is a toothless answer, as weak and harmless as a baby's mouth.

4   It is difficult for them to understand why a successful black woman would choose to return to the South and, worse yet, to Mississippi, which looms large in the public's imagination for its racist depredations, and rightfully so. In the early 1800s, there were more millionaires in Mississippi than anywhere else in the country, and all these white men were made rich by cotton, by slavery. Their fields were notorious for their brutality and their productivity. When this cornerstone of the state's foundation was hobbled by the Civil War

NOTES

and the 13th Amendment, those in power reacted immediately, violently, burning with the same sense of entitlement that had led them to settle this wild place. Black pain, Native pain, women's pain: if this was necessary in order to reap their lot, to build their wealth, to earn their leisure, so be it.

5   White Mississippi's **steadfast** belief in this idea was not only readily apparent but also burned into the national consciousness. There are many images of tortured and lynched people taken during that era in the South: white crowds milling under mangled bodies, men, women and children alight, smiling. In the '60s, civil rights demonstrators across the South faced dogs, water hoses and guns. These images remain with us. Mississippi is the memory America invokes whenever it wants to convince itself that racial violence and subjugation are mostly lodged in the past, that they have no space in our present moment, save in this backwoods, backward place.

6   This can be that place. The aggression is sometimes slight and interpersonal, as simple as me walking through a department store with my children, an obvious shopper, when an older white woman with perfectly coiffed hair and small hands walks up to ask me if a shirt or a pair of shoes is on sale. When my youngest sister stops at a gas station, a white man takes offense at the volume of her rap music and tells her to "turn that s*** down." When she visits her friend's apartment, the neighbor casually tosses the word n***** at her, as easily as an underhand softball toss.

7   Other times, it's when a black family in my neighborhood tries to buy a piece of property on the DeLisle Bayou and the white people who own property in the area do everything they can to block the purchase. Or when my mother's neighbor begins clearing his land to build his house, and the white people who live on the other side of the woods demand that he leave a strip of forest separating our black neighborhood from their white one.

8   Sometimes the aggression is deeper, systemic. It is black children in my family enrolling in free preschool programs where their teachers barely tolerate them, ignore them, do a terrible job of leading them to learning. It is my nephew being accused of selling drugs in middle school and being strip-searched. It is black children getting into fights at school, principals pressing charges, and those same children being suspended and sent to juvenile detention centers. It is a white drunk driver hitting my brother from behind, killing him and never being held accountable for the crime of murdering him— only for leaving the scene of an accident.

9   Living in the American South for generations, my family has collected so many accounts of racial terror, passed down over the decades. I carry every slur, every slight, every violent **malign** within me; they have become a part of me,

Skill:
Reasons and evidence

The author provides two pieces of evidence to illustrate how racism still exists in the South. Choosing examples from her own life makes her evidence more powerful for the reader.

Skill:
Connotation and Denotation

The word "slight" sometimes means "small." In this instance the word has a different meaning. It is a noun with a negative connotation. I think it means "insult" because it must be a synonym for "slur" and "violent malign."

NOTES

accreted in me year after year to settle in me and express themselves in my body: vascular inflammation, migraine headaches, diabetes, giving birth to both of my children prematurely.

. . .

10   There is an American assumption underlying every bit of this terror: I see you, I know you, and you are nothing. I remember this when the pressure of living as an adult with my family and children in the South seems like too much, when the poverty my family and community has been mired in for generations by design is too galling, too present. There are moments that would break me if they could, moments when I am all too aware of how we have been robbed of opportunities to create intergenerational wealth, when our schools fail us, when we are shuttled into the service sector, when we scrabble for demeaning job after demeaning job. Days when I see one of my cousins, struggling with addiction and untreated mental illness, walking the streets shirtless and shoeless, drowning in his life, and my heart breaks. It is on days like this when a white person will interview me and ask me how to make black people want more for themselves, and I've had enough.

11   I want to run away, at moments like that, to someplace where there is no humidity, where the light is golden over the hills and the specter of all that we have survived and died by is not present in every flag, every street name, every monument, every vote. I fantasize about living in that fabled America. And then I remember that one cannot escape an infinite room. Moving across a few state lines is not going to help me escape this place that tells me I am less. The racist, misogynistic sentiment I encounter every day in Mississippi is the same belief that put in place the economic and social caste systems that allowed America to become America. It is the bedrock beneath the soil. Racial violence and subjugation happen on the streets of St. Louis, on the sidewalks of New York City and in the BART stations of Oakland.

12   I breathe. I remain. I remember that Mississippi is not only its ugliness, its treachery, its willful ignorance. It is also my nephew, hurling his body down a waterslide, rocketing to the bottom, joy running from shoulder to heel. It is my godmother boiling pots and pots of shrimp and pouring them into a children's pool so we can eat the delicious spicy mess at our family gathering on the Fourth of July. It is my youngest sister smiling and dancing to Al Green in my godmother's driveway while the night enfolds like a hand and the insects hiss with summer's sibilant kiss. It is riding to a convenience store with my childhood friends with the windows down and the night wind caressing me on my cheekbones, UGK booming from the speakers in answer to the blooming Mississippi night. It is sitting on the porch with my 78-year-old grandmother, my children sandwiched between us on the swing, making idle

Skill:
Figurative
Language

The author wants to run away from all of the negative aspects of the South. She then compares racism in America to an infinite room. This metaphor shows she cannot escape racism simply by moving around the country.

Copyright © BookheadEd Learning, LLC

talk and watching hummingbirds zip through the air beyond her screen as she tells us stories. Flush with joy.

13   But there is more. Here is my local bookseller, a white middle-aged man, arranging a celebratory birthday dinner for my sister and hosting it even as he is **convalescing** from an illness, and doing it all with a quiet, gentle smile. Here is one of my best friends from high school, a white woman with two toddlers, who stops her car when she sees black people pulled over by the police, pulling out her phone and filming in an attempt to belay disaster, to hold authority accountable, fussy children be damned. And behold the Pass Christian Public Library leading an initiative to choose The Fire This Time, a book about black experience in America, for its citywide reading program in order to foster community dialogue about what it means to be bound together in this place. We are trying to understand that one person's fate predicates another's, that this illness of racial violence and oppression affects all of us—not just in Mississippi, but throughout the South, America and abroad.

14   I like to imagine that one day, I will build a home of cement, a home built to **weather** the elements, in a clearing in a piney Southern wood, riven with oak and dogwood. I'd like a small garden where I could grow yellow squash and bell peppers in the summer, collards and carrots in the winter, and perhaps keep a few chickens. I wish for one or two kind neighbors who will return my headstrong bulldog if she wanders off, neighbors who I can gift a gallon of water in the aftermath of a hurricane. I like to think that after I die, my children will look at that place and see a place of refuge, of rest. I hope they do not flee. I hope that at least one of them will want to remain here in this place that I love more than I loathe, and I hope the work that I have done to make Mississippi a place worth living is enough. I hope they feel more themselves in this place than any other in the world, and that if they do leave, they dream of that house, that clearing, those woods, when they sleep.

15   This is the answer with teeth. The reply that demands nuance, introspection and ruthless clarity, enough to see that this can be another place. Even as the South remains troubled by its past, there are people here who are fighting so it can find its way to a healthier future, never forgetting the lessons of its long, brutal history, ever present, ever instructive.

16   We stand at the edge of a gulf, looking out on a surging, endless expanse of time and violence, constant and immense, and like water, it wishes to swallow us. We resist. We dredge new beaches, build seawalls, fortify the shore and hold fast to each other, even as storm after storm pushes down on us. We learn how to bear the rain, the wind, the inexorable waves. We fear its power, respect its reach, but we learn how to navigate it, because we must. We draw

Skill:
Reasons and
evidence

The author contrasts her previous examples of racism in the South with examples of good amongst white Southerners. This evidence shows that the South is a complex place that still has much to offer despite its flaws.

NOTES

sustenance from it. We dream of a day when we will not feel the need to throw our children into its maw to shock them into learning how to swim. We stand. And we build.

From TIME.com, July 26, 2018 © 2018 Time Inc. Used under license. TIME.com and Time Inc. are not affiliated with, and do not endorse products or services of, Licensee.

MY TRUE SOUTH:
WHY I DECIDED TO RETURN HOME

First Read

Read "My True South: Why I Decided to Return Home." After you read, complete the Think Questions below.

 THINK QUESTIONS

1. How do the changing physical environment and climate affect the narrator's thoughts during her drive to Mississippi? Cite details from the text to support your response.

2. How does the narrator view racism in Mississippi compared to racism in other parts of the United States? Provide specific examples.

3. How does the author use the concept of "building" in the text? What is the importance of this concept to her?

4. Read the following dictionary definition:

weather
wea•ther /'we-thər/ *verb*

1. wear away or change the appearance or texture of something
2. come safely through, withstand
3. make boards or tiles overlap downward to keep out the rain

Which definition most closely matches the meaning of **weather** as it is used in the text? Write the correct definition of *weather* here and explain how you figured out the correct meaning.

5. In paragraph 5, the author describes white Mississippi as having a **steadfast** belief. Based on context clues, what do you think the word *steadfast* means? Write your best definition of *steadfast* here, and explain your reasoning.

Please note that excerpts and passages in the StudySync® library and this workbook are intended as touchstones to generate interest in an author's work. The excerpts and passages do not substitute for the reading of entire texts, and StudySync® strongly recommends that students seek out and purchase the whole literary or informational work in order to experience it as the author intended. Links to online resellers are available in our digital library. In addition, complete works may be ordered through an authorized reseller by filling out and returning to StudySync® the order form enclosed in this workbook.

Reading & Writing Companion   **373**

Skill: Figurative Language

Use the Checklist to analyze Figurative Language in "My True South: Why I Decided to Return Home." Refer to the sample student annotations about Figurative Language in the text.

••• CHECKLIST FOR FIGURATIVE LANGUAGE

In order to determine the meaning of a figure of speech in context, note the following:

✓ words that mean one thing literally and suggest something else

✓ similes, metaphors, or personification

✓ words with figurative meanings that are used throughout the course of a paragraph or text

✓ the context in which an author uses figurative language and how that context may have subtle effects on the meaning of words and phrases

In order to interpret a figure of speech in context and analyze its role in the text, consider the following questions:

✓ Where is there figurative language in the text and, what seems to be the purpose of the author's use of it?

✓ Why does the author use a figure of speech rather than literal language?

✓ Are there any words or phrases with figurative meanings that are used throughout the course of a paragraph or text? What might these words represent?

✓ What words and context around an example of figurative language might change how you interpret it?

Skill: Figurative Language

Reread paragraph 12 of "My True South: Why I Decided to Return Home." Then, using the Checklist on the previous page, answer the multiple-choice questions below.

↻ YOUR TURN

1. Which of the following is not an example of personification?

   ○ A. "the night unfolds like a hand"

   ○ B. "summer's sibilant kiss"

   ○ C. "UGK booming from the speakers"

   ○ D. "wind caressing me on my cheekbones"

2. What is the intended effect of the repeated use of personification in this paragraph?

   ○ A. The intended effect is to convey the idea that Mississippi is not only a place but is as familiar as a person to the author.

   ○ B. The intended effect is to continually remind the reader of the different physical attributes of Mississippi.

   ○ C. The intended effect is to create a more interesting piece of writing that keeps the reader engaged from start to finish.

   ○ D. The intended effect is to show the reader that Mississippi is a very interesting place to visit.

Please note that excerpts and passages in the StudySync® library and this workbook are intended as touchstones to generate interest in an author's work. The excerpts and passages do not substitute for the reading of entire texts, and StudySync® strongly recommends that students seek out and purchase the whole literary or informational work in order to experience it as the author intended. Links to online resellers are available in our digital library. In addition, complete works may be ordered through an authorized reseller by filling out and returning to StudySync® the order form enclosed in this workbook.

Reading & Writing Companion   375

Skill:
Connotation and Denotation

Use the Checklist to analyze Connotation and Denotation in "My True South: Why I Decided to Return Home." Refer to the sample student annotations about Connotation and Denotation in the text.

↻ CHECKLIST FOR CONNOTATION AND DENOTATION

In order to identify the denotative meanings of words, use the following steps:

✓ first, note unfamiliar words and phrases, key words, or words that inspire an emotional reaction

✓ next, determine and note the denotative meaning of words by consulting a reference material such as a dictionary, glossary, or thesaurus

✓ finally, analyze nuances in the meaning of words with similar denotations

To better understand the meaning of words and phrases as they are used in a text, including connotative meanings, use the following questions as a guide:

✓ What is the genre or subject of the text? Based on context, what do you think the meaning of the word is intended to be?

✓ Is your inference the same or different from the dictionary definition?

✓ Does the word create a positive, negative, or neutral emotion?

✓ What synonyms or alternative phrasings help you describe the connotative meaning of the word?

To determine the meaning of words and phrases as they are used in a text, including connotative meanings, use the following questions as a guide:

✓ What is the denotative meaning of the word? Is that denotative meaning satisfactory in this context?

✓ What possible positive, neutral, or negative connotations might the word have, depending on context?

✓ What textual details signal a particular connotation for the word?

Skill:
Connotation and Denotation

Reread paragraph 10 from "My True South: Why I Decided to Return Home." Then, using the Checklist on the previous page, answer the multiple-choice questions below.

YOUR TURN

1. Based on the passage, what is the connotation and denotation of the word *mired*?

   ○ A. The connotation of mired is positive and its denotative meaning is to make clean.
   ○ B. The connotation of mired is negative and its denotative meaning is to attack with great force.
   ○ C. The connotation of mired is negative and its denotative meaning is to get stuck.
   ○ D. The connotation of mired is positive and its denotative meaning is to achieve success.

2. Based on the passage, what is the connotation and denotation of the word *shuttled*?

   ○ A. The connotation is negative and it means to systematically direct people without their consent.
   ○ B. The connotation is neutral and it means to move someone via a method of transportation.
   ○ C. The connotation is negative and means to have walked at a slow pace.
   ○ D. The connotation is neutral and it means to make the choice to move one's family to another state.

Skill:
Reasons and Evidence

Use the Checklist to analyze Reasons and Evidence in "My True South: Why I Decided to Return Home." Refer to the sample student annotations about Reasons and Evidence in the text.

CHECKLIST FOR REASONS AND EVIDENCE

In order to delineate and evaluate the reasoning and evidence that support an author's claim(s) in an argument, note the following:

✓ the argument and claim the author presents in the text

✓ the reasons and evidence the author presents in support of the claim

✓ how reasons and evidence build on one another over the course of the text to strengthen the author's claim

✓ the extent to which reasoning and evidence directly support the author's claim

✓ instances where reasoning or evidence is unclear, irrelevant, or contradictory to the author's claim

To evaluate the reasoning and evidence that an author uses to support his or her claim, consider the following questions:

✓ What kind of argument is the author making?

✓ Is the reasoning, or the thinking behind the claim(s), sound and valid?

✓ Are the reasons and evidence the author presents to support the claim sufficient, or is more evidence needed? Why or why not?

✓ Do the author's reasoning and evidence build on each other over the course of the text to strengthen the author's claim?

✓ Does the author introduce irrelevant, unclear, or contradictory evidence? How do you know?

REASONS
AND
EVIDENCE

sync•skills

Skill:
Reasons and Evidence

Reread paragraphs 14–16 of "My True South: Why I Decided to Return Home." Then, using the Checklist on the previous page, answer the multiple-choice questions below.

↻ YOUR TURN

1. Which sentence in these paragraphs best summarizes the author's claim?

   ○ A. I like to imagine that one day, I will build a home of cement, a home built to weather the elements, in a clearing in a piney Southern wood, riven with oak and dogwood.

   ○ B. I like to think that after I die, my children will look at that place and see a place of refuge, of rest.

   ○ C. Even as the South remains troubled by its past, there are people here who are fighting so it can find its way to a healthier future, never forgetting the lessons of its long, brutal history, ever present, ever instructive.

   ○ D. We stand at the edge of a gulf, looking out on a surging, endless expanse of time and violence, constant and immense, and like water, it wishes to swallow us.

2. How does the author use the final paragraph to reinforce her claim?

   ○ A. Through an analogy of a storm, the author illustrates how the people of the South work together to resist the South's troubled history and present to build a better future.

   ○ B. The author uses figurative language to show the natural beauty of the South that people must work together to preserve.

   ○ C. The author shows that the people of the South work together when natural disasters occur, making them stronger.

   ○ D. The final paragraph shows how much the author appreciates living in the South even though life can be hard.

Please note that excerpts and passages in the StudySync® library and this workbook are intended as touchstones to generate interest in an author's work. The excerpts and passages do not substitute for the reading of entire texts, and StudySync® strongly recommends that students seek out and purchase the whole literary or informational work in order to experience it as the author intended. Links to online resellers are available in our digital library. In addition, complete works may be ordered through an authorized reseller by filling out and returning to StudySync® the order form enclosed in this workbook.

Reading & Writing
Companion

379

Close Read

Reread "My True South: Why I Decided to Return Home." As you reread, complete the Skills Focus questions below. Then use your answers and annotations from the questions to help you complete the Write activity.

◎ SKILLS FOCUS

1. Identify the comparison that Ward makes in the third paragraph of her essay. What is she comparing? Explain what you think she intends to show with this comparison?

2. What evidence does Ward provide to support the idea that white Mississippians were determined to uphold their racist institutions, even after the Civil War? Identify this evidence and explain how her evidence and reasoning support her claim.

3. Identify the word **scrabble** in paragraph 10. Using context, explain what connotation this word has and what you think the word means. Explain how you arrived at your answers.

4. Identify the comparison that Ward makes in the conclusion of her essay. What is she comparing? How does this figurative language help support her argument?

5. Ward seems to have a love/hate relationship with her home state. Which of these emotions wins out and why? Support your response with evidence from the text.

✏ WRITE

LITERARY ANALYSIS: In "My True South: Why I Decided to Return Home," Jesmyn Ward uses narrative nonfiction and employs figurative language to strengthen her argument that while she is critical of the South, it is her home and is worth fighting for. Identify the reasons and evidence that Ward provides to support her claim. Then, analyze how her use of figurative language throughout the essay serves to strengthen her claim. Use textual evidence to support your response.

What to the Slave Is the Fourth of July?

ARGUMENTATIVE TEXT
Frederick Douglass
1852

Introduction

Born into slavery, Frederick Douglass (1818–1895) escaped to freedom in 1838 and went on to become a leading abolitionist and social reformer. Acclaimed for his brilliant oratory skills and incisive writing, Douglass was invited by leading citizens of Rochester, New York, to speak at an Independence Day celebration in 1852. With his characteristic eloquence and even-handed logic, Douglass answers the question posed in the title of his speech.

"Your high independence only reveals the immeasurable distance between us."

1 Fellow Citizens, I am not wanting in respect for the fathers of this republic. The signers of the Declaration of Independence were brave men. They were great men, too great enough to give frame to a great age. It does not often happen to a nation to raise, at one time, such a number of truly great men. The point from which I am compelled to view them is not, certainly, the most favorable; and yet I cannot contemplate their great deeds with less than admiration. They were statesmen, patriots and heroes, and for the good they did, and the principles they contended for, I will unite with you to honor their memory. . . .

2 . . . Fellow-citizens, pardon me, allow me to ask, why am I called upon to speak here to-day? What have I, or those I represent, to do with your national independence? Are the great principles of political freedom and of natural justice, embodied in that Declaration of Independence, extended to us? And am I, therefore, called upon to bring our humble offering to the national altar, and to confess the benefits and express devout gratitude for the blessings resulting from your independence to us?

3 Would to God, both for your sakes and ours, that an affirmative answer could be truthfully returned to these questions! Then would my task be light, and my burden easy and delightful. For who is there so cold, that a nation's sympathy could not warm him? Who so **obdurate** and dead to the claims of gratitude, that would not thankfully acknowledge such priceless benefits? Who so stolid and selfish, that would not give his voice to swell the hallelujahs of a nation's jubilee, when the chains of servitude had been torn from his limbs? I am not that man. In a case like that, the dumb might eloquently speak, and the "lame man leap as an hart."

4 But such is not the state of the case. I say it with a sad sense of the **disparity** between us. I am not included within the pale of glorious anniversary! Your high independence only reveals the immeasurable distance between us. The blessings in which you, this day, rejoice, are not enjoyed in common. The rich inheritance of justice, liberty, prosperity and independence, bequeathed by your fathers, is shared by you, not by me. The sunlight that brought light and healing to you, has brought stripes and death to me. This Fourth July is

yours, not mine. You may rejoice, I must mourn. To drag a man in fetters into the grand illuminated temple of liberty, and call upon him to join you in joyous anthems, were inhuman mockery and sacrilegious irony. Do you mean, citizens, to mock me, by asking me to speak to-day? If so, there is a parallel to your conduct. And let me warn you that it is dangerous to copy the example of a nation whose crimes, towering up to heaven, were thrown down by the breath of the Almighty, burying that nation in **irrevocable** ruin! I can to-day take up the plaintive lament of a peeled and woe-smitten people!

5 "By the rivers of Babylon, there we sat down. Yea! We wept when we remembered Zion. We hanged our harps upon the willows in the midst thereof. For there, they that carried us away captive, required of us a song; and they who wasted us required of us mirth, saying, Sing us one of the songs of Zion. How can we sing the Lord's song in a strange land? If I forget thee, O Jerusalem, let my right hand forget her cunning. If I do not remember thee, let my tongue cleave to the roof of my mouth."[1]

6 Fellow-citizens, above your national, tumultuous joy, I hear the mournful wail of millions! whose chains, heavy and grievous yesterday, are, to-day, rendered more intolerable by the jubilee shouts that reach them. If I do forget, if I do not faithfully remember those bleeding children of sorrow this day, "may my right hand forget her cunning, and may my tongue cleave to the roof of my mouth!" To forget them, to pass lightly over their wrongs, and to chime in with the popular theme, would be treason most scandalous and shocking, and would make me a **reproach** before God and the world. My subject, then, fellow-citizens, is American slavery. I shall see this day and its popular characteristics from the slave's point of view. Standing there identified with the American bondman, making his wrongs mine, I do not hesitate to declare, with all my soul, that the character and conduct of this nation never looked blacker to me than on this 4th of July! Whether we turn to the declarations of the past, or to the professions of the present, the conduct of the nation seems equally hideous and revolting. America is false to the past, false to the present, and solemnly binds herself to be false to the future. Standing with God and the crushed and bleeding slave on this occasion, I will, in the name of humanity which is outraged, in the name of liberty which is fettered, in the name of the constitution and the Bible which are disregarded and trampled upon, dare to call in question and to denounce, with all the emphasis I can command, everything that serves to perpetuate slavery the great sin and shame of America! "I will not equivocate; I will not excuse"; I will use the severest language I can command; and yet not one word shall escape me that any man, whose judgment is not blinded by prejudice, or who is not at heart a slaveholder, shall not confess to be right and just.

1. **If I do not remember thee, let my tongue cleave to the roof of my mouth** "If I do not remember thee, let my tongue cleave to the roof of my mouth; if I prefer not Jerusalem above my chief joy" (Psalm 137:6)

7   But I fancy I hear some one of my audience say, "It is just in this circumstance that you and your brother abolitionists fail to make a favorable impression on the public mind. Would you argue more, and denounce less; would you persuade more, and **rebuke** less; your cause would be much more likely to succeed." But, I submit, where all is plain there is nothing to be argued. What point in the anti-slavery creed would you have me argue? On what branch of the subject do the people of this country need light? Must I undertake to prove that the slave is a man? That point is **conceded** already. Nobody doubts it. The slaveholders themselves acknowledge it in the enactment of laws for their government. They acknowledge it when they punish disobedience on the part of the slave. There are seventy-two crimes in the State of Virginia which, if committed by a black man (no matter how ignorant he be), subject him to the punishment of death; while only two of the same crimes will subject a white man to the like punishment. What is this but the acknowledgment that the slave is a moral, intellectual, and responsible being? The manhood of the slave is conceded. It is admitted in the fact that Southern statute books are covered with enactments forbidding, under severe fines and penalties, the teaching of the slave to read or to write. When you can point to any such laws in reference to the beasts of the field, then I may consent to argue the manhood of the slave. When the dogs in your streets, when the fowls of the air, when the cattle on your hills, when the fish of the sea, and the reptiles that crawl, shall be unable to distinguish the slave from a brute, then will I argue with you that the slave is a man!

8   For the present, it is enough to affirm the equal manhood of the Negro race. Is it not astonishing that, while we are ploughing, planting, and reaping, using all kinds of mechanical tools, erecting houses, constructing bridges, building ships, working in metals of brass, iron, copper, silver and gold; that, while we are reading, writing and ciphering, acting as clerks, merchants and secretaries, having among us lawyers, doctors, ministers, poets, authors, editors, orators and teachers; that, while we are engaged in all manner of enterprises common to other men, digging gold in California, capturing the whale in the Pacific, feeding sheep and cattle on the hill-side, living, moving, acting, thinking, planning, living in families as husbands, wives and children, and, above all, confessing and worshipping the Christian's God, and looking hopefully for life and immortality beyond the grave, we are called upon to prove that we are men!

9   Would you have me argue that man is entitled to liberty? That he is the rightful owner of his own body? You have already declared it. Must I argue the wrongfulness of slavery? Is that a question for Republicans?[2] Is it to be settled by the rules of logic and argumentation, as a matter beset with great difficulty,

2. **Republicans** Douglass is referring here to participants in a system of government in which the people have a representative stake.

involving a doubtful application of the principle of justice, hard to be understood? How should I look to-day, in the presence of Americans, dividing, and subdividing a discourse, to show that men have a natural right to freedom? Speaking of it relatively and positively, negatively and affirmatively. To do so, would be to make myself ridiculous, and to offer an insult to your understanding. There is not a man beneath the canopy of heaven that does not know that slavery is wrong for him.

10 What, am I to argue that it is wrong to make men brutes, to rob them of their liberty, to work them without wages, to keep them ignorant of their relations to their fellow men, to beat them with sticks, to flay their flesh with the lash, to load their limbs with irons, to hunt them with dogs, to sell them at auction, to sunder their families, to knock out their teeth, to burn their flesh, to starve them into obedience and submission to their masters? Must I argue that a system thus marked with blood, and stained with pollution, is wrong? No! I will not. I have better employment for my time and strength than such arguments would imply.

11 What, then, remains to be argued? Is it that slavery is not divine; that God did not establish it; that our doctors of divinity are mistaken? There is blasphemy in the thought. That which is inhuman, cannot be divine! Who can reason on such a proposition? They that can, may; I cannot. The time for such argument is passed.

12 At a time like this, scorching irony, not convincing argument, is needed. O! Had I the ability, and could reach the nation's ear, I would, to-day, pour out a fiery stream of biting ridicule, blasting reproach, withering sarcasm, and stern rebuke. For it is not light that is needed, but fire; it is not the gentle shower, but thunder. We need the storm, the whirlwind, and the earthquake. The feeling of the nation must be quickened; the conscience of the nation must be roused; the propriety of the nation must be startled; the **hypocrisy** of the nation must be exposed; and its crimes against God and man must be proclaimed and denounced.

13 What, to the American slave, is your 4th of July? I answer; a day that reveals to him, more than all other days in the year, the gross injustice and cruelty to which he is the constant victim. To him, your celebration is a sham; your boasted liberty, an unholy license; your national greatness, swelling vanity; your sounds of rejoicing are empty and heartless; your denunciation of tyrants, brass fronted impudence; your shouts of liberty and equality, hollow mockery; your prayers and hymns, your sermons and thanksgivings, with all your religious parade and solemnity, are, to Him, mere **bombast,** fraud, deception, impiety, and hypocrisy — a thin veil to cover up crimes which would disgrace a nation of savages. There is not a nation on the earth guilty of practices more shocking and bloody than are the people of the United States, at this very hour.

14 Go where you may, search where you will, roam through all the monarchies and despotisms of the Old World, travel through South America, search out every abuse, and when you have found the last, lay your facts by the side of the everyday practices of this nation, and you will say with me, that, for revolting barbarity and shameless hypocrisy, America reigns without a rival.

✏ WRITE

CORRESPONDENCE: Douglass delivered this speech in 1852, more than a decade before the abolition of slavery. How do you imagine citizens of the times might have reacted to this speech? What reflections or reservations might they have had? As a person of that time, sitting in the audience, write a letter to a family member describing and responding to Douglass's message. Use specific lines from the speech to support your opinions.

Barracoon:
The Story of the
Last "Black Cargo"

INFORMATIONAL TEXT
Zora Neale Hurston
2018

Introduction

Zora Neale Hurston (1891–1960) was an African American author and anthropologist and major figure in the Harlem Renaissance. In addition to publishing a collection of African American folklore she collected during her travels, Hurston also published works of fiction, including *Their Eyes Were Watching God* and *Moses, Man of the Mountain*. *Barracoon: The Story of the Last "Black Cargo,"* published nearly 60 years after her death, consists of interviews Hurston conducted in 1927. The main subject of the book, and this excerpt, is Oluale Kossula, sometimes known as Cudjo Lewis. At the time of his interview with Hurston, Cujdo was known to be one of the last living survivors of the Atlantic slave trade.

"Cudjo feel so lonely, he can't help he cry sometime. Whut you want wid me?"

NOTES

Skill:
Summarizing

Kossula begins to cry tears of joy one morning on his porch when the author calls him by his African name. He says that she is the only one in America that calls him by his real name and that she always does this.

1   It was summer when I went to talk with Cudjo so his door was standing wide open. But I knew he was somewhere about the house before I entered the yard, because I had found the gate unlocked. When Cudjo goes down into his back-field or away from home he locks his gate with an **ingenious** wooden peg of African invention.

2   I hailed him by his African name as I walked up the steps to his porch, and he looked up into my face as I stood in the door in surprise. He was eating his breakfast from a round enameled pan with his hands, in the fashion of his fatherland.

3   The surprise of seeing me halted his hand between pan and face. Then tears of joy welled up.

4   "Oh Lor', I know it *you* call my name. Nobody don't callee me my name from cross de water but you. You al-ways called me Kossula,[1] jus' lak I in de Affica soil!"

5   I noted that another man sat eating with him and I wondered why. So I said, "I see you have company, Kossula."

6   Yeah, I got to have somebody stay wid me. I been sick in de bed de five month. I needa somebody hand me some water. So I take dis man and he sleep here and take keer of Cudjo. But I gitee well now."

7   In spite of the recent illness and the fact that his well had fallen in, I found Cudjo Lewis full of gleaming, good will. His garden was planted. There was deep shade under his China-berry tree and all was well.

8   He wanted to know a few things about New York and when I had answered him, he sat silently smoking. Finally, I told him I had come to talk with him. He removed his pipe from his mouth and smiled.

---

1. **Kossula** Cudjoe Lewis (1840–1935) was the last known survivor of the Atlantic slave trade, originally named Oluale Kossula or Kossola, a name historians trace to the Yoruba tribe of present-day Benin.

9   "I doan keer," he said, "I lakee have comp'ny come see me." The the smile faded into a wretched weeping mask. "I so lonely. My wife she left me since de 1908. Cujo all by hisself."

10 After a minute or two he remembered me and said **contritely**, "Excuse me, You didn't do nothin' to me. Cudjo feel so lonely, he can't help he cry sometime. Whut you want wid me?"

11 "First, I want to ask you how you feel today?"

12 Another muted silence. Then he said, "I thank God I on prayin' groun' and in a Bible country."

13 "But didn't you have a God back in Africa?" I asked him.

14 His head dropped between his hands and the tears sprung fresh. Seeing the **anguish** in his face, I regretted that I had come to worry this captive in a strange land. He read my face and said "Excusee me I cry. I can't help it when I hear de name call. Oh, Lor'. I no see Afficky soil no mo'!"

Skill:
Summarizing

Kossula cries, and the author regrets bringing up his pain. He notices that she is sorry and tells her that hearing his real name makes him cry and that it reminds him that he will never see Africa again.

15 Another long silence. Then, "How come you astee me ifn' we had no God back dere in Afficky?"

16 "Because you said 'thank God you were on praying ground in a Bible country.'"

17 "Yeah, in Afficky we always know dere was a God; he name Alahua, bu po' Affickans we cain readee de Bible, so we doan know God got a Son. We ain' ignant— we jes doan know. Nobody doan tell us 'bout Adam eatee de apple, we didn't know de seven seals[2] was sealee 'gainst us. Our parents doan tell us dat. Dey didn't tell us 'bout de first days.[3] No, dass a right. We jes doan know. So dat whut you come astee me?"

18 I temporized. "Well, yes. I wanted to ask that, but I want to ask you many things. I want to know who you are and how you came to be a slave; and to what part of Africa do you belong, and how you fared as a slave, and how you have managed as a free man?"

19 Again his head was bowed for a time. When he lifted his wet face again he murmured, "Thankee Jesus! Somebody come ast about Cudjo! I want tellee somebody who I is, so maybe dey go in de Afficky soil some day and calle my name and somebody dere say, 'Yeah, I know Kossula.'" I want you everywhere you go to tell everybody whut Cudjo say, and how come I in Americky soil

2. **seven seals** the seals binding the Book of Revelation in the New Testament
3. **de first days** the creation of the heavens and earth as depicted in the Biblical story of Genesis

since de 1859 and never see my people no mo'. I can't talkee plain, you unnerstand me, but I calls it word by word for you so it won't be too crooked for you.

20   "My name, is not Cudjo Lewis. It Kossula. When I gittee in Americky soil, Mr. Jim Meaher he try callee my name, but it too long, you unnerstand me, so I say, 'Well, I yo' property?' He say, 'Yeah.' Den I say, 'You callee me Cudjo. Dat do.' But in Afficky soil my mama she name me Kossula.'"

21   "My people, you unnerstand me, dey ain' got no ivory by de door. When it ivory from de elephant stand by de door, den dat a king, a ruler, you unnerstand me, My father neither his father don't rule nobody. De ole folks dat live two hud'ed year befo' I born don't tell me de father (remote ancestor) rule nobody.

22   "My people in Afficky, you unnerstand me, dey not rich. Dass de truth, now. I not goin' tellee you my folks dey rich and come from high blood. Den when you go in de Afficky soil an' astee de people, dey say, 'Why Kossula over dere in Americky soil tellee de folks he rich?' I tellee you lak it is. Now, dass right, ain' it?

23   "My father's father, you unnerstand me, he a officer of de king. He don't live in de **compound** wid us. Wherever de king go, he go, you unnerstand me. De king give him plenty land, and got plenty cows and goats and sheep. Now, dass right. Maybe after while he be a little chief, I doan know. But he die when I was a lil boy. Whut he gointer be later on, dat doan reachee me.

24   "My grandpa, he a great man. I tellee how he go."

25   I was afraid that Cudjo might go off on a **tangent**, so I cut in with, "But Kossula, I want to hear about *you* and how *you* lived in Africa."

26   He gave me a look full of scornful pity and asked, "where is de house where de mouse is de leader? In de Affica soil I cain tellee you ''bout de son before I tellee you ''bout de father; and derefore, you unnerstand me, I cain talk about de man who is father *(et te)* till I tellee you bout de man who he father to him, *(et, te, te,* grandfather) now, dass right ain" it?"

Excerpted from *Barracoon: The Story of the Last "Black Cargo"* by Zora Neale Hurston, published by Amistad, an imprint of HarperCollins.

First Read

Read *Barracoon: The Story of the Last "Black Cargo."* After you read, complete the Think Questions below.

☁ THINK QUESTIONS

1. What details does Hurston include in the text that describe the kind of relationship she has with Kossula? What words would you use to describe their relationship?

2. What is Kossula's reaction when Hurston asks for his story? What can you infer about his past based on this reaction?

3. According to paragraphs 2–4, why does Kossula respond with "tears of joy" when Hurston greets him? Why is her greeting significant?

4. What is the meaning of the word **contritely** as it is used in the text? Write your best definition here, along with a brief explanation of how you arrived at its meaning.

5. Read the following dictionary entry:

tangent
tangent/ˈtanjənt/ *noun*

1. a straight line or plane that touches a curve or curved surface at a point, but if extended does not cross it at that point
2. a completely different line of thought or action.
3. touching

Use context to determine which of these definitions most closely matches the use of **tangent** in *Barracoon: The Story of the Last "Black Cargo."* Write the correct definition of *tangent* here, and explain how you figured it out.

Please note that excerpts and passages in the StudySync® library and this workbook are intended as touchstones to generate interest in an author's work. The excerpts and passages do not substitute for the reading of entire texts, and StudySync® strongly recommends that students seek out and purchase the whole literary or informational work in order to experience it as the author intended. Links to online resellers are available in our digital library. In addition, complete works may be ordered through an authorized reseller by filling out and returning to StudySync® the order form enclosed in this workbook.

Reading & Writing Companion   **391**

Skill: Summarizing

Use the Checklist to analyze Summarizing in *Barracoon: The Story of the Last "Black Cargo."* Refer to the sample student annotations about Summarizing in the text.

↻ CHECKLIST FOR SUMMARIZING

In order to determine how to write an objective summary of a text, note the following:

✓ answers to the basic questions *who, what, where, when, why,* and *how* about the text

✓ themes or central ideas that are developed over the course of the text, and how they interact and build on one another to produce a complex account

✓ that you stay objective, and do not add your own personal thoughts, judgments, or opinions to the summary

To provide an objective summary of a text, consider the following questions:

✓ What are the answers to the basic questions *who, what, where, when, why,* and *how* about the text?

✓ Does my summary include how the text's themes or central ideas are developed over the course of the text, and how they interact and build on one another?

✓ Is my summary objective, or have I added my own thoughts, judgments, and personal opinions?

SUMMARIZING

sync•skills

Skill: Summarizing

Reread paragraphs 20–26 of *"Barracoon: The Story of the Last 'Black Cargo.'"* Then, using the Checklist on the previous page, answer the multiple-choice questions below.

⟳ YOUR TURN

1. Which statement best summarizes the information Kossula provides about his family in Africa?

   ○ A. Kossula makes it clear that he will not lie and say that his people were rich but says his grandfather was a great man who could have become a little chief and may have become rich.

   ○ B. His people were not wealthy, nor rulers, but his grandfather was an officer to the king, who took good care of his grandfather and gave him land and livestock.

   ○ C. His people were not wealthy, nor had high blood, but his grandfather was a proud man, and Kossula looked up to him and loved him even though he was not African royalty.

   ○ D. His people were not wealthy, and they were not rulers; they, however, did have an elephant and ivory, and Kossula's grandfather worked for the king.

2. Which statement provides the most objective summary of why Kossula starts the story of his life by telling about his grandfather?

   ○ A. Kossula says that a child in a house is a little mouse and that on the soil of Africa you tell about a son, then the father. He asks if the author understands that you would not speak about a son before speaking about the father and the man who is the father of the father.

   ○ B. Kossula says that a child in a house is not the leader and that in Africa you would not speak about the son before speaking about the father. So he can't speak about himself or his father until he speaks about his grandfather.

   ○ C. Kossula says that he is a mouse, which is not true as his life is as important as his grandfather's life, so he should tell his story and then talk about his grandfather.

   ○ D. The mouse is the child and cannot be a leader in a house. Children should not talk about themselves before talking about those who came before them. Kossula's understanding of this shows his respect for his father and grandfather as well as for African tradition.

Copyright © BookheadEd Learning, LLC

Reading & Writing Companion

Close Read

Reread *Barracoon: The Story of the Last "Black Cargo."* As you reread, complete the Skills Focus questions below. Then use your answers and annotations from the questions to help you complete the Write activity.

◎ SKILLS FOCUS

1. Describe the relationship between Kossula and the author. Identify textual evidence to support your response.

2. Identify Kossula's response to the author's question about whether or not the people in Africa had a God. Summarize Kossula's explanation in your own words.

3. Identify Kossula's initial reaction when the author asks him to tell her about his life. Summarize his reaction in your own words.

4. Describe how the author's decision to write Kossula's words in vernacular (as they are spoken) enhances the reader's understanding of this excerpt. Cite textual evidence to support your answer.

5. How does Kossula's childhood in Africa continue to shape his identity, even long after he was forced to leave his home? Identify specific examples to support your explanation.

✏ WRITE

LITERARY ANALYSIS: The authors of both "What to the Slave Is the Fourth of July?" and *Barracoon: The Story of the Last "Black Cargo"* use writing to shed light as well as offer commentary on the institution of slavery. For each text, summarize what the author wants his or her audience to understand about the inherent brutality of slavery and what content or rhetorical choices the author makes to convey this message. Support your response with textual evidence.

As I Lay Dying

FICTION
William Faulkner
1930

Introduction

William Faulkner (1897–1962) was a Nobel Prize-winning novelist and short-story writer from Oxford, Mississippi, whose works are a cornerstone of American Southern literature. His novel *As I Lay Dying* is titled after a line from the *Odyssey* ("As I lay dying, the woman with the dog's eyes would not close my eyes as I descended into Hades"). It revolves around the death of the matriarch of the Bundren family, who are poor farmers in Mississippi. Her sons, Darl and Jewel, and her friend, Cora, each reveal their thoughts as Addie lies on her deathbed. The excerpt moves between their individual first-person accounts.

"And now them others sitting there, like buzzards. Waiting, fanning themselves."

NOTES

Darl

1   When I reach the top he has quit sawing. Standing in a litter of chips, he is fitting two of the boards together. Between the shadow spaces they are yellow as gold, like soft gold, bearing on their flanks in smooth **undulations** the marks of the adze blade: a good carpenter, Cash is. He holds the two planks on the trestle, fitted along the edges in a quarter of the finished box. He kneels and squints along the edge of them, then he lowers them and takes up the adze. A good carpenter. Addie Bundren could not want a better one, a better box to lie in. It will give her confidence and comfort. I go on to the house, followed by the
Chuck. Chuck. Chuck.
of the adze.

...

Cora

2   So I saved out the eggs and baked yesterday. The cakes turned out right well. We depend a lot on our chickens. They are good layers, what few we have left after the possums and such. Snakes too, in the summer. A snake will break up a hen-house quicker than anything. So after they were going to cost so much more than Mr Tull thought, and after I promised that the difference in the number of eggs would make it up, I had to be more careful than ever because it was on my final say-so we took them. We could have **stocked** cheaper chickens, but I gave my promise as Miss Lawington said when she advised me to get a good breed, because Mr Tull himself admits that a good breed of cows or hogs pays in the long run. So when we lost so many of them we couldn't afford to use the eggs ourselves, because I could not have had Mr Tull chide me when it was on my say-so we took them. So when Miss Lawington told me about the cakes I thought that I could bake them and earn enough at one time to increase the net value of the flock the **equivalent** of two head. And that by saving the eggs out one at a time, even the eggs wouldn't be costing anything. And that week they laid so well that I not only saved out enough eggs above what we had engaged to sell, to bake the cakes with, I had saved enough so that the flour and the sugar and the stove wood would not be costing anything. So I baked yesterday, more careful than

ever I baked in my life, and the cakes turned out right well. But when we got to town this morning Miss Lawington told me the lady had changed her mind and was not going to have the party after all.

3   "She ought to taken those cakes anyway," Kate says.

4   "Well," I say, "I reckon she never had no use for them now."

5   "She ought to taken them," Kate says. "But those rich town ladies can change their minds. Poor folks cant."

6   Riches is nothing in the face of the Lord, for He can see into the heart. "Maybe I can sell them at the bazaar Saturday," I say. They turned out real well.

7   "You cant get two dollars a piece for them," Kate says.

8   "Well, it isn't like they cost me anything," I say. I saved them out and swapped a dozen of them for the sugar and flour. It isn't like the cakes cost me anything, as Mr Tull himself realises that the eggs I saved were over and beyond what we had engaged to sell, so it was like we had found the eggs or they had been given to us.

9   "She ought to taken those cakes when she same as gave you her word," Kate says. The Lord can see into the heart. If it is His will that some folks has different ideas of honesty from other folks, it is not my place to question His decree.

10   "I reckon she never had any use for them," I say. They turned out real well, too.

11   The quilt is drawn up to her chin, hot as it is, with only her two hands and her face outside. She is propped on the pillow, with her head raised so she can see out the window, and we can hear him every time he takes up the adze or the saw. If we were deaf we could almost watch her face and hear him, see him. Her face is wasted away so that the bones draw just under the skin in white lines. Her eyes are like two candles when you watch them gutter down into the sockets of iron candle-sticks. But the eternal and the everlasting **salvation** and grace is not upon her.

12   "They turned out real nice," I say. "But not like the cakes Addie used to bake." You can see that girl's washing and ironing in the pillow-slip, if ironed it ever was. Maybe it will **reveal** her blindness to her, laying there at the mercy and the ministration of four men and a tom-boy girl. "There's not a woman in this section could ever bake with Addie Bundren," I say. "First thing we know she'll be up and baking again, and then we wont have any sale for ours at all."

Under the quilt she makes no more of a hump than a rail would, and the only way you can tell she is breathing is by the sound of the mattress shucks. Even the hair at her cheek does not move, even with that girl standing right over her, fanning her with the fan. While we watch she swaps the fan to the other hand without stopping it.

13 "Is she sleeping?" Kate whispers.

14 "She's just watching Cash yonder," the girl says. We can hear the saw in the board. It sounds like snoring. Eula turns on the trunk and looks out the window. Her necklace looks real nice with her red hat. You wouldn't think it only cost twenty-five cents.

15 "She ought to taken those cakes," Kate says.

16 I could have used the money real well. But it's not like they cost me anything except the baking. I can tell him that anybody is likely to make a miscue, but it's not all of them that can get out of it without loss, I can tell him. It's not everybody can eat their mistakes, I can tell him.

17 Someone comes through the hall. It is Darl. He does not look in as he passes the door. Eula watches him as he goes on and passes from sight again toward the back. Her hand rises and touches her beads lightly, and then her hair. When she finds me watching her, her eyes go blank.

· · ·

Jewel

18 It's because he stays out there, right under the window, hammering and sawing on that goddamn box. Where she's got to see him. Where every breath she draws is full of his knocking and sawing where she can see him saying See. See what a good one I am making for you. I told him to go somewhere else. I said Good God do you want to see her in it. It's like when he was a little boy and she says if she had some fertilizer she would try to raise some flowers and he taken the bread pan and brought it back from the barn full of dung.

19 And now them others sitting there, like buzzards. Waiting, fanning themselves. Because I said If you wouldn't keep on sawing and nailing at it until a man cant sleep even and her hands laying on the quilt like two of them roots dug up and tried to wash and you couldn't get them clean. I can see the fan and Dewey Dell's arm. I said if you'd just let her alone. Sawing and knocking, and keeping the air always moving so fast on her face that when you're tired you cant breathe it, and that goddamn adze going One lick less. One lick less.

One lick less until everybody that passes in the road will have to stop and see it and say what a fine carpenter he is.

Excerpted from *As I Lay Dying* by William Faulkner, published by Vintage Books.

✏ WRITE

ARGUMENTATIVE: What are the pros and cons of telling a story through multiple narrators? Using *As I Lay Dying* as an example, explain whether telling the story from the viewpoints of many characters improves the story or whether the converse is true. Cite specific examples from the text to support your claim.

Please note that excerpts and passages in the StudySync® library and this workbook are intended as touchstones to generate interest in an author's work. The excerpts and passages do not substitute for the reading of entire texts, and StudySync® strongly recommends that students seek out and purchase the whole literary or informational work in order to experience it as the author intended. Links to online resellers are available in our digital library. In addition, complete works may be ordered through an authorized reseller by filling out and returning to StudySync® the order form enclosed in this workbook.

Reading & Writing
Companion   **399**

Flowering Judas

FICTION
Katherine Anne Porter
1930

Introduction

Katherine Anne Porter (1890–1980) wrote fiction, essays, and journalism. She is best known for her short stories and her best-selling novel *Ship of Fools*; she was also a teacher and political activist. Born and raised in Texas, and later splitting her time between New York City and Mexico, Porter went on to win a Pulitzer Prize for her collected short stories. "Flowering Judas," first published in 1930, follows Laura, an American expatriate living in Mexico as a member of the revolutionary forces.

"Now she is free, and she thinks, I must run while there is time. But she does not go."

 NOTES

1   BRAGGIONI sits heaped upon the edge of a straight-backed chair much too small for him, and sings to Laura in a furry, mournful voice. Laura has begun to find reasons for avoiding her own house until the latest possible moment, for Braggioni is there almost every night. No matter how late she is, he will be sitting there with a surly, waiting expression, pulling at his kinky yellow hair, thumbing the strings of his guitar, snarling a tune under his breath. Lupe the Indian maid meets Laura at the door, and says with a flicker of a glance towards the upper room, "He waits."

2   Laura wishes to lie down, she is tired of her hairpins and the feel of her long tight sleeves, but she says to him, "Have you a new song for me this evening?" If he says yes, she asks him to sing it. If he says no, she remembers his favorite one, and asks him to sing it again. Lupe brings her a cup of chocolate and a plate of rice, and Laura eats at the small table under the lamp, first inviting Braggioni, whose answer is always the same: "I have eaten, and besides, chocolate thickens the voice."

3   Laura says, "Sing, then," and Braggioni heaves himself into song. He scratches the guitar familiarly as though it were a pet animal, and sings passionately off key, taking the high notes in a prolonged painful squeal. Laura, who haunts the markets listening to the ballad singers, and stops every day to hear the blind boy playing his reed-flute in Sixteenth of September Street, listens to Braggioni with pitiless courtesy, because she dares not smile at his miserable performance. Nobody dares to smile at him. Braggioni is cruel to everyone, with a kind of specialized insolence, but he is so vain of his talents, and so **sensitive** to slights, it would require a cruelty and vanity greater than his own to lay a finger on the vast cureless wound of his self-esteem. It would require courage, too, for it is dangerous to offend him, and nobody has this courage.

4   Braggioni loves himself with such tenderness and amplitude and eternal charity that his followers—for he is a leader of men, a skilled revolutionist, and his skin has been **punctured** in honorable warfare—warm themselves in the reflected glow, and say to each other: "He has a real nobility, a love of humanity raised above mere personal affections." The excess of this self-love

has flowed out, inconveniently for her, over Laura, who, with so many others, owes her comfortable situation and her salary to him. When he is in a very good humor, he tells her, "I am tempted to forgive you for being a gringa. Gringita!" and Laura, burning, imagines herself leaning forward suddenly, and with a sound back-handed slap wiping the suety smile from his face. If he notices her eyes at these moments he gives no sign.

5   She knows what Braggioni would offer her, and she must resist tenaciously without appearing to resist, and if she could avoid it she would not admit even to herself the slow drift of his intention. During these long evenings which have spoiled a long month for her, she sits in her deep chair with an open book on her knees, resting her eyes on the consoling rigidity of the printed page when the sight and sound of Braggioni singing threaten to identify themselves with all her remembered **afflictions** and to add their weight to her uneasy premonitions of the future. The gluttonous bulk of Braggioni has become a symbol of her many disillusions, for a revolutionist should be lean, animated by heroic faith, a vessel of abstract virtues. This is nonsense, she knows it now and is ashamed of it. Revolution must have leaders, and leadership is a career for energetic men. She is, her comrades tell her, full of romantic error, for what she defines as cynicism in them is merely "a developed sense of reality." She is almost too willing to say, "I am wrong, I suppose I don't really understand the principles," and afterward she makes a secret truce with herself, determined not to surrender her will to such expedient logic. But she cannot help feeling that she has been betrayed irreparably by the disunion between her way of living and her feeling of what life should be, and at times she is almost contented to rest in this sense of grievance as a private store of consolation. Sometimes she wishes to run away, but she stays. Now she longs to fly out of this room, down the narrow stairs, and into the street where the houses lean together like conspirators under a single mottled lamp, and leave Braggioni singing to himself.

6   Instead she looks at Braggioni, frankly and clearly, like a good child who understands the rules of behavior. Her knees cling together under sound blue serge, and her round white collar is not purposely nun-like. She wears the uniform of an idea, and has renounced vanities. She was born Roman Catholic, and in spite of her fear of being seen by someone who might make a scandal of it, she slips now and again into some crumbling little church, kneels on the chilly stone, and says a Hail Mary on the gold rosary she bought in Tehuantepec. It is no good and she ends by examining the altar with its tinsel flowers and ragged brocades, and feels tender about the battered doll-shape of some male saint whose white, lace-trimmed drawers hang limply around his ankles below the hieratic dignity of his velvet robe. She has encased herself in a set of principles derived from her early training, leaving no detail of gesture or of personal taste untouched, and for this reason she

will not wear lace made on machines. This is her private heresy, for in her special group the machine is sacred, and will be the salvation of the workers. She loves fine lace, and there is a tiny edge of fluted cobweb on this collar, which is one of twenty precisely alike, folded in blue tissue paper in the upper drawer of her clothes chest.

7 Braggioni catches her glance solidly as if he had been waiting for it, leans forward, balancing his paunch between his spread knees, and sings with tremendous emphasis, weighing his words. He has, the song relates, no father and no mother, nor even a friend to console him; lonely as a wave of the sea he comes and goes, lonely as a wave. His mouth opens round and yearns sideways, his balloon cheeks grow oily with the labor of song. He bulges marvelously in his expensive garments. Over his lavender collar, crushed upon a purple necktie, held by a diamond hoop: over his ammunition belt of tooled leather worked in silver, buckled cruelly around his gasping middle: over the tops of his glossy yellow shoes Braggioni swells with ominous ripeness, his mauve silk hose stretched taut, his ankles bound with the stout leather thongs of his shoes.

8 When he stretches his eyelids at Laura she notes again that his eyes are the true tawny yellow cat's eyes. He is rich, not in money, he tells her, but in power, and this power brings with it the blameless ownership of things, and the right to indulge his love of small luxuries. "I have a taste for the elegant refinements," he said once, flourishing a yellow silk handkerchief before her nose. "Smell that? It is Jockey Club, imported from New York." Nonetheless he is wounded by life. He will say so presently. "It is true everything turns to dust in the hand, to gall on the tongue." He sighs and his leather belt creaks like a saddle girth. "I am disappointed in everything as it comes. Everything." He shakes his head. "You, poor thing, you will be disappointed too. You are born for it. We are more alike than you realize in some things. Wait and see. Some day you will remember what I have told you, you will know that Braggioni was your friend."

9 Laura feels a slow chill, a purely physical sense of danger, a warning in her blood that violence, mutilation, a shocking death, wait for her with lessening patience. She has translated this fear into something homely, immediate, and sometimes hesitates before crossing the street. "My personal fate is nothing, except as the testimony of a mental attitude," she reminds herself, quoting from some forgotten philosophic primer, and is sensible enough to add, "Anyhow, I shall not be killed by an automobile if I can help it."

10 "It may be true I am as **corrupt**, in another way, as Braggioni," she thinks in spite of herself, "as callous, as incomplete," and if this is so, any kind of death seems preferable. Still she sits quietly, she does not run. Where could she go? Uninvited she has promised herself to this place; she can no longer

imagine herself as living in another country, and there is no pleasure in remembering her life before she came here.

11 Precisely what is the nature of this devotion, its true motives, and what are its obligations? Laura cannot say. She spends part of her days in Xochimilco, near by, teaching Indian children to say in English, "The cat is on the mat." When she appears in the classroom they crowd about her with smiles on their wise, innocent, clay-colored faces, crying, "Good morning, my titcher!" in **immaculate** voices, and they make of her desk a fresh garden of flowers every day. During her leisure she goes to union meetings and listens to busy important voices quarreling over tactics, methods, internal politics. She visits the prisoners of her own political faith in their cells, where they entertain themselves with counting cockroaches, repenting of their indiscretions, composing their memoirs, writing out manifestoes and plans for their comrades who are still walking about free, hands in pockets, sniffing fresh air. Laura brings them food and cigarettes and a little money, and she brings messages disguised in equivocal phrases from the men outside who dare not set foot in the prison for fear of disappearing into the cells kept empty for them. If the prisoners confuse night and day, and complain, "Dear little Laura, time doesn't pass in this infernal hole, and I won't know when it is time to sleep unless I have a reminder," she brings them their favorite narcotics, and says in a tone that does not wound them with pity, "Tonight will really be night for you," and though her Spanish amuses them, they find her comforting, useful. If they lose patience and all faith, and curse the slowness of their friends in coming to their rescue with money and influence, they trust her not to repeat everything, and if she inquires, "Where do you think we can find money, or influence?" they are certain to answer, "Well, there is Braggioni, why doesn't he do something?"

12 She smuggles letters from headquarters to men hiding from firing squads in back streets in mildewed houses, where they sit in tumbled beds and talk bitterly as if all Mexico were at their heels, when Laura knows positively they might appear at the band concert in the Alameda on Sunday morning, and no one would notice them. But Braggioni says, "Let them sweat a little. The next time they may be careful. It is very restful to have them out of the way for a while." She is not afraid to knock on any door in any street after midnight, and enter in the darkness, and say to one of these men who is really in danger: "They will be looking for you—seriously—tomorrow morning after six. Here is some money from Vicente. Go to Vera Cruz and wait."

13 She borrows money from the Roumanian agitator to give to his bitter enemy the Polish agitator. The favor of Braggioni is their disputed territory, and Braggioni holds the balance nicely, for he can use them both. The Polish agitator talks love to her over café tables, hoping to exploit what he believes is her secret sentimental preference for him, and he gives her misinformation

which he begs her to repeat as the solemn truth to certain persons. The Roumanian is more adroit. He is generous with his money in all good causes, and lies to her with an air of ingenuous candor, as if he were her good friend and confidant. She never repeats anything they may say. Braggioni never asks questions. He has other ways to discover all that he wishes to know about them.

14   Nobody touches her, but all praise her gray eyes, and the soft, round under lip which promises gayety, yet is always grave, nearly always firmly closed: and they cannot understand why she is in Mexico. She walks back and forth on her errands, with puzzled eyebrows, carrying her little folder of drawings and music and school papers. No dancer dances more beautifully than Laura walks, and she inspires some amusing, unexpected ardors, which cause little gossip, because nothing comes of them. A young captain who had been a soldier in Zapata's army attempted, during a horseback ride near Cuernavaca, to express his desire for her with the noble simplicity befitting a rude folk-hero: but gently, because he was gentle. This gentleness was his defeat, for when he alighted, and removed her foot from the stirrup, and essayed to draw her down into his arms, her horse, ordinarily a tame one, shied fiercely, reared and plunged away. The young hero's horse careered blindly after his stable-mate, and the hero did not return to the hotel until rather late that evening. At breakfast he came to her table in full charro dress, gray buckskin jacket and trousers with strings of silver buttons down the leg, and he was in a humorous, careless mood. "May I sit with you?" and "You are a wonderful rider. I was terrified that you might be thrown and dragged. I should never have forgiven myself. But I cannot admire you enough for your riding!"

15   "I learned to ride in Arizona," said Laura. "If you will ride with me again this morning, I promise you a horse that will not shy with you," he said. But Laura remembered that she must return to Mexico City at noon.

16   Next morning the children made a celebration and spent their playtime writing on the blackboard, "We lov ar ticher," and with tinted chalks they drew wreaths of flowers around the words. The young hero wrote her a letter: "I am a very foolish, wasteful, impulsive man. I should have first said I love you, and then you would not have run away. But you shall see me again." Laura thought, "I must send him a box of colored crayons," but she was trying to forgive herself for having spurred her horse at the wrong moment.

17   A brown, shock-haired youth came and stood in her patio one night and sang like a lost soul for two hours, but Laura could think of nothing to do about it. The moonlight spread a wash of gauzy silver over the clear spaces of the garden, and the shadows were cobalt blue. The scarlet blossoms of the Judas tree were dull purple, and the names of the colors repeated themselves

automatically in her mind, while she watched not the boy, but his shadow, fallen like a dark garment across the fountain rim, trailing in the water. Lupe came silently and whispered expert counsel in her ear: "If you will throw him one little flower, he will sing another song or two and go away." Laura threw the flower, and he sang a last song and went away with the flower tucked in the band of his hat. Lupe said, "He is one of the organizers of the Typographers Union, and before that he sold corridos in the Merced market, and before that, he came from Guanajuato, where I was born. I would not trust any man, but I trust least those from Guanajuato."

18   She did not tell Laura that he would be back again the next night, and the next, nor that he would follow her at a certain fixed distance around the Merced market, through the Zócalo, up Francisco I. Madero Avenue, and so along the Paseo de la Reforma to Chapultepec Park, and into the Philosopher's Footpath, still with that flower withering in his hat, and an indivisible attention in his eyes.

19   Now Laura is accustomed to him, it means nothing except that he is nineteen years old and is observing a convention with all propriety, as though it were founded on a law of nature, which in the end it might well prove to be. He is beginning to write poems which he prints on a wooden press, and he leaves them stuck like handbills in her door. She is pleasantly disturbed by the abstract, unhurried watchfulness of his black eyes which will in time turn easily towards another object. She tells herself that throwing the flower was a mistake, for she is twenty-two years old and knows better; but she refuses to regret it, and persuades herself that her negation of all external events as they occur is a sign that she is gradually perfecting herself in the stoicism she strives to cultivate against that disaster she fears, though she cannot name it.

20   She is not at home in the world. Everyday she teaches children who remain strangers to her, though she loves their tender round hands and their charming opportunist savagery. She knocks at unfamiliar doors not knowing whether a friend or a stranger shall answer, and even if a known face emerges from the sour gloom of that unknown interior, still it is the face of a stranger. No matter what this stranger says to her, nor what her message to him, the very cells of her flesh reject knowledge and kinship in one monotonous word. No. No. No. She draws her strength from this one holy talismanic word which does not suffer her to be led into evil. Denying everything, she may walk anywhere in safety, she looks at everything without amazement.

21   No, repeats this firm unchanging voice of her blood; and she looks at Braggioni without amazement. He is a great man, he wishes to impress this simple girl who covers her great round breasts with thick dark cloth, and who hides long, invaluably beautiful legs under a heavy skirt. She is almost thin except for the incomprehensible fullness of her breasts, like a nursing

mother's, and Braggioni, who considers himself a judge of women, speculates again on the puzzle of her notorious virginity, and takes the liberty of speech which she permits without a sign of modesty, indeed, without any sort of sign, which is disconcerting.

22   "You think you are so cold, gringita! Wait and see. You will surprise yourself some day! May I be there to advise you!" He stretches his eyelids at her, and his ill-humored cat's eyes waver in a separate glance for the two points of light marking the opposite ends of a smoothly drawn path between the swollen curve of her breasts. He is not put off by that blue serge, nor by her resolutely fixed gaze. There is all the time in the world. His cheeks are bellying with the wind of song. "O girl with the dark eyes," he sings, and reconsiders. "But yours are not dark. I can change all that. O girl with the green eyes, you have stolen my heart away!" then his mind wanders to the song, and Laura feels the weight of his attention being shifted elsewhere. Singing thus, he seems harmless, he is quite harmless, there is nothing to do but sit patiently and say "No," when the moment comes. She draws a full breath, and her mind wanders also, but not far. She dares not wander too far.

23   Not for nothing has Braggioni taken pains to be a good revolutionist and a professional lover of humanity. He will never die of it. He has the **malice**, the cleverness, the wickedness, the sharpness of wit, the hardness of heart, stipulated for loving the world profitably. He will never die of it. He will live to see himself kicked out from his feeding trough by other hungry world-saviors. Traditionally he must sing in spite of his life which drives him to bloodshed, he tells Laura, for his father was a Tuscany peasant who drifted to Yucatan and married a Maya woman: a woman of race, an aristocrat. They gave him the love and knowledge of music, thus: and under the rip of his thumbnail, the strings of the instrument complain like exposed nerves.

24   Once he was called Delgadito by all the girls and married women who ran after him; he was so scrawny all his bones showed under his thin cotton clothing, and he could squeeze his emptiness to the very backbone with his two hands. He was a poet and the revolution was only a dream then; too many women loved him and sapped away his youth, and he could never find enough to eat anywhere, anywhere! Now he is a leader of men, crafty men who whisper in his ear, hungry men who wait for hours outside his office for a word with him, emaciated men with wild faces who waylay him at the street gate with a timid, "Comrade, let me tell you. . ." and they blow the foul breath from their empty stomachs in his face.

25   He is always sympathetic. He gives them handfuls of small coins from his own pocket, he promises them work, there will be demonstrations, they must join the unions and attend the meetings, above all they must be on the watch for

spies. They are closer to him than his own brothers, without them he can do nothing—until tomorrow, comrade!

26   Until tomorrow. "They are stupid, they are lazy, they are treacherous, they would cut my throat for nothing," he says to Laura. He has good food and abundant drink, he hires an automobile and drives in the Paseo on Sunday morning, and enjoys plenty of sleep in a soft bed beside a wife who dares not disturb him; and he sits pampering his bones in easy billows of fat, singing to Laura, who knows and thinks these things about him. When he was fifteen, he tried to drown himself because he loved a girl, his first love, and she laughed at him. "A thousand women have paid for that," and his tight little mouth turns down at the corners. Now he perfumes his hair with Jockey Club, and confides to Laura: "One woman is really as good as another for me, in the dark. I prefer them all."

27   His wife organizes unions among the girls in the cigarette factories, and walks in picket lines, and even speaks at meetings in the evening. But she cannot be brought to acknowledge the benefits of true liberty. "I tell her I must have my freedom, net. She does not understand my point of view." Laura has heard this many times. Braggioni scratches the guitar and meditates. "She is an instinctively virtuous woman, pure gold, no doubt of that. If she were not, I should lock her up, and she knows it."

28   His wife, who works so hard for the good of the factory girls, employs part of her leisure lying on the floor weeping because there are so many women in the world, and only one husband for her, and she never knows where nor when to look for him. He told her: "Unless you can learn to cry when I am not here, I must go away for good." That day he went away and took a room at the Hotel Madrid.

29   It is this month of separation for the sake of higher principles that has been spoiled not only for Mrs. Braggioni, whose sense of reality is beyond criticism, but for Laura, who feels herself bogged in a nightmare. Tonight Laura envies Mrs. Braggioni, who is alone, and free to weep as much as she pleases about a concrete wrong. Laura has just come from a visit to the prison, and she is waiting for tomorrow with a bitter anxiety as if tomorrow may not come, but time may be caught immovably in this hour, with herself transfixed, Braggioni singing on forever, and Eugenio's body not yet discovered by the guard.

30   Braggioni says: "Are you going to sleep?" Almost before she can shake her head, he begins telling her about the May-day disturbances coming on in Morelia, for the Catholics hold a festival in honor of the Blessed Virgin, and the Socialists celebrate their martyrs on that day. "There will be two independent processions, starting from either end of town, and they will march until they meet, and the rest depends. . ." He asks her to oil and load

his pistols. Standing up, he unbuckles his ammunition belt, and spreads it laden across her knees. Laura sits with the shells slipping through the cleaning cloth dipped in oil, and he says again he cannot understand why she works so hard for the revolutionary idea unless she loves some man who is in it. "Are you not in love with someone?" "No," says Laura. "And no one is in love with you?" "No." "Then it is your own fault. No woman need go begging. Why, what is the matter with you? The legless beggar woman in the Alameda has a perfectly faithful lover. Did you know that?"

31 Laura peers down the pistol barrel and says nothing, but a long, slow faintness rises and subsides in her; Braggioni curves his swollen fingers around the throat of the guitar and softly smothers the music out of it, and when she hears him again he seems to have forgotten her, and is speaking in the hypnotic voice he uses when talking in small rooms to a listening, close-gathered crowd. Some day this world, now seemingly so composed and eternal, to the edges of every sea shall be merely a tangle of gaping trenches, of crashing walls and broken bodies. Everything must be torn from its accustomed place where it has rotted for centuries, hurled skyward and distributed, cast down again clean as rain, without separate identity. Nothing shall survive that the stiffened hands of poverty have created for the rich and no one shall be left alive except the elect spirits destined to procreate a new world cleansed of cruelty and injustice, ruled by benevolent anarchy: "Pistols are good, I love them, cannon are even better, but in the end I pin my faith to good dynamite," he concludes, and strokes the pistol lying in her hands. "Once I dreamed of destroying this city, in case it offered resistance to General Ortíz, but it fell into his hands like an overripe pear."

32 He is made restless by his own words, rises and stands waiting. Laura holds up the belt to him: "Put that on, and go kill somebody in Morelia, and you will be happier," she says softly. The presence of death in the room makes her bold. "Today, I found Eugenio going into a stupor. He refused to allow me to call the prison doctor. He had taken all the tablets I brought him yesterday. He said he took them because he was bored."

33 "He is a fool, and his death is his own business," says Braggioni, fastening his belt carefully.

34 "I told him if he had waited only a little while longer, you would have got him set free," says Laura. "He said he did not want to wait."

35 "He is a fool and we are well rid of him," says Braggioni, reaching for his hat.

36 He goes away. Laura knows his mood has changed, she will not see him any more for a while.

Please note that excerpts and passages in the StudySync® library and this workbook are intended as touchstones to generate interest in an author's work. The excerpts and passages do not substitute for the reading of entire texts, and StudySync® strongly recommends that students seek out and purchase the whole literary or informational work in order to experience it as the author intended. Links to online resellers are available in our digital library. In addition, complete works may be ordered through an authorized reseller by filling out and returning to StudySync® the order form enclosed in this workbook.

Reading & Writing Companion 409

37   He will send word when he needs her to go on errands into strange streets, to speak to the strange faces that will appear, like clay masks with the power of human speech, to mutter their thanks to Braggioni for his help. Now she is free, and she thinks, I must run while there is time. But she does not go.

38   Braggioni enters his own house where for a month his wife has spent many hours every night weeping and tangling her hair upon her pillow. She is weeping now, and she weeps more at the sight of him, the cause of all her sorrows. He looks about the room. Nothing is changed, the smells are good and familiar, he is well acquainted with the woman who comes toward him with no reproach except grief on her face. He says to her tenderly: "You are so good, please don't cry any more, you dear good creature." She says, "Are you tired, my angel? Sit here and I will wash your feet." She brings a bowl of water, and kneeling, unlaces his shoes, and when from her knees she raises her sad eyes under her blackened lids, he is sorry for everything, and bursts into tears. "Ah, yes, I am hungry, I am tired, let us eat something together," he says, between sobs. His wife leans her head on his arm and says, "Forgive me!" and this time he is refreshed by the solemn, endless rain of her tears.

39   Laura takes off her serge dress and puts on a white linen nightgown and goes to bed. She turns her head a little to one side, and lying still, reminds herself that it is time to sleep. Numbers tick in her brain like little clocks, soundless doors close of themselves around her. If you would sleep, you must not remember anything, the children will say tomorrow, good morning, my teacher, the poor prisoners who come every day bringing flowers to their jailor. 1–2–3–4–5—it is monstrous to confuse love with revolution, night with day, life with death— ah, Eugenio!

40   The tolling of the midnight bell is a signal, but what does it mean? Get up, Laura, and follow me: come out of your sleep, out of your bed, out of this strange house. What are you doing in this house? Without a word, without fear she rose and reached for Eugenio's hand, but he eluded her with a sharp, sly smile and drifted away. This is not all, you shall see—Murderer, he said, follow me, I will show you a new country, but it is far away and we must hurry. No, said Laura, not unless you take my hand, no; and she clung first to the stair rail, and then to the topmost branch of the Judas tree that bent down slowly and set her upon the earth, and then to the rocky ledge of a cliff, and then to the jagged wave of a sea that was not water but a desert of crumbling stone. Where are you taking me, she asked in wonder but without fear. To death, and it is a long way off, and we must hurry, said Eugenio. No, said Laura, not unless you take my hand. Then eat these flowers, poor prisoner, said Eugenio in a voice of pity, take and eat: and from the Judas tree he stripped the warm bleeding flowers, and held them to her lips. She saw that his hand was fleshless, a cluster of small white petrified branches, and his eye sockets were without light, but she ate the flowers greedily for they satisfied

both hunger and thirst. Murderer! said Eugenio, and Cannibal! This is my body and my blood. Laura cried No! and at the sound of her own voice, she awoke trembling, and was afraid to sleep again.

"Flowering Judas" from FLOWERING JUDAS AND OTHER STORIES by Katherine Anne Porter. Copyright 1930 and renewed 1958 by Katherine Anne Porter. Reprinted by permission of Houghton Mifflin Harcourt Publishing Company. All rights reserved.

✏ WRITE

ARGUMENTATIVE: Porter writes "for a revolutionist should be lean, animated by heroic faith, a vessel of abstract virtues." What attributes does Porter think make a good leader? Do you agree or disagree with her description of a leader? Write an essay arguing what characteristics you think are crucial for good leaders to have and use evidence from the text to explain whether or not Braggioni has these qualities.

Please note that excerpts and passages in the StudySync® library and this workbook are intended as touchstones to generate interest in an author's work. The excerpts and passages do not substitute for the reading of entire texts, and StudySync® strongly recommends that students seek out and purchase the whole literary or informational work in order to experience it as the author intended. Links to online resellers are available in our digital library. In addition, complete works may be ordered through an authorized reseller by filling out and returning to StudySync® the order form enclosed in this workbook.

Reading & Writing Companion   **411**

Their Eyes Were Watching God

FICTION
Zora Neale Hurston
1937

Introduction

First published in 1937, and eventually achieving widespread acclaim decades later, *Their Eyes Were Watching God* secured Zora Neale Hurston's legacy as a beloved and influential American writer. This novel tells the story of spirited, independent Janie Crawford, a woman who refuses to give up on love, despite the challenges of prejudice and poverty. In this excerpt, the locals of Eatonville, Florida note Janie's return and speculate about her mysterious past.

"What she doin coming back here in dem overhalls? Can't she find no dress to put on?"

Chapter One

1 Ships at a distance have every man's wish on board. For some they come in with the tide. For others they sail forever on the horizon, never out of sight, never landing until the Watcher turns his eyes away in **resignation**, his dreams mocked to death by Time. That is the life of men.

2 Now, women forget all those things they don't want to remember, and remember everything they don't want to forget. The dream is the truth. Then they act and do things accordingly.

3 So the beginning of this was a woman and she had come back from burying the dead. Not the dead of sick and ailing with friends at the pillow and the feet. She had come back from the **sodden** and the bloated; the sudden dead, their eyes flung wide open in judgment.

4 The people all saw her come because it was sundown. The sun was gone, but he had left his footprints in the sky. It was the time for sitting on porches beside the road. It was the time to hear things and talk. These sitters had been tongueless, earless, eyeless conveniences all day long. Mules and other brutes had occupied their skins. But now, the sun and the bossman were gone, so the skins felt powerful and human. They became lords of sounds and lesser things. They passed nations through their mouths. They sat in judgment.

5 Seeing the woman as she was made them remember the envy they had stored up from other times. So they chewed up the back parts of their minds and swallowed with **relish**. They made burning statements with questions, and killing tools out of laughs. It was mass cruelty. A mood come alive. Words walking without masters; walking altogether like **harmony** in a song.

6 "What she doin coming back here in dem overhalls? Can't she find no dress to put on? — Where's dat blue satin dress she left here in? — Where all dat money her husband took and died and left her? — What dat ole forty year ole 'oman doin' wid her hair swingin' down her back lak some young gal? Where

she left dat young lad of a boy she went off here wid? — Thought she was going to marry? — Where he left her? — What he done wid all her money? — Betcha he off wid some gal so young she ain't even got no hairs — why she don't stay in her class?"

7   When she got to where they were she turned her face on the bander log[1] and spoke. They scrambled a noisy "good evenin'" and left their mouths setting open and their ears full of hope. Her speech was pleasant enough, but she kept walking straight on to her gate. The porch couldn't talk for looking.

8   The men noticed her firm buttocks like she had grape fruits in her hip pockets; the great rope of black hair swinging to her waist and unraveling in the wind like a plume; then her **pugnacious** breasts trying to bore holes in her shirt. They, the men, were saving with the mind what they lost with the eye. The women took the faded shirt and muddy overalls and laid them away for remembrance. It was a weapon against her strength and if it turned out of no significance, still it was a hope that she might fall to their level some day.

9   But nobody moved, nobody spoke, nobody even thought to swallow spit until after her gate slammed behind her.

10   Pearl Stone opened her mouth and laughed real hard because she didn't know what else to do. She fell all over Mrs. Sumpkins while she laughed. Mrs. Sumpkins snorted violently and sucked her teeth.

11   "Humph! Y'all let her worry yuh. You ain't like me. Ah ain't got her to study 'bout. If she ain't got manners enough to stop and let folks know how she been makin out, let her g'wan! "

12   "She ain't even worth talkin' after," Lulu Moss drawled through her nose. "She sits high, but she looks low. Dat's what Ah say 'bout dese ole women runnin' after young boys."

13   Pheoby Watson hitched her rocking chair forward before she spoke. "Well, nobody don't know if it's anything to tell or not. Me, Ah'm her best friend, and Ah don't know."

14   "Maybe us don't know into things lak you do, but we all know how she went 'way from here and us sho seen her come back. 'Tain't no use in your tryin' to cloak no ole woman lak Janie Starks, Pheoby, friend or no friend."

15   "At dat she ain't so ole as some of y'all dat's talking."

---

1. **bander log** the talking monkeys of the Seeonee jungle in Rudyard Kipling's The Jungle Book

16   "She's way past forty to my knowledge, Pheoby."

17   "No more'n forty at de outside."

18   "She's way too old for a boy like Tea Cake."

19   "Tea Cake ain't been no boy for some time. He's round thirty his ownself."

20   "Don't keer what it was, she could stop and say a few words with us. She act like we done done something to her," Pearl Stone complained. "She de one been doin' wrong."

21   "You mean, you mad 'cause she didn't stop and tell us all her business. Anyhow, what you ever know her to do so bad as y'all make out? The worst thing Ah ever knowed her to do was taking a few years offa her age and dat ain't never harmed nobody. Y'all makes me tired. De way you talkin' you'd think de folks in dis town didn't do nothin' in de bed 'cept praise de Lawd. You have to 'scuse me, 'cause Ah'm bound to go take her some supper." Pheoby stood up sharply.

22   "Don't mind us," Lulu smiled, "just go right ahead, us can mind yo' house for you till you git back. Mah supper is done. You bettah go see how she feel. You kin let de rest of us know."

Excerpted from *Their Eyes Were Watching God* by Zora Neale Hurston, published by Harper Perennial.

✎ WRITE

LITERARY ANALYSIS: Analyze the first paragraph, which is about ships at a distance. What do the ships represent? What analogy is the author making? How do you see the meaning of the first paragraph playing itself out in the rest of the text? Support your response with evidence from the text.

Please note that excerpts and passages in the StudySync® library and this workbook are intended as touchstones to generate interest in an author's work. The excerpts and passages do not substitute for the reading of entire texts, and StudySync® strongly recommends that students seek out and purchase the whole literary or informational work in order to experience it as the author intended. Links to online resellers are available in our digital library. In addition, complete works may be ordered through an authorized reseller by filling out and returning to StudySync® the order form enclosed in this workbook.

Reading & Writing Companion   415

South

POETRY
Natasha Trethewey
2006

Introduction

Natasha Trethewey (b. 1966) is a Pulitzer Prize–winning poet who has twice been appointed the Poet Laureate of the United States. Born in Mississippi, her work often examines memory and racial legacy in America, and frequently visits the subject of the Civil War, a piece of American history that has fascinated her since childhood. "South" is an example of both, wherein the poet walks among fields and trees in the American South, contemplating the lives of her ancestors and the society around her.

"I returned to a stand of pines, bone-thin phalanx flanking the roadside"

Homo sapiens is the only species
to suffer psychological exile.
   —*E. O. Wilson*

1   I returned to a stand of pines,
2   bone-thin phalanx

3   flanking the roadside, tangle
4   of understory—a **dialectic** of dark

5   and light—and magnolias blossoming
6   like afterthought: each flower

7   a surrender, white flags draped
8   among the branches. I returned

9   to land's end, the swath of coast
10   clear cut and buried in sand:

11   mangrove, live oak, gulfweed
12   **razed** and replaced by thin palms—

13   palmettos—**symbols** of victory
14   or defiance, over and over

15   marking this vanquished land. I returned
16   to a field of cotton, hallowed ground—

17   as slave legend goes—each boll
18   holding the ghosts of **generations**:

19   those who measured their days
20   by the heft of sacks and lengths

21 of rows, whose sweat flecked the cotton plants
22   still sewn into our clothes.

23 I returned to a country battlefield
24   where colored troops fought and died—

25 Port Hudson where their bodies swelled
26   and blackened beneath the sun—unburied

27 until earth's green sheet pulled over them,
28   unmarked by any headstones.

29 Where the roads, buildings, and **monuments**
30   are named to honor the Confederacy,

31 where that old flag still hangs, I return
32   to Mississippi, state that made a crime

33 of me—mulatto, half-breed—native
34   in my native land, this place they'll bury me.

"South" from NATIVE GUARD: Poems by Natasha Trethewey. Copyright © 2006 by Natasha Trethewey. Used by permission of Houghton Mifflin Harcourt Company. All rights reserved.

WRITE

DISCUSSION: The E. O. Wilson quotation that is written before the poem describes a "psychological exile." In a discussion with your group, develop and refine a definition for "psychological exile." Who may have experienced it in the poem? How does the poet's use of imagery and descriptions contribute to the idea of psychological exile? Prepare for the discussion by writing down your initial thoughts on the prompt along with any textual evidence to support your ideas.

'N'em

POETRY
Jericho Brown
2014

Introduction

Jericho Brown (b. 1976) is an American poet and professor of creative writing at Emory University. He has published two highly regarded collections of poetry, *Please* and *The New Testament*, and is the recipient of numerous awards, including an American Book Award, a National Endowment for the Arts Poetry Fellowship, and a Guggenheim Fellowship. In "'N'em," Brown invokes elders and recent ancestors, whose names are now forgotten, but whose wisdom

"Some of their children Were not their children."

1   They said to say goodnight
2   And not goodbye, **unplugged**
3   The TV when it rained. They hid
4   Money in mattresses
5   So to sleep on **decisions**.
6   Some of their children
7   Were not their children. Some
8   Of their parents had no birthdates.
9   They could **sweat** a cold out
10   Of you. They'd wake without
11   An alarm telling them to.
12   Even the short ones reached
13   Certain shelves. Even the skinny
14   Cooked animals too quick
15   To get caught. And I don't care
16   How ugly one of them arrived,
17   That one got married
18   To somebody fine. They fed
19   Families with change and wiped
20   Their kitchens clean.
21   Then another **century** came.
22   People like me forgot their names.

Jericho Brown, "N'em" from The New Testament. Copyright © 2014 by Jericho Brown. Reprinted with the permission of The Permissions Company, Inc. on behalf of Copper Canyon Press, www.coppercanyonpress.org.

WRITE

PERSONAL RESPONSE: The poem evokes the way certain people lived in earlier times. What do you know of your own family history or a historical figure? How might their experiences have differed from your own? Write a creative account in a journal entry. Describe a daily routine he or she may have had. Use the poem for inspiration, and be sure to use plenty of descriptive details to bring your journal entry to life.

Given to Rust

POETRY
Vievee Francis
2015

Introduction

Written by poet Vievee Francis, "Given to Rust" is full of imagery and figurative language that lends new light to the concept of time offering unusual wisdom. In this rich lyrical poem, Francis examines her dynamic connection to the sound, and sometimes silence, of her own voice. Throughout "Given to Rust," the poet marvels and mourns, as the trials of her life—"Time and disaster"—inevitably bring about changes within her. Francis is an associate professor of English at Dartmouth College and was the 2017 recipient of the Kingsley Tufts Poetry Award.

"Still, I did once like my voice, the way it moved"

1 Every time I open my mouth my teeth reveal
2 more than I mean to. I can't stop tonguing them, my teeth.
3 Almost **giddy** to know they're still there (my mother lost hers)
4 but I am embarrassed nonetheless that even they aren't
5 pretty. Still, I did once like my voice, the way it moved
6 through the gap in my teeth like birdsong in the morning,
7 like the slow swirl of a creek at dusk. Just yesterday
8 a woman closed her eyes as I read aloud, and
9 said she wanted to sleep in the sound of it, my voice.
10 I can still sing some. Early cancer didn't stop the **compulsion**
11 to sing but
12 there's gravel now. An **undercurrent**
13 that also reveals me. Time and disaster. A heavy landslide
14 down the mountain. When you stopped speaking to me
15 what you really wanted was for me to stop speaking to you. To
16 **stifle** the sound of my voice. I know.
17 Didn't want the quicksilver of it in your ear.
18 What does it mean
19 to silence another? It means I **ruminate** on the hit
20 of rain against the tin roof of childhood, how I could listen
21 all day until the water rusted its way in. And there I was
22 putting a pan over here and a pot over there to catch it.

By Vievee Francis, 2017. Used by permission of Vievee Francis.

Skill:
Figurative
Language

The simile compares
the speaker's voice to
birdsong. At first, I saw it
as simply sound imagery,
showing that her voice
was high and bright. But
the verb *moved* shows
she also means she liked
the way her voice felt,
the vibration.

Skill:
Figurative
Language

One does not usually
sleep "in" a sound. The
fact that the woman
also closed her eyes
makes me think this is an
implied metaphor
comparing the speaker's
voice to a bed. It
suggests that her voice
is now deep and
comforting.

First Read

Read "Given to Rust." After you read, complete the Think Questions below.

 THINK QUESTIONS

1. According to the speaker, how has her voice changed over the course of her life? Use evidence from the poem to support your assertions.

2. What do you think the speaker means in the first two lines: "Every time I open my mouth my teeth reveal / more than I mean to"? Explain how you came to your understanding, citing evidence from other lines of the poem if necessary.

3. What do you think is the significance or the meaning of the title, and how does it connect to the content of the poem? Be sure to cite textual evidence to help explain your answer.

4. What does the word **undercurrent** mean in the context of this poem? Do you think the author is being figurative or literal in her use of the word in line 12? If necessary, consult a dictionary to confirm your definition. Write your answer to the second part of this question, citing evidence from the poem to support your explanation.

5. The Latin word *ruminatus* means "to chew over again" or "to chew the cud." With this definition in mind, as well as the context of the passage, write your own definition of the word **ruminate** as it is used in this poem. Cite any context clues that helped you determine its meaning.

Skill: Figurative Language

Use the Checklist to analyze Figurative Language in "Given to Rust." Refer to the sample student annotations about Figurative Language in the text.

••• CHECKLIST FOR FIGURATIVE LANGUAGE

In order to determine the meaning of a figure of speech in context, note the following:

- ✓ words that mean one thing literally and suggest something else

- ✓ similes, metaphors, or personification

- ✓ figures of speech, including

  - • extended metaphor, or a sustained metaphor used throughout a story or poem

  - • implied metaphor, or a metaphor that does not directly name, but rather implies, one of the two things being compared

In order to interpret a figure of speech in context and analyze its role in the text, consider the following questions:

- ✓ Where is there figurative language in the text and what seems to be the purpose of the author's use of it?

- ✓ Why does the author use a figure of speech rather than literal language?

- ✓ Where are contradictory words and phrases used to enhance the reader's understanding of the character, object, or idea?

- ✓ How does the figurative language develop the message or theme of the literary work?

Skill: Figurative Language

Reread lines 14–19 of "Given to Rust." Then, using the Checklist on the previous page, answer the multiple-choice questions below.

↻ YOUR TURN

1. The metaphor in this passage compares —

   ○ A. a mountain to the obstacle between the speaker and "you."
   ○ B. a mountain to quicksilver.
   ○ C. hearing too much of a person's annoying voice to having a worm in your ear.
   ○ D. the sound of the speaker's voice to quicksilver.

2. After analyzing the context of the metaphor in this passage, what is the best conclusion about its meaning?

   ○ A. The gulf between the speaker and "you" is so great that their relationship can never be repaired.
   ○ B. The speaker's voice is not easily controlled by others, and this quality threatened the person she calls "you."
   ○ C. It is impolite to ignore someone whose voice you find annoying.
   ○ D. The speaker feels like her voice is as daunting as a mountain and as elusive as quicksilver.

Close Read

Reread "Given to Rust." As you reread, complete the Skills Focus questions below. Then use your answers and annotations from the questions to help you complete the Write activity.

◎ SKILLS FOCUS

1. Locate the passage in "Given to Rust" where the speaker describes having cancer and what the illness did to her. Summarize that passage, maintaining the meaning and logical order of the original text.

2. Highlight an example of a metaphor in lines 12–16. What does this help the reader understand?

3. Locate the passage where the speaker uses figurative language to describe her voice. How does this passage help develop a theme in the poem?

4. How does the poet's childhood memory help remind her of who she is and the strength and power that she has?

✎ WRITE

LITERARY ANALYSIS: "Given to Rust," "South," and "'N'em" each present an individual navigating the connections between the past and the present. Compare and contrast how this idea is presented across each of the poems. Then analyze how the use of figurative language in "Given to Rust" emphasizes the author's message regarding this theme. Support your analysis with evidence from the text and original commentary.

Please note that excerpts and passages in the StudySync® library and this workbook are intended as touchstones to generate interest in an author's work. The excerpts and passages do not substitute for the reading of entire texts, and StudySync® strongly recommends that students seek out and purchase the whole literary or informational work in order to experience it as the author intended. Links to online resellers are available in our digital library. In addition, complete works may be ordered through an authorized reseller by filling out and returning to StudySync® the order form enclosed in this workbook.

Reading & Writing Companion   **427**

One
Today

POETRY
Richard Blanco
2013

Introduction

Richard Blanco (b. 1968) is an American poet who was chosen to read his poem "One Today" at President Barack Obama's second inauguration in 2013. Blanco is a Latin American immigrant, a member of the LGBTQ community, and his poem celebrates the diverse fabric of people, places, and experiences that make up American life.

"millions of faces in morning's mirrors, / each one yawning to life, crescendoing into our day"

1 One sun rose on us today, kindled over our shores,
2 peeking over the Smokies, greeting the faces
3 of the Great Lakes, spreading a simple truth
4 across the Great Plains, then charging across the Rockies.
5 One light, waking up rooftops, under each one, a story
6 told by our silent gestures moving behind windows.

7 My face, your face, millions of faces in morning's mirrors,
8 each one yawning to life, **crescendoing** into our day:
9 pencil-yellow school buses, the rhythm of traffic lights,
10 fruit stands: apples, limes, and oranges arrayed like rainbows
11 begging our praise. Silver trucks heavy with oil or paper—
12 bricks or milk, **teeming** over highways alongside us,
13 on our way to clean tables, read ledgers, or save lives—
14 to teach geometry, or ring-up groceries as my mother did
15 for twenty years, so I could write this poem.

16 All of us as vital as the one light we move through,
17 the same light on blackboards with lessons for the day:
18 equations to solve, history to question, or atoms imagined,
19 the "I have a dream"[1] we keep dreaming,
20 or the impossible vocabulary of sorrow that won't explain
21 the empty desks of twenty children marked absent
22 today, and forever. Many prayers, but one light
23 breathing color into stained glass windows,
24 life into the faces of bronze statues, warmth
25 onto the steps of our museums and park benches
26 as mothers watch children slide into the day.

27 One ground. Our ground, rooting us to every stalk
28 of corn, every head of wheat sown by sweat
29 and hands, hands gleaning coal or planting windmills

NOTES

Skill:
Poetic Elements and Structure

There are internal rhymes and repeating consonants and vowels in this stanza. The lines run together, and the pace feels faster like the busy start to a day. This is a catalog and the repeating sounds connect the items in it.

1. **"I have a dream"** reference to Dr. Martin Luther King Jr.'s August 28, 1963 speech at the March on Washington

Skill:
Media

The emphasis Blanco puts on certain words accentuates the poem's meaning. I noted that he stresses the words "our breath." Then he draws out the word "breathe." It's as if he wants us to absorb the wind and country we all share.

30 in deserts and hilltops that keep us warm, hands
31 digging trenches, routing pipes and cables, hands
32 as worn as my father's cutting sugarcane
33 so my brother and I could have books and shoes.

34 The dust of farms and deserts, cities and plains
35 mingled by one wind—our breath. Breathe. Hear it
36 through the day's gorgeous **din** of honking cabs,
37 buses launching down avenues, the symphony
38 of footsteps, guitars, and screeching subways,
39 the unexpected song bird on your clothes line.

40 Hear: squeaky playground swings, trains whistling,
41 or whispers across café tables, Hear: the doors we open
42 for each other all day, saying: hello / shalom,
43 buon giorno / howdy / namaste / or buenos días
44 in the language my mother taught me—in every language
45 spoken into one wind carrying our lives
46 without **prejudice**, as these words break from my lips.

47 One sky: since the Appalachians and Sierras claimed
48 their majesty, and the Mississippi and Colorado worked
49 their way to the sea. Thank the work of our hands:
50 weaving steel into bridges, finishing one more report
51 for the boss on time, stitching another wound
52 or uniform, the first brush stroke on a portrait,
53 or the last floor on the Freedom Tower[2]
54 jutting into a sky that yields to our resilience.

55 One sky, toward which we sometimes lift our eyes
56 tired from work: some days guessing at the weather
57 of our lives, some days giving thanks for a love
58 that loves you back, sometimes praising a mother
59 who knew how to give, or forgiving a father
60 who couldn't give what you wanted.

61 We head home: through the gloss of rain or weight
62 of snow, or the plum blush of dusk, but always—home,
63 always under one sky, our sky. And always one moon
64 like a silent drum tapping on every rooftop
65 and every window, of one country—all of us—
66 facing the stars

---

2. **Freedom Tower** the building that opened November 3, 2014, at One World Trade Center, on the site where the twin towers were destroyed on September 11, 2001

67 hope—a new **constellation**
68 waiting for us to map it,
69 waiting for us to name it—together.

"One Today: A Poem for Barack Obama's Presidential Inauguration January 21, 2013" by Richard Blanco, © 2013. All rights are controlled by the University of Pittsburgh Press, Pittsburgh, PA 15260. Used by permission of the University of Pittsburgh Press.

First Read

Read "One Today." After you read, complete the Think Questions below.

☁ THINK QUESTIONS

1. What pronouns does Blanco use throughout the text? What is the impact of using these pronouns on the overall message of the poem? Point to specific examples from the poem to support your answer.

2. What American values does Blanco emphasize in this poem? What poetic techniques does Blanco use to emphasize these values? Cite evidence from the text to support your response.

3. Blanco begins many stanzas with the word "One." Why do you think he does this? How does this choice reflect the message of the poem? Cite evidence from the text to support your answer.

4. Use context clues to determine the meaning of the word **teeming** as it is used in "One Today." Write your definition of *teeming* here, along with any words or phrases from the text that helped you arrive at it.

5. What is the meaning of the word **prejudice** as it is used in the text? Write your best definition here, along with a brief explanation of how you arrived at its meaning.

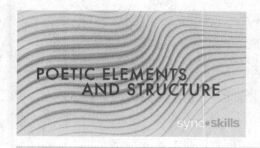

Skill:
Poetic Elements and Structure

Use the Checklist to analyze Poetic Elements and Structure in "One Today." Refer to the sample student annotations about Poetic Elements and Structure in the text.

♻ CHECKLIST FOR POETIC ELEMENTS AND STRUCTURE

In order to identify elements of poetic structure, note the following:

- ✓ how the words and lines are arranged

- ✓ the form and overall structure of the poem

- ✓ the rhyme and/or rhythm if present

- ✓ any pattern of stressed and unstressed syllables or meter if present

- ✓ how the arrangement of lines and stanzas in the poem contributes to the poem's theme, or message

To analyze how a particular stanza fits into the overall structure of a text and contributes to the development of the theme, consider the following questions:

- ✓ What poetic form does the poet use? What is the structure?

- ✓ How do the lengths of the lines and stanzas affect the meaning?

- ✓ How does a given stanza fit into the structure of the poem overall?

- ✓ How does the sound and rhythm contribute to the poem's meaning?

- ✓ How does the form and structure affect the poem's meaning?

- ✓ In what way does a specific stanza contribute to the poem's theme?

Skill:
Poetic Elements and Structure

Reread lines 40–69 of "One Today." Then, using the Checklist on the previous page, answer the multiple-choice questions below.

↻ YOUR TURN

1. What best describes the meter of lines 40–41?

   ○ A. A pattern of unstressed first syllables followed by a pattern of stressed first syllables
   ○ B. A pattern of unstressed first syllables followed by two unstressed syllables
   ○ C. A pattern of stressed first syllables followed by unstressed syllables
   ○ D. A pattern of stressed first syllables followed by a pattern of unstressed first syllables

2. What is the author's purpose for including many different languages in lines 42–43?

   ○ A. To indicate the number of languages the poet learned as a child
   ○ B. To vary the rhythm by mixing stressed initial syllables with unstressed
   ○ C. To highlight the diversity of voices that make up our national identity
   ○ D. To stimulate the reader to study several languages

3. How does the poem's ending in lines 55–69 relate to its beginning?

   ○ A. It closes the day begun in stanza 1, lines 1–6, by repeating its sounds, words, and ideas.
   ○ B. It repeats the day that dawned in stanza 1, lines 1–6, by repeating its images, language, and rhythms.
   ○ C. It indicates our national character as explorers and our interest in space exploration.
   ○ D. As a realistic picture of the end of the day, it contrasts with the idealistic picture in stanza 1, lines 1–6.

Skill: Media

Use the Checklist to analyze Media in "One Today." Refer to the sample student annotations about Media in the text.

CHECKLIST FOR MEDIA

Before analyzing multiple interpretations of a story, drama, or poem, note the following:

- ✓ similarities and differences in different media, such as the live production of a play as compared to the film version

- ✓ the similarities, differences, and nuances that can occur between the written version of a work and an audio version

- ✓ the different time periods and cultures in which the source material and interpretations were produced

To analyze multiple interpretations of a story, drama, or poem, evaluating how each version interprets the source text, consider the following questions:

- ✓ How does each version interpret the source text? What are the main similarities and differences between the two (or more) versions?

- ✓ In what ways does the medium affect the interpretations of the source text?

- ✓ How does a media interpretation of a source text influence or change the audience's understanding of the text?

- ✓ If each version is from a different time period and/or culture, what does each version reveal about the time period and culture in which it was written?

- ✓ Does information about the time period and culture allow you to make any inferences about the authors' objectives or intentions?

Skill: Media

Read along with the following passage of "One Today" as you listen to one reader's interpretation of stanzas 6 and 7. Then, using the Checklist on the previous page, answer the multiple-choice questions below.

🔄 YOUR TURN

Stanza 6 and 7, Lines 40–54 of "One Today"

Hear: squeaky playground swings, trains whistling,
or whispers across café tables, Hear: the doors we open
for each other all day, saying: hello / shalom,
buon giorno / howdy / namaste / or buenos días
in the language my mother taught me—in every language
spoken into one wind carrying our lives
without prejudice, as these words break from my lips.

One sky: since the Appalachians and Sierras claimed
their majesty, and the Mississippi and Colorado worked
their way to the sea. Thank the work of our hands:
weaving steel into bridges, finishing one more report
for the boss on time, stitching another wound
or uniform, the first brush stroke on a portrait,
or the last floor on the Freedom Tower
jutting into a sky that yields to our resilience.

1. Which statement best explains the reader's delivery of the words for "hello" in different languages (lines 42 and 43)?

   ○ A. The words for "hello" are read somberly with no inflection primarily to give them a formal tone.

   ○ B. The words for "hello" are read as they might be by native speakers of the languages, primarily to stress native inflection.

   ○ C. The words for "hello" are read in a friendly and lively tone primarily to capture the sense of community and warmth that is conveyed in this part of the poem.

   ○ D. The words for "hello" are read with natural stress with a pause after "hello" to indicate that foreign words follow.

2. Which statement best describes the reader's pacing of lines 50–53 and the primary intended effect of such pacing?

- ○ A. The pacing is slow and deliberate to stress the importance of each action.
- ○ B. The pacing is consistent with the rest of the poem to maintain an even flow.
- ○ C. The pacing is quick and rushed to mimic the fast pace of people getting work done.
- ○ D. The pacing is quick and lively to add interest to the delivery of the poem.

ONE TODAY

Close Read

Reread "One Today." As you reread, complete the Skills Focus questions below. Then use your answers and annotations from the questions to help you complete the Write activity.

◎ SKILLS FOCUS

1. Various portions of Blanco's poem include lists separated by commas. Identify at least one example of this, and explain what effect this structure has on the reader's understanding of the poem. Why would Blaco choose to use this structure repeatedly?

2. Re-watch the Richard Blanco's reading of "One Day." Highlight an instance where Blanco's spoken version and published version of the poem are different. Why do you think he would have made this change while reading at the inauguration?

3. Identify the use of the word *vital* in line 16. Explain whether the connotation of the word is positive, negative, or neutral as used in this context and why you think so.

4. While Blanco's poem could be about a typical day anywhere, it was written about the United States. Which lines of this poem make it distinctly about the United States? Cite examples and explain your choices.

✏ WRITE

LITERARY ANALYSIS: Blanco finishes the poem with the phrase "waiting for us to name it—together." How does Blanco use language and imagery along with poetic elements and structure in this poem to build a sense of togetherness? How does he further attain this sense of togetherness in his reading of the poem? Analyze the poetic elements and structure of the text along with Blanco's reading of the poem, and explain how they build a sense of togetherness. Be sure to use specific examples from the text and the media to support your analysis.

We Contain Multitudes

INFORMATIONAL TEXT
Lauren Groff
2018

Introduction

Lauren Groff (b. 1978) was born and raised in Cooperstown, New York, but makes her home in Gainesville, Florida. She is a highly acclaimed author of novels and short stories; her 2015 novel *Fates and Furies* was nominated for a National Book Award and declared by then-President Barack Obama as his favorite book of the year. In "We Contain Multitudes," Groff punctures the national punching bag of her adopted home state, attempting to explain what's beyond the images generated by news stories and cultural cliches.

"We are large, we contain multitudes."

1   We moved to Florida in the heat of the summer, when the termites swarming at night made golden haloes out of the streetlights, and our air conditioning wheezed and labored to keep our antique house below a sultry eighty degrees. Over half of the state's residents are transplants from other places, and like these interlopers, I was born and raised elsewhere—in upstate New York, where both the landscape and the people are full of lonely mountains and icy lakes. For a very long time in my new life in Florida, I was so bewildered by the humidity and heat, and wild and teeming life of the subtropics that I felt like an alien in my own skin.

2   I was unprepared for this sense of dislocation because, by the time I moved to Gainesville, I believed that I understood the real Florida. After all, I had visited the state dozens of times; first to the precise and plastic fantasia of Disney, then to the key lime sunlight of Miami, and finally to my parents-in-law's house in Gainesville, perched on the edge of a swamp, replete with its alligators and egrets and cypress knees. Now, twelve years later, I understand how little I knew when I first arrived. They say familiarity breeds contempt, but I'd say that it should instead breed complexity—a layered, complicated, and always deepening understanding. The longer you look, the more you should see. My changing vision of the state of Florida is a neat optical trick of **perspective**, the way that when you walk toward a window that frames a distant tree, each step lets the greater landscape into the picture so that, though the tree is coming closer, it appears to shrink.

3   Perhaps Florida is so vast and so various, so mutable and contradictory, that it can't actually be understood in any global sense; the Florida of the beaches is not the Florida of the swamps or the oak hummocks or the orange groves or the rolling pastures where racehorses graze. Not far from the Everglades that breathes like a great green lung in the center of the state, there are hundreds of miles of white sand beaches where sea turtles slowly bury their eggs before they creep back into the sea; how strange that we lump these wildly different places together and imagine that they make up a single place. This is a state where grown women pretend to be mermaids in the springs of

Weeki Wachee,[1] while billionaires blast their vanity rockets into space at Cape Canaveral.[2] This is a state haunted with strange and overlapping histories: look carefully enough and you can see the weary and malarial ghosts of Cabeza de Vaca's expedition[3] rattling by in their sixteenth-century Spanish armor; look harder and you can see the Native Americans burning their own villages and fleeing before the conquistadors' path. Here is the ghost of the peaceful African American village of Rosewood in January 1923, just before it was obliterated by drunken racists who had attended a Ku Klux Klan[4] meeting the day before; over here, not far from where Rosewood stood, walks the ghost of the noble Quaker naturalist William Bartram who traveled through Florida in 1774 and found the natural world a source of endless, almost ecstatic wonder. "How happily situated is this retired spot of earth! What an elisium [sic] it is!" he exults in his *Travels*. These things all coexist **simultaneously**, even while they are contradictory.

4 What's also true is that the more one knows of Florida, the more one sees how the rest of the country thinks we are our own least-flattering side: the toddlers eaten by gators, the sinkholes swallowing houses, the Spring Breakers vomiting in the dunes, and even social media's Florida Man, the worst superhero of all times. But these are stereotypes, and though there is a grain of truth in them, it's a grain the size of a speck of sand. The reality is that my experience of Florida is likely vastly different from yours: we are large, we contain multitudes. The good and the evil, the living and the dead, are tangled uneasily here together in a great **inextricable** knot. Ours is the Sunshine State, but the sunshine can have sharp teeth in it.

5 After these many years in Gainesville, the Florida that keeps me happy is the one that lives in the quiet and daily moment of grace. Today is the first cool day of October, and I am out on the front porch with no other humans in sight. The sun is thick and honeyed as it shines through the Spanish moss. My dog is snoring at my feet, my coffee is hot. Not far away, there's a wood thrush singing, which is rare and getting rarer with the bird's loss of **habitat**. On the sidewalk near the sago palm, a small, gray lizard is doing endless push-ups. For the moment, all is well; even in this good stillness I can sense the layers of this place shifting and sliding beneath me: the history, the changing natural world, the press of civilization, the weather. I am a small piece of a great web that is deepening and growing and becoming ever stranger and more

1. **Weeki Wachee** a Florida water park and tourist attraction with performing mermaids and mermen
2. **Cape Canaveral** the location of NASA's rocket base and the departure point for American space exploration
3. **Cabeza de Vaca's expedition** the Spanish exploratory expedition through the Caribbean, Florida, and the Gulf Coast to Mexico City (1527–1536) led by Pánfilo de Narváez, and after his death, by Álvar Núñez Cabeza de Vaca
4. **Ku Klux Klan** a racist group formed by whites in the former Confederacy during the Reconstruction Era (1863–1877) with the purpose of terrorizing black citizens

fascinating with each **accumulated** moment. This, I would say to any neighbor passing by, is the real Florida, a place that continually renews itself through change.

✏ WRITE

ARGUMENTATIVE: Groff argues that while the stereotypes about Florida have a "grain of truth in them, it's a grain the size of a speck of sand." Think about a stereotype, whether controversial or commonly held, about a group of people. You can think about something mentioned in Groff's essay, or about another stereotype. Then, write a response in which you argue to what extent this stereotype holds true. Support your argument with examples and reasoning from your own knowledge and experience.

Bartram's Travels

INFORMATIONAL TEXT
William Bartram
1791

Introduction

*B*artram's Travels is an eponymous travel journal by William Bartram (1739–1823) and the first book of its kind that unabashedly presented scientific perspectives alongside personal experience. At once an illustrated field guide, a travelogue, a religious meditation and cultural history, Bartram's Travels documents the botanist and author's journey through the southeastern territories of the Carolinas, Georgia, and Florida over three years in the late 18th century. Although the book received mixed reactions from reviewers upon publication because of its lush language and hybrid nature, it would soon become a torchlight for the Romantic poets and future generations of novelists and nonfiction writers. Aside from the literary reverberations of Bartram's Travels, the book also documented several new species in the animal kingdom and was one of the first nuanced portrayals of tribal nations of the American South.

"I find myself alone in the wilderness of Florida, on the shores of Lake George."

Part 2, Chapter 5

1　HAVING agreeably diverted away the intolerable heats of sultry noon in fruitful fragrant groves, with renewed vigour I again resume my **sylvan** pilgrimage. The afternoon and evening moderately warm, and exceeding[1] pleasant views from the river and its varied shores. I passed by Battle lagoon and the bluff,

The title page of *Bartram's Travels* with with frontispiece "Mico Chlucco the Long Warrior."'

without much opposition; but the crocodiles were already assembling in the pass. Before night I came to, at a charming Orange grove bluff, on the East side of the little lake, and after fixing my camp on a high open situation, and collecting a plenty of dry wood for fuel, I had time to get some fine trout for supper and joyfully return to my camp.

2　WHAT a most beautiful creature is this fish before me! gliding to and fro, and figuring in the still clear waters, with his orient attendants and associates: the yellow bream*

*Cyprinus coronarius.

or sun fish. It is about eight inches in length, nearly of the shape of the trout, but rather larger in proportion over the shoulders and breast; the mouth large, and the branchiostega opens wide; the whole fish is of a pale gold (or burnished brass) colour, darker on the back and upper sides; the scales are of a proportionable size, regularly placed, and every where variably powdered with red, russet, silver, blue and green specks, so laid on the scales as to appear like real dust or opaque bodies, each apparent particle being so projected by light and shade, and the various attitudes of the fish, as to

1. **exceeding** (archaic intensifier) quite or very; exceptional

deceive the sight; for in reality nothing can be of a more plain and polished surface than the scales and whole body of the fish; the fins are of an Orange colour; and like all the species of the bream, the ultimate angle of the branchiostega terminate by a little stula, the extreme end of which represents a crescent of the finest ultramarine blue, encircled with silver, and velvet black, like the eye in the feathers of a peacock's train; he is a fish of **prodigious** strength and activity in the water; a warrior in a gilded coat of mail, and gives no rest or quarters to small fish, which he preys upon; they are delicious food and in great abundance.

3   THE Orange grove, is but narrow, betwixt the the river banks and ancient Indian fields, where there are evident traces of the habitations of the ancients, surrounded whith groves of Live Oak, Laurel Magnolia, Zanthoxilon, Liquid-amber, and others.

4   How harmonious and soothing is this native sylvan music now at still evening! inexpressibly tender are the responsive cooings of the innocent dove, in the fragrant Zanthoxilon groves, and the variable and tuneful warblings of the nonparel; with the more sprightly and elevated strains of the blue linnet and golden icterus; this is indeed harmony even amidst the **incessant** croaking of the frogs; the shades of silent night are made more chearful, with the shrill voice of the whip-poor-will* and active mock-bird.

*Caprimulgus rufus called chuck-will's-widow, from a fancied resemblance of his notes to these words: they inhabit the maritime parts of Carolina and Florida, and are more than twice the size of the night hawk or whip-poor-will.

5   My situation high and airy, a brisk and cool breeze steadily and incessantly passing over the clear waters of the lake, and fluttering over me through the surrounding groves, wings its way to the moon-light savannas, while I repose on my sweet and healthy couch of the soft Tillandsi ulnea-adscites, and the latter gloomy and still hours of night passed rapidly away as it were in a moment; I arose, strengthened and chearful, in the morning. Having some repairs to make in the tackle of my vessel, I paid my first attention to them; which being accomplished, my curiosity prompted me to penetrate the grove and view the illumined plains.

6 WHAT a beautiful display of vegetation is here before me! seemingly unlimited in extent and variety; how the dew-drops twinkle and play upon the fight,[2] trembling on the tips of the lucid, green savanna, sparkling as the gem that flames on the turban of the Eastern prince; fee the pearly tears rolling off the buds of the expanding Granadilla*;

*Passiflora incarnata, called May-Apple.

behold the azure fields of cerulean Ixea! what can equal the rich golden flowers of the Canalutea, which ornament the banks of yon **serpentine** rivulet, meandering over the meadows; the almost endless varieties of the gay Phlox, that enamel the swelling green banks, associated with the purple Verbena corymbosa, Viola, pearly Gnaphalium, and silvery Perdicium; how fantastical looks the libertine Clitoria, mantling the shrubs, on the vistas skirting the groves. My morning excursion finished, I returned to the camp, breakfasted, then went on board my boat, and gently descended the noble river and passed by several openings of extensive plains and meadows, environing the East Lake, charming beyond compare; at evening I came to at a good harbour, under the high banks of the river, and rested during the night, amidst the fragrant groves, exposed to the constant breezes from the river: here I made ample collections of specimens and growing roots of curious vegetables, which kept me fully employed the greatest part of the day, and in the evening arrived at a charming spot on the East bank, which I had marked on my ascent up the river, where I made some addition to my collections, and the next day I employed myself in the same manner, putting into shore frequently, at convenient places, which I had noticed; and in the evening arrived again at the upper store, where I had the pleasure of finding my old friend, the trader, in good health and chearful, and his affairs in prosperous way. There were also a small party of Indians here, who had lately arrived with their hunts to purchase goods. I continued a few days at this post, searching its environs for curious vegetable productions, collecting seeds and planting growing roots in boxes, to be transported to the lower trading house.

---

2. **fight** The text preserves this typographical oddity of the word 'sight'; in calligraphy of the 17th and 18th centuries, an *f* resembled a contemporary cursive *s*.

7   Now, having procured necessaries to accommodate me on my voyage down to the lower store, I bid adieu to my old friend and benefactor, Mr. Job Wiggens, embarked alone on board my little fortunate vessel, and sat sail; I chose to follow the Eastermost channel of the river to the Great Lake, because it ran by high banks and bluffs of the Eastern main the greatest part of the distance, which afforded me an opportunity of observing a far greater variety of natural subject, than if I had taken the Western or middle channel, which flowed thro' swamps and marshes.

8   AT evening I arrived at Cedar Point, my former safe and pleasant harbour, at the East cape of the Great Lake, where I had noticed some curious shrubs and plants; here I rested, and on the smooth and gentle current launch again into the little ocean of Lake George, meaning now, on my return, to coast his Western shores in search of new beauties in the bounteous kingdom of Flora.

9   I WAS however induced to deviate a little from my intended course, and touch at the inchanting little Isle of Palms. This delightful spot, planted by nature, is almost an entire grove of Palms, with a few pyramidal Magnolias, Live Oaks, golden Orange, and the animating Zanthoxilon; what a beautiful retreat is here! blessed unviolated spot of earth! rising from the limpid waters of the lake; its fragrant groves and blooming lawns invested and protected by encircling ranks of the Yucca gloriosa; a fascinating atmosphere surrounds this blissful garden; the balmy Lantana, ambrosial Citra, perfumed Crinum, perspiring their mingled odours, wafted through Zanthoxilon groves. I at last broke away from the enchanting spot, and stepped on board my boat, hoisted sail and soon approached the coast of the main, at the cool eve of day; then traversing a capacious semicircular cove of the lake, verged by low, extensive grassy meadows, I at length by dusk made a safe harbour, in a little lagoon, on the sea shore or strands of a bold sandy point, which descended from the surf of the lake; this was a clean sandy beach, hard and firm by the beating surf when the wind sets from the East coast; I drew up my light vessel on the sloping shore, that she might be safe from the beating waves in case of a sudden storm of wind in the night. A few yards back the land was a little elevated, and overgrown with thickets of shrubs and low trees, consisting chiefly of Zanthoxilon, Olea Americana, Rhamus frangula, Sideroxilon, Morus, Ptelea, Halesia, Querci, Myrica cerifera and others; these groves were but low, yet sufficiently high to shelter me from the chilling dews; and being but a few yards distance from my vessel, here I fixed my encampment. A brisk wind arising from the lake, drove away the clouds of mosquitoes into the thickets. I now, with difficulty and industries, collected a sufficiency of dry wood to keep up a light during the night, and to roast some trout which I had caught when descending the river; their heads I stewed in the juice of Oranges, which, with boiled rice, afforded me a wholesome and delicious supper: I hung the remainder of my broiled fish on the snags of some shrubs over my head. I at last, after reconnoitring my habitation, returned, spread abroad my

skin and blanket upon the clean sands by my fire side, and betook myself to repose.

10 How glorious the powerful sun, minister of the Most High, in the rule and government of this earth, leaves our hemisphere, retiring from our sight beyond the western forests! I behold with gratitude his departing smiles, tinging the fleecy roseate clouds, now riding far away on the Eastern horizon; behold they vanish from sight in the azure skies!

11 ALL now silent and peaceable, I suddenly fell asleep. At midnight I awake; when raising my head effect, I find myself alone in the wilderness of Florida, on the shores of Lake George. Alone indeed, but under the care of the Almighty, and protected by the invisible hand of my guardian angel.

12 WHEN quite awake, I started at the heavy tread of some animal, the dry limbs of trees upon the ground crack under his feet, the close shrubby thickets part and bend under him as he rushes off.

13 I REKINDLED up my sleepy fire, lay in contact the exfoliated smoking brands damp with the dew of heaven.

14 THE bright flame ascends and illuminates the ground and groves around me.

15 WHEN looking up, I found my fish carried off, though I had thought them safe on the shrubs, just over my head, but their scent, carried to a great distance by the damp noctournal breezes, I suppose were too powerful attractions to resist.

16 PERHAPS it may not be time lost, to rest awhile here, and reflect on the unexpected and unaccountable incident, which however pointed out to me an extraordinary deliverance, or protection of my life, from the **rapacious** wolf that stole my fish from over my head.

17 HOW much easier and more eligible might it have been for him to have leaped upon my breast in the dead of sleep, and torn my throat, which would have instantly deprived me of life, and then glutted his stomach for the present with my warm blood, and dragged off my body, which would have made a feast afterwards for him and his howling associates; I say would not this have been a wiser step, than to have made protracted and circular approaches, and then after, by chance, espying the fish over my head, with the greatest caution and silence rear up, and take them off the snags one by one, then make off with them, and that so cunningly as not to awaken me until he had fairly accomplished his purpose.

WRITE

NARRATIVE: Compose your own travelogue with *Bartram's Travels* as your guide. Think about a natural landscape of your choosing, be it as seemingly unspectacular as an abandoned lot or as revered as the Everglades. Record your examination of this natural landscape and your reactions to it. Use both scientific and figurative language typical of Bartram's style.

The Midnight Zone

FICTION
Lauren Groff
2018

Introduction

Lauren Groff (b. 1978) is an American writer whose body of work include the novels *The Monsters of Templeton*, *Arcadia*, and *Fates and Furies*, as well as the short story collection *Florida*. Her work has been featured in *The New Yorker*, *The Atlantic*, and several *Best American Short Stories* anthologies. "The Midnight Zone," which was included in *Florida*, is the tale of a middle-aged woman who suffers a debilitating concussion while camping with her two sons and has an

"Time would not care if you fell out of it."

1   It was an old hunting camp shipwrecked in twenty miles of scrub. Our friend had seen a Florida panther sliding through the trees there a few days earlier. But things had been fraying in our hands, and the camp was free and silent, so I walked through the resistance of my cautious husband and my small boys, who had wanted hermit crabs and kites and wakeboards and sand for spring break. Instead, they got ancient sinkholes filled with ferns, potential death by cat.

2   One thing I liked was how the screens at night pulsed with the tender bellies of lizards.

3   Even in the sleeping bag with my smaller son, the golden one, the March chill seemed to blow through my bones. I loved eating, but I'd lost so much weight by then that I carried myself delicately, as if I'd gone translucent.

4   There was sparse electricity from a gas-powered generator and no Internet and you had to climb out through the window in the loft and stand on the roof to get a cell signal. On the third day, the boys were asleep and I'd dimmed the lanterns when my husband went up and out and I heard him stepping on the metal roof, a giant brother to the raccoons that woke us thumping around up there at night like burglars.

5   Then my husband stopped moving, and stood still for so long I forgot where he was. When he came down the ladder from the loft, his face had blanched.

6   Who died? I said lightly, because if anyone was going to die it was going to be us, our skulls popping in the jaws of an endangered cat. It turned out to be a bad joke, because someone actually had died, that morning, in one of my husband's apartment buildings. A fifth-floor occupant had killed herself, maybe on purpose, with aspirin and vodka and a bathtub. Floors four, three, and two were away somewhere with beaches and alcoholic smoothies, and the first floor had discovered the problem only when the water of death had seeped into the carpet.

Skill:
Figurative
Language

A metaphor is used to describe her kids, comparing something growing in petri dishes that fascinates her. This fascination contrasts with her emotions towards motherhood where she feels frustrated by imposed expectations.

7   My husband had to leave. He'd just fired one handyman and the other was on his own Caribbean adventure, eating buffet food to the sound of cruise-ship calypso. Let's pack, my husband said, but my rebelliousness at the time was like a sticky fog rolling through my body and never burning off, there was no sun inside, and so I said that the boys and I would stay. He looked at me as if I were crazy and asked how we'd manage with no car. I asked if he thought he'd married an incompetent woman, which cut to the bone, because the **source** of our problems was that, in fact, he had. For years at a time I was good only at the things that interested me, and since all that interested me was my work and my children, the rest of life had sort of inched away. And while it's true that my children were endlessly fascinating, two petri dishes growing human cultures, being a mother never had been, and all that seemed assigned by default of gender I would not do because it felt insulting. I would not buy clothes, I would not make dinner, I would not keep schedules, I would not make playdates, never ever. Motherhood meant, for me, that I would take the boys on monthlong adventures to Europe, teach them to blast off rockets, to swim for glory. I taught them how to read, but they could make their own lunches. I would hug them as long as they wanted to be hugged, but that was just being human. My husband had to be the one to make up for the depths of my lack. It is exhausting, living in debt that increases every day but that you have no intention of repaying.

8   Two days, he promised. Two days and he'd be back by noon on the third. He bent to kiss me, but I gave him my cheek and rolled over when the headlights blazed then dwindled on the wall. In the banishing of the engine, the night grew bold. The wind was making a low, inhuman muttering in the pines, and, inspired, the animals let loose in call-and-response. Everything kept me alert until shortly before dawn, when I slept for a few minutes until the puppy whined and woke me. My older son was crying because he'd thrown off his sleeping bag in the night and was cold but too sleepy to fix the situation.

9   I made scrambled eggs with a vengeful amount of butter and Cheddar, also cocoa with an inch of marshmallow, thinking I would **stupefy** my children with calories, but the calories only made them stronger.

10 Our friend had treated the perimeter of the clearing with panther deterrent, some kind of synthetic superpredator urine, and we felt safe-ish near the cabin. We ran footraces until the dog went wild and leapt up and bit my children's arms with her puppy teeth, and the boys screamed with pain and frustration and showed me the pink stripes on their skin. I scolded the puppy harshly and she crept off to the porch to watch us with her chin on her paws. The boys and I played soccer. We rocked in the hammock. We watched the circling red-shouldered hawks. I made my older son read *Alice's Adventures in Wonderland* to the little one, which was a disaster, a book so punny and Victorian for modern children. We had lunch, then the older boy tried to make

fire by rubbing sticks together, his little brother attending solemnly, and they spent the rest of the day constructing a hut out of branches. Then dinner, singing songs, a bath in the galvanized-steel horse trough someone had converted to a cold-water tub, picking ticks and chiggers off with tweezers, and that was it for the first day.

11   There had been a weight on us as we played outside, not as if something were actually watching but because of the possibility that something could be watching when we were so far from humanity in all that Florida waste.

12   The second day should have been like the first. I doubled down on the calories, adding pancakes to breakfast, and succeeded in making the boys lie in pensive digestion out in the hammock for a little while before they ricocheted off the trees.

13   But in the afternoon the one light bulb sizzled out. The cabin was all dark wood and I couldn't see the patterns on the dishes I was washing. I found a new bulb in a closet, dragged over a stool from the bar area, and made the older boy hold the spinning seat as I climbed aboard. The old bulb was hot, and I was passing it from hand to hand, holding the new bulb under my arm, when the puppy leapt up at my older son's face. He let go of the stool to whack at her, and I did a quarter spin, then fell and hit the floor with my head, and then I surely blacked out.

14   After a while, I opened my eyes. Two children were looking down at me. They were pale and familiar. One fair, one dark; one small, one big.

15   Mommy? the little boy said, through water.

16   I turned my head and threw up on the floor. The bigger boy dragged a puppy, who was snuffling my face, out the door.

17   I knew very little except that I was in pain and that I shouldn't move. The older boy bent over me, then lifted an intact light bulb from my armpit, triumphantly; I a chicken, the bulb an egg.

18   The smaller boy had a wet paper towel in his hand and he was patting my cheeks. The pulpy smell made me ill again. I closed my eyes and felt the dabbing on my forehead, on my neck, around my mouth. The small child's voice was high. He was singing a song.

19   I started to cry with my eyes closed and the tears went hot across my temples and into my ears.

Skill:
Figurative
Language

Hyperbole is used to capture the seriousness of the situation and the protagonist's mental state. She is immobile and they are stuck in a cabin with no lifeline to the outside world. If the boys attempt to go get help they may die.

20   Mommy! the older boy, the solemn dark one, screamed, and when I opened my eyes both of the children were crying, and that was how I knew them to be mine.

21   Just let me rest here a minute, I said. They took my hands. I could feel the hot hands of my children, which was good. I moved my toes, then my feet. I turned my head back and forth. My neck worked, though fireworks went off in the corners of my eyes.

22   I can walk to town, the older boy was saying, through wadding, to his brother, but the nearest town was twenty miles away. Safety was twenty miles away and there was a panther between us and there, but also possibly terrible men, sinkholes, alligators, the end of the world. There was no landline, no umbilical cord, and small boys using cell phones would easily fall off such a slick, pitched metal roof.

23   But what if she's all a sudden dead and I'm all a sudden alone? the little boy was saying.

24   O.K., I'm sitting up now, I said.

25   The puppy was howling at the door.

26   I lifted my body onto my elbows. Gingerly, I sat. The cabin dipped and spun and I vomited again.

27   The big boy ran out and came back with a broom to clean up. No! I said. I am always too hard on him, this beautiful child who is so brilliant, who has no **logic** at all.

28   Sweetness, I said, and couldn't stop crying, because I'd called him Sweetness instead of his name, which I couldn't remember just then. I took five or six deep breaths. Thank you, I said in a calmer voice. Just throw a whole bunch of paper towels on it and drag the rug over it to keep the dog off. The little one did so, methodically, which was not his style; he has always been adept at cheerfully watching other people work for him.

29   The bigger boy tried to get me to drink water, because this is what we do in our family in lieu of applying Band-Aids, which I refuse to buy because they are just flesh-colored landfill.

30   Then the little boy screamed, because he'd moved around me and seen the bloody back of my head, and then he dabbed at the cut with the paper towel he had previously dabbed at my pukey mouth. The paper disintegrated in his hands. He crawled into my lap and put his face on my stomach. The bigger

NOTES

boy held something cold on my wound, which I discovered later to be a beer can from the fridge.

31 They were quiet like this for a very long time. The boys' names came back to me, at first dancing coyly out of reach, then, when I seized them in my hands, mine.

32 I'd been a soccer player in high school, a speedy and aggressive midfielder, and head trauma was an old friend. I remembered this constant lability from one concussive visit to the emergency room. The confusion and the sense of doom were also familiar. I had a flash of my mother sitting beside my bed for an entire night, shaking me awake whenever I tried to fall asleep, and I now wanted my mother, not in her diminished current state, brittle retiree, but as she had been when I was young, a small person but gigantic, a person who had blocked out the sun.

33 I sent the little boy off to get a roll of dusty duct tape, the bigger boy to get gauze from my toiletry kit, and when they wandered back I duct-taped the gauze to my head, already mourning my long hair, which had been my most expensive pet.

34 I inched myself across the room to the bed and climbed up, despite the sparklers behind my eyeballs. The boys let the forlorn puppy in, and when they opened the door they also let the night in, because my fall had taken hours from our lives.

35 It was only then, when the night entered, that I understood the depth of time we had yet to face. I had the boys bring me the lanterns, then a can opener and the tuna and the beans, which I opened slowly, because it is not easy, supine, and we made a game out of eating, though the thought of eating anything gave me chills. The older boy brought over Mason jars of milk. I let my children finish the entire half gallon of ice cream, which was my husband's, his one daily reward for being kind and good, but by this point the man deserved our disloyalty, because he was not there.

36 It had started raining, at first a gentle thrumming on the metal roof.

37 I tried to tell my children a cautionary tale about a little girl who fell into a well and had to wait a week until firefighters could figure out a way to rescue her, something that maybe actually took place back in the dimness of my childhood, but the story was either too **abstract** for them or I wasn't making much sense, and they didn't seem to grasp my need for them to stay in the cabin, to not go anywhere, if the very worst happened, the unthinkable that I was skirting, like a pit that opened just in front of each sentence I was about to utter. They kept asking me if the girl got lots of toys when she made it out

Please note that excerpts and passages in the StudySync® library and this workbook are intended as touchstones to generate interest in an author's work. The excerpts and passages do not substitute for the reading of entire texts, and StudySync® strongly recommends that students seek out and purchase the whole literary or informational work in order to experience it as the author intended. Links to online resellers are available in our digital library. In addition, complete works may be ordered through an authorized reseller by filling out and returning to StudySync® the order form enclosed in this workbook.

Reading & Writing Companion   455

of the well. This was so against my point that I said, out of spite, Unfortunately, no, she did not.

38　I made the boys keep me awake with stories. The younger one was into a British television show about marine life, which the older one maintained was babyish until I pretended not to believe what they were telling me. Then they both told me about cookie-cutter sharks, who bore perfect round holes in whales, as if their mouths were cookie cutters. They told me about a fish called the humuhumunukunukuāpua'a, a beautiful name that I couldn't say correctly, even though they sang it to me over and over, laughing, to the tune of "Twinkle Twinkle, Little Star." They told me about the walking catfish, which can stay out of water for days and days, meandering about in the mud. They told me about the sunlight, the twilight, and the midnight zones, the three depths of water, where there is transparent light, then a murky, darkish light, then no light at all. They told me about the world pool, in which one current goes one way, another goes another way, and where they meet they make a tornado of air, which stretches, my little one said, from the midnight zone, where the fish are blind, all the way up up up to the birds.

39　I had begun shaking very hard, which my children, sudden gentlemen, didn't mention. They piled all the sleeping bags and blankets they could find on me, then climbed under and fell asleep without bathing or toothbrushing or getting out of their dirty clothes, which, anyway, they sweated through within an hour.

40　The dog did not get dinner but she didn't whine about it, and though she wasn't allowed to, she came up on the bed and slept with her head on my older son's stomach, because he was her favorite, being the biggest puppy of all.

41　Now I had only myself to sit vigil with me, though it was still early, nine or ten at night. I had a European novel on the nightstand that filled me with dimness and fret, so I tried to read *Alice's Adventures in Wonderland*, but it was incomprehensible with my scrambled brains. Then I looked at a hunting magazine, which made me remember the Florida panther. I hadn't truly forgotten about it, but could manage only a few terrors at a time, and others, when my children had been awake, were more urgent. We had seen some scat in the woods on a walk three days earlier, enormous scat, either a bear's or the panther's, but certainly a giant predator's. The danger had been abstract until we saw this bodily proof of existence, and my husband and I led the children home, singing a round, all four of us holding hands, and we let the dog off the leash to circle us joyously, because, as small as she was, it was bred in her bones that in the face of peril she would sacrifice herself first.

42　The rain increased until it was deafening and still my sweaty children slept. I thought of the waves of sleep rushing through their brains, washing out the tiny unimportant flotsam of today so that tomorrow's heavier truths could wash in. There was a nice solidity to the rain's pounding on the roof, as if the noise were a barrier that nothing could enter, a stay against the looming night.

43 I tried to bring back the poems of my youth, and could not remember more than a few floating lines, which I put together into a strange, sad poem, Blake and Dickinson and Frost and Milton and Sexton, a tag-sale poem in clammy meter that nonetheless came alive and held my hand for a little while.

44 Then the rain diminished until all that was left were scattered clicks from the drops falling from the pines. The batteries of one lantern went out and the light from the remaining lantern was sparse and thwarted. I could hardly see my hand or the shadow it made on the wall when I held it up. This lantern was my sister; at any moment it, too, could go dark. I feasted my eyes on the cabin, which in the oncoming black had turned into a place made of gold, but the shadows seemed too thick now, fizzy at the edges, and they moved when I shifted my eyes away from them. It felt safer to look at the cheeks of my sleeping children, creamy as cheeses.

45 It was elegiac, that last hour or so of light, and I tried to push my love for my sons into them where their bodies were touching my own skin.

46 The wind rose again and it had personality; it was in a sharpish, meanish mood. It rubbed itself against the little cabin and played at the corners and broke sticks off the trees and tossed them at the roof so they jigged down like creatures with strange and scrabbling claws. The wind rustled its endless body against the door.

47 Everything depended on my staying still, but my skin was stuffed with itches. Something terrible in me, the darkest thing, wanted to slam my own head back against the headboard. I imagined it over and over, the sharp backward crack, and the wash and spill of peace.

48 I counted slow breaths and was not calm by two hundred; I counted to a thousand.

49 The lantern flicked itself out and the dark poured in.

50 The moon rose in the skylight and backed itself across the black.

51 When it was gone and I was alone again, I felt the dissociation, a physical shifting, as if the best of me were detaching from my body and sitting down a few feet distant. It was a great relief.

52 For a few moments, there was a sense of mutual watching, a wait for something definitive, though nothing definitive came, and then the bodiless me stood and circled the cabin. The dog moved and gave a soft whine through her nose, although she remained asleep. The floors were cool underfoot. My head

brushed the beams, though they were ten feet up. Where my body and those of my two sons lay together was a black and pulsing mass, a hole of light.

53   I passed outside. The path was pale dirt and filled with sandspur and was cold and wet after the rain. The great drops from the tree branches left a pine taste in me. The forest was not dark, because darkness has nothing to do with the forest—the forest is made of life, of light—but the trees moved with wind and subtle creatures. I wasn't in any single place. I was with the raccoons of the rooftop, who were now down fiddling with the bicycle lock on the garbage can at the end of the road, with the red-shouldered hawk chicks breathing alone in the nest, with the armadillo forcing its armored body through the brush. I hadn't realized that I'd lost my sense of smell until it returned hungrily now; I could smell the worms tracing their paths under the pine needles and the mold breathing out new spores, shaken alive by the rain.

54   I was vigilant, moving softly in the underbrush, and the palmettos' nails scraped down my body.

55   The cabin was not visible, but it was present, a sore at my side, a feeling of density and airlessness. I couldn't go away from it, I couldn't return, I could only circle the cabin and circle it. With each circle, a terrible, stinging anguish built in me and I had to move faster and faster, each pass bringing up ever more wildness. What had been built to seem so solid was fragile in the face of time because time is impassive, more animal than human. Time would not care if you fell out of it. It would continue on without you. It cannot see you; it has always been blind to the human and the things we do to stave it off, the taxonomies, the cleaning, the arranging, the ordering. Even this cabin with its perfectly considered angles, its veins of pipes and wires, was barely more stable than the rake marks we made in the dust that morning, which time had already scrubbed away.

56   The self in the woods ran and ran, but the running couldn't hold off the slow shift. A low mist rose from the ground and gradually came clearer. The first birds sent their questions into the chilly air. The sky developed its blue. The sun emerged.

57   The drawing back was gradual. My older son opened his brown eyes and saw me sitting above him.

58   You look terrible, he said, patting my face, and my hearing was only half underwater now.

59   My head ached, so I held my mouth shut and smiled with my eyes and he padded off to the kitchen and came back with peanut-butter-and-jelly sandwiches, with a set of Uno cards, with cold coffee from yesterday's pot for the low and constant thunder of my headache, with the dog whom he'd let out and then fed all by himself.

60   I watched him. He gleamed. My little son woke but didn't get up, as if his face were attached to my shoulder by the skin. He was rubbing one unbloodied lock of my hair on his lips, the way he did after he nursed when he was a baby.

61   My boys were not unhappy. I was usually a preoccupied mother, short with them, busy, working, until I burst into fun, then went back to my hole of work; now I could only sit with them, talk to them. I could not even read. They were gentle with me, reminded me of a golden retriever I'd grown up with, a dog with a mouth so soft she would go down to the lake and steal ducklings and hold them intact on her tongue for hours until we noticed her sitting unusually erect in the corner, looking sly. My boys were like their father; they would one day be men who would take care of the people they loved.

62   I closed my eyes as the boys played game after game after game of Uno.

63   Noon arrived, noon left, and my husband did not come.

64   At one point, something passed across the woods outside like a shudder, and a hush fell over everything, and the boys and the dog all looked at me and their faces were like pale birds taking flight, but my hearing had mercifully shut off whatever had occasioned such swift terror over all creatures of the earth, save me.

65   When we heard the car from afar at four in the afternoon, the boys jumped up. They burst out of the cabin, leaving the door wide open to the blazing light, which hurt my eyes. I heard their father's voice, and then his footsteps, and he was running, and behind him the boys were running, the dog was running. Here were my husband's feet on the dirt drive. Here were his feet heavy on the porch.

66   For a half-breath, I would have vanished myself. I was everything we had fretted about, this passive Queen of Chaos with her bloody duct-tape crown. My husband filled the door. He is a man born to fill doors. I shut my eyes. When I opened them, he was **enormous** above me. In his face was a thing that made me go quiet inside, made a long slow sizzle creep up my arms from the fingertips, because the thing I read in his face was the worst, it was fear, and it was vast, it was elemental, like the wind itself, like the cold sun I would soon feel on the silk of my pelt.[1]

---

1. **pelt** an animal's skin and fur

THE MIDNIGHT ZONE

First Read

Read "The Midnight Zone." After you read, complete the Think Questions below.

☁ THINK QUESTIONS

1. Briefly explain how the protagonist's sons felt upon seeing their mother wake up from her concussion. Use evidence from the text to support your explanation.

2. How does the presence of the panther contribute to the theme of isolation in the story? Be specific and be sure to cite evidence from the text.

3. How does the protagonist's attitude in relation to her role as a mother change towards the end of the story? Cite evidence from the text to support your answer.

4. The word **stupefy** comes from the Latin *stupefacere*, which means "to be struck senseless." With that information in mind and using context clues, write a definition of *stupefy* as it is used in this story. How does your definition compare or contrast to the Latin definition? Explain, and cite context clues that helped you arrive at your understanding of the word.

5. Read the following dictionary entry:

   abstract
   abstract \ abˈstrakt \ *adjective*

   1. existing in thought or as an idea without physical or concrete existence
   2. relating to art
   3. consider theoretically or separately from something else
   4. a summary of the contents of a book, article, or formal essay

   Which definition most closely matches the meaning of **abstract** as it is used in the story? Write the correct definition of *abstract* here and explain how you figured out its meaning.

Skill:
Figurative Language

Use the Checklist to analyze Figurative Language in "The Midnight Zone." Refer to the sample student annotations about Figurative Language in the text.

⟳ CHECKLIST FOR FIGURATIVE LANGUAGE

In order to determine the meaning of a figure of speech in context, note the following:

✓ words that mean one thing literally and suggest something else

✓ similes, metaphors, or personification

✓ figures of speech, including

- hyperbole, or exaggerated statements not meant to be taken literally, such as

  > a child saying " I'll be doing this homework until I'm 100!"

  > a claim such as, "I'm so hungry I could eat a horse!"

In order to interpret a figure of speech in context and analyze its role in the text, consider the following questions:

✓ Where is there figurative language in the text, and what seems to be the purpose of the author's use of it?

✓ Why does the author use a figure of speech rather than literal language?

✓ What impact does exaggeration or hyperbole have on your understanding of the text?

✓ How does the figurative language develop the message or theme of the literary work?

Copyright © BookheadEd Learning, LLC

Skill:
Figurative Language

Reread paragraphs 44–46 of "The Midnight Zone." Then, using the Checklist on the previous page, answer the multiple-choice questions below.

⟳ YOUR TURN

1. This question has two parts. First, answer Part A. Then, answer Part B.

   Part A: In the first paragraph, how does the use of figurative language in describing the protagonist's surroundings reveal her mental and physical state as well as enhance the reader's understanding of the plot?

   ○ A. The inventive descriptions and use of figurative language help the reader grasp the depth of her mental illness as well as build tension and suspense.

   ○ B. The inventive descriptions and use of figurative language help the reader grasp the reality that she is about to die as well as build tension and suspense.

   ○ C. The inventive descriptions and use of figurative language help the reader grasp the severity of her injury as well as build tension and suspense.

   ○ D. The inventive descriptions and use of figurative language help the reader grasp the love that she has for her children as well build tension and suspense.

   Part B: Which line from the passage uses a metaphor to best support your answer in Part A?

   ○ A. "This lantern was my sister; at any moment it, too, could go dark."

   ○ B. ". . .but the shadows seemed too thick now, fizzy at the edges, and they moved when I shifted my eyes away from them"

   ○ C. "It felt safer to look at the cheeks of my sleeping children, creamy as cheeses."

   ○ D. "I could hardly see my hand or the shadow it made on the wall when I held it up."

2. What is the predominant use of figurative language being used in the final paragraph and what message does it convey?

○ A. Personification is being used to convey the idea that the narrator and her sons are at the mercy of their natural surroundings, which are more hostile than they are friendly.

○ B. Hyperbole is being used to convey the idea that the narrator and her sons are at the mercy of their natural surroundings, which are more hostile than they are friendly.

○ C. Simile is being used to convey the idea that the narrator and her sons are at the mercy of their natural surroundings, which are more hostile than they are friendly.

○ D. Metaphor is being used to convey the idea that the narrator and her sons are at the mercy of their natural surroundings, which are more hostile than they are friendly.

THE MIDNIGHT ZONE

Close Read

Reread "The Midnight Zone." As you reread, complete the Skills Focus questions below. Then use your answers and annotations from the questions to help you complete the Write activity.

◎ SKILLS FOCUS

1. What is the narrator's attitude towards motherhood? Identify evidence to support your answer, and explain why you think she feels this way.

2. Identify an example of figurative language used to describe the setting of the story. How does such figurative language contribute to the story's meaning?

3. The panther is like an unseen character in this story. Identify multiple mentions of the panther, and explain what role the "character" plays in the story.

4. Identify the part of the story in which the narrator dreams she has gone outside in the night. Explain the transformation that is suggested through the author's word choice in this passage.

5. How does the setting of this story operate as an additional character? Identify a place where the setting is described in a human way, and explain the impact that the setting has on plot or theme.

✏ WRITE

COMPARE AND CONTRAST: In both "The Midnight Zone" and *Bartram's Travels*, the authors use intense imagery and figurative language to describe their natural surroundings. Compare and contrast how each writer's use of figurative language affects the reader's impression of Florida's natural environment. How does each writer's descriptions of similar landscapes produce different effects on the reader? Support your response with evidence from the text.

Extended
Writing
Project and
Grammar

EXTENDED
WRITING
PROJECT
LITERARY ANALYSIS
WRITING

Literary Analysis Writing Process: Plan

PLAN	DRAFT	REVISE	EDIT AND PUBLISH

As America entered its adolescence, its territory stretching from coast to coast and its cities supporting ever-growing numbers of people, authors portrayed the relationship between individuals and the features of their regional environment. The authors in this unit are particularly focused on exploring the connections between individuals and their immediate surroundings. These relationships reveal issues that are important to specific characters as well as themes that connect the texts to readers and their own world.

WRITING PROMPT

How does place shape the individual?

From texts in this unit, select three individuals. In a literary analysis, examine how these individuals are shaped by and interact with their immediate surroundings. In your analysis, explain how these interactions either give readers a deeper understanding of the characters or give characters a deeper understanding of themselves. Be sure your literary analysis essay includes the following:

- an introduction
- a thesis
- successful transitions
- solid reasons and the use of relevant evidence
- a conclusion

Introduction to Literary Analysis Writing

A literary analysis is a form of argumentative writing that tries to persuade readers to accept the writer's interpretation of one or more literary texts. Good literary analysis writing builds an argument with a strong thesis, relevant textual evidence, and a clear structure with an introduction, body, and conclusion. The characteristics of literary analysis writing include:

- an introduction with an engaging hook and an original thesis statement
- a logical organizational structure
- textual evidence and reasoning that support the thesis
- a formal style
- a conclusion that wraps up your ideas in a thoughtful way

In addition to these characteristics, literary analysis writers also carefully craft their work through their use of transitions. An author's choices help to shape the tone and overall impact of the text. Effective literary analysis writing combines these genre characteristics and craft to engage the reader.

As you continue with this Extended Writing Project, you'll receive more instruction and practice in crafting each of the characteristics of literary analysis writing to create your own analytical essay.

Before you get started on your own literary analysis, read this essay that one student, Connor, wrote in response to the writing prompt. As you read the Model, highlight and annotate the features of literary analysis that Connor included in his essay.

NOTES

≡ STUDENT MODEL

Setting as Character

1   *Barracoon: The Story of the Last "Black Cargo"* by Zora Neale Hurston, "The Midnight Zone" by Lauren Groff, and "Flowering Judas" by Katherine Anne Porter are three texts rich with details about an individual's immediate surroundings. Although the three works are dramatically different, the emphasis on each text's setting acts as a technique by which the author reveals an inner realization or the growth of self-knowledge in a character or individual. In a sense, the setting is a character in itself. In *Barracoon: The Story of the Last "Black Cargo,"* "The Midnight Zone," and "Flowering Judas," rich environmental details provide a deeper understanding of the characters' inner conflicts and growth, sometimes for the reader and sometimes for the characters themselves.

2   Zora Neale Hurston uses the setting in *Barracoon: The Story of the Last "Black Cargo"* to deepen the reader's understanding of the depth of Kossula's pain. Initially, the setting subverts the reader's understanding of how having been enslaved has traumatized Kossula. Kossula's peaceful surroundings are in stark contrast to his inner pain. In spite of Kossula's illness and loneliness, Hurston comments, "His garden was planted. There was deep shade under his China-berry tree and all was well." Hurston's descriptions of Kossula's home and immediate surroundings suggest that Cudjo has found his place in this new land; he has a garden, a caretaker, and a home. Nevertheless, as the conversation moves from Kossula's present situation to his life in Africa, the details of his immediate surroundings take on a new meaning.

3   When Hurston and Kossula begin discussing Africa, the narrative takes an unexpected turn. Kossula does not describe Africa with concrete features such as the style of his home, the color of the sky, or the type of food he ate. Instead, he starts by quickly clarifying for Hurston, "My people in Afficky, you unnerstand me, dey not rich. Dass de

truth, now. I not goin' tellee you my folks dey rich and come from high blood." For Kossula, his life in Africa was defined by his family and their status in the community. Africa, in Kossula's mind, is his family and community. While Hurston's descriptions of Kossula's home and land initially show what he has achieved in America, as Kossula describes his life in Africa, the reader comes to understand just how much he has lost. His solitary surroundings in America are in direct opposition to the family and community that he was stolen from and longs to return to. The reader's understanding of Kossula and his inner turmoil about having been enslaved is enhanced through the author's descriptions of the setting to contrast the past and present.

4   In "The Midnight Zone," Lauren Groff uses the setting as a way to provoke a change in a mother's understanding of her fitness as a parent as she watches over her sons, alone in the wilderness. Instead of providing details about the characters directly, the author prioritizes details about the setting, with the first sentence stating, "It was an old hunting camp shipwrecked in twenty miles of scrub." The next figure introduced in the story is a "Florida panther sliding through the trees," further emphasizing that the setting is an essential part of the characters' experiences throughout the story. Later, after the protagonist has suffered a concussion and is alone on the couch, the rain is described as "a barrier that nothing could enter, a stay against the looming night." As the story progresses, the camp, the wildlife, and the natural elements become characters through which the protagonist has revelations about herself.

5   For example, when faced with being alone in the wilderness with her children, the protagonist immediately feels insecure, asking about her husband "if he thought he'd married an incompetent woman, which cut to the bone, because the source of our problems was that, in fact, he had." The setting of the camp pushes the protagonist to further consider her inadequacies as a mother when she begins to view her children as part of the natural world, thinking, "It's true that my children were endlessly fascinating, two petri dishes growing human cultures, being a mother never had been." The protagonist experiences a shift after suffering a concussion and having a dream about floating above the cabin and through the Florida wilderness. The following morning, after her dream, she feels differently about her abilities and says that her sons are not unhappy, therefore giving

NOTES

herself credit for her competency as a mother. This shift following her accident and dream shows how much the surroundings of the camp play into the protagonist's feelings about herself. When her husband finally returns, she feels the emotion as a "wind" and describes her skin as a "silk . . . pelt," further illustrating how embracing her natural surroundings and embracing her role as a mother went hand in hand.

6   Another text in which the setting helps the reader understand a major change in the protagonist's life is "Flowering Judas" by Katherine Anne Porter. Porter uses the setting to show that Laura's disillusionment with her life as an expatriate revolutionary in Mexico is not so simple. Descriptions of Braggioni dominate Laura's inner thoughts in the beginning of the text, which may initially make him seem like the major source of discontent in Laura's life. While the story begins describing Braggioni, it is the brief descriptions of the settings that reveal Laura's true feelings about the revolution and her life in Mexico. For Laura, her students, the prisoners, and her secret moments at the altar are what fulfill her; being a revolutionary leaves her empty. Between long descriptions of Braggioni's awful singing and hypocrisy, Porter uses the setting to reveal how being a revolutionary has pushed Laura from being a mere cynic to someone who wakes up in the night screaming.

7   Laura's cynical attitude toward the revolution is revealed at several points in the text. Details about the setting, such as "the street where the houses lean together like conspirators under a single mottled lamp," reveal Laura's increasing cynicism toward her life as a revolutionary. Laura's discontent grows upon the arrival of a young man who serenades her outside her window. Porter's vivid descriptions of the setting at this point in the story draw the reader's attention to the importance of this event. She writes, "The moonlight spread a wash of gauzy silver over the clear spaces of the garden, and the shadows were cobalt blue" and "the scarlet blossoms of the Judas tree were dull purple." As Laura listens to the singing youth and stares at the Judas tree, she is lost in thought. It isn't until the closing of the story that the reader fully understands the significance of this moment. In a dream, Laura gives in to her cynicism and doubt by eating the leaves of the Judas tree in a symbolic act of betrayal. Throughout the story, it is Porter's use of the setting that ultimately

Copyright © BookheadEd Learning, LLC

NOTES

reveals Laura's feelings of existential dread over the life she is living in Mexico.

8   Authors use setting to accomplish a variety of goals in a text. In *Barracoon: The Story of the Last "Black Cargo"* by Zora Neale Hurston, the author uses details about Alabama and Africa to illustrate Kossula's pain and trauma from having been enslaved. In "The Midnight Zone" by Lauren Groff, the wilderness setting deepens a mother's understanding of her ability as a parent. Finally, in "Flowering Judas" by Katherine Anne Porter, the streets and gardens of Mexico contribute to the character's self-discovery. In each of these stories, the setting becomes an agent of change or revelation. Through the use of rich details about these individuals' environments, the reader sees how place shapes the individual. Reading these individuals' stories shows us how our surroundings shed light on who we are and where we come from.

✎ WRITE

Writers often take notes before they sit down to write. Think about what you've learned so far about literary analysis writing to help you begin prewriting.

- **Purpose:** What topic do you want to write about? Why is it worth analyzing across texts?

- **Audience:** Who is your audience? What message do you want to express to your audience? How do you want your audience to view the texts differently?

- **Introduction:** How will you introduce the topic and thesis of your essay? Do your topic and thesis present a unique perspective on the texts?

- **Organizational Structure:** What strategies will you use to organize your response to the prompt? How can you make the progression of your ideas logical and coherent? Will you spend equal time analyzing each of the texts?

- **Textual Evidence:** What kinds of textual evidence might you use to support your ideas? Which quotations best demonstrate how the characters think about and interact with their surroundings? How can you ensure that you provide sufficient original commentary?

- **Style:** Is the tone formal or conversational? What kinds of information might you remove to make sure your essay is clear and concise?

- **Conclusion:** How will you rephrase your thesis in a new way? How did performing an analysis transform the way you read the texts? How can you connect ideas from the body of your essay to a larger concept?

Response Instructions

Use the questions in the bulleted list to write a one-paragraph summary. Your summary should describe the texts and characters you will analyze as well as your observations about how these characters interact with their surroundings.

Don't worry about including all of the details now; focus only on the most essential and important elements. You will refer to this short summary as you continue through the steps of the writing process.

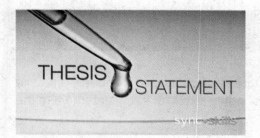

Skill:
Thesis Statement

••• CHECKLIST FOR THESIS STATEMENT

Before you begin writing your thesis statement for your literary analysis essay, ask yourself the following questions:

- What is the prompt asking me to write about?
- What claim do I want to make about the topic of this essay?
- Is my claim precise? How is it specific to my topic?
- Does my thesis statement introduce the body of my essay?
- Where should I place my thesis statement?

Here are some methods for introducing and developing a topic as well as a precise thesis:

- think about your central claim of your essay

  > identify a clear claim you want to introduce, thinking about:

    o how closely your claim is related to your topic and how specific it is to your supporting details

    o any alternate or opposing claims (counterclaims)

  > identify as many claims as you intend to prove

- your thesis statement should:

  > let the reader anticipate the content of your essay

  > help you begin your essay in an organized manner

  > present your opinion clearly

  > respond completely to the writing prompt

- consider the best placement for your thesis statement

  > if your response is short, you may want to get right to the point and present your thesis statement in the first sentence of the essay

  > if your response is longer (as in a formal essay), you can build up to your thesis statement and place it at the end of your introductory paragraph

↻ YOUR TURN

Read the statements below. Then, complete the chart by sorting the statements into two categories: effective thesis statements and ineffective thesis statements. Write the corresponding letter for each statement in the appropriate column.

	Statement Options
A	The protagonist's inability to protect her children from the harsh natural environment highlights her inadequacies as a mother.
B	Braggioni's persistence in making Laura feel part of a community throughout the course of the story actually drives her further away.
C	The author's descriptions of Kossula's home and life as a free man help the reader visualize what he was like.
D	The contrast between Kossula's past and present environments serves to draw the reader's attention to his inner turmoil.
E	The setting of the story prompts the protagonist to confront her attitude toward the movement she's dedicated her life to.
F	Natural surroundings play a large role in the main character's injury.

Effective Thesis Statement	Ineffective Thesis Statement

✏ WRITE

Follow the steps in the checklist to draft a thesis statement for your literary analysis.

Skill: Organizing Argumentative Writing

CHECKLIST FOR ORGANIZING ARGUMENTATIVE WRITING

As you consider how to organize your writing for your literary analysis essay, a type of argumentative essay, use the following questions as a guide:

- What kinds of evidence could I find that would support my claim?
- What types of information could I look for to establish the significance of my claim?

Follow these steps to organize your argumentative essay in a way that logically sequences claim(s), reasons, and evidence:

- identify your precise, or specific, claim or claims and the evidence that supports them

- establish the significance of your claim

- choose an organizational structure that logically sequences and establishes clear relationships between your claims, reasons, and the evidence presented to support your claims

⟳ YOUR TURN

Read the statements from a student's literary analysis essay about *Their Eyes Were Watching God* below. Then, determine where each statement belongs in the outline in the chart. Write the corresponding letter for each statement in the appropriate row.

	Statement Options
A	The men stare at Janie's body in an aggressive manner.
B	The first person to ridicule Janie talks about her appearance, asking why she couldn't find a dress.
C	When a person makes an unusual decision, he or she often suffers ridicule and becomes the target of gossip.
D	Lulu Moss says that because Janie had a younger husband, Janie thinks she is better than other people.
E	In *Their Eyes Were Watching God,* Janie must endure particularly cruel judgment by her community for her choices because she is a woman.

Outline	Statement
Introductory Statement	
Thesis	
Supporting Detail 1	
Supporting Detail 2	
Supporting Detail 3	

⟳ YOUR TURN

Complete the chart below by writing a short summary of what you will focus on in each paragraph of your essay.

Outline	Summary
Introductory Statement	
Thesis	
Main Idea 1	
Main Idea 2	
Main Idea 3	

Skill: Reasons and Relevant Evidence

••• CHECKLIST FOR REASONS AND RELEVANT EVIDENCE

As you begin to determine what reasons and relevant evidence will support your claim(s), use the following questions as a guide:

- Is my claim precise, specific, and clearly stated?

- How can I make my claim more specific to my topic and ideas?

- What relevant evidence do I have? Where could I add more support for my claim?

Use the following steps as a guide to help you introduce a precise claim(s) and support your claim with reasons and relevant evidence:

- identify the precise claim you will make in your argument, and refine it by:

  > eliminating any vague ideas

  > using vocabulary that clarifies your ideas

- choose an organizational structure, such as compare and contrast, that will establish a clear relationship between your claim, reasons, and evidence

- find the most relevant evidence that supports the claim

- decide what explanation or reasoning you need to include with your evidence to support and strengthen your claim

↻ YOUR TURN

Read each piece of textual evidence from *Barracoon: The Story of the Last "Black Cargo"* below. Then, complete the chart by determining whether the evidence is relevant or not relevant to the claim that the author uses the setting to contrast Kossula's past environment with his present. Write the corresponding letter for each piece of evidence in the appropriate column.

	Textual Evidence Options
A	"He wanted to know a few things about New York and when I had answered him, he sat silently smoking. Finally, I told him I had come to talk with him. He removed his pipe from his mouth and smiled."
B	"I was afraid that Cudjo might go off on a tangent, so I cut in with, 'But Kossula, I want to hear about you and how you lived in Africa.'"
C	"My father's father, you unnerstand me, he a officer of de king. He don't live in de compound wid us. Wherever de king go, he go, you unnerstand me."
D	"He was eating his breakfast from a round enameled pan with his hands, in the fashion of his fatherland."

Relevant	Not Relevant

Please note that excerpts and passages in the StudySync® library and this workbook are intended as touchstones to generate interest in an author's work. The excerpts and passages do not substitute for the reading of entire texts, and StudySync® strongly recommends that students seek out and purchase the whole literary or informational work in order to experience it as the author intended. Links to online resellers are available in our digital library. In addition, complete works may be ordered through an authorized reseller by filling out and returning to StudySync® the order form enclosed in this workbook.

Reading & Writing Companion   **479**

⟳ YOUR TURN

Complete the chart below by identifying evidence from each text you've chosen for your literary analysis essay. Identifying evidence will help you develop your own writing ideas.

Text	Textual Evidence	Observation/Reaction
Selection 1 Title:		
Selection 2 Title:		
Selection 3 Title:		

Literary Analysis Writing Process: Draft

| PLAN | DRAFT | REVISE | EDIT AND PUBLISH |

You have already made progress toward writing your literary analysis. Now it is time to draft your literary analysis.

✏ WRITE

Use your plan and other responses in your Binder to draft your literary analysis essay. You may also have new ideas as you begin drafting. Feel free to explore those new ideas as you have them. You can also ask yourself these questions to ensure that your writing is focused, organized, and developed:

Draft Checklist:

☐ **Focused:** Have I made my thesis clear to readers? Have I included only relevant information and details and nothing extraneous that might confuse my readers?

☐ **Organized:** Does the organization of ideas in my analysis make sense? Does the organization of my essay help readers understand how my thesis applies to each text?

☐ **Developed:** Does my writing include evidence? Will my readers be able to easily follow my argument and understand my use of relevant evidence to support my claims?

Before you submit your draft, read it over carefully. You want to be sure that you've responded to all aspects of the prompt.

Here is Connor's literary analysis draft. As you read, notice how Connor ensures that his draft is focused, organized, and developed. As he continues to revise and edit his analysis, he will find and improve weak spots in his writing, as well as correct any language or punctuation mistakes.

☰ STUDENT MODEL: FIRST DRAFT

Setting as Character

~~*Barracoon: The Story of the Last "Black Cargo"* by Zora Neale Hurston, "The Midnight Zone" by Lauren Groff, and "Flowering Judas" by Katherine Anne Porter are three texts with lots of information about an individual's immediate surroundings and how they force individuals to confront inner realizations about personal growth and change. Whether it is the tale of becoming enslaved, the inner thoughts of a mother alone in the wilderness, or the cynical thoughts of an expatriate revolutionary, the emphasis on each text's setting acts as a technique by which the author reveals an inner realization or growth of self knowledge in a character or individual. In *Barracoon: The Story of the Last "Black Cargo,"* "The Midnight Zone," and "Flowering Judas," rich environmental details reveal the characters' inner conflicts and growth.~~

Barracoon: The Story of the Last "Black Cargo" by Zora Neale Hurston, "The Midnight Zone" by Lauren Groff, and "Flowering Judas" by Katherine Anne Porter are three texts rich with details about an individual's immediate surroundings. Although the three works are dramatically different, the emphasis on each text's setting acts as a technique by which the author reveals an inner realization or the growth of self-knowledge in a character or individual. In a sense, the setting is a character in itself. In *Barracoon: The Story of the Last "Black Cargo,"* "The Midnight Zone," and "Flowering Judas," rich environmental details provide a deeper understanding of the characters' inner conflicts and growth, sometimes for the reader and sometimes for the characters themselves.

~~Zora Neale Hurston uses setting in *Barracoon: The Story of the Last "Black Cargo"* to deepen the reader's understanding of the depth of Kossula's pain. The setting subverts the reader's understanding of how having been enslaved has traumatized Kossula. Kossula's peaceful surroundings are in stark contrast to his inner pain. Hurston describes~~

Skill: Introductions

Connor strengthens his introduction by refining his thesis and eliminating repetition. In addition, he hooks the reader's interest by adding the sentence "In a sense, the setting is a character in itself." By using these techniques, Connor creates a more focused, precise, and engaging introduction.

Zora Neale Hurston uses the setting in *Barracoon: The Story of the Last "Black Cargo"* to deepen the reader's understanding of the depth of Kossula's pain. Initially, the setting subverts the reader's understanding of how having been enslaved has traumatized Kossula. Kossula's peaceful surroundings are in stark contrast to his inner pain. In spite of Kossula's illness and loneliness, Hurston comments, "His garden was planted. There was deep shade under his China-berry tree and all was well." Hurston's descriptions of Kossula's home and immediate surroundings suggest that Kossula has found his place in this new land; he has a garden, a caretaker, and a home. Nevertheless, as the conversation moves from Kossula's present situation to his life in Africa, the details of his immediate surroundings take on a new meaning.

When Hurston and Cudjo begin discussing Africa, the narrative takes an unexpected turn. Kossula does not describe Africa with concrete features. He does not describe the style of his home. He does not describe the color of the sky. He does not describe the type of food he ate. Instead, he starts by saying "My people, you unnerstand me, dey ain' got no ivory by de door." For Kossula, his life in Africa, was defined by his family and there status in the community. Africa in, Kossula's mind, is his family and community. While Hurston's descriptions of Kossula's home and land initialy show what he has achieved in America, as Kossula describes his life in Africa, the reader comes to understand just how much he's lost. The reader's understanding of Kossula and his inner turmoil about having been enslaved is enhanced through the author's descriptions of setting to contrast the past and present. His solitary surroundings in America are in direct opposition to the family and community that he was stolen from and longs to return to.

In "The Midnight Zone," Lauren Groff uses setting as a way to provoke a change in a mother's understanding of her fitness as a

Skill:
Transitions

Connor realizes that the relationships between his ideas in the second paragraph are not always clear. So he adds the transitions initially, in spite of, *and* nevertheless *to connect his ideas and create cohesion.*

Copyright © BookheadEd Learning, LLC

parent as she watches over her sons; alone in the wilderness. Instead of providing details about the characters directly, the author prioritizes details about the setting, with the first sentence stating "It was an old hunting camp shipwrecked in twenty miles of scrub." The next figure introduced in the story is a "Florida panther sliding through the trees," further emphasizing that the setting is an essential part of the characters' experiences throughout the story. Later, after the protagonist has suffered a concussion and is alone on the couch, the rain is described as "a barrier that nothing could enter, a stay against the looming night." As the story progresses, the camp, the wildlife, and the natural elements become characters through which the protagonist has revelations about herself.

For example, when faced with being alone in the wilderness with her children, the protagonist's imediate reaction is to feel bad, asking about her husband "if he thought he'd married an incompetent woman, which cut to the bone, because the source of our problems was that, in fact, he had." The setting of the camp pushes the protagonist to further consider her inadequacies as a mother when she begins to view her children as part of the natural surrounding, thinking "it's true that my children were endlessly fascinating, two petri dishes growing human cultures, being a mother never had been." The protagonist experiences a shift after suffering a concussion and having a dream about floating above the cabin and through the Florida wilderness. The following morning after her dream. She feels differently about her abilities and says that her sons are not unhappy, thus giving herself credit for her competency as a mother. This shift following her accident and dream shows how much the surroundings of the camp play into the protagonist's feelings about herself. When her husband finally returns she feels the emotion as a "wind" and describes her skin as a "silk pelt," further illustrating how embracing her natural surroundings and embracing her role as a mother went hand in hand.

In yet a another text the setting helps the reader understand a major change in the protagonist's life. Porter uses setting to show that Laura's dislike of her life as an expatriate revolutionary in Mexico is not so simple. Descriptions of Braggioni dominate Laura's inner thoughts in the beginning of the text, which may initially make him seem like the cruddiest part of Laura's life. Despite him occupying a large portion of Laura's life and inner thoughts, I think it is the brief descriptions of the settings away from Braggioni that reveal her true feelings about the revolution and her life in Mexico. For Laura, her students, the prisoners, and her secret moments at the altar are how she chills out, being a revolutionary leaves her empty. Between long descriptions of Braggionis awful singing and hypocrisy, Porter uses the setting to reveal how being a revolutionary has pushed Laura from a mere cynic to someone who wakes up in the night screaming.

Laura's cynical attitude toward the revolution is revealed at several points throughout the text. Details about the setting reveal Laura's increasing cynicism toward her life as a revolutionary. Laura's discontent grows upon the arrival of a young man who serenades her outside her window. Porter emfasizes the significance of the event when she vividly describes it as "the moonlight spread a wash of gauzy silver over the clear spaces of the garden, and the shadows were cobalt blue" and "the scarlet blossoms of the Judas tree were dull purple." The singing youth, and the colors of the Judas tree, push Laura to further doubt her choice to become a revolutionary. It isn't until the closing of the story that the reader fully understands the significance of this moment which is very important for the narrator. In a dream, Laura gives in to her cynicism and doubt by eating the leaves of the Judas tree in a symbolic act of betrayal. "Flowering Judas" may be a story full of memorable characters, but it is Porter's use of setting that ultimately reveals, Laura's feelings of existential dread over the life she is living in Mexico.

~~Authors use setting to accomplish a variety of goals in a text. In *Barracoon: The Story of the Last "Black Cargo,"* the author uses details about Alabama and Africa to illustrate pain and trauma from having been enslaved. In "The Midnight Zone," the wilderness setting deepens a mother's understanding of her ability as a parent. And in "Flowering Judas," descriptions of the streets and gardens of Mexico serve as instigators for a character's self discovery. Through the use of rich details about these individuals' environments, the reader sees how place shapes the individual. Reading these individuals' stories shows us how engaging with our surroundings is a valuable tool to have.~~

NOTES

Skill:
Conclusions

Connor strengthens his conclusion by adding a sentence that rephrases his thesis in a thoughtful way. He then realizes that his last sentence does not take into account all the points in his essay. He revises the sentence to make it more accurate, convey the significance of his topic, and end with a memorable idea.

Authors use setting to accomplish a variety of goals in a text. In *Barracoon: The Story of the Last "Black Cargo"* by Zora Neale Hurston, the author uses details about Alabama and Africa to illustrate Kossula's pain and trauma from having been enslaved. In "The Midnight Zone" by Lauren Groff, the wilderness setting deepens a mother's understanding of her ability as a parent. Finally, in "Flowering Judas" by Katherine Anne Porter, the streets and gardens of Mexico contribute to the character's self-discovery. In each of these stories, the setting becomes an agent of change or revelation. Through the use of rich details about these individuals' environments, the reader sees how place shapes the individual. Reading these individuals' stories shows us how our surroundings shed light on who we are and where we come from.

Skill:
Introductions

Before you write your introduction, ask yourself the following questions:

- What is my claim? In addition:

  > How can I make it more precise and informative?

  > Have I included why my claim is significant to discuss?

- How can I introduce my topic? Have I organized complex ideas, concepts, and information so that each new element builds on the previous element and creates a unified whole?

- How will I "hook" my reader's interest? I might:

  > start with an attention-grabbing statement

  > begin with an intriguing question

Below are two strategies to help you introduce your precise claim and topic clearly in an introduction:

- Peer Discussion

  > Talk about your topic with a partner, explaining what you already know and your ideas about your topic.

  > Write notes about the ideas you have discussed and any new questions you may have.

  > Review your notes, and think about what your claim or controlling idea will be.

  > Write a possible "hook."

- Freewriting

  > Freewrite for 10 minutes about your topic. Don't worry about grammar, punctuation, or having fully formed ideas. The point of freewriting is to discover ideas.

  > Review your notes, and think about what your claim or controlling idea will be.

  > Write a possible "hook."

YOUR TURN

Choose the best answer to each question.

1. The following introduction is from a previous draft of Connor's essay. Connor needs to add a hook to grab his audience's attention and introduce his topic. Which sentence could he add to help achieve this goal?

> *Barracoon: The Story of the Last "Black Cargo"* by Zora Neale Hurston, "The Midnight Zone" by Lauren Groff, and "Flowering Judas" by Katherine Anne Porter are three texts where the setting is important. Whether it is the tale of becoming enslaved, the inner thoughts of a mother alone in the wilderness, or the cynical thoughts of an expatriate revolutionary, the emphasis on each text's setting acts as a technique by which the author reveals an inner realization or growth of self knowledge in a character or individual. In each of these texts, the use of environmental details illustrates how the setting forces individuals to confront inner realizations about personal growth and change.

- A. The texts in this unit portrayed a range of characters.
- B. Sometimes in literature, a setting is so vividly portrayed that it becomes a character itself.
- C. "The Midnight Zone" is a narrative written in the form of a short story.
- D. The texts I will discuss cover a variety of themes.

2. The following is Connor's revised introduction. Which sentence is his thesis?

> (1) *Barracoon: The Story of the Last "Black Cargo"* by Zora Neale Hurston, "The Midnight Zone" by Lauren Groff, and "Flowering Judas" by Katherine Anne Porter are three texts rich with details about an individual's immediate surroundings. (2) Although the three works are dramatically different, the emphasis on each text's setting acts as a technique by which the author reveals an inner realization or the growth of self-knowledge in a character or individual. (3) In a sense, the setting is a character in itself. (4) In *Barracoon: The Story of the Last "Black Cargo,"* "The Midnight Zone," and "Flowering Judas," rich environmental details provide a deeper understanding of the characters' inner conflicts and growth, sometimes for the reader and sometimes for the characters themselves.

- A. Sentence 1
- B. Sentence 2
- C. Sentence 3
- D. Sentence 4

 WRITE

Use the checklist to revise the introduction of your literary analysis essay.

Skill:
Transitions

••• CHECKLIST FOR TRANSITIONS

Before you revise your current draft to include transitions, think about:

- the key ideas you discuss
- the major sections of your essay
- the organizational structure of your essay
- the relationships between complex ideas and concepts

Next, reread your current draft and note places in your essay where:

- the organizational structure is not yet apparent

  > For example, if you are comparing and contrasting two texts, your explanations about how the two texts are similar and different should be clearly stated.

- the relationship between ideas from one paragraph to the next is unclear

  > For example, when you describe a process in sequential order, you should clarify the order of the steps by using transitional words like *first, then, next,* and *finally.*

- your ideas do not create cohesion, or a unified whole
- your transition and/or syntax is inappropriate

Revise your draft to use appropriate and varied transitions to link the major sections of your essay, create cohesion, and clarify the relationships between complex ideas and concepts, using the following questions as a guide:

- What kind of transitions should I use to make the organizational structure clear to readers?
- Are my transitions linking the major sections of my essay?
- What transitions create cohesion between complex ideas and concepts?
- Are my transitions varied and appropriate?
- Have my transitions clarified the relationships between complex ideas and concepts?

Please note that excerpts and passages in the StudySync® library and this workbook are intended as touchstones to generate interest in an author's work. The excerpts and passages do not substitute for the reading of entire texts, and StudySync® strongly recommends that students seek out and purchase the whole literary or informational work in order to experience it as the author intended. Links to online resellers are available in our digital library. In addition, complete works may be ordered through an authorized reseller by filling out and returning to StudySync® the order form enclosed in this workbook.

Reading & Writing
Companion

489

⟳ YOUR TURN

Choose the best answer to each question.

1. Below is a section from a previous draft of Connor's essay. The connection between the paragraphs is unclear. What transition should Connor add to the beginning of the second paragraph to make his writing more coherent?

> Later, after the protagonist has suffered a concussion and is alone on the couch, the rain is described as "a barrier that nothing could enter, a stay against the looming night." As the story progresses, the camp, the wildlife, and the natural elements become characters through which the protagonist has revelations about herself.
>
> When faced with being alone in the wilderness with her children, the protagonist's immediate reaction is to feel bad, asking about her husband "if he thought he'd married an incompetent woman, which cut to the bone, because the source of our problems was that, in fact, he had."

○ A. Eventually

○ B. For example

○ C. Given these points

○ D. On the other hand

2. Below is a section from a previous draft of Connor's essay. Connor did not use an appropriate transition to show the relationship between ideas in the underlined sentence. Which of the following transitions is the best replacement for the word *so*? Choose the transition that makes his writing more coherent.

> The following morning after her dream. <u>She feels differently about her abilities and says that her sons are not unhappy, so giving herself credit for her competency as a mother.</u> This shift following her accident and dream shows how much the surroundings of the camp play into the protagonist's feelings about herself.

○ A. thus

○ B. with attention to

○ C. whereas

○ D. to illustrate

✏ WRITE

Use the questions in the checklist to revise your use of transitions in a section of your literary analysis.

Skill:
Conclusions

••• CHECKLIST FOR CONCLUSIONS

Before you write your conclusion, ask yourself the following questions:

- How can I rephrase the thesis or main idea?

- How can I write my conclusion so that it supports and follows from the information I presented?

- How can I communicate the importance of my topic? What information do I need?

Below are two strategies to help you provide a concluding statement or section that follows from and supports the information or explanation presented:

- Peer Discussion

  > After you have written your introduction and body paragraphs, talk with a partner about what you want readers to remember, writing notes about your discussion.

  > Think about how you can articulate, or express, the significance of your topic in the conclusion.

  > Rephrase your main idea to show the depth of your knowledge and support for the information you presented.

  > Write your conclusion.

- Freewriting

  > Freewrite for 10 minutes about what you might include in your conclusion. Don't worry about grammar, punctuation, or having fully formed ideas. The point of freewriting is to discover ideas.

  > Think about how you can articulate, or express, the significance of your topic in the conclusion.

  > Rephrase your main idea to show the depth of your knowledge and support for the information you presented.

  > Write your conclusion.

↻ YOUR TURN

Choose the best answer to each question.

1. The following passage is from a previous draft of Connor's conclusion. Connor would like to revise the underlined sentence to suit the purpose of his essay and improve the style and tone so that they are appropriate for a formal academic context. Which is the best revision of the underlined sentence?

> <u>I like when authors get creative when describing setting.</u> In *Barracoon: The Story of the Last "Black Cargo"* the author uses details about Alabama and Africa to illustrate pain and trauma from having been enslaved. In "The Midnight Zone" the wilderness setting deepens a mother's understanding of her ability as a parent. And in "Flowering Judas," descriptions of the streets and gardens of Mexico contribute to the character's self discovery.

- ○ A. Authors are very talented in that they can describe setting in creative ways.
- ○ B. I think it is brave when an author uses setting to say something about society at large.
- ○ C. Out of the three texts I analyzed, "The Midnight Zone" is my favorite because of its fascinating setting.
- ○ D. In complex works of fiction, the setting reveals much more than just where the story takes place.

2. Below is Connor's conclusion from a previous draft. What is one piece of information that Connor needs to include as he continues to revise?

> Authors use setting to accomplish a variety of goals in a text. In *Barracoon: The Story of the Last "Black Cargo"* the author uses details about Alabama and Africa to illustrate pain and trauma from having been enslaved. In "The Midnight Zone" the wilderness setting deepens a mother's understanding of her ability as a parent. And in "Flowering Judas," descriptions of Mexico are very vibrant. Through the use of rich details about these individuals' environments, the reader sees how place shapes the individual.

- ○ A. Connor neglects to discuss setting, which is part of his thesis.
- ○ B. Connor discusses only one of the texts, "The Midnight Zone," rather than all three.
- ○ C. Connor needs to discuss other texts besides the three mentioned in his essay.
- ○ D. Connor neglects to mention how the setting of "Flowering Judas" helps the protagonist process her feelings.

✎ WRITE

Use the checklist to revise the conclusion of your literary analysis essay.

Literary Analysis Writing Process: Revise

PLAN	DRAFT	REVISE	EDIT AND PUBLISH

You have written a draft of your literary analysis essay. You have also received input from your peers about how to improve it. Now you are going to revise your draft.

⬅ REVISION GUIDE

Examine your draft to find areas for revision. Keep in mind your purpose and audience as you revise for clarity, development, organization, and style. Use the guide below to help you review:

Review	Revise	Example
Clarity		
Identify the names of selections, authors, and the individuals you discuss. Annotate any places where it is unclear whom or what you're describing.	State the titles of texts and individuals' names to make it clear whom you are talking about.	~~In yet a~~ Another text in which the setting helps the reader understand a major change in the protagonist's life is "Flowering Judas" by Katherine Anne Porter.
Development		
Identify the textual evidence that supports your claims, and include commentary. Annotate places where you feel there is not enough textual evidence to support your ideas.	Focus on a single idea or claim, and add support in the form of textual evidence or original commentary.	Details about the setting, such as "the street where the houses lean together like conspirators under a single mottled lamp," reveal Laura's increasing cynicism toward her life as a revolutionary.

Review	Revise	Example
Organization		
Review your body paragraphs. Identify and annotate any sentences that don't flow in a clear and logical way.	Rewrite the sentences so they appear in a clear and logical order, starting with a strong transition or topic sentence. Delete details that are repetitive or not essential to support the thesis.	It isn't until the closing of the story that the reader fully understands the significance of this moment ~~which is very important for the narrator~~.
Style: Word Choice		
Identify weak or repetitive words or phrases that do not clearly convey your ideas to the reader.	Replace weak and repetitive words and phrases with more descriptive ones that better convey your ideas.	For example, when faced with being alone in the wilderness with her children, the protagonist's ~~imediate~~ immediately ~~reaction is to feel~~ feels ~~bad~~ insecure, asking about her husband "if he thought he'd married an incompetent woman, which cut to the bone, because the source of our problems was that, in fact, he had."
Style: Sentence Fluency		
Read aloud your writing and listen to the way the text sounds. Does it sound choppy? Or does it flow smoothly with rhythm, movement, and emphasis on important details and events?	Rewrite a portion of your essay, making your sentences longer or shorter to achieve a better flow of writing and the emotion you want your reader to feel.	When Hurston and Kossula begin discussing Africa, the narrative takes an unexpected turn. Kossula does not describe Africa with concrete features: ~~such as He does not describe~~ the style of his home,: ~~He does not describe~~ the color of the sky, or: ~~He does not describe~~ the type of food he ate.

✏ WRITE

Use the revision guide, as well as your peer reviews, to help you evaluate your literary analysis to determine areas that should be revised.

Skill:
Style

••• CHECKLIST FOR STYLE

First, reread the draft of your literary analysis essay and identify the following:

- slang, colloquialisms, contractions, abbreviations, or a conversational tone

- places where you could use academic language in order to help persuade your readers

- the use of the first person (*I*) or the second person (*you*)

- statements that express judgment or emotion, rather than objective statements that rely on facts and evidence

- places where you could vary sentence structure and length by using compound, complex, and compound-complex sentences

  > for guidance on effective ways of varying syntax, use a style guide

- incorrect uses of the conventions of standard English for grammar, spelling, capitalization, and punctuation

Establish and maintain a formal style in your essay, using the following questions as a guide:

- Have I avoided slang in favor of academic language?

- Did I consistently use a third-person perspective, using third-person pronouns (*he*, *she*, *they*)?

- Have I maintained an objective tone without expressing my own judgments and emotions?

- Have I used varied sentence lengths and different sentence structures? Did I consider using style guides to learn about effective ways of varying syntax?

  > Where should I make some sentences longer by using conjunctions to connect independent clauses, dependent clauses, and phrases?

  > Where should I make some sentences shorter by separating independent clauses?

- Have I correctly followed the conventions of standard English?

↻ YOUR TURN

Choose the best answer to each question.

1. Which type of stylistic error did Connor make in this line from a previous draft?

> Based on how Hurston describes Kossula's life, I think he is very depressed.

- ○ A. Connor's use of capitalization is incorrect.
- ○ B. The sentence is too complex.
- ○ C. Connor uses the pronoun *I* and makes a statement based on his feelings.
- ○ D. Connor uses slang.

2. Below are two sentences from a previous draft of Connor's essay. How should these sentences be rewritten to improve the style?

> The following morning after her dream, she feels better and says that her sons are not unhappy. This means she gives herself credit for being a good mother.

- ○ A. The following morning, after her dream, she feels differently about her abilities and says that her sons are not unhappy. I think this is giving herself credit for her competency as a mother.
- ○ B. The following morning after her dream she feels differently about her abilities and says that her sons are not unhappy therefore giving herself credit for her competency as a mother.
- ○ C. The following morning, after her dream, she feels differently about her abilities. She says that her sons are not unhappy. She is giving herself credit for her competency as a mother.
- ○ D. The following morning, after her dream, the narrator acknowledges that her sons are not unhappy, thus giving herself credit for her competency as a mother.

✎ WRITE

Use the checklist to revise a paragraph of your literary analysis to improve the style.

Grammar: Semicolons

A semicolon does the same thing as a comma and a coordinating conjunction (*and, but, or, nor, for, yet,* or *so*)—it joins two independent clauses. Never use a semicolon with a coordinating conjunction.

Correctly Edited	Incorrect
I love jazz; the blues are my favorite kind of jazz.	I love jazz; and the blues are my favorite kind of jazz.

Follow these additional rules when using semicolons:

Rule	Text
Use a semicolon to join two clauses that are closely connected.	I also now first saw the use of the quadrant; I had often with astonishment seen the mariners make observations with it, and I could not think what it meant. The Interesting Narrative of the Life of Olaudah Equiano, or Gustavus Vassa, the African
Use a semicolon to join two independent clauses with a conjunctive adverb (such as *however*) or another transition word or phrase (such as *for example*). A comma may follow the transition word or phrase.	Slavery was legal in the North, too; **however,** conditions were different. American Literature & History: The Civil War Era (1850-1880)
Use a semicolon to separate items in a series when one or more of the items already contain commas.	Congress shall make no law respecting the establishment of religion, or prohibiting the free exercise thereof; or abridging the freedom of speech, or of the press; or the right of people peaceably to assemble, and to petition the Government for a redress of grievances. Founding Documents of the United States of America: Preamble to the United States Constitution and First Ten Amendments (The Bill of Rights) 1787-1791

↻ YOUR TURN

1. How should this sentence be changed?

> The Antarctic continent covers five and one-half million square miles this is an area larger than the United States and Central America combined.

- ○ A. Insert a semicolon after the word **continent**.
- ○ B. Insert a colon after the word **miles**.
- ○ C. Insert a semicolon after the word **miles**.
- ○ D. No change needs to be made to this sentence.

2. How should this sentence be changed?

> The paint in the 100-year-old mansion is peeling; therefore, the owners plan to put a fresh coat of paint on the walls with some help from family and friends.

- ○ A. Replace the semicolon with a colon.
- ○ B. Delete the comma after the word **therefore**.
- ○ C. Insert a semicolon after the word **walls**.
- ○ D. No change needs to be made to this sentence.

3. How should this sentence be changed?

> Wireless TV systems are competing with cable systems and I say it's about time that we have a choice.

- ○ A. Remove the word **and**, and add a semicolon after **systems**.
- ○ B. Add a semicolon after the word **time**.
- ○ C. Add a semicolon after the word **say**.
- ○ D. No change needs to be made to this sentence.

4. How should this sentence be changed?

> Which state has the most interesting place names would be a hotly contested topic for a debate, however, Maine, with names such as Passamaquoddy Bay, would certainly be in the running for first place.

- ○ A. Change the comma after **however** to a semicolon.
- ○ B. Change the comma after **debate** to a semicolon.
- ○ C. Change the commas after **debate** and **Passamaquoddy Bay** to semicolons.
- ○ D. No change needs to be made to this sentence.

commonly confused words

sync skills

Grammar: Commonly Confused Words

There are many words that are similar and are sometimes misused.

Its and It's

- *Its* is the possessive form of *it*.
- *It's* is a contraction of *it is* or *it has*.

There, Their, and They're

- *There* refers to a physical or abstract place. It can also be used as a pronoun.
- *Their* is the possessive form of the pronoun *they*.
- *They're* is a contraction of the words *they are*.

Than and Then

- *Than* is a conjunction that is used to introduce the second element in a comparison; it also shows exception.
- *Than* can also function as a preposition, depending on what is being compared: You like Jan more *than* I [do]. (conjunction)
  You like Jan more *than* [you like] *me*. (preposition)
- *Then* is an adverb meaning "at that time."

Affect and Effect

- *Affect* is a verb that means "to cause a change in" or "to influence."
- *Effect* is a noun that means "a result" or "that which has been brought about."
- *Effect* is also a verb that means "to bring about or accomplish."

Lie and Lay

- *Lay* means "to put" or "to place."
- *Lie* means "to rest or recline" or "to be positioned."

It's helpful to remember that the verb *lie* in all its forms is intransitive and does not take a direct object. The verb *lay* in all its forms is transitive and takes a direct object: You *lie* down, but you *lay something* down.

⟳ YOUR TURN

1. Which sentence is written correctly?

> 1. The doctor told the patient she should lay on the cot.
>
> 2. Even throughout the thunderstorm last night, the baby lay in her crib fast asleep.
>
> 3. I went back to the couch to find the cat laying in the spot where I had been.

○ A. 1   C. 3
○ B. 2   D. All sentences are written correctly.

2. Which sentence is written correctly?

> 1. The student council wants to effect change in the dress code.
>
> 2. Receiving a good grade will affect the student's motivation.
>
> 3. Playing sports can have an effect on students' academic performance.

○ A. 1   C. 3
○ B. 2   D. All sentences are written correctly.

3. Which sentence is written correctly?

> 1. Its not always easy to fall asleep quickly.
>
> 2. The food lost its flavor after sitting in the fridge for so long.
>
> 3. This pillow is too big for it's case.

○ A. 1   C. 3
○ B. 2   D. All sentences are written correctly.

4. Which sentence is written correctly?

> 1. I wonder if they're planning to go on vacation with us.
>
> 2. You'll find the book on that shelf over their.
>
> 3. People sometimes wear sweaters when there cold.

○ A. 1   C. 3
○ B. 2   D. All sentences are written correctly.

Grammar:
Misuse of Commas

One common error to avoid is the comma splice, when two main clauses in a compound sentence are joined only by a comma. They should be joined either by a semicolon or by a comma and a conjunction. Another common error is using a comma between two parts of a compound predicate in a simple sentence. Commas can also be incorrectly inserted between a subject and its verb or between a verb and its complement.

In many cases, such as after short introductory prepositional phrases, commas are optional. When you are deciding whether to use or take out a comma, clarity is the first standard you should apply.

Text	Explanation
The **widow she cried** over me, **and called** me a poor lost lamb, **and she called** me a lot of other names, too, **but she never meant** no harm by it. Adventures of Huckleberry Finn	In this compound sentence, the first comma separates two parts of a compound predicate, which is an error to avoid. The three main clauses are separated by commas plus conjunctions, which is correct as it avoids comma splices.
But that which was most sad and lamentable **was, that** in two or three months' time half of their company died . . . Of Plymouth Plantation	This text from the 1600s includes a comma that separates a verb, *was*, from its complement, the clause beginning with *that*. Today we would consider this a comma error.
Britain, with an army to enforce her tyranny, has declared that she has a right (not only to TAX) but "to BIND us in ALL CASES WHATSOEVER" **and if being bound in that manner, is not slavery,** then is there not such a thing as slavery upon earth. The Crisis	This sentence from a 1776 pamphlet contains a comma that separates the subject of a clause from its verb, which we would consider an error today.
The influence of factious leaders **may kindle** a flame within their particular States, **but will be** unable to spread a general conflagration through the other States. The Federalist Papers: No. 10	In this sentence, written in 1787, a comma separates two parts of a compound predicate. Today, this would be considered a misuse of a comma.

⟳ YOUR TURN

1. How should you correct the comma usage in this sentence?

> Adams was at the Constitutional Convention and Abigail Adams wrote to her husband, she reminded him to "remember the ladies."

- ○ A. Add a comma after **Convention**
- ○ B. Add a semicolon instead of a comma after **husband**
- ○ C. Add a comma after *him*
- ○ D. No change needs to be made to this sentence.

2. How should you correct the comma usage in this sentence?

> The account of how Lee surrendered to Grant, showed that both men were capable leaders.

- ○ A. Delete the comma after **Grant**
- ○ B. Add a comma after **showed**
- ○ C. Add a comma after **men**
- ○ D. No change needs to be made to this sentence.

3. How should you correct the comma usage in this sentence?

> The children of immigrants write about generational differences in adjusting to their new homes, they explore wider human themes such as compassion and loyalty.

- ○ A. Add a comma after **immigrants**
- ○ B. Add a comma after **write**
- ○ C. Add the conjunction **and** after **homes**,
- ○ D. No change needs to be made to this sentence.

4. How should you correct the comma usage in this sentence?

> In his Sonnet 18, one of his best-known poems, Shakespeare compares his love to a summer's day, and he uses the comparison to meditate on beauty and immortality.

- ○ A. Delete the commas after **Sonnet 18** and **poems**
- ○ B. Delete the comma after **day**
- ○ C. Delete the conjunction **and**
- ○ D. No change needs to be made to this sentence.

Literary Analysis Writing Process: Edit and Publish

PLAN	DRAFT	REVISE	EDIT AND PUBLISH

You have revised your literary analysis essay based on your peer feedback and your own examination.

Now it is time to edit your essay. When you revised, you focused on the content of your essay. You probably looked at your introduction, conclusion, and your reasons and evidence. When you edit, you focus on the mechanics of your essay, paying close attention to things like grammar and punctuation.

Use the checklist below to guide you as you edit:

☐ Have I followed the rules for semicolons?

☐ Have I misused commas?

☐ Have I misused commonly confused words?

☐ Do I have any sentence fragments or run-on sentences?

☐ Have I spelled everything correctly?

Notice some edits Connor has made:

• Removed a comma that was used between the subject and the verb of a sentence

• Corrected the spelling of a commonly confused word

• Corrected a spelling mistake

For Kossula, his life in Africa~~,~~ was defined by his family and ~~there~~ **their** status in the community. Africa, in Kossula's mind, is his family and community. While Hurston's descriptions of Kossula's home and land ~~initialy~~ **initially** show what he has achieved in America, as Kossula describes his life in Africa, the reader comes to understand just how much he has lost.

✏ WRITE

Use the questions on the previous page, as well as your peer reviews, to help you evaluate your literary analysis to determine areas that need editing. Then, edit your essay to correct those errors.

Once you have made all your corrections, you are ready to publish your work. You can distribute your writing to family and friends, hang it on a bulletin board, or post it on your blog. If you publish online, share the link with your family, friends, and classmates.

After the Ball

FICTION

Introduction

The novels of Jane Austen are filled with examples of wealthy young women who struggle against the limitations placed on them by society due to their gender. But what about the maidservants who serve them? What options do they have? This work of historical fiction showcases the challenges of one such

VOCABULARY

endeavor

to attempt intensely to accomplish something

aspire

to desire or aim for something

abruptly

in a way that is very sudden and unexpected

dominion

authority; the power to rule

blunt

direct; clear and to the point without considering others' feelings

 NOTES

☰ READ

1 "Do not yawn, Amelia. It is very rude," Mrs. Henry scolded. "Even though you worked the ball last night instead of dancing at it, you should still **endeavor** to act like a lady." Mrs. Henry served the Sinclair family with pride. She expected no less from the maidservants she managed.

2 Amelia covered her mouth, unable to stop the yawn. She cleared her throat. "I cannot help it. I am exhausted after yesterday's endless chores. Scrubbing the manor from ceiling to floor. Beating the curtains. Preparing the fires. And then cleaning the manor again after the guests had gone. I hardly closed my eyes for two hours before the sun pulled me out of bed."

3 Ollie, the youngest member of the staff, tore through the kitchen like a tornado. He sent a pile of apples cascading off the table when he tried to nab one. They thundered against the wooden floor. Amelia sighed heavily. "And now I have to clean up after the servants, too." She crouched down and

gathered the fruit in her apron. "These apples are already starting to bruise. I wanted to bake a pie as a treat. Will this nightmare ever end?"

4   "Such a hardship you have suffered," Mrs. Henry chuckled. She gave a knowing smile. She had once been a lowly maid-of-all-work just like Amelia. Over time she had risen in the ranks. "It is just a few spoiled apples. Be patient. One day perhaps you will be standing where I am. The head of the household. Would not that be a worthy goal to focus on?"

5   Amelia stood up **abruptly**. The apples tumbled to the ground. "If I may be **blunt**, Mrs. Henry, I do not **aspire** to your position. You may have **dominion** over the maidservants. But you are no more free than I am. The Sinclairs decide our fate. Any day they may toss us out. Without their recommendation, we would never secure a position with another respected family. You may be in charge of this kitchen, Mrs. Henry. But you are not the head of the household."

6   Mrs. Henry's own mouth fell open at Amelia's disrespectful tirade. Amelia continued.

7   "What hope do I have for a future? Last evening, I overheard many young women lamenting their limited options for suitable husbands. At least their marriages may raise them up in society. Women of our profession are not even supposed to marry. You have never taken a husband. If I marry, my groom will likely be an actual groom! I will spend my life washing the horse smell from his clothing. If I do not marry, I will live out my days serving the Sinclairs. There is no way out of servitude. I am trapped."

8   Mrs. Henry's usually kind eyes narrowed. "You speak of the Sinclairs as if they are tyrants. They are the kindest, most generous family I have ever known." Then, she took Amelia's hand.

9   "You are right, Amelia. Some women may move up through marriage. But your life is not so bleak. Have you ever thought about where you might be if you did not have a place in this household? You have a roof over your head and food in your stomach. You may not get to enjoy a slice of pie whenever you want, but you are not starving. There are plenty out there who are. Before I met Mr. Sinclair's mother in a shop when I was a girl, I used to be one of them. Whether you choose to marry and leave this life or stay here and serve, never forget that you do have choices."

10 Amelia had no response. She felt her cheeks turn pink. She hurried to look away. To her surprise, Mrs. Henry smiled brightly again. "Now, let us see if we can salvage these apples."

11 Amelia returned a weak smile and got back to work.

First Read

Read "After the Ball." After you read, complete the Think Questions below.

☁ THINK QUESTIONS

1. Who are the main characters in the story? What is their relationship?

   The main characters are _____.

   Their relationship is _____.

2. Why is Amelia so tired?

   Amelia is so tired because _____.

3. How do the views of Amelia and Mrs. Henry differ regarding their positions?

   Amelia thinks that _____.

   Mrs. Henry thinks that _____.

4. Use context to confirm the meaning of the word *aspire* as it is used in "After the Ball." Write your definition of *aspire* here.

   Aspire means _____.

   A context clue is _____.

5. What is another way to say that Amelia's answers are *blunt*?

   Amelia's answers are _____.

Skill:
Analyzing Expressions

★ DEFINE

When you read, you may find English expressions that you do not know. An **expression** is a group of words that communicates an idea. Three types of expressions are idioms, sayings, and figurative language. They can be difficult to understand because the meanings of the words are different from their **literal**, or usual, meanings.

An **idiom** is an expression that is commonly known among a group of people. For example, "It's raining cats and dogs" means it is raining heavily. **Sayings** are short expressions that contain advice or wisdom. For instance, "Don't count your chickens before they hatch" means do not plan on something good happening before it happens. **Figurative** language is when you describe something by comparing it with something else, either directly (using the words *like* or *as*) or indirectly. For example, "I'm as hungry as a horse" means I'm very hungry. None of the expressions are about actual animals.

••• CHECKLIST FOR ANALYZING EXPRESSIONS

To determine the meaning of an expression, remember the following:

✓ If you find a confusing group of words, it may be an expression. The meaning of words in expressions may not be their literal meaning.

• Ask yourself: Is this confusing because the words are new? Or because the words do not make sense together?

✓ Determining the overall meaning may require that you use one or more of the following:

• context clues

• a dictionary or other resource

• teacher or peer support

✓ Highlight important information before and after the expression to look for clues.

⟳ YOUR TURN

Read each sentence in the first column. Then, identify the expression found in each sentence and write what you think it means.

Expression Options	
A	"the sun pulled me out of bed"
B	"thundered against"
C	"cascading off"

Sentence	Expression	Meaning
I hardly closed my eyes for two hours before the sun pulled me out of bed.		
He sent a pile of apples cascading off the table when he tried to nab one.		
They thundered against the wooden floor.		

Skill:
Developing Background Knowledge

★ DEFINE

Developing background knowledge is the process of gaining information about different topics. By developing your background knowledge, you will be able to better understand a wider variety of texts.

First, preview the text to determine what the text is about. To **preview** the text, read the title, headers, and other text features and look at any images or graphics. As you are previewing, identify anything that is unfamiliar to you and that seems important.

While you are reading, you can look for clues that will help you learn more about any unfamiliar words, phrases, or topics. You can also look up information in another resource to increase your background knowledge.

••• CHECKLIST FOR DEVELOPING BACKGROUND KNOWLEDGE

To develop your background knowledge, do the following:

✓ Preview the text. Read the title, headers, and other features. Look at any images and graphics.

✓ Identify any words, phrases, or topics that you do not know a lot about.

✓ As you are reading, try to find clues in the text that give you information about any unfamiliar words, phrases, or topics.

✓ If necessary, look up information in other sources to learn more about any unfamiliar words, phrases, or topics. You can also ask a peer or teacher for information or support.

✓ Think about how the background knowledge you have gained helps you better understand the text.

YOUR TURN

Read each quotation from "After the Ball" below. Then, complete the chart by identifying the background knowledge that helps you understand each quotation.

Background Knowledge Options	
A	It's hard to get a job without a good recommendation.
B	Bruised and damaged apples aren't good for baking pies.
C	It's common for young people to want to rush through entry-level jobs and be the boss before they're ready.

Quotation	Background Knowledge
"These apples are already starting to bruise. I wanted to bake a pie as a treat."	
"Be patient. One day perhaps you will be standing where I am. The head of the household."	
"Without their recommendation, we would never secure a position with another respected family."	

Close Read

✏️ **WRITE**

LITERARY ANALYSIS: The two characters in this story look at life differently. Choose one of the characters and write a paragraph in which you explain her point of view and why she looks at life the way she does. Pay attention to and edit for verb tenses.

Use the checklist below to guide you as you write.

☐ What is the point of view of the character you have chosen to write about?

☐ Why does she have this point of view?

☐ What does she think about her life?

Use the sentence frames to organize and write your literary analysis.

Amelia's point of view is that her life _____

_____.

She feels this way because she does not have the freedom to _____.

Mrs. Henry always _____.

Maidservants should not _____.

Amelia thinks she will always be _____.

Please note that excerpts and passages in the StudySync® library and this workbook are intended as touchstones to generate interest in an author's work. The excerpts and passages do not substitute for the reading of entire texts, and StudySync® strongly recommends that students seek out and purchase the whole literary or informational work in order to experience it as the author intended. Links to online resellers are available in our digital library. In addition, complete works may be ordered through an authorized reseller by filling out and returning to StudySync® the order form enclosed in this workbook.

Reading & Writing
Companion

513

Finding Time for Fun

INFORMATIONAL TEXT

Introduction

Daily responsibilities can stop us from pursuing creative outlets such as drawing, writing, or painting, but these activities add so much more to our lives than just "fun." Studies have shown that having hobbies that involve creating can have positive social, emotional, and mental effects on us. No matter how busy our lives are, there should always be room for a little playtime.

VOCABULARY

priority

something that is seen as more important than another

function

use, task, or purpose

improve

to make better or become better

potential

quality or ability that can lead to success

≡ READ

 NOTES

1   The day starts quickly. Rush to school or work while grabbing a quick bite to eat on the way. Then, answer emails, forget to eat lunch, work late, make dinner, clean the house, and finally fall into bed. An average person's day is full of responsibilities. For most people, being busy is a way of life. Getting through daily tasks is a **priority**. However, living our lives without making any room for fun can have serious consequences. Everybody should set aside time to have a creative outlet—an opportunity to make, explore, or enjoy something. Making time for creative outlets can actually **improve** one's life and social, mental, and emotional health.

2   Have you ever seen a group of people sitting around knitting? Have you seen a group of friends go to a painting class? Creating something new brings people together. Having a creative hobby improves your mood and can make you feel part of a community. When people are involved in an activity with others, they make friends. They feel like they belong. This leads to a healthier life. It's common for young children to make friends and play together, creating games or participating in fun activities. However, as people get older, it's uncommon to take up hobbies and make new friends. Having a creative outlet allows people to have a social life. Plus, studies have found that adults who socialize are 55% less likely to have memory loss later on in life.

3   In addition to decreasing the risk of memory loss, engaging in creative outlets can improve mental health in other ways. Participating in crafts or other

creative projects increases brain **function**. Having a creative outlet can actually cause your brain to grow neurons. These are important cells that help keep your whole body working. People who enjoy creative activities are also less likely to develop Alzheimer's disease. This disease affects the brain. It makes people confused as they lose memory of things and people they once knew. Therefore, finding time to be creative can actually be life-saving.

4   Finding time for creative pursuits can also positively influence your emotional health. Studies have shown that even observing something creative, like attending a concert, can serve as an antidote for stress. When people are less stressed, their overall health improves. In addition, creative projects give people a purpose. In turn, they become happier and more confident. People often realize their full **potential** when they decide to try something new and succeed. Instead of focusing on day-to-day errands, which can cause unhappiness, enjoying a creative outlet gives you a chance to focus on something fun and fulfilling.

5   Think about the last time you dropped everything to do something creative. If it's been awhile, you should try it. Even though it can be difficult to find the time to do something creative, it really can save your life. Creative activities are not only fun, but they have been proven to prevent diseases, memory loss, and stress. They can also improve people's social lives and overall happiness. Finding time for fun isn't just for kids anymore.

First Read

Read "Finding Time for Fun." After you read, complete the Think Questions below.

☁ THINK QUESTIONS

1. What should everyone set aside time for?

   Everyone should set aside time for _____.

2. How can doing fun and creative things help people?

   Doing fun and creative things can help people by _____

   _____.

3. Write two or three sentences to describe how doing a specific creative activity can benefit a person's life. Base your answers on the text.

   Doing a specific creative activity can benefit a person's life by _____

   _____.

4. Use context to confirm the meaning of the word *priority* as it is used in "Finding Time for Fun." Write your definition of *priority* here.

   Priority means _____.

   A context clue is _____.

5. What is another way to say that creative outlets can *improve* someone's life?

   Creative outlets can _____.

Reading & Writing
Companion

Copyright © BookheadEd Learning, LLC

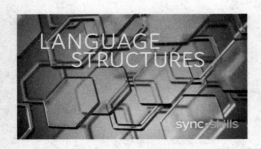

Skill:
Language Structures

★ DEFINE

In every language, there are rules that tell how to **structure** sentences. These rules define the correct order of words. In the English language, for example, a **basic** structure for sentences is subject, verb, and object. Some sentences have more **complicated** structures.

You will encounter both basic and complicated **language structures** in the classroom materials you read. Being familiar with language structures will help you better understand the text.

••• CHECKLIST FOR LANGUAGE STRUCTURES

To improve your comprehension of language structures, do the following:

✓ Monitor your understanding.

- Ask yourself: Why do I not understand this sentence? Is it because I do not understand some of the words? Or is it because I do not understand the way the words are ordered in the sentence?

✓ Pay attention to **perfect tenses** as you read. There are three perfect tenses in the English language: the present perfect, past perfect, and future perfect. The word *perfect* means "completed." These tenses describe actions that are completed or finished.

- **Present perfect tense** expresses an action that occurred at some indefinite time in the past.

  > Combine *have* or *has* with the past participle of the main verb.
  Example: **I have played** basketball for three years.

- **Past perfect tense** describes an action that happened before another action or event in the past.

  > Combine *had* with the past participle of the main verb.
  Example: **I had learned** how to dribble a ball before I could walk!

- **Future perfect tense** expresses one future action that will begin and end before another future event begins.

    > Use *will have* or *shall have* with the past participle of a verb.

    Example: Before the end of the year, **I will have played** more than 100 games!

✓ Break down the sentence into its parts.

- Ask yourself: What actions are expressed in this sentence? Are they completed or are they ongoing? What words give me clues about when an action is taking place?

✓ Confirm your understanding with a peer or teacher.

⟳ YOUR TURN

Read each sentence below and notice the perfect tense in each one. Then, complete the chart by determining if the sentence uses a present perfect, past perfect, or future perfect tense.

	Sentence Options
A	Miguel had studied his notes before he took the test.
B	Has Kyree taken the package to the post office?
C	The game will have already started by the time we leave the house.
D	They have arrived.
E	I had already finished my homework when Katie called.
F	Sierra will have completed high school before she moves to Tokyo.

Present Perfect	Past Perfect	Future Perfect

Skill:
Supporting Evidence

★ DEFINE

In some informational or argumentative texts, the author may share an opinion. This **opinion** may be the author's **claim** or **thesis**. The author must then provide readers with **evidence** that supports their opinion. Supporting evidence can be details, examples, or facts that agree with the author's claim or thesis.

Looking for supporting evidence can help you confirm your understanding of what you read. Finding and analyzing supporting evidence can also help you form your own opinions about the subject.

••• CHECKLIST FOR SUPPORTING EVIDENCE

In order to find and analyze supporting evidence, do the following:

✓ Identify the topic and the author's claim or thesis.

  • Ask yourself: What is this mostly about? What is the author's opinion?

✓ Find details, facts, and examples that support the author's claim or thesis.

  • Ask yourself: Is this detail important? How does this detail relate to the thesis or claim?

✓ Analyze the supporting evidence.

  • Ask yourself: Is this evidence strong? Do I agree with the evidence?

⟳ YOUR TURN

Read each claim below. Then, complete the chart by deciding which piece of supporting evidence best supports each claim.

Supporting Evidence Options	
A	Participating in crafts or other creative projects increases brain function. Having a creative outlet can actually cause your brain to grow neurons.
B	In addition, creative projects give people a purpose. In turn, they become happier and more confident.
C	When people are involved in an activity with others, they make friends. They feel like they belong.

Claim	Supporting Evidence
In addition to decreasing the risk of memory loss, engaging in creative outlets can improve mental health in other ways.	
Having a creative hobby improves your mood and can make you feel part of a community.	
Finding time for creative pursuits can also positively influence your emotional health.	

Close Read

✏ WRITE

ARGUMENTATIVE: At the end of the article, the author says that making time for a creative outlet can save your life. Do you agree or disagree? Write a paragraph explaining your opinion. Use details from the text to justify your response. Pay attention to and edit for spelling words correctly when doubling final consonants and adding prefixes as you write.

Use the checklist below to guide you as you write.

☐ What is your opinion on the author's statement?

☐ What evidence from the text supports your opinion?

☐ How does the evidence justify your opinion?

Use the sentence frames to organize and write your argumentative paragraph.

I _____ with the author. Setting aside time for a creative outlet _____ save your life.

One piece of supporting evidence is that _____

_____.

Today, people _____.

This _____ hurt a person. Therefore, having a creative outlet _____ save a

person's life.

PHOTO/IMAGE CREDITS:

p. 353, ©iStock.com/WerksMedia
p. 353, ©iStock.com/eyewave, ©iStock.com/subjug, ©iStock.com/Ivantsov, iStock.com/borchee, iStock.com/seb_ra
p. 355, iStock.com/
p. 356, William Bartram - The Picture Art Collection/Alamy Stock Photo
p. 356, Richard Blanco - Larry Busacca/Staff/Getty Images Entertainment
p. 356, Jerico Brown - Paul Marotta/Contributor/Getty Images Entertainment
p. 356, Frederick Douglass - Archive Photos/Library of Congress/Stringer/Getty Images
p. 356, William Faulkner - Eric Schaal/Contributor/The LIFE Images Collection/Getty Images
p. 357, Lauren Groff - Agence Opale/Alamy Stock Photo
p. 357, Zora Neale Hurston - Archive Photos/Fotosearch/Stringer/Getty Images
p. 357, Katherine A. Porter - Hulton Archive/Staff/Hulton Archive/Getty
p. 357, Natasha Trethewey - The Washington Post/Contributor/The Washington Post/Getty Images
p. 357, Jesmyn Ward - Ulf Andersen/Contributor/Getty Images Entertainment
p. 358, iStock.com/Jasmina007
p. 360, Public Domain Image
p. 361, Bettmann/Bettmann/Getty Images
p. 363, Public Domain Image
p. 364, Public Domain Image
p. 366, iStock.com/Jasmina007
p. 367, ©iStock.com/azuki25
p. 373, ©iStock.com/azuki25
p. 374, ©iStock.com/fotogaby
p. 375, ©iStock.com/fotogaby
p. 376, ©iStock.com/Orla
p. 377, ©iStock.com/Orla
p. 378, ©iStock/Pali Rao
p. 379, ©iStock/Pali Rao
p. 380, ©iStock.com/azuki25
p. 381, ©iStock.com/phive2015
p. 387, iStock.com/NicolasMcComber
p. 391, iStock.com/NicolasMcComber
p. 392, iStock.com
p. 393, iStock.com
p. 394, iStock.com/NicolasMcComber
p. 395, ©iStock.com/kentarcajuan
p. 400, ©iStock.com/borchee
p. 412, iStock.com/salimoctober
p. 416, ©iStock.com/valio84sl
p. 419, ©iStock.com/SVPhilon
p. 422, ©iStock.com/AlexLinch
p. 424, ©iStock.com/AlexLinch
p. 425, ©iStock.com/fotogaby
p. 426, ©iStock.com/fotogaby
p. 427, ©iStock.com/AlexLinch
p. 428, ©iStock.com/igorirge
p. 432, ©iStock.com/igorirge
p. 433, ©iStock.com/Andrey_A
p. 434, ©iStock.com/Andrey_A
p. 435, ©iStock.com/Hohenhaus
p. 436, ©iStock.com/Hohenhaus
p. 438, ©iStock.com/igorirge
p. 439, ©iStock.com/franckreporter

p. 443, iStock.com/viki, melkiu
p. 444, Public Domain Image
p. 445, Public Domain Image
p. 446, Public Domain Image
p. 450, iStock.com/
p. 460, iStock.com/
p. 461, ©iStock.com/fotogaby
p. 462, ©iStock.com/fotogaby
p. 464, iStock.com/
p. 465, iStock.com/hanibaram, iStock.com/seb_ra, iStock.com/Martin Barraud
p. 466, ©iStock.com/Martin Barraud
p. 473, ©iStock.com/gopixa
p. 475, ©iStock.com/fstop123
p. 478, ©iStock.com/domin_domin
p. 481, ©iStock.com/Martin Barraud
p. 487, ©iStock.com/bo1982
p. 489, ©iStock/Jeff_Hu
p. 491, ©iStock.com/stevedangers
p. 493, ©iStock.com/Martin Barraud
p. 495, ©iStock/Fodor90
p. 497, iStock.com/
p. 499, iStock.com/
p. 501, iStock.com/
p. 503, ©iStock.com/Martin Barraud
p. 505, iStock.com/knape
p. 506, maghakan/iStock.com
p. 506, alphaspirit/iStock.com
p. 506, Lighthaunter/iStock.com
p. 506, DarrenMower/iStock.com
p. 506, AlexBrylov/iStock.com
p. 508, iStock.com/knape
p. 509, ©iStock.com/Ales_Utovko
p. 511, ©iStock.com/Mlenny
p. 513, iStock.com/knape
p. 514, iStock.com/
p. 515, ©iStock.com/bankrx
p. 515, ©iStock.com/DNY59
p. 515, ©iStock.com/evgenyatamanenko
p. 515, ©iStock.com/republica
p. 517, iStock.com/
p. 518, iStock.com/BlackJack3D
p. 520, ©iStock.com/BlackJack3D
p. 522, iStock.com/

studysync®

Text Fulfillment Through StudySync

If you are interested in specific titles, please fill out the form below and we will check availability through our partners.

ORDER DETAILS

Date:

TITLE	AUTHOR	Paperback/ Hardcover	Specific Edition *If Applicable*	Quantity

SHIPPING INFORMATION

Contact:

Title:

School/District:

Address Line 1:

Address Line 2:

Zip or Postal Code:

Phone:

Mobile:

Email:

BILLING INFORMATION ☐ *SAME AS SHIPPING*

Contact:

Title:

School/District:

Address Line 1:

Address Line 2:

Zip or Postal Code:

Phone:

Mobile:

Email:

PAYMENT INFORMATION

☐ CREDIT CARD

Name on Card:

Card Number:

Expiration Date:

Security Code:

☐ PO

Purchase Order Number:

StudySync Text Fulfillment, BookheadEd Learning, LLC
610 Daniel Young Drive | Sonoma, CA 95476